T0303084

The Life of Buzzards

Peter Dare

Whittles Publishing

Published by
Whittles Publishing Ltd.,
Dunbeath,
Caithness, KW6 6EG,
Scotland, UK
www.whittlespublishing.com

© 2015 Peter Dare

ISBN 978-184995-130-2

All rights reserved.
The right of Peter Dare
to be identified as the author of this work
has been asserted by him in accordance with
the Copyright, Design and Patents Act 1988.
No part of this publication may be reproduced,
stored in a retrieval system, or transmitted,
in any form or by any means, electronic,
mechanical, recording or otherwise
without prior permission of the publisher.

Printed by
CPI Group (UK) Ltd, Croydon, CR0 4YY

CONTENTS

For Gillian and our daughter, Sarah

Preface

More than sixty-five years have passed since I saw my first Buzzards, on 26 August 1948, when, as a 14-year-old, I was taken on a boat trip, by the marine biologist and naturalist Owen D. Hunt, along the beautiful Yealm Estuary in south-west Devon. On a perfect summer afternoon, my attention was held by six of these large hawks, calling as they wheeled slowly in circles above the steep oak woods clothing the river banks. This memorable first encounter was followed by others as I explored the wooded countryside east of my home in Plymouth, looking for and recording bird nests. In the summer of 1949, I found my first Buzzard nest, holding three youngsters which fledged in late July. Then, exactly a year later, I learned to recognise the hunger calls of juveniles by tracking down a noisy fledgling in the Yealm Valley woods. Already, I had become intrigued by the Buzzard's lifestyle and fascinated by its effortless soaring flight. This early interest was fostered further by another local naturalist, H. G. Hurrell, who gave stimulating wildlife talks at school. I did not suspect then, of course, that I would spend much of my life, albeit intermittently, studying Buzzards in Devon, then during sojourns in Wales and latterly in East Anglia.

The first opportunity arose in the autumn of 1955 when, having gained my degree in Zoology, the University of Exeter offered me the chance of a PhD study to investigate the effects on Buzzards in Devon of a newly introduced Rabbit disease, myxomatosis. At that time, the then Nature Conservancy were concerned about widespread reports of heavy mortalities and breeding failures among Buzzard populations in many western counties following the almost complete extermination of Rabbits, which were known to be the major prey of Buzzards. At that time, virtually nothing was known of Buzzard ecology in Britain, unlike in Germany. The findings from these field investigations on Dartmoor form the focus for this volume.

Dartmoor in the 1950s was a largely undisturbed new National Park where no detailed ornithological studies had yet been undertaken. My selection of a study area there proved to be not only rewarding for the project but also provided stimulating physical challenges. I enjoyed making more than 400 unaided tree climbs when inspecting Buzzard broods, during which I learned the physical features of each tree species in varying weather conditions. Thus, in strong winds one can see, when looking down, that the top of a Sitka spruce does not merely sway from side to side but describes an elliptical path. The most intensive field work was undertaken during periodic stays at a traditional rustic-style caravan sited on a common and beside a trout stream in which Water Voles swam. From here Buzzards, and occasionally a local Merlin or Montagu's Harrier, could be seen hunting across the common. I was able to experience the full gamut of Dartmoor's weather and its effects on Buzzards – from cold which froze the milk on my table, to summer heat and drought, thunderstorms and river spates, and the more typical days of rain, gales and hill fog. The farming community and forestry workers were most supportive, taking an interest in the studies and often providing useful information on 'their' Buzzards and the local distribution of preys and predators in the district.

Within weeks of completing my last Buzzard field season, an irresistible offer of an applied research post in Africa found me arriving at a government research station beside the Blue Nile, to work as the government agricultural ornithologist in the newly independent Republic of Sudan. From this base, over the next three years, I was able to travel throughout this vast and very hot country while assessing the damage to crops being caused annually by immense swarms of *Quelea* weaver birds and other known avian pests, more especially across the broad semi-arid Sahelian zone. In addition, I recorded the distribution, abundance and seasonal movements of African raptors and of Palaearctic migrants. Meanwhile, my Buzzard thesis was written in spare time between travels, often being overseen in the evenings by geckos hunting insects that were attracted to the wall behind my table lamp. The literature on Buzzards was very sparse in those days but two books about raptor ecology in Africa (*Eagles* by Leslie Brown, 1955) and in North America (*Hawks, Owls and Wildlife* by the Craighead brothers, 1956) made inspiring reading and spurred me on. During leave periods in Devon I was able to revisit and monitor the Buzzard population in my Dartmoor study area and to submit my doctoral thesis.

Upon returning permanently to Britain in 1962, I became immersed in what would become a marine biological career in government shellfisheries research. The initial projects, whilst stationed in North Wales, were related to the needs of a team investigating, and providing advice on, the then perceived problems of Oystercatcher predation upon commercially important stocks of estuarine bivalve molluscs – cockles and mussels. Several years were devoted to extensive field surveys of the national distribution and abundance of wintering and breeding Oystercatchers in conjunction with large-scale ringing and colour-banding programmes to reveal their origins, migration routes and local movements between, and site fidelity within, winter feeding areas. The population surveys involved winter visits to virtually every estuary and bay around the British and Irish coastlines. Breeding surveys took me to coastal sites and inland along most of the river systems in Scotland and northern England. This was a fruitful period that linked up with studies of Oystercatcher feeding behaviour being undertaken at Oxford and Aberdeen universities, and with the pioneering work by the Wash Wader Ringing Group and others. Subsequent fisheries research then led progressively, via invertebrate predators of molluscs, and 'down the food chain' from Oystercatchers to ecological and cultivation studies of the mussel populations themselves.

During this phase I managed to continue monitoring the Dartmoor Buzzard population, 300 miles away, in each breeding season until 1969. Then, in the mid- 1970s I began a lengthy (leisure-time) study of the Buzzards, and Ravens, close to my home, in the mountains of Snowdonia and on the nearby Denbighshire moorlands around the upper Conwy valley.

Annual census work and breeding assessments covered more than 1,300 square kilometres in these rugged terrains, and improved my physical condition very satisfactorily! It was during these years that Leslie Brown, the renowned Kenyan raptor ecologist and author, liaised with and visited me to discuss his proposal to include some of my unpublished thesis material in his forthcoming book *British Birds of Prey*. He had shown a keen interest in the Dartmoor findings when I had first met him in Nairobi back in 1961. Years later, in 1976, he generously drove my wife and I on a memorable safari to some of his raptor study sites, culminating in a brisk ascent of his famous 'Eagle Hill' where, among other eagles, we were privileged to watch the resident pair of superb Ayre's Hawk Eagles at close quarters.

In 1982 the Snowdonia studies were curtailed abruptly upon my being transferred to a coastal laboratory in north Suffolk to work on the offshore fisheries for scallops (*Pecten maximus*) in the English Channel and Irish Sea. Suffolk at that time was as far removed from Buzzard country as one could get. Buzzards were still only scarce visitors there in the 1980s. Indeed, the skies then were virtually devoid of any raptors apart from Kestrels and an occasional Marsh Harrier, Sparrowhawk and Hobby. As for Buzzards, I had to be satisfied for many years with sporadic sightings of one or two passage migrants flying over in spring. Instead, return visits were made whenever possible to my old haunts in North Wales and on Dartmoor, the latter for a fresh assessment of the study area population during 1990–93. In that last year I made my last climb to a Buzzard nest, having realised that, after too many years exiled in Suffolk, I had lost the requisite fitness in my arms and legs.

All was not lost in Suffolk, however. Unexpectedly, in the late 1990s, increasing numbers of Buzzards were being reported passing north along the coast in early spring and within three kilometres of my home. This novel behaviour required closer examination. I and fellow 'sky watchers' therefore made personal observations of these movements each spring at a nearby watch point. These watches showed not only the scale of movements but, more excitingly, revealed that some groups of Buzzards actually flew out to sea towards the coast of Holland. These emigrants were thought most likely to be of Scandinavian origin and provided the first confirmation of such behaviour in eastern Britain.

Meanwhile, Buzzards had been spreading eastwards across central England and into East Anglia. Then, in summer 2006, following a report of apparent breeding behaviour on two nearby private estates, I found a nest with young close to fledging at one and a fledged brood at the other, only two kilometres from my garden. These were the first records of Buzzards breeding in north Suffolk for a century or more. I had never thought that breeding Buzzards would one day come to join me in the rather flat farmlands of East Anglia! Now they are affording an unforeseen opportunity for me to assess how well they are adapting in a landscape vastly different from those of my previous studies in western Britain.

FORMAT OF THIS BOOK

This book is not intended to be a comprehensive species monograph. Rather, I have set out to provide an up-to-date summary of our knowledge of Common Buzzards in Britain in a way that may not only interest raptor ecologists and enthusiasts but will also inform local conservation bodies and other land managers, especially those landowners with game bird-rearing interests. It is hoped that the format will also encourage and assist fresh field studies by a new generation of raptor enthusiasts, particularly in those regions now being resettled by Buzzards after an absence of more than a hundred years. The current reclamation of former breeding haunts has brought Buzzards into many areas where rural communities and many naturalists are unfamiliar with this imposing raptor.

The accounts describe the life history and ecology of Common Buzzards, mainly those living in the British uplands where, historically, this hawk had always been most numerous and where the main research work has been undertaken. Buzzard populations are followed through the seasons and the successive stages of their annual cycle. Information drawn from my own studies is integrated with findings from elsewhere in Britain and Europe in order to show how Buzzards cope with various seasonal challenges, posed notably by constantly fluctuating food supplies, the demands of breeding and by occasional weather extremes. This is also the story of how Buzzards are able to adapt so well to living in our modern and rapidly changing landscapes.

The book comprises two main sections. Following a general introduction to the species and descriptions of my own upland study areas, the first section (of nine chapters) follows the activities of Buzzards in those habitats progressively through the year from the start of winter to the end of the following autumn. Accounts are given of the sequential changes in the composition and behaviour of a population, the seasonal patterns of food habits and hunting methods, and the successive stages of the breeding season from courtship until fledging of the broods and their subsequent dispersal. A general theme explains how Buzzards constantly adapt their habits in response to continuously changing prey resources and environmental conditions, particularly in regard to the added demands of winter survival and rearing offspring.

The second section, comprising six chapters, expands on the six key aspects of Buzzard ecology that recur throughout the annual life cycle accounts: territory, energy and food needs, predation, food supply and breeding success, demography and population dynamics, and long-term population changes. These chapters collate research findings from many British and continental studies of Common Buzzards. These inter-related topics are perhaps of more interest to raptor enthusiasts and specialists. For easier accessibility to more general readers, the accounts are couched as far as possible in non-technical terms and without recourse to current 'eco-jargon'.

ACKNOWLEDGEMENTS

Many people have helped me over the years with the various projects. Sadly, those in Devon who made my doctoral study possible have now passed on. Above all, I am forever indebted to Professor L. A. Harvey and to my supervisor, Ian J. Linn, for their full support and advice throughout those years; and to Neville Barratt and his staff for crucial assistance with the care of my captive Buzzards. Grateful thanks are owed also to Dr. Norman Moore, at the former Nature Conservancy, who obtained permission for me to keep wild Buzzards at the laboratory; and equally to H. G. Hurrell, the Devon naturalist and falconer, who not only assisted with obtaining the young hawks but also 'hacked' them back into the wild. From visits to H.N. ('Mick') Southern, at the Bureau of Animal Population in Oxford, I learned much about predator-prey relationships and the then new small mammal sampling techniques used for his pioneering study of Tawny Owl ecology in Wytham Wood. Later, H.N.S. was also my external examiner.

On Dartmoor, the farmers (most now deceased) allowed me free access to their lands, thus enabling field work to proceed unhindered. Their interest and full cooperation is gratefully acknowledged, especially that of Mr. A. Brown (Archerton), Richard Coker (Runnage), Gordon Hambley (Challacombe), Lieutenant-General Sir Robert Sturges (Cator Court) and Jack, Wilf and Colin Irish (Grendon). I am particularly grateful also to the Webb family (Bill, Tom and Emmy) in Postbridge for their welcome hospitality on many a cold wet day as well as for information on some Buzzard nest sites and land use changes around the village.

During the North Wales studies my efforts were greatly assisted in some districts by local naturalists who supplied details of, or showed me, Buzzard nest areas in their localities. In particular, I am most grateful to Griff Jones-Ellis (Ysbyty Ifan), Gareth Parry (Llan Ffestiniog), Robin Fisher (Colwyn Bay) and Julian Driver (Llanfairfechan). Special thanks are due to J.D. also for providing data from his own and more recent long-term Buzzard studies in Snowdonia and for allowing me to include many of his photographs in this book. Dr Derek Ratcliffe kindly provided historical details for those mountain Buzzard sites he had noted whilst undertaking his famous Peregrine and Raven surveys in Snowdonia. As on Dartmoor, the hill farmers were helpful in many ways. During the 1970s, the Institute of Terrestrial Ecology was funding research on Buzzard ecology in mid-Wales and on Speyside in the Highlands of Scotland, as will be described later. Peter Davis encouraged my studies and provided information about the Wales project. During a 1977 visit to Speyside, Douglas

Weir generously took my wife and me to visit the area where he and Nick Picozzi had studied territorial behaviour and breeding performance.

The Suffolk study would not have been possible without the cooperation of those interested estate owners, keepers and farmers who allowed access to their woodlands. Local enthusiasts reported sightings of migrants and likely new breeding pairs in their districts. Particular thanks go to Miles Barne, John Buck, Colin Carter, Chris Darby, Derek Eaton, Fred Mallett, Alec and Kay Watson, and David Watson.

Special thanks are due to Peter Goodfellow for his encouragement, thoughtful comments and sundry improvements of the texts. I am much indebted also to Robin Prytherch who kindly sent details of his pioneering long-term Buzzard study in North Somerset. It was reassuring to learn that we shared similar views about so many aspects of Buzzard behaviour and population ecology.

The book is greatly enhanced by contributions from photographers whose fine digital images portray various aspects of Buzzard plumages, behaviour and upland habitats. I am most grateful for their generosity to Mike Alexander, John Anderson, Roy & Marie Battell (www.moorhens.me.uk), John Chapman, Steve Culley, Mark Darlaston, John Davis, Julian Driver, Paul Freestone, Steven Round, Roger Smaldon and Colin Whittle. Splendid photographs by eminent past photographers were made available from archived material by the kind efforts of Kay Kays (National Museum of Wales) and Kristie Cannings (Photoshot). The absence of modern high-quality images of Buzzards at nests is a sad reflection of current trends in digital bird photography. Roger Riddington, editor of *British Birds*, kindly allowed me to use diagrams from that journal; and Dr Peter Lack and Dawn Balmer (British Trust for Ornithology) obtained permission for me to reproduce the Buzzard distribution maps from the national atlas surveys.

Finally, I owe much to family support at critical periods. My early days as a budding naturalist were spent amid the ruins of post-war Plymouth and, with a friend, on short bus trips into the nearby countryside. My widowed mother was very tolerant and allowed me to keep, in my bedroom, sundry mice, voles, amphibians and caterpillars as well as collections of butterflies (then abundant), in addition to my collections of abandoned bird nests, feathers and bird wings, these last taken from chance finds or by purchases of wildfowl and game from poulterers' shops. Her support and understanding were crucial, not least when at school I decided at the last minute to switch my career path from the Classics to biology. More recently, my wife Gillian has been tremendously supportive in many ways: actively encouraging my so-called 'Buzzard bashing' up and down the steep woods and slopes of Snowdonia; ferrying me to and from hides located sometimes miles from home; and lastly, in the preparation of these 'memoirs' which otherwise might not have hatched after such prolonged incubation, let alone reached the fledging stage.

1

THE COMMON BUZZARD: AN INTRODUCTION

The Common Buzzard *Buteo buteo* is a Palaearctic (Old World) member of the hawk family Accipitridae. The nominate subspecies *B. b. buteo*, which includes British birds, breeds more or less throughout Europe from about the Arctic Circle in Fenno-Scandia south to the northern shores of the Mediterranean and eastwards into the Baltic States, Poland, the Balkans, south-east Russia, and around the Black Sea including northernmost Turkey (Cramp & Simmons 1980). Its limits in eastern Europe, where it overlaps with the eastern Palaearctic subspecies *B. b. vulpinus* or Steppe Buzzard are, however, often ill-defined and inter-breeding may occur. Other subspecies have been described from central Asia and Japan; and on islands in the western Mediterranean (Corsica and Sardinia); and on Atlantic (Macaronesian) island groups from the Azores south to Madeira and the Canary Islands (Cramp & Simmons 1980). In the field, however, there is considerable similarity between the island forms and the variable plumages of our familiar Buzzards. Indeed, recent DNA genetics and morphological studies found no differences between these endemic island buzzards and those in continental Europe (Kruckenhauser *et al.* 2004). An even more remote Atlantic buzzard population is found further south, at 15°N, on the tropical Cape Verde archipelago off West Africa. These birds appear to be more closely related genetically to Long-legged Buzzard, which breeds in North Africa than, as was formerly thought, to Common Buzzard (Clouet & Wink. 2000).

In Europe two other and quite distinctive buzzard species breed and overlap slightly with the Common Buzzard at the northern and south-eastern limits of its range. They are the Rough-legged Buzzard (*B. lagopus*) on the fells and tundras of Fenno-Scandia and Russia, and the Long-legged Buzzard (*B. rufinus*) inhabiting the drier and more mountainous parts of the Balkans and Caucasus (Hagemeijer *et al.* 1997). Worldwide, the genus *Buteo* itself is well represented by about 28 species in all continents except Australasia (del Hoyo *et al.* 1994). They can be found in a wide range of habitat zones from tundras to tropical forests and savannahs, sub-deserts and montane regions.

COMMON BUZZARDS IN BRITAIN

When viewed at rest, adult Common Buzzards will be seen to have large dark brown eyes, rather uniform dark brown upperparts but with the under parts variously mottled, barred

Above: Figure 1.1 Portraits of Buzzards: adult (upper) and juvenile (lower); showing the sturdy build and dark brown plumages with individual patterns on the under parts. Juveniles can be identified by their streaked markings on throat and breast, and a paler iris. Note also the strong beak, legs and talons. (Photos: Wirral © Steven Round)

Opposite: Figure 1.2 Buzzards in Britain vary greatly in plumage from near-uniformly dark brown to part-white and even, rarely, all-white leucistic birds. (Photos: (a–c) adults © Steven Round; (d) Wales © John Davis)

and streaked in shades of brown and buff on a paler or white background (Figures 1.1, 1.2). Extensively streaked Buzzards with pale eyes are typically juveniles or first-year birds (Figure 1.1b, 1.4). The acquisition of adult plumage takes about three years, during which time confusing intermediate patterns may be observed, as have been described (with photographs) for Buzzards breeding in North Somerset (Prytherch 2009). Adult plumage patterns, especially on the underparts, show considerable individual variability in both sexes (Figure 1.2). Some adult Buzzards are predominantly dark brown all over while others display pale or even white areas anywhere on the body. Exceptional birds that are all-white (leucistic) are recorded both

Figure 1.3 Buzzards low overhead show conspicuous under-wing patterns and body markings: a juvenile (left) and an adult (below). Note the juvenile's more streaked and spotted breast and belly compared with the uniformly dark breast and ventral barring of the adult. (North Wales © Steven Round)

in Britain and on the Continent. To the French it is known, appropriately, as *la Buse variable*. A considerable degree of plumage variability is a characteristic of buzzard species nearly everywhere though the advantages and underlying genetic basis are not clear (Schreiber *et al.* 2001). In southern Germany, five different plumage morphs have been described although 98% of the breeding birds were uniformly dark above with dark brown patterned underparts, and thus similar to the bird in Figure 1.2a (Dittrich 1985). On the other hand, Kruger (2001) recognized just three colour morphs in his study population: dark (6% of birds), intermediate (65%) and light (29%). Although intermediate birds were the most successful in terms of life-time breeding productivity, the other morphs persisted in the population because each morph can produce more than one type of offspring.

In Britain, Common Buzzards (hereinafter Buzzards) probably are best known for, and readily recognised by, their distinctive loud calls and grand soaring flight, when individuals or groups of these large and vocal hawks soar and sweep in wide circles high around the sky, the adults sometimes performing spirited aerobatic displays. They spiral and glide effortlessly on up-curved wings with deeply emarginated primary tips ('fingers') and their lightly-barred tails broadly fanned (Figure 1.3). The undersides of their large wings then usually show a contrasting pattern of dark coverts and a large white area or 'flash' across the base of the dark-tipped primaries. The secondaries are variably barred or spotted with brown and pale tones, their tips forming a dark bar along the trailing edge. More detailed descriptions, with photographs, can be consulted in Forsman (1999).

Structure

In size, the Buzzard is a medium to large diurnal bird of prey, of robust build, and measures roughly 51–57 cm (20–22 inches) in overall length of body and tail, with broad wings spanning 113–128 cm (about 4 feet). Adults typically weigh 800–1,200 g (1.5–2.2 lb). Adult females are heavier, by 20–30% on average, than males but are only slightly larger in linear dimensions (Cramp & Simmons 1980). This sex size dimorphism is seldom reliably apparent in the field except when some pairs are seen perched together or at the nest. The bill has a bright yellow basel cere, and is large and strongly hooked, the yellow legs and talon-bearing feet sturdy (Figure 1.1). The eye sockets of Buzzards occupy a large proportion of the skull's cavity (Figure 1.5) and indicate the supreme importance of these sensory organs. The ultra-keen eyesight (visual acuity) of Buzzards is evident especially when one witnesses them hunting. Good accounts of the eye structure and the vision of Buzzards are given by Leslie Brown (1976).

Although predators predominantly of small mammals, Buzzards are well equipped to catch and kill prey as large as Rabbits and crows. In some north European countries their predilection for small mammals, particularly rodents, is reflected in the vernacular names meaning 'mouse hawk' or 'mouse buzzard': thus, *Mäusebussard* (Germany), *Musvåge* (Denmark), *Musvåk* (Norway), *Hiirihaukka* (Finland) and *Busardo Ratónero* (Spain).

Longevity

Given their size, one would expect Buzzards to have a fairly long potential life span, and now this is being confirmed. Formerly, few ringed youngsters survived 5–10 years, many having been trapped, shot or poisoned. Nowadays, their chances have greatly improved following the easing of persecution. The longest-lived British bird was found dead in a recent winter 25.5 years after being ringed and very near to its birthplace in North Wales, and several other life spans have exceeded 20 years (*per* British Trust for Ornithology (BTO) reports). Other British ringed birds have survived well into their teens. A long-term field study in North Somerset of Buzzards recognizable by their individual plumage patterns is showing that some birds have lived at least 16 years in the same small locality (Prytherch 1997). Indeed, at the time of writing, the average age of birds in this unpersecuted population is likely now to be around 15 years (Robin Prytherch, pers. comm.). In Devon, a nearly all-white bird lived for 21 years near the farm where it was born (Hurrell 1974). The two oldest continental Common Buzzards were in their 29th year (Cramp & Simmons 1980, citing Rydzewski 1974).

Distribution

Today, the Buzzard is the most conspicuous and widely distributed diurnal raptor across most of Britain, by virtue of its generalised feeding habits and habitat needs. Its current status, however, belies its past fluctuations in fortune at the hands of farming and game-bird rearing interests. Somehow, Buzzards have weathered intense and prolonged persecution, the recent and insidious threats from pesticides pollution, and losses or reduction of important prey resources caused by rabbit diseases released by man (as will be chronicled in Chapter 15). Buzzards traditionally are associated most with the thickly wooded valleys, hills and livestock farms of the West Country and Wales. In some of those regions it has long been common to see half-a-dozen or more of the big hawks on the wing and displaying together in spring, or assemblies of several dozen juveniles feeding in fields. In mid-Wales, Buzzards gathering with Red Kites at special feeding stations have become a popular tourist attraction. Wilder landscapes also support many Buzzards, notably the mountains and moorlands of North Wales, Lakeland and the western Scottish Highlands and Islands. In contrast to these classic Buzzard haunts, the flatter and more intensively farmed lowlands of central and eastern England, previously depleted of Buzzards, are now being resettled after absences of a century or more. All these events are chronicled in later chapters.

Where they are not persecuted, Buzzards are found at densities according to the mix of habitats and the amount and variety of prey animals which each sustains. Buzzard densities in Britain tend to be highest on rich farmland in lower hilly regions with a mosaic of deciduous or mixed woodlands scattered amid pastures, numerous hedgerows with trees, and patches of rough grassland and scrub. Densities are lowest where there are extensive deciduous forests or conifer plantations and also in high open moorland and mountain regions. In the early 1990s by far the highest relative densities of Buzzards, as mapped from a BTO atlas survey, were found in central and west Wales, Devon and Cornwall. Other but smaller areas with good numbers were found in the Lake District and in western Scotland from Galloway north to Skye (Gibbons *et al.* 1993, Chapter 15). In Ireland, where Buzzards had been exterminated, their recolonisation – by birds wandering across the sea from south-west Scotland – initially was very slow and restricted to northern counties before subsequently spreading south.

Above: Figure 1.4 Buzzard head close up; the pale eye colour denotes a juvenile. (© Steven Round)

Left: Figure 1.5 A Buzzard skull shows the relatively enormous size of the eyes. (© Colin Whittle)

Buzzards are now the most numerous diurnal bird of prey in Britain, at least 30,000 pairs being estimated by the British Trust for Ornithology (Chapter 15). For such a large bird of prey they can achieve surprisingly high localized densities, as on some small study areas usually covering less than 100 km^2 (Appendix 26). For example, on three areas of rich farmland in North Somerset, the West Midlands and near the Welsh border during the 1990s, each resident pair on average occupied just one square kilometre of land (data collated by Clements 2002). Such high values are not representative for Buzzards across wider agricultural landscapes, however. In 1974 and 1983, two extensive surveys of large samples of rich Devon farmland recorded 3–4 km^2 per Buzzard pair (Sitters 1988) although densities there may since have risen. In upland regions, despite poorer soils and reduced productivity, Buzzard densities of 2 km^2 per pair in one small area and 3–10 km^2 per pair over five large study districts (Appendix 26) have been measured. This subject will be revisited in later chapters.

COMMON BUZZARDS IN EUROPE

Across Continental Europe the Common Buzzard is by far the most numerous raptor, having an estimated population of 370,000–470,000 pairs; with a further 400,000–600,000 pairs of the Steppe Buzzard race in western Russia (Hagemeijer & Blair 1997). The European population, having decreased in central and western countries during the pesticide era, has recovered somewhat and is thought to be possibly stable despite continuing persecution in some regions. More than half of the Common Buzzards are considered to live in Germany (140,000 pairs), Poland (40,000) and France (50,000) compared to around 20,000 pairs in the British Isles (Hagemeijer *et al.* 1997). Their British estimate is now far too low in view of the recent increases in densities and range noted above.

On the Continent, in the breeding season, high densities (similar to those in Britain) have been recorded in several countries. In Germany the average on four farmland study areas ranged from 1.5–8 (average 2.8) km^2 per breeding pair (Mebs 1964). Across a 1,336 km^2 region of Denmark, the average density was 2.6 km^2 per pair (Holstein 1956) while the corresponding figure in France for Buzzards in 148 km^2 of Lorraine was 1.3 km^2 (Thiollay 1967).

Unlike the sedentary British Isles population, those Common Buzzards in Europe that breed in the coldest regions are annual short-medium range migrants. Birds from Norway and Sweden spend winter in the south and west of Europe, though some remain all winter in southern Sweden (Cramp & Simmons 1980, Sylvén 1982). No ringed bird from Scandinavia has yet been recovered in the British Isles although a few of these migrants appear to pass north in spring along the coasts of Kent and East Anglia, and occasional birds might arrive in autumn with Rough-legged Buzzards (Dare 2006). Buzzards from Germany and central Europe are partially migratory and make shorter movements. By contrast, Steppe Buzzards are all long distance migrants and almost all pass through the Middle East in huge flocks to spend winter between north-east and southern Africa. However, small numbers stay in the Middle East and around the Mediterranean Basin while others cross that sea at various points and head for West Africa.

The evident success of the Common Buzzard, at a time when many other European raptors are declining or endangered, can be attributed (as we shall see later) to it being a versatile predator, though mainly a small mammal hunter, with no special habitat or breeding site requirements. Common Buzzards occupy an ecological niche between the bird-hunting specialists of well-wooded country (Sparrowhawk) and the large mammal-hunting eagles of mountainous and other wilderness areas. Moreover, if not persecuted, our Common Buzzards also tolerate human presence more readily than do any other raptors except the Kestrel. Such attributes have enabled them to adapt to diverse and changing environments where, if left undisturbed, they can thrive in many of our modern farmed landscapes.

2

BUZZARD COUNTRY: STUDY AREAS AND METHODS

This chapter describes the physical and ecological features, as well as the Buzzard preys and competitors, found in those upland areas inhabited by the Buzzards whose life stories form the basis for much of this book. I have been fortunate to be able to study Buzzards in three of the most scenic hill regions in western Britain. Their locations, and the sites of other researchers' studies, are mapped in Figure 2.1. An invaluable regional and chronological guide to all this work has been compiled by another Buzzard enthusiast (Whittle 2013).

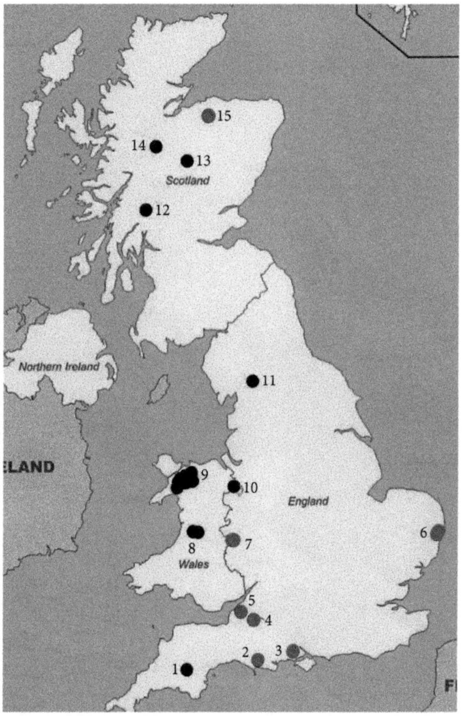

Figure 2.1 Locations of the 15 areas where Buzzard populations have been studied; upland areas in black, lowland in red. 1 Dartmoor; 2 Dorset; 3 New Forest; 4 Somerset; 5 N Somerset; 6 Suffolk; 7 W. Midlands; 8 Mid-Wales; 9 N. Wales; 10 N.E. Wales; 11 N.W. Pennines; 12 Argyll; 13 Strathspey; 14 Glen Urquhart; 15. W Moray.

Although nowadays, happily, Buzzards can be found breeding in most lowland counties further east, it is in the uplands where their aerial performances are seen best, in clear and exhilarating air above splendid panoramas and sometimes in contests with those other superb flyers, Ravens, Red Kites or Peregrines. My first study, on Dartmoor in south-west England, was a very detailed research programme over three years, 1956–58; its aims and field work programmes are outlined in Appendices 2a–2c. I continued to monitor this population during 1962–69, and again during 1990–93. The other studies were made during 1977–84 in north-west Wales, amid the mountains of Snowdonia and across an adjoining hill farming district around the moors of Migneint and Hiraethog, situated in parts of Merioneth and Denbighshire. There, my main interest was to census the total populations and to compare densities and breeding performance with that of the Dartmoor Buzzards and with upland populations then being studied by others in central Wales. The Snowdonia study has been continued by a resident fellow enthusiast, Julian Driver, and now spans 34 years. These study locations are broadly characteristic of uplands elsewhere in Wales, northern England and Scotland where other Buzzard studies have been made. Since 2005, I have been monitoring the recolonisation of an area in the lowlands of East Anglia in north-east Suffolk.

DARTMOOR STUDY AREA

The broad and seemingly desolate expanses of Dartmoor, covering 1,045 km^2 (400 square miles), comprise the highest, largest and wildest upland region in southern England. The moor rises prominently on all sides above the rich farming lowlands of southern Devon to elevations of 210–620 m (690–2,035 ft) above sea level. Geologically, it is a granite massif intrusion, now greatly eroded and weathered down to a gently undulating plateau that is dissected by many river valleys. Here and there, eroded granite outcrops remain on hill tops and ridges to form the well-known rocky tors. Much of the land above 450 m (1,500 ft) is covered by heather moorland and peat bogs devoid of trees. Below about 350 m (1,150 ft), the broadening valleys have largely long been converted to enclosed pastures to support hill farming of sheep and cattle. These are gentler landscapes with scattered spinneys, small woods and shelter-belts of both deciduous and coniferous trees. On common grazing land there are patches of scrub hawthorns, rowans, willows and gorse (scientific species names are listed in Appendix 1). Other commons, particularly on the eastern moor, have been afforested with extensive plantations of conifers.

The study area covers 33 km^2 (12 square miles) of eastern Dartmoor around the hamlet of Postbridge which nestles in a broad shallow basin relatively high up at around 300 m (980 ft). This is a typical, sparsely inhabited hill farming district set amidst heather and grass moors and rough bracken-clad hillsides. About 20% of the land is enclosed grass fields, mainly along the relatively sheltered West Webburn and East Dart valley bottoms. The main crop is winter fodder – formerly hay and root crops, but nowadays mainly silage – for the hardy sheep and cattle, many of which, together with feral ponies, graze over the hills and moors throughout the year. Across the higher northern parts, numerous Bronze Age stone huts and other structures remain as a testament to times when a warmer climate allowed pastoralists to settle and flourish as high as about 500 m (1,600 ft).

The area (Figure 2.2) is bounded on three sides by prominent hills and ridges topped by small rocky tors. It is traversed north to south by four fast-flowing rivers and streams – the East Dart river and the Cherry, Walla and West Webburn brooks descending from the treeless northern moor. The latter area is seldom visited by Buzzards, and thus forms a clear zone in the local Buzzard distribution. The eastern boundary comprises the 5 km long and prominent 'whaleback' ridge of Hameldown rising from 365 m (1,200 ft) at its southern end to 530 m (1,740 ft) in the north, just above the Bronze Age settlement of Grimspound. From

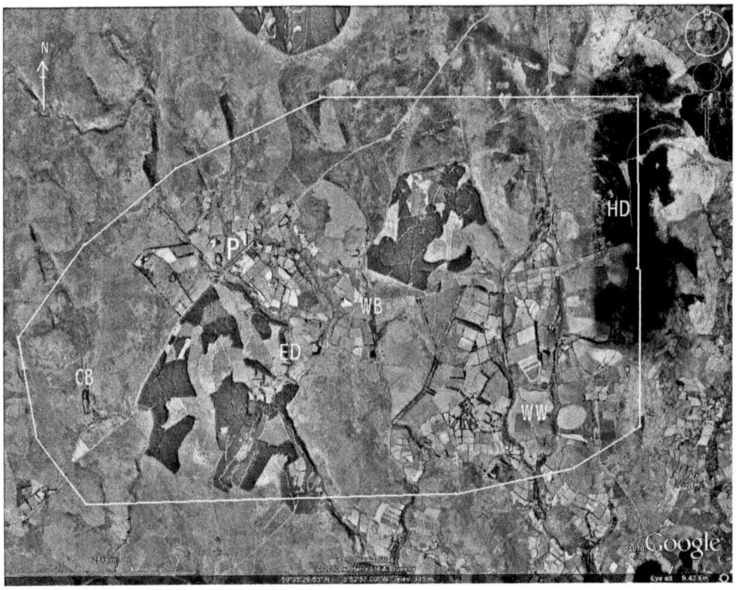

Figure 2.2 Dartmoor (Postbridge) study area in spring showing boundaries and land use patterns. Principal features are: the brown, high, eastern heather ridge of Hameldown (HD); bright green fields in the West Webburn Valley (WW) and around Postbridge (P) separated by moorland areas and dark green conifer plantations (showing recent large clear-fell areas); the East Dart river (ED), Cherry Brook (CB) and Walla Brook (WB). The open moorland of northern Dartmoor extends to the north and west. (© Image, Google Earth)

its summit there are panoramic vistas westwards across the study area (Figure 2.3) to Bellever Tor where the western side of the study area abuts onto open grass moor and bog at 300–350 m (1,000–1,150 ft) elevation. Only the southern (east-west) boundary has no obvious defining topographical features. Instead, it crosses the north-south aligned ridges and river systems with their associated valley bottom cultivations. Buzzards are plentiful immediately downstream beyond this southern margin to the study area.

Habitats

Little more than 20% of land in the study area is enclosed fields. The remainder comprises a mosaic of five major habitats (Figures 2.4, 2.5) which Buzzards utilise fully: heather and grass moors (47%), bogs (4%), coniferous plantations (23%), and mature deciduous or mixed woodland (<1%). The predominantly open nature of this hilly landscape greatly facilitated observations of the daily movements and behaviour of Buzzards through the year.

Heather and grass moors together cover some 1,560 ha of the study area. They are important hunting grounds for the Buzzards, particularly in the breeding season. Above

Figure 2.3 Dartmoor study area viewed in 2013 from (upper) its eastern limit on Hameldown, westwards across northern area with mature conifer plantations; (lower) south-west to the valley farms and southern Dartmoor on the horizon. The landscape has changed little since the 1950s apart from the maturing plantations. (© Roger Smaldon)

Figure 2.4 Dartmoor study area from the air: a soaring Buzzard's eye view north over the central farms, and nest woods of four Buzzard pairs, to the northern moors beyond. (May 1963)

400 m (1,300 ft) in the northern sector, heather moor predominates and still supports a few Red Grouse. Meadow Pipits and Skylarks are plentiful here while Whinchats, Stonechats and Wheatears are more local. Lower down, heather gives way to grass moors between the rivers (Figures 2.2, 2.5b) due to spring burning ('swaling') and heavier grazing pressure. On the lower slopes of some hills, hawthorns are scattered plentifully and bracken smothers large areas. Since 1960 several rough grazing grounds have been fenced and their *Nardus/Agrostis/Molinia* grasses, rush and sedge vegetation, together with scrub hawthorns and gorse, have been replaced by so-called 'improved grassland'. As a result, breeding Curlew and Lapwing have been lost though a few Skylarks may still remain. Along valley bottoms bogs cover some 4% (140 ha) of the study area, some forming extensive cotton grass and *Sphagnum* moss mires. These are important breeding grounds for Snipe and Mallard, and formerly of Lapwing and Curlew. In the larger valley bogs, small thickets of willow scrub flourish and provide hunting perches for Buzzards.

Two large conifer forests at Bellever and Soussons Down, of 660 ha and 265 ha respectively, now cover former grass and heather moors between the 320 m (1,050 ft) and 420 m (1,400 ft) contours in northern and western parts (Figures 2.2, 2.3a). Besides greatly augmenting the amount of woodland around Postbridge, these plantations, in their early stages and after recent clear-felling and regeneration of sections, have provided an entirely new suite of important successional habitats, from dense scrub to mature forest and, latterly, clear-fell

Figure 2.5 (a–c) Dartmoor study area in the 1960s: views eastwards from three western Buzzard territories to the Hameldown ridge boundary.

sections. Buzzards hunt frequently over scrub and clear-fell areas, and nowadays nest in the mature conifers. The main crop is Sitka spruce with some Norway spruce, Scots pine and alien *Pinus contorta*. The breeding Black Grouse and Montagu's Harriers of the 1950s are long gone from the young plantings, but the varied habitats from scrub to mature forest and later the post-harvesting re-growth benefit such breeding specialities as Nightjar, Siskin, Lesser Redpoll and Crossbill, as well as Tree Pipit and various warblers.

In contrast, old deciduous and mixed conifer-deciduous 'woodlands' amount to less than 12 ha and are still decreasing as a result of neglect and storm damage. Nevertheless, virtually all Buzzard nests are sited in shelter-belts, small scattered spinneys and isolated clusters of old timber, sites much favoured also by Redstarts. Other mature deciduous trees are scattered along hedgerows and around Postbridge habitations while the West Webburn valley is comparatively well-wooded on its sheltered western slopes. The predominant deciduous tree is beech, while sycamore, Scots pine and larch are all common. Few ash, oak and birch are found.

Potential preys for Buzzards

Buzzards are known to take a wide range of prey animals, but especially small mammals, and so it was important to gather information on which potential preys inhabited the study area, as well as some idea of their distributions, habitat preferences and comparative abundance from one district and season to another. Estimating prey numbers was impossible and so I relied upon a combination of general field observations and live-trapping of small mammals, supplemented by information from farmers, to obtain broad assessments for ten species of mammal, many birds, two amphibians and three reptiles.

Rabbits during the first years (1956–58) of my study were only beginning to re-colonise the area following the ravages of myxomatosis. This virus epizootic had spread northwards through the area from lower farms in the summer of 1954, by which time Rabbit numbers had reached 'near-plague proportions' around Postbridge. Initially, the few survivors were confined to a few sites in remoter north-west parts, being rare on lower farms. By 1958, however, Rabbits had reappeared in many places though only in small pockets here and there, and their densities were reported to be still far below the pre-myxomatosis levels. Even 50 years later, Rabbits, though now more widespread and plentiful, are being kept in check by periodic recurrent outbreaks of disease.

Of the small mammals, the Short-tailed (Field) Vole was common and widely distributed. They were found especially in young conifer plantings and other rough tussocky grass habitats, though they apparently were never unusually numerous. Farmers sometimes reported small and localised increases when numbers of voles and nests were seen when cutting hay in June or July. Bank Voles were scarcer though widely distributed. The Wood Mouse appeared to be widely distributed in deciduous spinneys and was fairly plentiful in the young conifer plantations. Common Shrews were almost certainly widespread. Moles, or at least their hills, were conspicuously plentiful in pasture fields but were unusual on farms with much moorland terrain.

Four other small mammals were scarce. Both the Brown Rat and House Mouse were reported around many habitations where their numbers were controlled. A few Water Voles lived along all four main waters and their side streams and in associated bogs. The Water Shrew was recorded only in Barn Owl pellets at one farm.

The bird fauna was very diverse, with 98 species from 30 families being observed. However, only a few of the commonest resident species could be considered, either numerically or on a weight basis, to be possibly important Buzzard preys through the year or especially in the breeding season: Carrion Crow, Magpie, Wood Pigeon and Blackbird. During the breeding season many small passerines were present in all habitats, whereas the winter numbers and diversity were very low.

Three reptile species were found here. The Adder (Viper) and Common Lizard were observed and reported to be widespread in small numbers, especially on the heaths, commons and sunny hedge banks. The earliest lizard emergence was noted on 10 February (1957). Slow-worms apparently were rare. Of the amphibians the Common Frog was locally plentiful each year at spawning assemblies in many bogs and beside all rivers and streams. The earliest seen was on 9 February. In contrast, the mainly nocturnal Common Toad was rarely noted.

Associated predators and competitors

Buzzards were not the only predators of small mammals and other vertebrates in the study area. Several mammals and two other birds of prey were potentially important competitors, particularly in the early years following the 1954–55 'crash' in Rabbit numbers. Foxes hunted throughout the area and Badgers occupied at least five setts. Weasels and Stoats, however, appeared to be scarce. Of the two other birds of prey that feed mainly on small mammals, there were 10–12 pairs of sedentary and nocturnal Tawny Owls but not more than three pairs of Kestrel. Possible competitors for carrion, other than Foxes, were the 1–2 pairs of breeding Ravens and 100–150 pairs of Carrion Crows. The latter corvid also competed for nest sites and proved to be an important predator of Buzzard eggs.

Climate

Buzzards on Dartmoor, as in other uplands, must cope with more rigorous weather conditions than do their lowland neighbours, particularly in winter and through the breeding season. The moor forms a major barrier to the prevailing moisture-laden Atlantic winds. Its climate is thus characterized by high rainfall, frequent hill fogs and strong winds throughout the year and by more frequent and heavier snowfalls than occur elsewhere in south-west England. At Postbridge, annual precipitation averages around 2,000 mm (80 in.). Rainfall can be very prolonged even during the Buzzard breeding season, April to July, amounting usually to 350–450 mm (14–18 in.) spread over some 60 rain-days. The adverse effects of such wet weather upon breeding success will become evident later. Snowfalls occur mainly between December and March, but vary greatly in amount. During the early years of my study there were usually fewer than 20 days of actual snow-cover in a year. In severe winters such as 1962–63, however, when several blizzards struck the area, a deep snow-cover and drifts could remain for many weeks. By contrast, the recent run of milder winters (1990–2008) have produced little snow.

The annual mean temperature at Postbridge is about 8°C, and 4°C in winter. Frosts may last several weeks uninterrupted during very cold winters. The coldest weather during my detailed study was in February 1956, when the temperature stayed below freezing on 21 days and remained between –10°C and –11°C on 21 February. In the chick-rearing period the average temperature is approximately 12°C. Frosts can still occur when the first Buzzard clutches are hatching, and clear nights could still be frosty even as late as 26 June. In contrast, prolonged summer heat and comparative drought may also happen at Postbridge, as I recorded in 1957.

Stormy weather is frequent in autumn and winter, when gale-force winds – often with heavy rain and thick hill fog – may lash the moor for days on end. Even in spring and summer, one- and two-day gales or near-gales are not uncommon. Thick hill fogs (low cloud) are frequent and may persist for several days, especially above 300 m, where they often reduce visibility to 20–30 m.

North-west Wales study areas

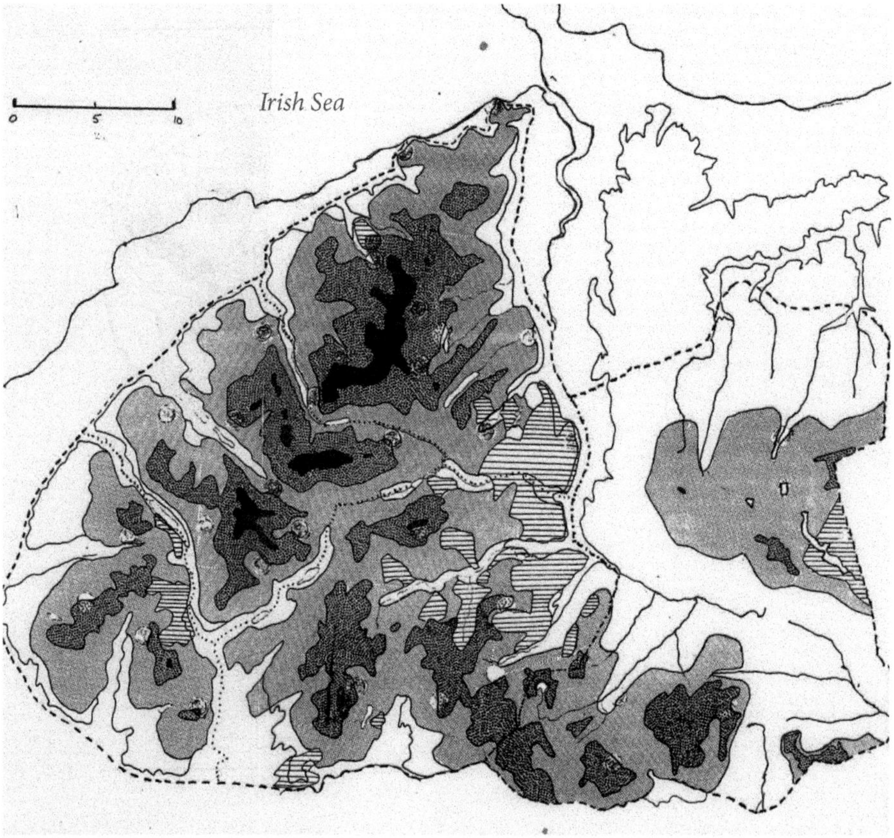

Figure 2.6 Map of the two North Wales study areas: Snowdonia mountains (left) and Migneint-Hiraethog moorlands (right) separated by the Conwy River valley. Lowest contour is at 150 m. White areas are enclosed farmland; shaded areas are open sheepwalk above 150 m, the darkest being above 750 m. Conifer forests are shown by horizontal hatching.

NORTH-WEST WALES STUDY AREAS

Two very large study areas were chosen for the 1977–84 census studies (Figure 2.6). They spanned a wide range of upland topography and habitats. The two regions are separated by the Conwy River and its broad north-south aligned valley. The larger (926 km^2) western area comprised the mountainous region of Snowdonia); while the smaller (440 km^2) area was a contiguous moorland region of hill farms set on and around the moors of Migneint and Hiraethog. These two study sites are thus about 40 and 13 times larger, respectively, than the Dartmoor area. However, as the Welsh moorland area also more closely resembles Dartmoor in its physical, habitats and land use features it will be described first.

1. MIGNEINT-HIRAETHOG MOORS

Much of this delightful region is a gently undulating plateau landscape at around 300–450 m, with the highest ridge at 688 m, and affords wide vistas all around, but especially of the Snowdonia mountain ranges to the west. Given a geological origin predominately of Silurian shales and mudstones, any rocky outcrops are rare although the upper reaches of the Conwy river system descend through narrow rocky gorges at several places. There are only five small villages and 55% of the 1-km squares are either uninhabited or only sparsely inhabited. The area selected is a sample from a far greater upland region across North Wales that extends far to the south and south-east.

From the eastern slopes of the upper Conwy valley the study area encompasses (roughly) a 25 x 17 km block of country dominated by hill sheep farms and moors (Figures 2.7, 2.8). It reaches south to the Llyn Celyn reservoir and nearby mountain of Arenig Fach. Lower and smooth grassy ridges demarcate the south-east and eastern boundaries close to Llangwm and

Figure 2.7 Migneint-Hiraethog study area: view south over hill farms east of the Conwy Valley, to the Hiraethog moor on the horizon (many wooded valleys not visible).

Figure 2.8 Moorland edge farm along the upper Conwy river at 300 m elevation; prime Buzzard habitats.

Figure 2.9 The Migneint study area includes extensive treeless heather and grass moor sheep-walk where Buzzards forage occasionally.

Cerrigydrudion villages; thence northwards to the high moor of Mynydd Hiraethog (496 m) before descending into the Aled valley at Llansannan. The northern boundary, set arbitrarily at the 150 m contour, runs westwards across ridges and small valleys from Llansannan back to the 1 km-wide flood plain of the Conwy valley near Llanrwst town.

Two extensive moors together comprise nearly half (48%) of this study area. Both are used as sheep-walk, as are the rough grazing and heather terrain found in valleys and on hills in the south-east section (Figure 2.9). In the south-west, the lower Migneint moor starts around the source of the River Conwy and presents a 17 km^2 wilderness of cotton-grass blanket bogs, heathery peat hummocks and drier rough grass mounds. Buzzards occasionally hunt across this area from nest sites nearby. From the study area's western limit the land rises abruptly into the bordering mountains of Snowdonia around the vast slate quarries at Blaenau Ffestiniog. The more northerly and higher Hiraethog moor, at around 400 m, is a mosaic of heather and rough grass, with scattered rowans, hawthorns, deciduous tree spinneys and 15 km^2 of conifer plantations that are occupied by breeding Buzzards, Black Grouse, Siskin and Crossbill. Both of the moors are breeding haunts for a few Golden Plover and Dunlin in addition to Lapwing, Snipe, Red Grouse, and scattered Wheatears and Whinchats. With luck, an occasional hunting Merlin, Hen Harrier or Short-eared Owl still may be glimpsed. Carrion Crows and Ravens are ubiquitous scavengers here, as elsewhere, while Meadow Pipits and Skylarks are numerous.

These two moorlands are separated by a broad swathe of pasture fields and damp meadows set in a shallow basin. Together with farms around the edges of the moors, 47% of land is enclosed as sheep and cattle pastures and hay meadows. The damper meadows were favoured by many breeding Lapwing, Curlew, Snipe and Whinchat during my survey period (though all are now much scarcer). Hill farm pastures also extend down the northern slopes from Hiraethog and the eastern flanks of the broad Conwy valley (Figure 2.7). Breeding Buzzards are scattered widely over this predominantly open country where they nest in the few small shelterbelts and groups of trees.

Woodland covers a mere 5% (4% conifers, 1% deciduous). Fine old sessile oak woods here and there line both the upper Conwy river and the narrow sheltered valleys along several small rivers draining down from Hiraethog towards the Irish Sea coast some 10 km to the north. These often steep oak woods harbour most of the Buzzards together with breeding Wood Warblers, Redstarts, Pied Flycatchers and many commoner species. Spinneys and clumps of birch and alder are common in damp valley bottoms while mature trees grow along most valley hedges. On the higher ground away from the River Conwy there are only scattered deciduous and coniferous shelterbelts, small woods and spinneys containing a wide mix of trees. Hedgerows usually retain scattered large oaks, sycamores and birch while rowans and hawthorns grow on rough hillsides.

Potential Buzzard preys and associated fauna

Although the mammal fauna of this area has not been documented, my general observations and local reports indicate that the main preys for Buzzards are all present, with Rabbits, Short-tailed Voles, Moles and Frogs being widespread and locally plentiful. Shrews and Common

Lizards are widespread while Water Voles are found on the Migneint and in other boggy areas and nearby streams (Snowdonia Mammal Group Newsletter, 2007). Brown Hares, Weasels and Stoats also are present on and around Migneint and doubtless elsewhere. Adders appear to be rare or absent. Sheep carrion is available on open moorlands. Foxes roam everywhere but Badgers are restricted to valley woodlands. Carrion Crows are numerous (>200 pairs) but the breeding density of Ravens during the study was much lower (20 pairs at 23.9 km^2 per pair) than in Snowdonia. Kestrels and Tawny Owls were scattered throughout suitable habitats.

Climate

Weather conditions here are intermediate between those in neighbouring Snowdonia and on Dartmoor. Annual rainfall decreases away from Snowdonia; it averages 2,235 mm (88 in.) on the Migneint in the west and about 1300 mm (52 in.) in the east of this moorland region. Snow falls less frequently than in Snowdonia but more often and for longer periods than on Dartmoor, especially in spring. A notably heavy fall occurred in late April 1981, soon after Buzzards had started egg-laying. Temperatures, however, appear to be broadly similar to those noted on Dartmoor for much of the year though at times appreciably colder in the winter.

2. SNOWDONIA

This study area (Figure 2.6) forms the northern sector of the Snowdonia National Park and has long been pre-eminently the domain of Raven and Peregrine. Recently, however, these cliff-nesters have been joined by an increasing number of mountain-dwelling Buzzards. Space permits only a very brief overview of a superb region and its dramatic landscapes of ancient mountain ranges formed from Ordovician rocks, igneous intrusions and Cambrian slates that reach up to 1085 m (3,560 ft) above sea-level. The high ranges are separated by glacially-formed valleys with numerous side valleys, some still harbouring remnants of a subarctic flora. There are also many scenic lakes, high-level tarns, and fast-flowing rivers noted for their salmon and trout fishing. The region is clearly demarcated all round by coastal lowlands and major valleys (Figure 2.6). Many books and articles have been written concerning the landscape, sheep farming, human impacts and general natural history of Snowdonia (notably, North *et al.* 1949 and Condry 1976). However, few detailed ornithological studies have been published other than on the crow family and raptors.

The mountain blocks vary considerably in topography and character. Overlooking the Irish Sea in the north, and the Conwy valley to the east, is the smooth 1,062 m-high 'whaleback' ridge of the Carneddau, which descends steeply at its southern end into the spectacular pass of Nant Ffrancon with its broad and classic U-shape indicating its Ice Age origins. The rugged Glyderau range (Figure 2.10) with their glacially carved hanging *cwms* then rise dramatically across the pass to 999 m before they drop steeply further south into the narrow Llanberis Pass (Figure 2.11). Here, cliff faces tower on both sides above boulder screes, with those on the south side rising precipitously, via still higher *cwms* and cliffs, to the 1,085 m summit of Yr Wyddfa (Snowdon) itself. Crags and cliffs, many fearsome to all but expert rock-climbers,

Figure 2.10 (a) Snowdonia: Nant Ffrancon, view down this glacial valley; Buzzards nest on crags along the far side. (© Mike Alexander)

abound at all elevations but especially along the sides of these two passes. Here, the sonorous croaks of Ravens and strident calls of Peregrines echo around the rock walls. On several cliffs both species nowadays share their formerly secluded haunts with rock climbers while some must share their air space with fast and ultra-low-flying military aircraft; Buzzard pairs in Nant Ffrancon can look down upon RAF Hawk jet trainers routinely roaring down the pass below them. In a nearby valley I watched as one jet missed a soaring Buzzard by less than 100 m. Collisions with aircraft have been documented officially elsewhere in Britain. Twelve Buzzards were known to have been killed during the eleven years 1966–76, mainly at low levels in mountain and moorland areas (Rochard & Horton 1977).

From high on Snowdon's central massif can be seen several lesser ranges and intervening valleys that are all occupied by Buzzards, Peregrines and Ravens. These include the notably verdant and wooded Nantgwynant (Figure 2.12). To the north-east is the isolated 872m peak of Moel Siabod (Figure 3.8a) and, beyond it, the more distant wooded valleys along the Conwy tributaries. Away to the south-east, across the attractive valley and lakes of Nantgwynant, are

Figure 2.10 (b) Snowdonia: Nant Ffrancon; view up the valley; Buzzards nest on crags along both sides.

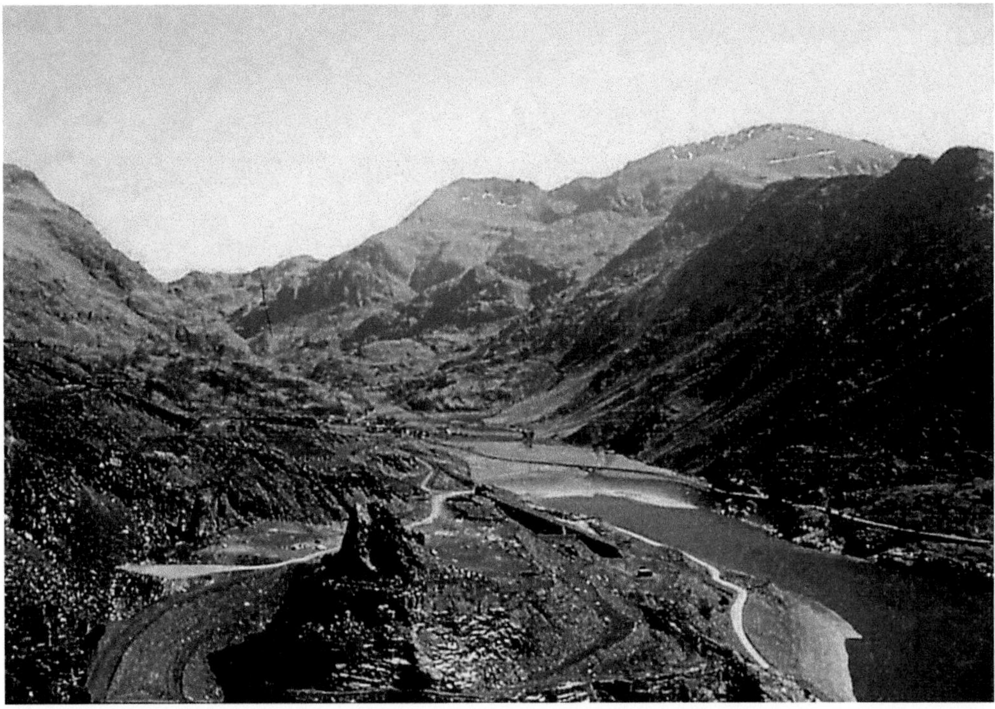

Figure 2.11 Snowdonia: Llanberis Pass beneath the massif of Yr Wyddfa (Snowdon).

Figure 2.12 (a) Snowdonia: Nantgwynant below the eastern flank of Yr Wyddfa; view south upper sector (© Mike Alexander).

Figure 2.12 (b) Snowdonia: Nantgwynant below the eastern flank of Yr Wyddfa; lower sector view south to Moel Hebog.

the imposing outlier blocks of the Moelwynion (770 m), hidden beyond which is the thickly wooded and deep Vale of Ffestiniog, which forms a natural southern boundary to the park and my survey area. Due south is Moel Hebog (782 m) with Tremadoc Bay visible beyond on a clear day. Then, around to the south-west, are the lower (*c*.700 m) but still prominent ranges either side of the Nantlle Valley. Finally, westwards beyond the foothills of Snowdon and the coastal lowlands, can be seen the Irish Sea and the Isle of Anglesey (Ynys Môn). Such are the panoramas that can seen by Buzzards soaring above central Snowdonia.

Habitats

Hill sheep farming prevails throughout the park. In terms of land use, 66% of Snowdonia is sheep-walk (Figure 2.13), 16% is enclosed pastures, 11% woodlands (8% coniferous, 3%

Figure 2.13 Snowdonia: mountain sheep-walk above Nantgwynant; foraging ground for Buzzards.

deciduous), 3% lakes, 3% quarry sites and only 1% is urbanized. Human habitations are restricted to foothill farmsteads and cottages, and widely scattered villages and small towns in the valley bottoms and around the borders. Working farmsteads are scattered widely. Even so, some 55% of the 1 km squares are uninhabited or contain only isolated, and mostly holiday, cottages.

On many mountain sides there are huge expanses of mountain sheep-walk carpeted with rough acid-loving grasses and patches of heather moor (Figure 2.13). These make up about two-thirds of the survey area. Meadow Pipits are numerous up here to the highest levels. On rocky slopes with bilberry and heather, Ring Ouzels and Wheatears are widespread. There is a large and ubiquitous sheep population which was increased rapidly during recent decades,

Figure 2.14 Snowdonia: most Buzzards nest in deciduous and conifer woodlands, as here along the upper Conwy valley.

causing environmental damage by overgrazing, a trend now being eased by a reversal in hill-farming support policies. However, whereas the high grazing intensity adversely affected vegetation cover, the greater availability of sheep carcasses on the mountains has benefited Buzzards, Ravens and Carrion Crows as well as, doubtless, Foxes and other scavengers (Driver & Dare 2009).

Many mountains bear the scars of industrial quarrying and mining, most notably for slate, and in a few places for hard igneous rocks, on a vast and impressive scale though activities now have virtually ceased. Despite being 'blots on the landscape' for some people, many long-abandoned quarries have weathered and are becoming havens for flora and birds. Notable birds that utilise the man-made cliff ledges and caverns are Ravens, Buzzards, Kestrels, Peregrines and occasionally Choughs and Ring Ouzels.

The valley floors and lower slopes, below 300 m, form a patchwork of enclosed low-grade farmland, for sheep and cattle grazing, wet patches and many woods (Figures 2.12, 2.14). Delightful deciduous woodlands of sessile oak, some mixed with ash and birch, are a prominent feature. They are significant habitats for breeding Buzzards, Redstarts, Pied Flycatchers and Wood Warblers as well as for many common woodland birds. Clumps of old Scots pines grow here and there. Bracken and scrub cover is extensive in places. Several large plantation forests of conifers (80 km^2) were planted 35–90 years ago in some eastern and south-eastern valleys, even on steep rugged slopes (Figure 2.14). The mature stands of spruces and firs are important for breeding Siskins, occasionally Crossbills and for Sparrowhawks. On the steepest slopes, even at low levels, craggy outcrops, cliff faces and disused slate quarries are widespread. Many attract nesting Ravens, Jackdaws, Kestrels and Buzzards. Immediately above the woodland zone are unenclosed rough grass slopes (*ffridd*) with bracken, scrub, scattered rowan, birch and hawthorn as well as some rougher terrain where, among the numerous sheep, typical breeding birds include Wheatears, Tree Pipits and Willow Warblers.

Potential Buzzard preys and associated fauna

Snowdonia supports all the potential mammalian, bird and other vertebrate prey species found on Dartmoor and the Migneint-Hiraethog study areas. However, given the greater size, altitudinal range and habitat diversity of Snowdonia, species with restricted distributions are not available to many Buzzards. The following general account of the current status of mammals, reptiles and amphibians has been gleaned mainly from the recent observations of Julian Driver (*in litt.* 2009), made during the course of his own long-term Buzzard and Raven field work, supplemented by older information published by Condry (1974).

Only five prey species are found at almost all elevations – Short-tailed (Field) Vole, Common Shrew, Pygmy Shrew, Common Lizard and Common Frog. Of these, the vole is widespread and often numerous on high grass slopes while the frogs spawn up to 900–1,000 m in boggy pools, despite partial ice and snow cover at times in spring. Adders are surprisingly scarce on the hills except in a few favoured locations. Moles are found throughout richer grasslands, even up to 890 m. Brown Hares, though uncommon, range up grassy slopes to 400–500 m, occasionally higher. Rabbits are restricted to lower slopes, seldom reaching 400 m, and seem nowhere to be numerous. All the above species also occupy lower valley habitats, where both Bank Vole and Wood Mouse are abundant, Grey Squirrel common in woodlands, Common Toads are plentiful, and Slow-worm locally common. Both Water Vole and Water Shrew seem to be scarce, perhaps because many stream flows are too fast and frequently in spate. Of the predatory mammals that may compete with Buzzards, both Fox and Stoat are common and hunt also high up the mountains, the Fox having increased markedly since the 1970s. Weasels, however, seem to be confined to lower regions. Badger numbers have risen with a spread from valley woodlands up onto lower but exposed mountain slopes. Sheep carrion, often widely available on the mountain sides, is of prime importance for Buzzards breeding at higher elevations (Driver & Dare 2009). In the late spring of 2013 a pair of Buzzards was observed scavenging from the carcasses of mountain ponies that had died on the tops during a severe late March blizzard (J. Driver, *in litt.*).

Potential avian competitors with Buzzards for food and (or) nest sites are Carrion Crows which are abundant and ubiquitous, with perhaps more than 2,000 pairs plus non-breeders. Ravens are common and nest at all levels. Their numbers have increased rapidly in recent decades from 98 breeding pairs in the early 1980s (Dare 1986) to around 175 pairs by 2005 (Driver 2006). Tawny Owls occupy many woodlands, but Kestrels are scattered thinly and well outnumbered by Buzzards (Dare 1986).

Climate

The climate of Snowdonia below about 600 metres is broadly similar to that of Dartmoor, a reflection of their exposure predominantly to Atlantic weather systems. In the central Snowdonian valley of Dyffryn Mymbyr, at 215 m (710 ft) at Capel Curig, the average annual precipitation is around 2,450 mm (88 in.) with an average temperature of 9.1°C. However, at higher elevations the montane climate is much more extreme. Buzzards residing on the treeless upper slopes face particularly tough conditions even during the breeding season. Up there, annual precipitation exceeds 3,000 mm (120 in.) around the highest ranges where much may fall as snow through winter and early spring. Cloud base often is well down the mountain sides at any time of year while severe gales off the nearby Irish Sea are funnelled through the passes during stormier periods. The wide altitudinal range also results in temperatures on the high summits being on average 5°C colder than those in valley bottoms. The upper slopes are especially inhospitable for birds in winter when temperatures usually remain close to or below freezing. Snow falls are much more frequent and heavier than on Dartmoor. Above 450 m periods of snow cover are common during December to March, and often last many weeks on the high ranges. Heavy though short-lived snowfalls in April are not unusual down to 150 m; one such occurred in late April 1981 soon after Buzzards had started egg-laying. Light falls on the highest tops may happen briefly in May or even in early June, as I observed on 2 June 1975.

3

BUZZARDS IN WINTER
(DECEMBER–FEBRUARY)

Winter in the British uplands is a testing time for our sedentary Buzzards. Not only must they survive often rigorous weather conditions but also, despite the short day lengths available for hunting, find sufficient food to be in good physical condition for the start of the next breeding season. This chapter describes how Buzzards prepare for and maintain themselves through an average winter, and respond to any severe cold weather that may occur from December into February, and even in March.

Mid-winter is a period of relative stability in a Buzzard population. As a result, this is, perhaps surprisingly, a good time to begin a field study of Buzzards. The brighter mild interludes can provide good opportunities for observing these hawks and to become familiar with the habitats in a chosen study area. During December and January the Buzzards are least mobile, instead spending most of the short day on rest and hunting perches. From careful observations, using telescopes or binoculars, many Buzzards can then be recognised individually from distinctive variations in plumage patterns, some of which were shown in the introductory chapter. The recent advent of high definition digi-scoping photographic techniques should make this approach very practical, thereby obviating the formidable problems that otherwise would be associated with trapping fully-grown hawks for colour marking or for fitting with radio-tracking devices. The ability to distinguish individual Buzzards in the field enables one to discern, for example, how adults and juveniles in the local population are dispersed across the area, their social interactions in winter and through their yearly cycle, and to follow the breeding fortunes of each pair for a number of years.

BUZZARDS AS INDIVIDUALS

The highly variable plumage markings of Buzzards can, with care, be used not only to identify individual adults but also to distinguish between adults and fully-fledged young birds (juveniles) through their first autumn and winter. By photographing individuals, one perhaps may be able even to identify older immatures or sub-adults in their intermediate plumage stages, as is being done with Buzzards in a North Somerset study (Prytherch 2009). Plumage patterns are not sex specific; instead, one must rely on behavioural clues to distinguish between the sexes.

The overall colour tone may vary from rich dark brown to a colder ash-brown or even rufous (Figure 3.2c). Among adult Buzzards in Britain the most typical features that can be used, either singly or in combination, are the presence and extent of a pale U-shaped band across the lower breast, coupled with the pattern of dark areas of mottled brown on the throat and upper breast, and of any brown and white barring or dark patches on the belly and flanks (Figure 1.3). The under-wing pattern sometimes might also be a useful additional guide. Many adults have dark under-wing coverts, often a darker carpal patch, and broad dark ends to the flight feathers. These contrast to a greater or lesser degree with a broad white central zone, patch or 'flash' across both the bases of the secondaries and especially the primaries. The rear edge of the wings generally has a dark border. The upperparts are usually too uniform to be of reliable use.

Most juvenile Buzzards (Figure 1.2) can be identified readily, given a good view, in their first autumn and winter, perhaps even into the following spring or summer. They often show pale creamy throats and central breast areas with variable amounts of prominent brown streaks and 'tear drops'. These distinctive markings may extend onto the lower breast and belly or merge into a variegated patchwork of mottling, spots and pale areas. The juveniles lack pectoral bands and ventral barring. At close range their eyes (irides) are seen to be markedly paler than those of adults, being a tawny, even yellowish colour in contrast to the warm deep (Tawny Owl-like) brown of adults. Nearly all published photographs of Buzzards feeding at carrion baits are clearly juveniles, with prominent pale eyes and streaked throats and breasts. The under-wings of juveniles generally are darker than those of adults. They have a less contrasting pattern owing to more extensive transverse rows of brown spotting or barring across the flight feathers (Figure 1.4, and see also Forsman 1999).

A few Buzzards can be very pale and show uniform creamy-white areas on various parts of the body and wings (Figure 1.3d). Such leucistic birds are most likely to have pale under-parts and under-wing surfaces; others may have pale heads or patches on the upper wing coverts and back. Some combinations produce strikingly handsome looking Buzzards and 10–15 such birds have been reported over the years in the Devon county bird reports (DBRs), with a few others from elsewhere in western Britain. Exceptionally, virtually all-white Buzzards have been observed in Devon. I saw one such handsomely marked bird which stayed briefly in my Dartmoor study area one autumn. The presence of any unusually marked Buzzard in an area is, of course, a bonus for the observer.

A remarkable female, all-white save for a few pale buff patches, lived for 21 years (1952–73) in south Devon (photograph in Hurrell 1974). Her mate and all offspring were 'normal' Buzzards. Two similar birds lived for 19 and 11 years in mid-Devon while a dead white Buzzard was found in 1947 in east Devon (DBRs). In my study area a 'practically white' Buzzard was reported twice during spring in the myxomatosis outbreak year of 1954, not long before my study began. A similarly white Buzzard seen in 1950 less than 5 km outside the study area might have been the same bird. All leucistic Buzzards retain the normal dark eye coloration. Other strikingly variant Devon Buzzards have been recorded on seven occasions: two otherwise normal Buzzards but with clear white rump patches such that they resembled 'ringtail' Hen Harriers, a bird with Osprey-like head and body markings, two very dark or melanistic individuals, another with a rufous tail and, finally, one with its plumage suffused with a blue-grey hue. In the late 1800s single 'ginger' and 'almost black' specimens were collected (D'Urban & Mathew 1892). Continental populations of this hawk are even more variable, and display a higher incidence of leucistic and melanistic individuals.

Value of individual recognition in field studies

The value of being able to recognise particular Buzzards was first demonstrated during my 1955–58 study on Dartmoor (Dare 1961). There, individual plumages were documented or sketched in the field from observations using a pocket telescope (x 20 magnification). Nowadays, one could employ digital still and video cameras fitted with zoom lenses, and then examine plumages in detail and at leisure on a computer screen. On Dartmoor the Buzzards, especially when perched in winter, often could be approached closely enough to check identities, and in almost all weathers and terrains, from a 4-wheel drive Land Rover. Frequent prolonged watches showed crucially how appearances could change with different lighting, weather and state of the annual moult. A log of each bird's sightings was kept. Using these simple, if time consuming, methods enabled identification of most of the 20–30 Buzzards

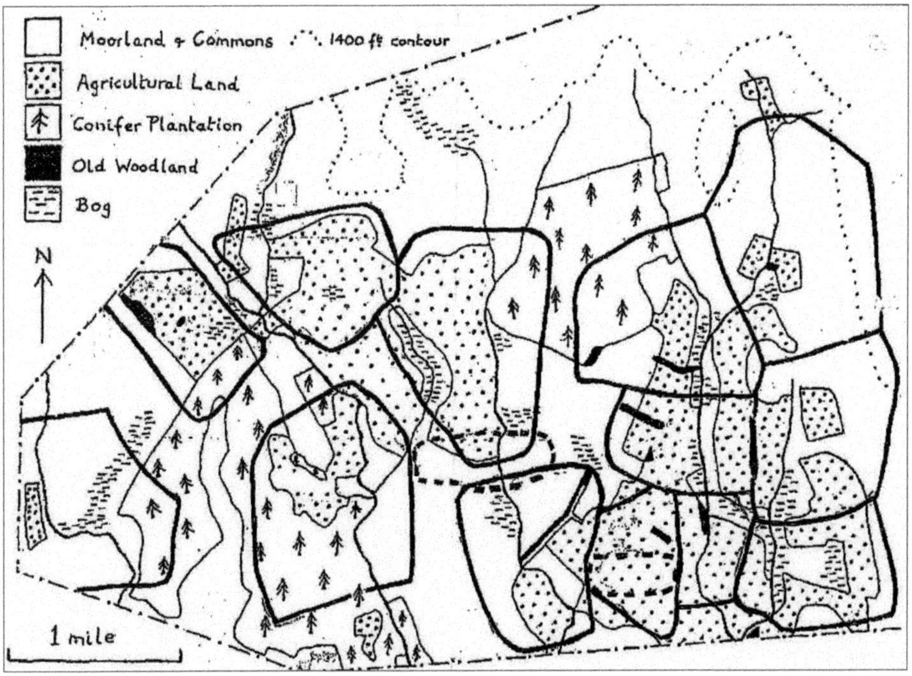

Figure 3.1 Sketch map of the consistent pattern of Buzzard territories determined by observing individual pairs in winter and spring in a Dartmoor study area. Two temporary breeding territories are shown by broken lines. The basic pattern was still recognisable in 1990–94. (Dare 1961, 1998)

living in the study area. By following their daily locations and movements, a clear pattern of their local distributions was mapped showing their winter home ranges and main hunting areas. During subsequent spring and breeding season months any changes in distribution were plotted (Figure 3.1). It soon became evident that the population was made up of pairs occupying and defending discrete territories – the first confirmation of such behaviour among Common Buzzards (Dare 1961).

In spring, birds could be sexed during courtship and from other behaviour. Although female Buzzards are slightly larger, being around 10% heavier than males, they can seldom be reliably distinguished in the field on physical dimensions.

Plumage patterns later were used by other workers for more detailed behavioural studies of Buzzards. On Speyside, in the Scottish Highlands, Douglas Weir and Nick Picozzi were able, among other aspects, to study behavioural interactions and reveal the existence of dominance hierarchies between age groups and individuals through the year (Weir & Picozzi 1975, 1983). More recently in North Somerset, Robin Prytherch has been studying social interactions within a Buzzard population (Prytherch 2009). Some of the findings from these meticulous observers are featured in later chapters.

POPULATION STRUCTURE

On Dartmoor and in other upland study areas, the Buzzards present in winter were found to be predominantly paired adults residing in territories which they used and defended for feeding and breeding purposes, as will be described later. Many of these adults would have bred here in the previous spring. A few of their offspring remained with their parents through the winter before leaving to find their own places to settle (Dare 1961). A third and minor component of the winter population comprised itinerant older immature birds from elsewhere that were seeking mates and territories. In lowland regions Buzzard populations appear to be similar in composition in both North Somerset (R. Prytherch, *in litt.*) and Dorset (Walls & Kenward 1995, Tyack *et al.* 1998).

A good example of an upland winter Buzzard population is that occupying the Dartmoor area where usually 12–14 pairs resided in 33 km^2 around Postbridge. During three successive winters some 95% of the birds were territorial adults. Juveniles still staying with their parents comprised 4–6% of the resident Buzzards in December and January and 0–3% in February. The last youngster was seen on 20 February. In mid-Wales and Speyside study areas a few juveniles were still present into early March (Newton *et al.* 1982, Picozzi & Weir 1976). Some were in peripheral areas of the parental territories. Additionally, a very small number of wandering (itinerant) Buzzards, of unknown age and origins, were occasionally detected at Postbridge, sometimes by the defensive reactions of adults towards such intruders. The first wanderers might appear as early as mid-January and take up any vacant ground resulting from deaths or other 'disappearances' of previous occupants. In one instance, a replacement male for a 'widowed' female arrived in late February, some six weeks after I had found her mate dead. This spring replacement phase was completed by mid-March. It seems very likely, from the tracking of radio-tagged young Dorset Buzzards, by Sean Walls and Robert Kenward, that Postbridge newcomers would have been reared in this part of Dartmoor and were returning to settle close to their natal areas after one or more years spent wandering in Devon, or perhaps further afield (Walls & Kenward 1995).

TERRITORIES

The Buzzard pairs on Dartmoor in winter kept within limited hunting ranges, as did the few single adults. Range borders were marked by certain hedges, favourite trees, fence posts or other prominent features. These perches enabled Buzzards to advertise passively their presence and to observe the activities of neighbours. Many such markers also served as hunting perches where birds spent most of each winter day, particularly in valley bottoms and other relatively sheltered locations. The Buzzards flew very little, mainly short distances between hunting stations, and were generally silent except for occasional brief '*pee-ya*' contact calls. Some would call once or twice as they flew in to roost in a wood at dusk. Roosting flights, from over 200–300 metres away, were quite distinctive, being direct and purposeful at tree-top height with rapid wing beats, as described for Cornish birds (Ryves 1948). Mates roosted near one another. The members of one pair were seen to arrive only five minutes apart even though coming from different directions. Five such roosting flights were observed between 19–38 minutes (average 28 minutes) after local sunset on clear afternoons in December and January. On dull days birds could be expected to roost earlier. Further evidence that Buzzards may utilise all available daylight for hunting are found in a continental study (Schuster 1949). In Germany, the roosting flight times varied from 29 minutes before to 24 minutes after dusk, though neither month nor definition of dusk are evident. The Buzzards left roosts early, between 29–55 minutes before sunrise.

Overt signs of territorial behaviour towards neighbours were seldom noticed until late winter (see next chapter). On dull, cold or windy days many birds could be unobtrusive and difficult to locate as they kept within tree cover or hunted from the lee side of copses and shelterbelts. One Buzzard even flew into the centre of a large hawthorn, in Sparrowhawk fashion. On such days, not more than 30–50% of birds could be located, even after searching some territories three times. Buzzards in Snowdonia likewise became inconspicuous in winter and seldom appeared much above the tree tops.

Those Dartmoor pairs with smaller territories, of 50–100 ha, in valley bottom farmland hunted regularly over most of their area. Those with larger territories that included much treeless moorland and open hillsides concentrated their hunting in core areas on lower ground where hunting perches were more available. The subject of Buzzard territories will be covered in detail in Chapter 10. In Snowdonia many of the lower altitude Buzzards likewise withdrew to valley bottoms for much of the winter in the earlier study years around 1980. More recently, however, at the currently much higher population density (Driver & Dare 2009, Appendix 24), the Buzzards appear to have occupied their entire territories, even at high elevations, during the milder 1990–2005 winters with reduced snow-cover. With winter sheep carrion nowadays scarcer here, the flocks instead being wintered on low ground, the montane Buzzards are thought to subsist instead on Short-tailed (Field) Voles and shrews found on snow-free wind-cleared slopes. These preys may be supplemented by Frogs that have been seen emerging intermittently during mild spells even at such high elevations (Julian Driver, *in litt.*). The ability of Buzzards to withstand lengthy privation in severe cold is discussed below. On upper Speyside the Buzzards retreated down to valley bottom sections of their territories in colder winters where they defended smaller core areas of 45–200 ha, on average 105 ha (Weir & Picozzi 1983).

WINTER CHALLENGES

At this coldest and darkest time of year the Buzzards (like other birds) need to find sufficient food to satisfy their daily energy requirements, including higher thermoregulation demands to maintain body temperature when hunting time is at a premium. Day length (sunrise to sunset) at the latitude of Dartmoor ranges from a mere 8 hours in December to nearly 11 hours at the end of February; and, of course, it is shorter still in the Scottish areas where Buzzards have also been studied. Furthermore, food abundance is declining, as mammalian prey populations approach the lowest points of their annual cycles (Chapter 12), while prey availability may suddenly be cut off at the coldest time by heavy and prolonged snow cover. The survival strategies evolved by Buzzards involve: first, the accumulation of body fat reserves in autumn, followed in winter by conserving energy through reducing physical activities to the minimum needed to obtain food. In southernmost Sweden, where Buzzards likewise stay in their breeding areas, at the same latitude as southernmost Scotland, their daily activity patterns (time budgets) were measured through the year by Magnus Sylvén (Sylvén 1982). In winter the birds conserved energy by reducing active flight to only 22 minutes a day during December and January, after which it rose to 66 minutes in February with the approach of spring. Otherwise, they rested or hunted statically from perches. A third and vital requirement is the possession of an exclusive hunting territory supporting an adequate supply of catchable prey animals.

Preparing for winter

The accumulation of body fat reserves in autumn, when food is most plentiful, is crucial for Buzzards to have a good chance of surviving the harshest conditions they may encounter in winter at latitudes similar to those of the British Isles. Fat deposition begins in adults during the summer, after breeding, but mainly from September into November when small mammals are most numerous. As the reserves are used progressively through winter, so body weights fall. In central Germany, the average weight of reserves, measured in 195 dead Buzzards at the start of winter in December, amounted to 183 g (15.6% of body weight) in females and 130 g (14.2%) in the smaller males. Over winter the average Buzzard weight fell by 12%, from 992 g to 872 g (Piechocki 1970, in Sylvén 1982). The fat reserves of Swedish Buzzards are nearly exhausted by April. In southern Sweden, where 109 Buzzards were trapped for ringing, the average weight fell by 7% over a normal winter, from 989 g in December to 917 g by March (Sylvén 1982).

Comparable information for British Buzzards is lacking although three Devon birds that I examined in the 1955–56 autumn and winter contained substantial fat reserves. An adult female (killed by road traffic) in January was in excellent condition and weighed 1,220 g of which 63 g (5%) were visible fat deposits. These comprised: a 3-15 mm thick 'shield' over the viscera, a thick coating to the whole intestine, fat around the kidneys and on the dorsal wall of both abdominal and thoracic cavities, a thick layer over the posterior pectoral muscles, as well as up to 7 mm of subcutaneous fat over the ventral abdominal cavity. Two other adults examined in good condition with large visceral fat deposits were: a 1,130 g female killed by a train in October, and a 860 g male that had been shot in January.

DAILY FOOD REQUIREMENTS

The amount of food that a bird needs to catch each day varies continuously in relation to the vital need to maintain body temperature at all times, despite fluctuating ambient air temperatures, and the physical activities essential to each season of its annual life cycle. Food requirements can be estimated for each month by, first, calculating the energetic costs (in kilocalories or kcal) of each activity (such as thermoregulation, resting, flight, moult) and then applying these rates of energy expenditure to the average amount of time spent daily (24 hours) on each activity. The integrated final values then indicate the daily energy expenditure (DEE) which needs to be balanced by the energy obtained from food consumed. Finally, using the average size and energy (caloric) value of various Buzzard preys, the DEE can be expressed in terms of total prey weight (biomass) or as the numbers of each prey animal required. Such laborious investigations have been undertaken for Buzzards that were observed throughout the year in southern Sweden (Sylvén 1982). His findings help to explain many aspects of the Buzzard's lifestyle not previously examined; these will be detailed in Chapter 11.

During the three winter months, the average DEE of Buzzards in south Sweden was estimated to be 143 kcal for males and 160 kcal for the larger females; which approximates to the energy value of 100 g fresh weight of mammalian flesh (Appendix 3) or to about 10% of a Swedish Buzzard's average winter weight. In prey terms 100 g equates to, for example, four or five adult Short-tailed Voles of 20–25 g body weight. The DEE of Dartmoor Buzzards should be somewhat lower because the southern Sweden winter is colder; it averaged 0.2°C during Magnus Sylvén's study compared with about 4°C at Postbridge (Dare 1961). The milder temperatures on Dartmoor, however, could be offset by higher 'wind and rain chill' levels that are often experienced there. In Red-tailed Hawks (*B. jamaicensis*), and other North American raptors, it is known that energy expenditure increases under these conditions (Hayes & Gessaman 1980, Wilson *et al.* 2004). Nevertheless, using the Swedish values, the need for a Buzzard to obtain at least 100 g of food a day to balance its energy demands may be adopted as a reasonable first estimate. These calculations give a fair idea of the hunting challenges faced daily by Buzzards irrespective of fluctuating weather conditions. We shall return later to explore the topic of food requirements (Chapter 11).

FINDING FOOD

In winter Buzzards on the moor, and probably widely elsewhere, routinely employ two unspectacular but energy-efficient hunting methods: searching for small mammals from perches, supplemented by foraging on the ground for invertebrates as a back-up when larger prey activity is depressed by wet weather conditions.

Hunting from perches

Every Buzzard home range contained a number of favourite hunting perches (Figure 3.2a–c) which were used with great regularity, probably at least once a day, by one or both members of a pair. Although a pair might associate together when hunting, cooperative hunting was never suspected. The partners searched quite independently and were often out of sight of one another or at opposite ends of their land. Small kills (voles etc.) were not shared, even if mates were not far apart. On the other hand, sharing a large kill (young Rabbit) was observed once, and is probably normal behaviour. The perches appeared to be prime requisites of a good territory and were guarded against trespassers at all times. Visits to perches lasted from two minutes to over two hours and, sometimes perches seemed to be used in some sort of sequence. One bird worked systematically along a row of fence posts one way and then

Figure 3.2 (a–c): In winter, Buzzards hunt small mammals predominantly from perches in trees and on fence posts. Birds on posts are easiest for individual identification. Fig 3.2c is an unusually rufous bird. (© a and b: Mark Darlaston; c: Steven Round)

Figure 3.2 c

back again. Another pair, watched for 2.25 hours, hunted independently and silently, each thoroughly searching from posts the ground along the boggy sides of a stream.

Many perches commanded an extensive field of view for detecting prey, as well as intruders and potential threats. Situations most favoured were tall stout fence posts, roadside telegraph poles, isolated bush tops and, above all, bare or dead prominent limbs of tall trees, visited frequently. Other trees provided inconspicuous and sheltered resting places, especially on the margin of a belt of trees. Pellets were found at times under these trees. Where high perches were scarce, Buzzards made do with much lower sites such as small bushes, old stone walls, prominent rocks and even grassy banks on slopes.

Perching quietly, head to wind and motionless on its vantage point, a Buzzard would scan its surroundings, occasionally showing interest in some detected movement by a sudden shifting of its gaze and quick forward jerking motions of its head. These slight head movements (as in other raptors) aid distance perception and focusing, even for a hawk possessing binocular vision and great visual acuity (Tucker 2000). Prey was captured by a swift glide down and away from the perch for distances up to 40 m, depending to a great extent on the perch height. Occasionally, prey was caught close beneath a perch by a quick pounce, sometimes with an oblique side-slipping motion. Small vertebrate prey, typically small mammals, would then be eaten on the ground or taken to a nearby perch.

Evidence of sharp visual acuity, or ability to discern fine details at distance, in Buzzards hunting from perches was demonstrated on several occasions by some impressive performances. One bird glided about 5 m away from a 0.5 m-high post to take beetles in a sheep pasture. Another bird on a 4 m-high bush top suddenly flew off low over freshly snow-covered ground for 20–30 m, then dropped into an open patch of rushes and emerged with a Frog in its talons! The visual acuity of Buzzards is probably about three times greater than that of the human eye, as has been measured for various American hawks and other raptors (Fox *et al.* 1976).

Hunting from perches is the most energy efficient method, particularly in winter, for catching ground-dwelling prey ranging from invertebrates to (especially) Rabbits. However, as a certain minimum time must be spent at each station, to allow prey a chance to appear, an entire Buzzard territory can be searched only slowly by using perches. Instead, in winter, the Buzzards concentrated their efforts on certain habitat patches, favouring especially areas of scrub with rough tussocky grass and other coarse ground vegetation where small mammals were most likely to be found, as the following account based on my field notes describes:

> *On a sunny December day, after an early frost, a Buzzard hunts from 3-4 m high bush tops beside a large patch of rough grass bordering the West Webburn stream. Its posture is tense as it not only peers down but also seems to be listening for prey movements and squeaks in the ground cover. It catches no fewer than four full-grown Short-tailed Voles within 30 minutes! Each vole is captured by gliding out some 8-10 m from the perches. In taking the third vole the hawk evidently misses at first strike, for it pauses alert in the grass for a moment then strides forward a few paces and lashes out with a talon to make the kill. Each victim is then swiftly torn up and eaten either*

on the ground or on nearby fence posts before the hawk moves to a new vantage point. A few discarded viscera are snatched by a bold Carrion Crow as soon as the Buzzard returns to its hunting perch. After the last kill the Buzzard moves to a new and lower (1.5 m) perch, from which it soon glides out 6 m to its last catching place. There, it pauses some 30 seconds, as if listening, before returning to the perch. After such unusual hunting success the Buzzard then flies away low and out of sight.

Undoubtedly, Buzzards at times also hunted more covertly, from trees within or around the edges of spinneys and small woods. Occasionally, birds were noted at dusk stationed in trees overlooking hedge banks known to be harbouring Rabbits which in winter emerge to feed only at dusk. Crepuscular hunting is perhaps frequent through the year and may be especially vital in winter when daylight is so short and Buzzards can just be seen flying at last light to their roosts.

Attempts to catch bird prey from perches were rarely witnessed in this area. One Buzzard made an opportunistic winter attack on birds which it chanced upon while changing hunting perches. This hawk was gliding low down across a sloping field and just rising to clear a low hedge, or perhaps perch on top, when suddenly it threw itself sideways down into a shallow rushy depression in the hedge bottom. Its lightning dive narrowly missed several Snipe and a Blackbird which flushed in alarm, but the hawk rose without a kill and promptly made off to perch in the lower field.

Juvenile (first-winter) birds still in parental territories on the moor maintained a low profile and were seldom seen hunting, though one was catching small mammals by December. Usually, they were noticed only when noisily but unsuccessfully begging for food. One youngster, however, did succeed in obtaining a Blackbird kill from a parent in early February.

Ground foraging

On a dank, calm and gloomy but mild day in January, with hill mist draping the slopes of Hameldown across the valley, a Buzzard forages from fence posts along a low bank bordering a pasture field. The turf is sprinkled with Mole hills among which a small mixed flock of Lapwing and Golden Plover is feeding. The hawk drops into the field at intervals to pick up invertebrates. Standing on the short grass, it is alert with head held high as it pauses every few steps before running with a surprisingly nimble but rather ungainly gait to snatch a beetle or surfacing earthworm 1–3m away. The plovers meanwhile take little notice of the Buzzard and some even allow it to land within 5–10 m of them. After 15 minutes or so the Buzzard flies off to hunt elsewhere.

At all times of year, but especially in autumn and winter, the moor Buzzards hunted for beetles, earthworms and other ground-dwelling invertebrates by 'grubbing' about in pastures and arable fields (Figures 3.3, 3.4). This behaviour was particularly prevalent during rain and misty weather when small mammals probably kept deep in cover. Certain fields were favoured, especially those infested by Moles and oft frequented by wintering plover flocks, which indicated that worms and insects (beetles mainly) would be plentiful there. On occasion (as above) a Buzzard would forage in among the plover. Although individual foraging periods

Figure 3.3 A Buzzard lands in a field to forage for earthworms and other soil invertebrates. (Wirral © Steven Round)

Figure 3.4 Buzzard eating earthworm. (Scotland © John Anderson)

did not normally exceed 15 minutes, before the Buzzard flew up to a perch, it was clear from pellet contents composed entirely of plant and invertebrate remains that 'grubbing' was the major feeding activity on some winter days (see below).

Likewise, in lowland Devon one Buzzard was reported foraging among a flock of feeding Curlew near an estuary and another 'grubbed' to within 3m of an unconcerned Song Thrush (DBRs). A juvenile Buzzard feeding among corvids and gulls can be watched on a video taken by the BBC Natural History Unit (www.arkive. org). Occasionally, up to five Buzzards have been reported as 'following-the-plough'. In recent years these ground-foraging habits have become increasingly observed throughout Devon, parts of North Somerset (R. Prytherch, *in litt.*) and in parts of Wales, as will be discussed in the autumn chapter.

From mid-January onwards, as the days start to lengthen perceptibly, the Dartmoor Buzzards began to change their hunting behaviour. The first fine sunny and mild day of the year, even as early as 8 January, would usually induce a bird or two to rise and hover briefly above a hill slope. In dull or colder years the first hovering bird could be delayed until mid-March. Thereafter, hovering became an important hunting method for searching across treeless hillsides and moor, as will be described in the next chapter.

WINTER DIETS

Prey remains in pellets

The only practical way to obtain a reasonable picture of what individual Buzzards eat in winter, and at other times outside the breeding period, is to examine prey remains found in their regurgitated pellets. Direct observation of kills is highly time-consuming and reliant upon chance though it can provide useful supplementary information on hunting method, prey handling and location. A Buzzard usually regurgitates one pellet a day when sufficient food is available (Dare 1961). Pellet dimensions and appearance vary with the food eaten (Chapter 11, Appendix 4). A typical pellet is a tightly compacted and elongated fur ball containing small amounts of undigested skeletal fragments of preys and, occasionally, also a few feathers or reptile scales. Birds that have fed intensively on invertebrates produce looser pellets made up of grass and other vegetable material.

Winter is a good time to start searching for pellets dropped beneath roost trees and other perches that are used regularly; pellets also are easier to find when ground vegetation is minimal. However, Buzzards are far less obliging than owls for such studies. Pellets may be difficult to find in quantity despite frequent and thorough searches of known and potential resting sites. Many pellets appear to be dropped in unsearchable places. Others can be disintegrated by frost action, melting snow or by heavy rain washing them into the ground. As a result, fewer than 15% of the estimated number of winter and spring pellets produced in my Dartmoor area could be found. In the hills of mid-Wales, too, pellets were difficult to locate outside the breeding season because birds changed roosts frequently (Newton *et al.* 1982).

The second major problem with Buzzard pellets is that digestion of bones and teeth of small mammals and similar size preys is not only far more complete than it is in owls but it also differs according to prey groups ('differential digestion'). This can lead to serious biases in interpretation when relying solely upon prey numbers identifiable in the sparse skeletal remains. Corrections for this source of bias were made from feeding trials with captive Buzzards (Dare 1961, Chapter 11). These showed that many of the small prey animals eaten were not detectable in pellet material. Importantly, only about one third of Short-tailed (Field) Voles and other small rodents, one quarter of Frogs, and just one fifth of shrews eaten could be traced in pellets. On the other hand, Rabbits and other large preys tended to be over-represented in the raw pellet data.

An allowance for digestive effects thus can be obtained by using multiplication (correction) factors: for voles (x3), Frogs (x4) and shrews (x5). By applying such adjustments

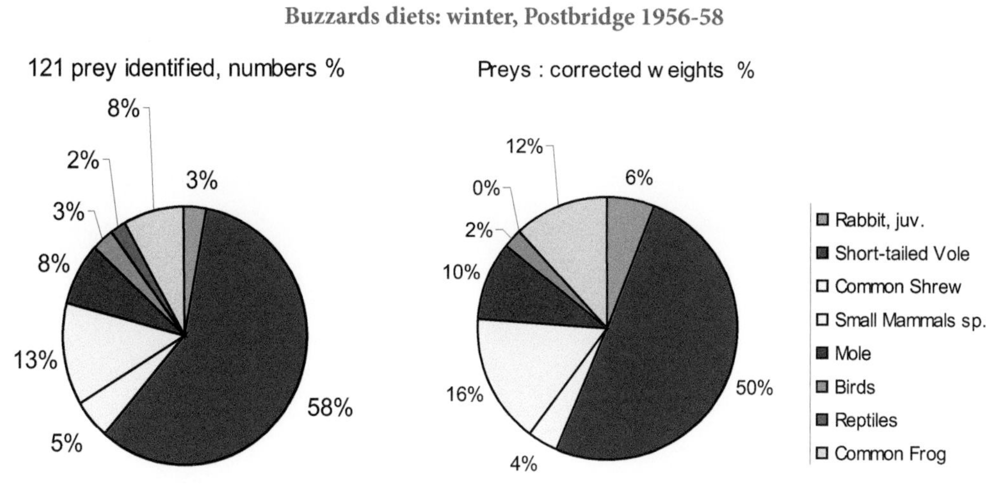

Figure 3.5 Winter (December–February) diet of Buzzards at Postbridge, Dartmoor, 1956–58. Charts show, as proportions: left – the numbers of prey animals identified in pellets; right – their estimated biomass contributions after correcting for differential digestion. [Colour codes are to be read clockwise from the top of each pie chart]

Figure 3.6 The Field or Short-tailed Vole is the most important small mammal prey of Buzzards, especially in upland areas. (© Steven Round)

to prey counts in pellets the original proportions in which these species were eaten can be reconstructed more realistically. Their nutritional contributions, which are vital factors from a Buzzard perspective, are calculated then by converting prey numbers to weight (biomass) using an average body weight for each species (Appendix 5). Large and less frequently taken preys such as Rabbits and many birds pose fewer such problems, while uncommon reptiles are always detectable from their scales.

Prey composition of diets

Vertebrates: On Dartmoor, the remains of 121 vertebrate prey animals were found in the 90 pellets gathered from six Dartmoor territories during 1956–58 (Figure 3.5).

Six species of small mammals comprised more than 80% of the food, both by numbers and biomass, with Short-tailed Voles (Figure 3.6) being the main food. Very few shrews were taken and only four Rabbits. Winter Rabbits are adults and not easily caught as they stay underground during the short winter days and surface only at dusk. Three unidentified small birds, two Brown Rats and a Water Vole were also recorded. Moles and, surprisingly, Frogs both made small but important contributions (10% and 12% by weight). Frogs were taken in all three winter months during very mild interludes but especially as they began emerging from hibernation. Then, Buzzards were seen to catch three Frogs in mid-February and to discard the oviducts below hunting perches on fence posts. Several vertebrae of a small Brown Trout in December and scales of two Common Lizards in February were most unexpected! The lizards evidently had newly emerged from hibernation during mild weather and were still torpid. Sheep wool was present in 4% of pellets collected in January and February. In addition, Buzzards were watched catching five voles and carrying a Blackbird while a farmer reported seeing a Buzzard in a lambing field trying, but failing, to pick up a fresh placenta frozen to the ground.

Elsewhere in Britain, other observers have witnessed Buzzards taking a remarkable variety of medium to large size birds in winter. There are Devon records (in county bird reports) of Buzzards catching Carrion Crow and Wood Pigeon, chasing a Green Woodpecker, striking at a Little Grebe (which escaped by diving) and even snatching a Chaffinch from a garden bird table. Buzzards also were seen carrying or eating unidentified gulls and an Oystercatcher at estuaries. At some Starling roosts in Devon as many as 12 Buzzards have been watched 'waiting on' and hunting birds coming in to a winter roost, much as Hen Harriers do at reed bed roosts in Suffolk. A trawl through other county and regional bird reports doubtless would yield further unusual preys. Four other Buzzards visited Devon gardens in winter, one to peck at a meat bone on the lawn, one to eat most of a windfall apple which it held down with its talons (Tyler 2000), and the others to land on a bird table and a bird feeder.

In Wales winter Buzzards have taken a Lapwing from a flying flock, a Starling in level flight (Robinson 1951), a Carrion Crow was struck down in flight 'with considerable force' and, remarkably, one Buzzard was seen carrying a Barn Owl that managed to escape (*Nature in Wales* 1955–1957). In Wiltshire during severe cold weather, a Buzzard swooped from a tree and killed a Tufted Duck sitting with several others on a frozen pond (Bright 1955). Clearly, there seems to be no limit to the enterprise of some Buzzards.

Carrion: Sheep carrion (Figure 3.7) was eaten only very occasionally by my Dartmoor Buzzards because carcasses were scarce and confined to higher ground in just a few territories. On Welsh uplands, where snow cover is more prevalent (Figure 3.8) and the sheep-walks have been stocked with high densities of ewes, carrion has been a plentiful and important winter resource. In the Cambrian Mountains of mid-Wales, pellet analyses showed that hill Buzzards utilised dead sheep throughout the year but more especially outside the breeding season (Newton *et al.* 1982). In Snowdonia, on the other hand, sheep carcasses recently have become scarce between early November and late March because stocks nowadays are wintered on lower ground. Buzzards in those mountains must have a particularly hard time to stay in high altitude territories through the winter, though many apparently do so by glide-hunting low across the exposed upper slopes, as if attempting to flush small birds (J. Driver, *in litt.*)

Buzzards are quite capable of holding their own against competing corvid scavengers at sheep and Rabbit carcasses, as experiments in the Highlands of western Scotland have shown (Hewson 1981). There, the Buzzards were dominant over Ravens and Hooded Crows. This seems generally to be the case in other hill areas as was confirmed by detailed observations of carrion feeders at dead sheep in mid-Wales (Davies & Davis 1973). There, individual Buzzards were capable of fending off competitors; one held at bay a Red Kite, a Raven and several Carrion Crows for 75 minutes while it gorged to repletion. However, crows and Magpies can outwit Buzzards when pair members cooperate, one distracting the hawk to allow its mate to dash in and seize a piece of meat before they reverse roles. On Anglesey, however, Buzzards currently appear to be dominated around dead sheep by the far more numerous and wily Ravens (J. Driver, *in litt.*). Buzzards feeding at sheep carcasses, while being pestered by Magpies and crows, can be seen on a fine BBC Natural History Unit video (www.arkive.org).

All types of carrion are acceptable to Buzzards including, from other Devon winter records, corpses of Mute Swan and a gull sp., a shot Cormorant, and even that of another Buzzard. Dead fish found beside estuaries and a Salmon on a river bank have provided sustenance, while one Buzzard even carried away the leg of a Fox that had been killed by a local hunt. Some Devon Buzzards, hunting from roadside telegraph poles and other perches,

Figure 3.7 Dead hill sheep are a vital resource for many Buzzards in winter and spring.

Figure 3.8 Some Buzzards scavenge from road kills but in turn may be hit by traffic. This Scottish bird had found a Brown Hare. (© John W. Anderson)

are attracted to road-kills of Rabbits, birds and other animals (Figure 3.8). This is a very hazardous habit as regular obituaries in the county bird reports testify. Other Buzzards hunt and are found dead beside railway tracks, presumably having been struck by trains. Three such casualties were found at the same place one day in early March (DBR 2006).

Invertebrates: Earthworms were on occasion a surprising and important reserve food for the Dartmoor Buzzards in winter, particularly on wet and windy days when conditions were unfavourable for hunting larger prey. That large quantities of earthworms could be taken was indicated by characteristic pellets of vegetable fibres containing their microscopic 'bristles' (setae) and mineral grains, but no fur or skeletal traces of Moles, shrews or other potential worm-eaters were found. Predation on worms was greatest in January and February when 13% of pellets were of the fibrous type. Beetles were also taken frequently, notably the slow-

Figure 3.9 Prolonged snow cover in the uplands reduces availability of small mammals for the sedentary Buzzards. They then rely increasingly on sheep carcasses, and chance catches of birds. These wintry scenes show Buzzard breeding territories in Snowdonia (above) and on the Hiraethog moors (below).

moving *Geotrupes* and *Ceratophyus* dung-beetles as well as faster carabid ground-beetles, and an occasional 'leatherjacket' larva of a tipulid cranefly, or turf-dwelling caterpillars of a noctuid moth.

In lowland Devon, Buzzards were first reported taking earthworms, along with beetles and earwigs (*Forficula* sp.), in the late 1800s (D'Urban & Mathew 1892). In 1929 two birds were seen 'hovering' and dropping into a ploughed field to pick up food (DBR). Since the 1950s, however, ground foraging has become a common and widely- reported habit, from September into March, particularly in re-seeded grass and arable fields. This habit, rarely reported before myxomatosis, had become established in Devon by the late 1960s (Hayman 1970). Nowadays in this county, large gatherings of 20–50 Buzzards, predominantly or entirely juveniles, are an annual occurrence (Dare 1999, DBRs). In parts of mid- and south Wales, a similar trend has become apparent since 1990 with assemblies of up to 57 Buzzards in winter (James 2000). This behaviour has spread latterly to north-east Wales (J. Lawton Roberts, *in litt.*). On the other hand, in Snowdonia, where sheep-rearing predominates, ground foraging is still uncommon, being limited to those coastal pairs with access to ploughed fields (J. Driver, *in litt.*). A detailed account of ground-foraging aggregations will be found in the autumn chapter.

COLD WEATHER RESPONSES AND MORTALITIES

Snow cover, particularly when combined with hard frosts, seriously reduces the availability of all Buzzard preys except, perhaps, for some birds. Short spells of snow had little discernible effect, however, on the Buzzards in my Dartmoor study area. For example, in January 1958 birds remained in their territories during six days with up to 12 cm depth of snow cover, perhaps by subsisting on chance captures. On one such day, unusually, all the Buzzards were perching prominently and conspicuously against the snowy background.

It was a different matter during nearly three weeks in February 1956 when there was continuous if thin (5 cm) snow cover and temperatures remained well below freezing, not rising above –10°C on the coldest day at nearby Princetown. My observations showed that the Buzzards appeared to remain in territories for the first nine days but then most disappeared during the next four days after a further 8–10 cm snowfall. A thorough (5-hour) search on foot located only one bird from the 12 present at the start of this severe spell. Most birds reappeared, however, within two days of a rapid thaw, suggesting that they had moved only short distances to lower ground. A few Buzzards possibly found sheep carrion on the more remote hillsides. Mortality was low but one Buzzard that did stay was shot during its second raid on poultry at a farm. Several others also tended to haunt the close vicinity of farmsteads and small-holdings for some time, probably for the few rodents and birds still frequenting habitations. Even more confiding behaviour was reported from three places in mid-Wales during severe weather in early 1963 when Buzzards became remarkably tame, even coming to gardens and taking food thrown out for them (Panting *et al.* 1963).

The prolonged and extremely cold and snowy winter of January and February 1963 on Dartmoor had more profound and long-lasting effects on Buzzard numbers in my area. Several birds were found dead by farmers, including two under the same roost trees about a week apart and some three weeks after the onset of deep snow cover. By the spring only 8–9 pairs had survived on territory, about one third of the 1962 adult population having died.

Buzzard deaths were reported also from the south-western fringes of the moor where five were picked up by foresters in the sheltered Plym valley woodlands (DBR 1963).

In Germany, and elsewhere in central Europe, where harsh 1963-type snow-winters are not unusual, many Buzzards may die from starvation. Mortality is then the highest among all raptors wintering in Germany because rodent preys then are hidden beneath deep snow (Olsson 1958, quoting Burr 1936 and Drost & Schuz 1940). Under these conditions many Buzzards rely increasingly upon carrion, for which competition may be intense and lead to fights (Figure 3.10). Others switch to bird preys such as poultry and game-birds, Barn Owls (themselves weakened by the cold) and, on the coast, to Herring Gulls.

How long Buzzards can survive without food in severe cold conditions is not known but must depend largely upon the amount of fat reserves available at the onset of snow cover coupled with finding occasional meals from chance kills or carrion. This complex and poorly understood subject is examined in Chapter 11. Suffice it to note here that field and experimental results from Dartmoor Buzzards, and post-mortem data from Germany, provide some indications. These suggest that Buzzards with good fat deposits should be able to withstand total starvation for two weeks and then quickly recoup lost weight when favourable conditions return.

SIGNS OF SPRING

As the days gradually become longer and brighter through January, some Buzzard pairs may already be preparing, albeit surreptitiously, for the breeding season, as winter searches for old nests in the north Wales woods revealed. Even in mid-January there is sometimes evidence that

Figure 3.10 Buzzards fight over food in cold weather. Such contests are more common in very cold central European winters when many birds may starve to death. (Scotland © John Chapman)

birds visit or even start to repair old nests which, unlike those on Dartmoor, are often in steep woods and thus easily viewed from up-slope. Many Buzzard pairs initially place conspicuous green foliage sprays, freshly picked from conifers or ivy, onto one or more flattened old nests. These are encouraging signs and all such potential nests in a territory should then be checked at intervals until that pair finally selects one for breeding. On Dartmoor, the Buzzards sometimes spent long periods on mild winter days within the tree cover and were then difficult to locate. In retrospect, they too might have been inspecting old nests.

In the Lake District such early 'decoration' of old nests appears to be more prevalent and conspicuous than in my areas. Close observations (Fryer 1986) showed that some male Buzzards placed green sprays, mostly of holly, onto former crag nest ledges within their territories, even where few traces of old nests remained. Furthermore, some birds continued to add 'decorative' sprays to these former sites even after their mates had begun incubating clutches elsewhere. These male Buzzards were considered to be using green sprays as 'markers' to advertise ownership of former nest sites to neighbours and to any wandering intruders (Fryer 1986).

In North Wales the more advanced Buzzard pairs may already be repairing nests by mid-January. One Buzzard was seen on 10 January carrying a long stick in its talons onto an already substantial nest on a crag at 380 m elevation, and with snow on the ground. Another nest was being repaired during a light snow shower on 13 January. By mid-February the rims of several nests had been rebuilt and birds were seen at other nests, with one female even arranging or shaping the nest cup on 20 February.

Meanwhile, as these nesting preparations are progressing covertly, some Buzzards may begin to show overt signs of territorial displays and courtship flights on the occasional warmer and sunny days in February. In the very mild 1956–57 winter, Dartmoor pairs were engaged in soaring manoeuvres on 12 February, coition posturing on the 14th and aerial 'talon-tangling' displays on the 17th. These are the first signs of the Buzzards emerging from their enforced state of seeming winter lethargy to become dynamic aerobatic performers, as the next chapter will describe.

4

BUZZARDS IN EARLY SPRING
(MARCH–MID-APRIL)

These six weeks see the Buzzards suddenly 'come alive' after their long winter spent conserving energy. Pairs once often difficult to locate now take to the skies and find their voices to proclaim territory ownership and to indulge in courtship as breeding preparations accelerate by the day. This is an equally busy and exciting time for Buzzard enthusiasts as they assess the occupancy and sizes of breeding territories, check carefully for potential nests and observe seasonal changes in hunting behaviour and food habits.

Weather in the hills is fickle in early spring, however, and it can switch almost overnight from balmy sunshine and southerly breezes to brisk chill north-westerlies bringing squalls of hail and snow. March snowfalls are not uncommon, though usually ephemeral, on Dartmoor but they are often substantial and more long-lasting on Welsh and northern hills. Short-lived wintry spells, even in late April, are also possible. Nevertheless, many typical upland-breeding birds are returning in March: Meadow Pipits, Skylarks, Curlew, Snipe, Lapwing, Wheatears and Ring Ouzels to moors, bogs and rocky slopes, while Redstarts, Pied Flycatchers and warblers reappear in the woods during April. The Buzzards are always very active whenever the weather permits.

Early spring is the best time to enjoy 'sky-watching' for Buzzards as they demonstrate their flying skills by soaring and performing exuberant and noisy displays; ideally seen against a blue sky high above the nearby skyline of a hill tinged rusty with dead bracken and topped with sparkling snow. Buzzards are most active between 1000–1500 h, on sunny days with light to moderate winds, clear visibility and a scatter of cumulus or 'fair weather' clouds indicating good thermal lift conditions. Any additional high-level veils of cirrus ('mare tails') or patchy sheets of thin cirro-stratus enhance the chances of detecting distant soaring Buzzards, as well as an occasional Buzzard or other raptor passing over at very high altitude. Various species may join Buzzards to soar in the same thermal. These include Sparrowhawk, Kestrel and, commonly in Wales, Ravens, with maybe also Red Kites, a Peregrine or Merlin; as well as noisy parties of crows and Jackdaws. Both Merlin and male Sparrowhawk sometimes stoop 'playfully' at a high-soaring Buzzard.

Strong interactions of crows with perched and circling Buzzards are a common sight in spring, especially when single Buzzards first start to rise. The hawks are often pestered vigorously by one or several raucous crows until they reach a height of 50–100 m, when their assailants generally break away and drop down, leaving the Buzzards to soar alone in peace. The Buzzards normally are impassive but occasionally may call in annoyance or roll slightly and show their talons if a crow should come too close. On rare occasions a pair of crows may actually hit a Buzzard sufficiently hard as to knock off feathers (DBR 1942). The tables may be turned, however, as when one Buzzard in Devon was seen to strike and kill its assailant (Hurrell 1952). The reason for such mobbing surely stems from the regular predation by Buzzards of fledgling crows (Chapter 6).

POPULATION FEATURES

After the winter period of stability, apart from the departure of the last few juveniles and any deaths, the arrival of spring brings new Buzzards into a study area. Some of these visitors may recruit to the local population by settling into vacant places. Others are transients, either itinerant prospectors ('floaters') or, in a few cases, true passage migrants that fly through or high over the area without stopping. By the time that egg-laying starts the population essentially is stable once again.

The first four months of the year were when full-grown Buzzards were most likely to be found dead in the Dartmoor study area. In 1956, eight birds were found or reported dead in five territories: four during severe weather (as noted previously) and four in March. Of the latter, three had died beside poisoned baits set for Foxes, and one died in March from an unknown cause. Most birds, if not all, were territorial adults. Five of the birds, including two pairs, were replaced in the same March during the spring influx. In contrast, during the following two years (1957–58) only one spring death was recorded, in April. In the 1960s, a further three local Buzzards were found dead in spring by Postbridge farmers during April and May; one with a smashed wing was being attacked by Carrion Crows.

Buzzards that were seen passing directly through this area were detected by chance, when watching resident birds, and doubtless others went unobserved. More than a dozen low-fliers were seen heading, in all compass directions, between 15 April and 22 May. They provoked responses from territory owners ranging from mild vocal protests to chases by males guarding incubating mates. One intruder was struck sufficiently hard as to dislodge a dorsal feather. In May 1990 several late intruders that were moulting flight feathers were clearly immature birds. All evidence suggests that such Buzzards probably were mainly 2–3 year old immature, or possibly unattached mature, birds that had been raised not far away. These age groups search either for vacant niches which they can fill or for suitable unclaimed sites where they can establish their own territories. Such behaviour has been confirmed recently in Dorset by tracking for several years a number of young Buzzards that had been fitted with radio tags just before they fledged (Walls & Kenward 1995, 1999).

The recruitment of young Buzzards into a breeding population therefore is spread across several age groups, depending on its density and stability. Where, as on Speyside, persecution provided frequent vacancies (higher turnover), more Buzzards could find or refill breeding territories within their first two years (Picozzi & Weir 1976). On the other hand, in areas where densities are high or stable the young Buzzards may experience considerable difficulties because they tend to stay or return close to their natal areas. For example, in mid-Wales the average age at which colour-marked young Buzzards were first found breeding was at 3.5 years (range 2–5 years) with males possibly breeding sooner than the females (Davis & Davies 1992). In Dorset the youngest ages at first breeding were 2–4 years but it was thought that many birds were delayed until they were 5–7 years old (Walls & Kenward 1998). Unusually, this population contained a persistently high proportion (60%) of non-breeding pairs (Kenward *et al.* 2000), apparently a consequence of too many offspring returning and settling in the natal area.

Such high fidelity of young Buzzards to birth areas is similar to that found in Sparrowhawks where the great majority (*c.*75 %) settle within 20 km of their natal place (Newton 1979). Ring recoveries show that British Buzzards are the most sedentary in temperate or northern Europe. On the Continent the mean distances between birth and breeding places were 60 km in western and central regions but 146 km in eastern and northern parts, from where most Buzzards move south in autumn to avoid the harsher winters.

A second and distinct category of transient spring Buzzards comprises occasional birds passing over the Dartmoor study area at considerable height and on steady courses. These show all the features of long-distance flights or passage migration, being similar to that of migrant Steppe Buzzards I have watched passing north in spring over the desert in Jordan. The passage Buzzards over Dartmoor appeared between mid-March and early May and were of two types. A few single birds passed across the entire study area, in fine clear weather with light westerly to northerly breezes, at altitudes far above those attained by residents. They glided steadily over on bearings between WNW and NNW. Other Buzzards have been watched here rising on fine mornings from the upper slopes of Hameldown ridge before heading away northwards. One such bird soared into a cumulus base. An exceptional party of 15 non-local Buzzards reported as circling high above the same site in early May (1966) had perhaps also rested there overnight.

These Dartmoor observations are consistent in dates and behaviour with similar spring sightings elsewhere in Devon (Dare 1999). More than 90% of these birds were reported as heading between NW and NNE. They included a party of 14 moving north following the Avon valley, south of Dartmoor, on 11 April, and flying in a manner similar to that of migrating raptors the observer had watched on the Continent (DBR). More recently, and further east at Haldon ridge on 24 April, an exceptional 71 Buzzards flew high NE in three dispersed flocks, the largest of 37 birds. North of Dartmoor, a total of 23 Buzzards flew north over a site on several dates one March. Other spring reports in Devon of more than a dozen Buzzards circling together also seem likely to refer to transient birds. Such, surely, were the spectacular assemblies of 39, 31 and 27 Buzzards seen in spring 1955 above three localities in north Devon, as would have been the four gatherings in fields elsewhere of 9–21 Buzzards seen in March or April (DBR 1999).

An alternative explanation, prompted by the large group sizes involved on those dates, is that these Buzzards could have been immatures that had over-wintered in groups locally and now were shifting to new feeding grounds or, perhaps, they were heading back towards their more northerly natal areas. Devon is probably too far west for these movements to have involved true passage migrants from south-west Europe returning north-eastwards to Scandinavian breeding areas. In south-eastern England and East Anglia, however, similar but smaller northerly coasting movements also occur in fine March-April weather. Small groups of Buzzards then seen departing E or ENE out to sea from the north Suffolk coast (the most easterly part of Britain) were considered most likely to be Scandinavian birds (Dare 2006).

TERRITORIES

During March the final sizes of the Dartmoor territories in which Buzzard pairs would attempt to breed were defined and reinforced, where need be, by means of boundary contests. Only minor adjustments were made to their winter territories. The pairs now visited all parts regularly instead of concentrating activities in their core winter hunting areas. Territories could now be mapped and the relative proportions of different habitats measured. The territories varied in size from 50–230 ha (130–545 acres) and some Buzzards bred successfully with as little as 53 ha of valley farmland. The reported sizes of territories in other uplands vary enormously depending on the productivity of the land, its habitats and availability of nest sites. Mountain Buzzards in Snowdonia occupied territories as large as 260–630 ha (Dare 1995). In general, Buzzards prefer a mosaic of habitats offering a diversity of preys. These and other aspects of breeding territories are examined in Chapter 10.

Territorial behaviour

Throughout winter the Buzzards in my Dartmoor study area had employed passive means to signify the boundaries of their land claims. Suddenly, in early March, all pairs began to use far more conspicuous and vocal methods, notably soaring and various aerial displays, both to advertise possession and to strongly defend what were now their breeding territories. These behaviour types were seasonally interlinked also with courtship, and some at times appeared to serve a dual function (see also Melde 1956). Similar behaviours have since been well described, some with sketches, for *Buzzards of the New Forest* by Colin Tubbs (Tubbs 1966) and on Speyside by Douglas Weir and Nick Picozzi (Weir & Picozzi 1975). Recently, in North Somerset, the intricate social behaviour of Buzzards through the year is being revealed in fine detail by Robin Prytherch. His drawings of the sequences of manoeuvres deployed in aerial courtship, territorial and aggressive displays provide an instructive guide for less experienced observers (Prytherch 2009). Many aspects of these displays can be watched in a fine video illustrating the Speyside studies (www.itvwild.com).

Soaring

This familiar Buzzard activity is performed either by the male alone, or mutually by the pair, but is quite seasonal. In all my study areas, and probably elsewhere, it begins with the first fine weather of the year – sometimes as early as mid-January on Dartmoor – and then rapidly increases in frequency, intensity and duration until it becomes almost daily, being inhibited only by rain, mist or strong winds. On fine spring days, from a good vantage point, three or four pairs of soaring Buzzards may be watched over their respective territories 'making lazy circles in the sky' (as so aptly described, for related North American 'hawks' in Oklahoma, by song writers Rodgers and Hammerstein in 1943). Soaring Buzzards themselves can probably see others circling and displaying over a radius of at least 5 km, given the sharp acuity of raptors. Indeed, Herberigs (1953) considered the visual range of Common Buzzards to be at least 15 km.

When females are sitting on eggs, the males often soar alone for long periods, though 15–20 minutes is perhaps more usual. Later, however, when there are young to be fed, the males have little time for soaring until their young have fledged. They may resume soaring throughout summer, but at a lower and steadily decreasing tempo. There is usually a brief resurgence of soaring and general aerial activities during fine autumn weather, but soaring is seldom seen after October.

Soaring Buzzards exploit any rising patches of warm air (thermals), as well as the up-draughts from windward hillsides. In favourable conditions, and like many other raptors, they can spiral up rapidly and remain effortlessly aloft for long periods, circling and counter-circling on broad out-stretched wings and fanned tails In strong thermals, vertical air speeds of 1–5 m/s (200–1,000 ft/min) are typical; and eagles have been measured rising at such rates (Spaar & Bruderer 1996, Koch 2006, Akos *et al.* 2008). Buzzards may even disappear into a cumulus cloud base, some 600-1000 m above the ground, in under five minutes, as I have observed on Dartmoor and in Suffolk. High Buzzards, well above 250 m altitude, often are first detected by their far-carrying so-called 'mewing' cries, *peee-ee-ya* and *pee-yaaaa,* with the emphasis varying with context and state of excitement. When, as often happens, mates soar together around one another, the male may break away to execute courtship dives and tumbling displays, as both birds utter loud screams in evident excitement. On Speyside the Buzzards required the same weather conditions as on Dartmoor for extended soaring sessions, when some birds reached heights exceeding an estimated 600 m (Weir & Picozzi 1975).

Frequent soaring visits to territory limits are made, when two or three neighbouring pairs often meet above common boundaries. In this instance, the Buzzards often circle one another and call, but with little or no overt aggression, for perhaps 10–15 minutes before separating and returning into their own territories. At the peak of the courtship and display season, however, many boundary encounters can develop into brief but lively and noisy exhibitions of diving, tumbling and close swerving manoeuvres, after which the pairs glide or drift away back into their respective airspace.

Diving displays

This impressive behaviour is confined to male Buzzards although incipient dives by females accompanying their mates very occasionally were observed. Dive displays first appear, very briefly and at low intensity, during rare sunny and mild days early in the year – even on 8 January (1958) and 9 February (1957) on Dartmoor. Their frequency and intensity rise with the tempo of other aerial activities to peak in March or April. During the busy nestling period the dives become spasmodic or are discontinued, but may re-appear after the breeding season for a short time before the moult period and the quiescent weeks of late summer and autumn

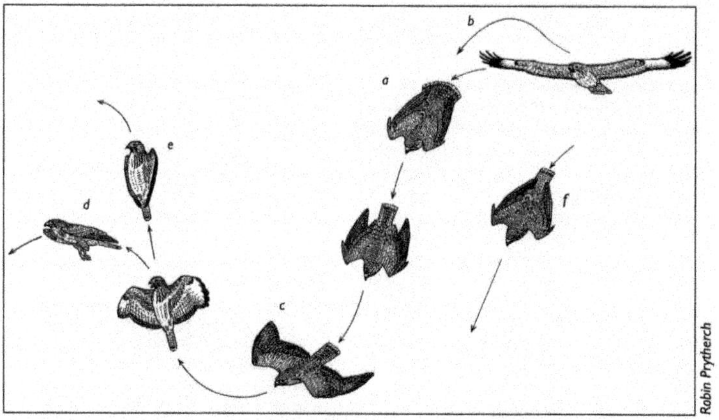

Figure 4.1 Display-diving male Buzzards perform a series of steep 10–15 m dives. (© Robin Prytherch, and reproduced with the permission of British Birds)

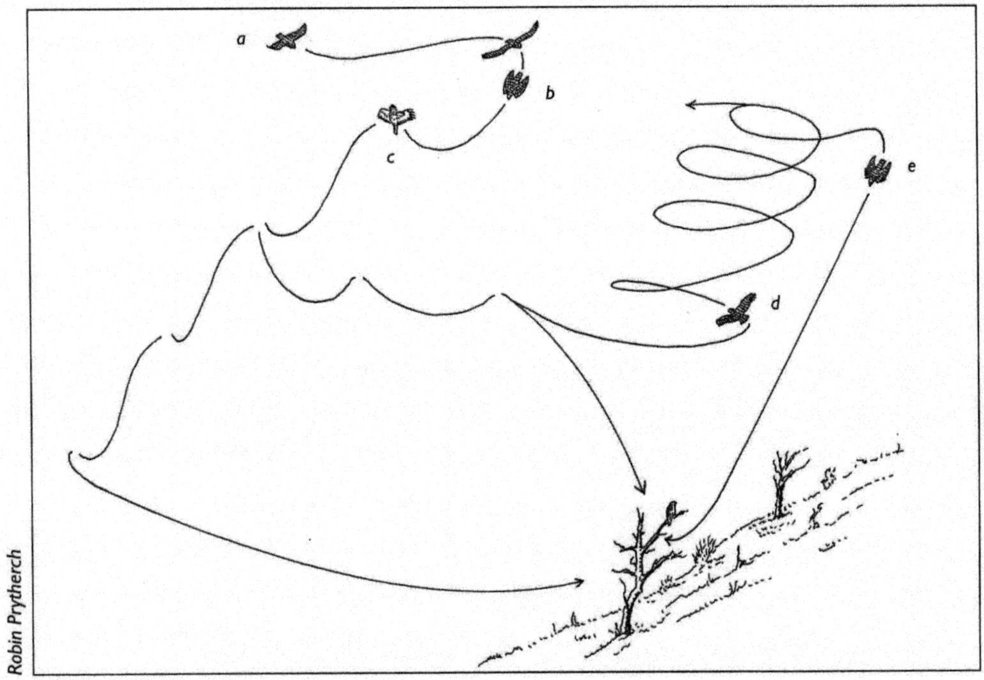

Figure 4.2 Schematic diagram of a display-diving male Buzzard (top left) and some alternative sequences of aerial manoeuvres by which it may descend to land near its mate or close to a nest site. (© Robin Prytherch, and reproduced with the permission of British Birds)

arrive. In October, display-diving was twice observed on Dartmoor on sunny days during the temporary resurgence in soaring activity already noted. Studies elsewhere have described this male behaviour in more detail; for Buzzards on Speyside (the 'roller-coaster' of Weir & Picozzi 1975) and in North Somerset (the 'dive stooping' of Prytherch 2009, whose sketch is reproduced here as Figure 4.1). More generally, nowadays, it is known among birdwatchers as 'sky dancing', a generic term applied also to the aerial displays of the Marsh and then Harriers and some other large raptors.

Display-diving is usually performed from a height of at least 100 m and often in the presence of the female. It is initiated during soaring by the male uttering loud *peee-ee-ya* cries, nearly closing his wings, and then dropping 10–20 m or more in a quite steep dive. At the bottom of the dive the wings are partly opened and the hawk throws up steeply with wings partially open. At the summit of his ascent he stalls, tilts forward and again folds his wings and tips forward smoothly into another plunge. As many as ten dives may follow in rapid succession as he gradually loses height. The display is terminated either by resumed soaring or by a leisurely descent to a perch. At peak intensity, display-diving can be an exhilarating performance to watch as the large hawk, calling excitedly, stoops and rises above its territory in great arcs. One should watch any of these displays to completion for sometimes the male may finish with a near-vertical plunge down to the close vicinity of its, perhaps as yet undiscovered, nest site. A number of woodland nests in Snowdonia valleys have been found by following-up these behavioural clues. The commonest sequence of events, as illustrated schematically by Robin Prytherch (2009) is reproduced here (Figure 4.2) though other permutations may be observed.

These conspicuous aerial activities serve several functions: territorial advertisement and reinforcement of boundaries. The mutual soaring of a mated pair is also an expression of the pair bond and the male's diving displays close to his mate contain elements of courtship behaviour.

Exaggerated wing beat displays

From time to time a soaring male Buzzard may switch to a conspicuously different mode of display in which, sometimes preceded by a sharp call, it flies a more or less level and straight or curving path while beating its wings slowly through a wide vertical arc. This conspicuous flight mode has been termed 'display flapping, slow-flapping flight or deep wing-beat flight' by Prytherch (2009). The hawk may then resume soaring or initiate another display activity. This display would seem to be another form of advertisement though the context in which it is deployed is not clear. The following excerpt from field notes gives a flavour of one particular sky-watch experience:

> *On a fine morning in mid-April I am scanning for the occupants of a territory at the foot of Hameldown ridge. Distant sharp calls alert me to three Buzzards soaring above the summit ridge, which is some 200 m higher than my position. Events then show that these are the territorial male protesting at an intruding pair. The male is calling aggressively as it dives several times at one intruder which rolls over with talons outstretched before gliding away rapidly over the ridge and out of sight. The male then evicts the other trespasser in similar fashion, after which he returns to join his mate who, meanwhile, has risen to meet him. The pair now soar very high, probably to almost 150 m above the summit and nearly 400 m above the valley bottom. Then, the*

male begins to display, first by flying level with exaggerated slow and deep wing beats, followed by a series of short dives and upward loops while intermittently uttering shrill and drawn-out 'peee-ee-yaa' calls. Twice he dives close past his mate who responds by rolling over on her side as he flashes by. The finale of his performance is a prolonged set of wide sweeping display dives and upward loops to and fro, covering wide arcs across the blue sky, as he drops into the valley. Finally, he starts a fast, long and slanting glide down towards the nest copse near where he rolls past his mate who, meanwhile, has descended more sedately. She tumbles over in greeting as the pair drop into the trees. An exhilarating performance to witness despite inducing (temporary) neck ache!

Defence of territories

Male Buzzards on Dartmoor were far more active and vocal than females in defending territories, though females sometimes acted in support. Trespassing incidents, and the intensity of defensive responses, were both at a peak early in the year, and especially during courtship and incubation. The Buzzards both recognised and respected one another's lengthy territory boundaries; infringements by neighbours were infrequent. Most airspace intrusions were brief and at a considerable height (100–150 m) and neighbours seldom trespassed to perch in unfamiliar ground. However, one pair was unusually persistent in entering an adjoining territory when the owners were not in view. Indeed, one trespasser actually settled briefly on a favourite perch of the owning pair some 300 m inside that territory. However, perching trespassers were always 'alert and uneasy', and retreated hastily when disturbed by the owner (or even by the observer). Buzzards on Speyside behaved in similar fashion (sketch in Weir & Picozzi, 1975). Hunting in a neighbour's territory was not witnessed.

Defensive responses varied with individual males and were often not predictable. The mildest form of positive reaction was to call sharply at distant intruders seen flying across boundaries; by adopting postures similar to that shown in Figure 4.3. Some owners uttered challenging and far carrying '*pee-ee-yaaa*' calls towards a trespasser, whereupon the latter promptly retreated. Other soaring intruders were approached more closely and 'escorted' out of the territory. Twice, when their mates were out of view, females were seen to rout trespassers – one actually left her eggs for a few minutes to demonstrate. A third female left eggs to support her mate. Juvenile Buzzards passing through during their autumn dispersal kept a low profile and seemed to be tolerated. Resentment towards them was limited to intimidatory vocal demonstrations. After all such incidents of mild responses, the owners quickly resumed their interrupted activities.

These defensive responses normally succeeded in swiftly evicting intruders from Dartmoor territories. However, two exceptions occurred, the first involving a new pair of Buzzards that persisted in remaining in another pair's territory for a considerable time one spring. The newcomers had settled just outside the study area, in open moorland terrain lacking breeding sites, and repeatedly intruded to hunt over the northern part of the resident pair's domain. The owners, surprisingly, seemed to protest little, perhaps because they were not themselves breeding that year. Alternatively, their failure to breed could conceivably have been due in part to the intruders' presence. In the second case, early one autumn, a new pair successfully

A POETIC DIVERSION

The soaring flight of Buzzards has inspired the following evocative verses, taken from two poems. The first excerpt is from *The Buzzards* by Martin Armstrong (b.1882). The second is from *Wings over Exmoor* by the late R. A. Richardson, and was first published by Moss Taylor (2002) in his book, recounting the life of the Norfolk artist and entitled *Guardian of the East Bank: A Celebration of the Life of R.A. Richardson.*

Serenely far there swam in the sunny height
A buzzard and his mate who took their pleasure
Swirling and poising idly in golden light.
On great pied motionless moth-wings borne along,
So effortless and so strong,
Cutting each other's paths together they glided,
Then wheeled asunder till they soared divided
Two valleys' width (as though it were a delight
To part like this, being sure they would unite
So swiftly in their empty, free dominion),
Curved headlong downward, towered up the sunny steep,
Then, with a sudden lift of the one great pinion,
Swung proudly to a curve, and from its height
Took half a mile of sunlight in one long sweep.

Sailing aloft with brown canvas set square,
Spread primaries cleaving the keen moorland air
A Buzzard is soaring with effortless grace,
Beneath, purple heather, above azure space.
Wide mottled pinions spread to the breeze,
Drifting and tacking high over the trees,
Sweeping away 'cross the bracken-clad vale
Steering serenely with fanwise-spread tail.

Figure 4.3 Territorial Buzzards may adopt similar poses to challenge noisily a potential intruder. (Wirral © Steven Round)

established a small territory (60 ha) on an extensive rough grass common, around a small spinney, that was in virtual 'no-man's-land' between two large occupied territories. The new pair bred in this spinney in the following spring but lost their eggs and departed. The responses of the established pairs were not observed, but the newcomers may have been helped by the large sizes of the two existing territories, the remoteness of their owners' nest sites from the newcomers, and by the new pair restricting activities to apparently sub-optimal terrain.

Stronger reactions by territorial males towards both low and high flying strangers, that were wanderers or transients, were occasionally observed. Male owners would utter frequent challenging and far-carrying cries of '*peee-ee-ee-ya*' and '*pee-yaaaaa*' as they closed on and intercepted the trespasser. Their tactics then ranged from shallow dives at, or half-hearted pursuits of, intruders to vigorous dives and prolonged noisy chases. One male took off and, calling repeatedly, climbed rapidly to intercept an intruder which was then chased away in a high, fast and twisting pursuit with the owner keeping close on its tail; one Snowdonia male did likewise. In the latter region in spring, five Buzzard were also seen engaging in noisy, fast and furious high chases during which they performed plunge dives, pursuit dives and tumbling; it was the best aerobatics 'show' I have ever witnessed.

The most aggressive encounter that I have witnessed was on Dartmoor when a defending male actually struck a low-flying bird on the back with its feet and displaced a few body feathers. That intruder uttered low and anxious squeals, circled its assailant for a moment and then retreated hastily; after which the defending male returned to a perch near its nest area. In extreme cases, which I have at times witnessed, a male diving at an intruder may force the latter to roll over with talons extended to ward off its attacker. The two Buzzards even may entangle talons and whirl downwards a short way before separating. Apparently interlocked opponents have twice been observed in Devon to tumble down until they hit the ground (DBRs). One such encounter was photographed in its various stages in Devon in April 2006 (www.charliesblog.com). Similar instances of 'fierce fights high in the sky' resulting in Buzzards 'tumbling' or 'crashing to the ground' have been reported also from Wales. One such encounter ended with a Buzzard somehow landing on the neck of a horse that was being ridden! (Anon. 1951). An even more unfortunate Welsh Buzzard which had retreated to an oak tree after a 'fierce and very noisy battle' was then seen to fall stunned to the ground. When examined, the unconscious bird had blood on its beak but no clear sign of injury; six hours later, it flew away (Haworth 1984). Similar fights among eagles and other raptors have been documented frequently (Newton 1979).

FOOD: THE SPRING CHALLENGE

Although the generally warming spring weather means that Buzzards now expend less energy in maintaining body temperature, this saving is more than offset by new energy demands needed to fuel their increasing activities in preparing for the breeding season. In southern Sweden it was found that by early April the overall daily energy expenditure (DEE) of male Buzzards was 35% higher (at 186 kcal/day) than it had been in December, the result of their greatly increased flying activities (Sylvén 1982 and Chapter 11). Female Buzzards showed a similar rise despite spending less time than their mates on flying. Instead, during April, increasingly more of their energy was being diverted into egg production. In mid-April, females spent 15% of their DEE on egg development and only 4% was used for flying. Females in Sweden effectively stopped flying some time before egg-laying began, a behavioural change that was obvious also among all my study populations (Chapter 5).

In prey terms the Buzzards now need to catch about 120 g of food daily, equivalent to five or six adult voles, but at a time when the total prey abundance is at or close to its annual lowest level (Chapter 12). Small mammal populations are now much depleted, and become more difficult to find once ground cover begins re-growing. Furthermore, these preys are still being taken by local Tawny Owls, Kestrels and Foxes. Few young Rabbits are as yet appearing above ground and small birds are only just returning to the hills from winter grounds elsewhere. This deficit of preys was compensated for in some Dartmoor territories by the emergence from hibernation of Frogs and, to a lesser extent, of reptiles. In Welsh uplands, until recently, some sheep carrion remained from winter casualties and that was supplemented later by larger and fresher amounts of mutton during the lambing season. Nowadays, however, this food resource is probably dwindling owing to changes in farming methods, at least in Snowdonia (J. Driver, pers.comm.).

Buzzards lose a considerable amount of their body weight through the winter and some will have used all their fat reserves by April (Sylvén 1982), as mentioned earlier. The inevitable differences in individual weight losses and ability to recover condition quickly (in 4–6 weeks) therefore could be significant factors in determining which Buzzard pairs will be fit enough to attempt breeding (lay eggs) as well as their chances of success in hatching broods.

HUNTING METHODS

Despite the arrival of favourable flying conditions, the hill Buzzards continue with their two winter hunting methods, particularly during inclement weather, but they now extend their capabilities in finer weather by adding hovering to their repertoire (Figure 4.4). This seasonal skill enables them to find more prey on the extensive open grass and heather moors, which lack hunting perches, as well as to search more efficiently the larger patches of rough grassland, scrub and bogs in valley bottoms. This behaviour had not been documented in Britain before the Dartmoor study though, at around this time, Buzzards in Germany also were noted hovering, to catch voles in summer (Melde 1956). From their hovering positions Buzzards often dive steeply (stoop) to capture these small mammals and similar preys (Figure 4.5).

There are two types of hovering according to flight attitude: active hovering and passive hanging. In active hovering a Buzzard adopts the Kestrel's typical pose – stationing itself into the wind on extended wings, tail fanned and depressed at a slight or moderate angle, and the remarkably stable head peering downwards to scan the ground. In favourable breezes only a delicate flickering of the spread primary tips is perceptible whereas in light and in turbulent winds, heavy flapping may be needed to maintain stability. The other type, hanging passively, is adopted to maintain a stationary position in a faster but smoother air-flow such as often occurs low above a grass or heather hillside (Figure 4.4). The primaries then may be swept back at a more or less acute angle and the tail is only partially opened; the Buzzard rides the up-draught with an absolute minimum of effort.

Figure 4.4 A Buzzard hovers ('hangs') in a hillside up-draught, head into wind and still, as it scans for prey. Note the widely spread primaries including the tiny first one (alula) and the smooth airflow across the wing surfaces evident on the lower bird. (Scotland © John Anderson)

An intriguing anatomical feature of a Buzzard's spread wing, clearly revealed by the above photographs, is the tiny first primary feather, the alula or bastard wing, which grows from the first digit ('thumb') and visibly protrudes from the leading edge of the wing. Its function, for long a mystery, has now been explained by aerodynamics engineers. It is a high lift device that helps to increase wing lift and prevent wing stalling at low speeds, and is automatically deployed when landing (as shown in Figure 3.3) or during hovering (Alvarez *et al.* 2001). Together with the prominent wing tip primary 'slats', which reduce turbulence, the alula smooths the air flow over the wing surface and thus, in this instance, improves hovering performance; a fine adaptation found also on Kestrels and many large birds of prey.

In this energy efficient way, a Buzzard may scour a hill slope for hours with scarcely a wing beat, dropping, sometimes in stages, for beetles and other small fare before rising to renew its position once more, as if suspended from an invisible thread. A Buzzard, swinging smoothly from one hunting station along the slope to the next with effortless ease, can match the skills of Kestrels. Small mammals, reptiles, beetles and, it seems, the nests of ground-nesting birds, are detected in the vegetation from heights of 15–30 m or more, a further indication of the Buzzard's keen eyesight.

For persistent hovering, dry bright days with a moderate breeze are most favoured. Wind speeds in the range 10–25 km/hr (Beaufort force 3–4) appeared to provide ideal conditions irrespective of air temperature. One bird in January continued to hover through a brief light snow shower. Blustery or strong winds on an otherwise sunny day inhibit hovering, while in very light airs the hawks cannot support themselves without excessive effort. Very dull, wet or misty weather depresses all aerial activities.

Hover-searching on Dartmoor is strictly seasonal, being employed mainly from March into September, but rarely later and never in December. The onset of hovering in each year is determined by prevailing weather conditions. The first fine sunny days of mid-January usually induce a bird to rise and hover briefly, just as they might also stimulate one or two males into performing incipient display-dives. It can, though, be delayed by persistently

Figure 4.5 Buzzards sometimes dive steeply to make a kill or to land after display-diving. (© John Anderson)

dull or cold weather until early March. By mid-March each year, hovering is widespread, thereafter becoming used extensively by all pairs until well into September. In some places, 4–5 hovering Buzzards can be in view at one time. Very prolonged hovering is commonly seen and later, with a brood to feed, a pair sometimes hunts nearly all day by this method.

The variable heights when hovering probably depend upon wind speed, ground contours and the type of prey being hunted. Low altitude hanging, below 3–5 m, was employed in stronger winds and when taking invertebrates, which needed frequent drops. On the other hand, widely scattered vertebrate preys, such as small mammals, require the scanning of large areas from heights perhaps as great as 50–100 m, though 15–30 m was more usual. The seasonal onset in March of hovering suggests that it is, at least in part, a response to a declining food supply at a time of higher energy requirements. On Dartmoor, hovering intensified further from late May onward once Buzzard broods had hatched. It was finally abandoned in early autumn, by which time juvenile Buzzards were attaining independence and just when mammal preys were at or near their annual peak of abundance.

The hovering habit has since been reported from other parts of Britain. On Speyside the Buzzards sometimes used similar methods ('slope soaring') over windward slopes (Weir & Picozzi 1975). It was certainly common behaviour in my North Wales study areas by the 1970s. Of particular interest, the Buzzards that are currently resettling Suffolk have adopted high-hovering techniques to scan the broad flat expanses of arable farmland, usually from heights of 100 m and more (Dare 2008). Many a hovering Common Buzzard has been misidentified by unwary bird-watchers as a Rough-legged Buzzard, a scarce winter visitor to Britain, which most literature emphasises as habitually hovering over open terrain.

EARLY SPRING DIET

Assessing preys taken at this season is still reliant upon pellet contents. On Dartmoor, important changes to the diet were revealed when compared with that in winter; based on the 214 preys found in 147 pellets collected from nine of the territories (Figure 4.6).

These reflected the seasonal trends in availability of the different species already noted. Thus, although Short-toed Voles were still the most frequently identifiable prey, in weight terms they were only half as important as small Rabbits and roughly equal to Frogs. Many Buzzards clearly were compensating for the spring shortage of small mammals by targeting the first 'crop' of young and unwary Rabbits to appear above ground (Figure 4.7); and also by concerted predation on recently emerged Frogs that were now conspicuous and easily caught at spawning assemblies in bogs and other wet areas. Few small birds, Moles and shrews were recorded along with single specimens of Brown Rat, Bank Vole and Water Vole. Sheep wool in four pellets indicated chance carrion feeding in one moorland edge territory.

Buzzards were observed on several occasions catching Frogs by pouncing from fence posts or bushes, once during a brief March snowfall. Oviducts were removed and dropped on the ground where they would swell (with rain) into gelatinous masses – the mysterious 'star slime' or 'star jelly' of folklore and legend. Fresh Starling and Magpie remains found beneath one nest some time before eggs were laid perhaps related to courtship feeding during nest building. Farmers reliably reported instances of a Buzzard pair eating sheep placentae and

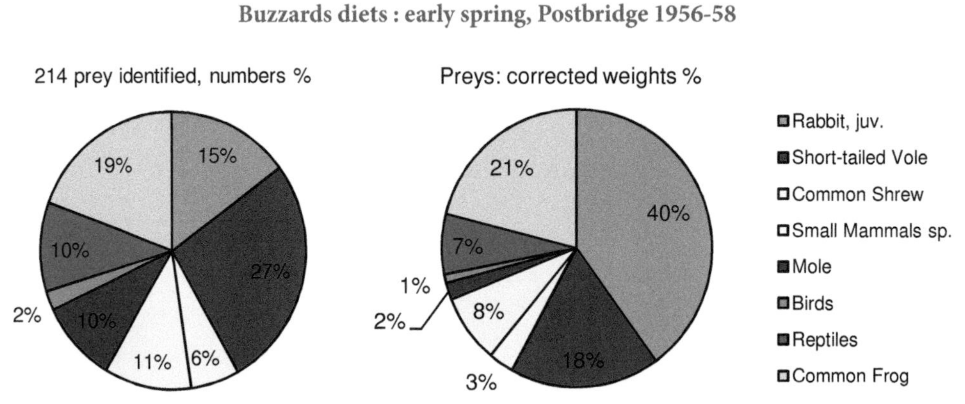

Figure 4.6 Early spring (March–April) diet of Buzzards at Postbridge, Dartmoor, 1956–58. Charts show as proportions: left – numbers of prey animals identified in pellets; right – their estimated biomass contributions after correcting for differential digestion. [Colour codes to be read clockwise]

Figure 4.7 Recently-emerged Rabbit kits are prime food for Buzzards and their broods in spring and summer. (© W. Paton/Photoshot)

of another 'exceptional' bird that was shot after killing two chickens in March. On wet days some Buzzards again resorted to ground foraging for earthworms, beetles and insect larvae but generally less intensively than in winter.

Ten Adders were present and made a small but interesting contribution to the diet. They were doubtless taken when basking semi-torpid on warm days, though still not without considerable risk. In April 1963, just outside the southern boundary of the study area, a farmer found a Buzzard 'dying in agony, its wings flapping, with a headless Adder on the hedge bank 20 m away'. In Germany, an adult Buzzard was found dead on its nest beside a live Adder (Melde 1956, citing Űttendorfer 1952).

Other Devon Buzzards, during early spring, have captured diverse preys by a variety of tactics. Several have been noted carrying Adders on moors or cliff tops; Toads (six taken by one bird) and once a Tawny Owl (DBRs). Carrion comprised sheep placentae and Mute Swan while two Dartmoor birds fed from a bullock carcass on the open moor. A hungry Buzzard even tried to break into a Magpie nest to catch the sitting bird, which escaped when her mate distracted the hawk. Another Buzzard stole an Eel from a Grey Heron that was fishing in an estuary. On Exmoor a gathering of 15 Buzzards was observed 'waiting on' a heather fire (during swaling) to catch fleeing voles and mice; a habit of many raptors in Africa that gather around grass and bush wild fires.

Feeding upon earthworms in spring has become increasingly common in lowland Devon since 1951. More unexpected, perhaps, some Buzzards 'follow the plough' in spring to take earthworms and beetles, with as many as six birds gathered in one field (DBRs). Near the Pembrokeshire coast this habit was first noted in 1940 (Davis 1955, Lockley 1955, Panting 1955, Smith 1955). From hedgerow perches the hawks dropped onto the fields near the ends of furrows, and well behind the attendant flocks of gulls and corvids, to pick up exposed invertebrates and, very occasionally, a small mammal. One Cornish observation was exceptionally interesting. A group of four Buzzards not only scared away the gulls, but then actually followed the wooden beam plough. Amazingly, the two boldest Buzzards, thought to be juveniles, eventually used the rear mole-board as a convenient mobile perch! (Smith 1986). Such observations demonstrate once again the ability of Buzzards to adapt to and exploit farming operations.

In Snowdonia the Buzzards, like Ravens, utilise sheep carrion throughout spring, particularly in the higher regions where it is considered likely to be essential for bringing birds into breeding condition (Julian Driver, pers. comm.). Buzzards in mid-Wales also take more sheep carrion in spring than do Dartmoor birds, along with some Rabbits and small mammals, but apparently no Moles, Frogs or reptiles (Newton *et al.* 1982). Elsewhere in Wales during early spring Buzzards have been seen opportunistically killing a Herring Gull, catching a flying Wood Pigeon, stooping (unsuccessfully) on an incubating Carrion Crow and snatching a Trout as it was being landed by a Grey Heron ! (*Nature in Wales* 1956–57).

COUNTING DOWN TO BREEDING

Courtship

In addition to fiercely defending their territories, the Buzzard pairs also spend much time engaged in unseen (but sometimes audible) courtship, nest site selection and building activities within the tree cover. Nest construction itself is a furtive business; birds are rarely seen carrying sticks into a site. In February and March, one might hear a hidden bird give a rapid series of excited '*pee-ya, pee-ya, pee-ya, pee-ya*' calls (the type 4 of Weir & Picozzi 1975). Much courtship or pair bonding seems to be incorporated into some of the aerial displays, as noted earlier. In particular, mutual soaring sometimes develops into talon-touching, as when a circling female rolls over and presents her clenched feet to the male as he passes so close above her that occasionally their feet may touch momentarily. Talon contacts may also occur when a pair glides silently and very slowly ('floating'), almost touching one another, just above their nest wood. Some birds may weave in and out of the woodland canopy, even as early as 10 February. This may be part of nest site selection perhaps, for I have located some nests from such clues. One male held grass in his talons while soaring with his mate over their nest copse.

Copulation

As the egg-laying period neared, the Buzzards on Dartmoor could be observed mating. Males mounted their mates either after standing beside them on a prominent tree branch, by flying in from another perch, or even by a steep descent from a display flight. In some matings, the females solicited by crouching forward. The act was accompanied by loud squealing sounds that were audible from at least 100 m away. According to the literature (Witherby *et al.* 1939) copulation takes place on the nest. In my area, however, all observed matings except one (on an old crow nest) took place on exposed perches on nearby trees or posts; and in high Snowdonia on a mountain crag. In North Somerset, similarly conspicuous copulations, even on electricity pylons, are thought also to signal clearly that the territory is occupied by a mated pair (Prytherch 2009).

Premature mating attempts (pair bonding) may occur long before eggs are laid; as on Dartmoor on 14 February and 5 March, and on Speyside even in mid-January (Weir & Picozzi 1975). On the moor, a total of 15 presumed effective copulations were noted between 20 March and 22 April but mainly from 10 April, which was within a week or so of the first eggs being laid. A very late but successful pair was seen mating on 11 May. In North Somerset, where first copulations are seen in early March, the peak period likewise is in early April when a pair may copulate more than twice in an hour (Prytherch 2009).

Elements of nest selection and courtship were shown by one Dartmoor male when it broke off a sycamore twig with its beak and flew first to the nest then, with twig now in its talons, he took off to circle up for two minutes. Suddenly, dropping its twig, the male then dived down to copulate with his mate who was standing on the ground. She laid her eggs 3–4 weeks later, but in a different nest.

Courtship feeding

Courtship feeding by the male Buzzard may be noted near the nest site a week or two before egg laying begins. In lowland Devon in early April, a male accompanied by his mate was seen circling high with a small Rabbit in his talons in a form of display (DBR). Another male was reported as passing a squealing young Rabbit to his mate in mid-air. A female near or at a nest might be heard begging for food by uttering shrill *seee-ee-yuk* calls like those of a hungry large nestling; as also was described for Speyside Buzzards (Weir & Picozzi 1975). Two Dartmoor females that were heard food-begging from their tree nests then flew off when their mates did not appear. Two bird kills beneath other nests at this season suggest that males had brought the food to mates that were either at the nest or perching nearby.

The food so obtained by the female is really an essential supplement because, in order to minimise damaging her developing eggs, she retires from hunting in the last week or so before laying. In Sweden female Buzzards were found to reduce their flying time and energy costs by about 75% in the final week or two before laying eggs (Sylvén 1982). Their withdrawal from active flight was clearly evident in early April in my Dartmoor and North Wales study areas. Instead, they became increasingly elusive, staying under cover for most of the day, presumably while collecting materials for lining and shaping the nest cup. The males, therefore, then started hunting for both partners and they soared and displayed alone in the skies. Thus, any pairs seen still soaring together in early May are signs either of non-breeding that spring, late breeding or perhaps an early loss of eggs.

And so, with all the above preliminaries having been completed, most Buzzard pairs should be ready to begin laying eggs by the middle of April.

5

BREEDING SEASON
I. Nests, eggs and incubation

The period from mid-April to mid-May is probably the most exciting time for Buzzard enthusiasts as the birds start to breed in one's study area. Frequent but careful searches will be made to locate all occupied nests and determine what proportion of the pairs actually lays eggs. A thorough knowledge of the area is essential as Buzzards with known alternative refurbished nests may not make their final decision until very close to laying, or even then may switch to a new and unsuspected site in a supposedly unlikely location. In addition, new pairs may have settled into the area, especially in those less accessible parts of a large upland region that one may have neglected to visit earlier in the year. More detailed information on methods for surveying and monitoring Buzzards, and other British birds of prey populations, can be found in the field guide for raptor study groups and individuals (Hardey *et al.* 2005).

Field work in the uplands now brings many fine days although brief returns of colder conditions are to be expected; heavy snowfalls are not unknown during the first week or so after Buzzards have begun incubating clutches in North Wales. The moors, bogs, woods and farms are now alive once again with the sounds and sights of song birds and waders. Later summer migrants from Africa, such as Cuckoos and Whinchats, have returned to the moors and mountain slopes. Those Buzzards nesting in the valleys share the canopy of ancient oak woods with singing Wood Warblers, Redstarts and Pied Flycatchers. The hill walker is seldom out of sight or earshot of Carrion Crows and Ravens. In the mountains of Snowdonia, where Ravens are ever-present, some Buzzard territories also harbour Peregrines, Kestrels and even Choughs.

POPULATION FEATURES

By the time that most Buzzards are sitting on eggs the population is once again settled. Territorial pairs comprise the basic structure once the early spring movements of dispersing or wandering immatures have slowed to a trickle. On Dartmoor, only occasional transient territory-seekers were seen into May in certain years; and even fewer were noted in North Wales. Such 'floating' birds comprise a largely unseen and difficult to assess element inhabiting a large area.

Of the territorial Buzzards, a variable proportion, but often around a quarter, fails to lay eggs in any given year. The reasons are often difficult to ascertain but generally are most likely to be food- or age-related. After severe winters, with associated food shortages, some surviving Buzzards perhaps are still weakened. However, even following 'normal' winters some long-established pairs may have an 'off year', possibly because one or both partners (especially the female) could not achieve sufficient fitness by April. Some pairs occupy territories where breeding is infrequent, presumably reflecting inadequate prey resources. The age and experience of individual Buzzards are other critical but indeterminate factors. For example, a non-breeding pair could include a recent and inexperienced replacement partner for a mate lost since the previous breeding season, or both birds may be newly-settled immatures that are re-occupying a vacated territory or perhaps establishing a new territory.

Confirmation of non-breeding can be difficult to obtain unless all territories are inspected cautiously at least weekly during April. It is important to exclude, if possible, the chance that eggs were laid then lost soon afterwards to predators, particularly to crows. The absence of a fully-prepared nest coupled with frequent views of both birds flying around during late April into early May, and lack of even weak anxiety responses to human presence near the nest, are normally indicators that eggs have not been laid. Using these criteria, the annual incidence of non-breeding in my most thoroughly studied population, on Dartmoor, varied between 21–33% of the pairs in 1956–58, 27–33% throughout the 1960s, and from 25–41% during 1990–93. In a similar but larger (and less intensively covered) moorland study area in North Wales, the proportion of non-breeding pairs varied between 23–36% over the four years 1979–82, but the proportion may have been slightly lower because some pairs were thought to have lost clutches soon after laying and between nest inspections (Dare 1995). By contrast, in a 120 km^2 Dorset farming area, supporting around 60 Buzzard pairs, 75–79% of pairs did not lay eggs, a remarkably low breeding rate. Radio-tracking revealed that there were three resident non-breeding adults for each breeding individual (Walls *et al.* 2000). It seems likely that such low breeding rates are atypical and may reflect the high population density (Appendix 24) coupled with probably insufficient food.

Bigamy, in which a male breeds simultaneously with two females at different nests, is rare among Buzzards. It has been recorded just four times in Wales and seven times in Scotland. This behaviour is difficult to detect and confirm, especially in wooded habitats, unless all the individual Buzzards can be recognised. However, four certain and three 'very probable' cases have been fully documented in mid-Wales (Davis & Davis 2002). Some bigamous pairings successfully reared young from both nests. In another (probably unique) triangle both females laid clutches, each of two eggs, in the same nest but one female then appeared not to play any further part in rearing the two young that fledged. . In Snowdonia no more than two suspected instances of bigamy have been noted during more than 30 years (J. Driver, *in litt.*). In a North Somerset population a more complex social arrangement was revealed by intensive observations. This involved a male Buzzard which defended two territories for two years, with two females – a mother and daughter in one, and a single female in the other

(Prytherch 2009). Both females bred successfully in the first year, fledging broods of two and one, but one female failed in the second year (R. Prytherch, in *litt.*).

On Speyside, the seven bigamous cases referred to four territories (Picozzi & Weir 1974). At least twelve of the fourteen females laid eggs but only once did both females in a territory rear young successfully, producing one and three fledglings respectively. In territories where bigamy happened twice, at least one of the females was different on the second occasion; but male identifications were uncertain. Two females were considered probably to be first-time breeders

Territorial behaviour

The breeding male Buzzards continue to advertise and defend their domains although their flying activities are gradually easing down. Instead, they now spend more time on guard from look-out and hunting perches near the nest site, and on providing food for their mates during incubation. These females effectively disappear from view for about six weeks from early April, leaving the males to patrol above their territories. As a result, the visible Buzzard population is virtually halved and a quieter period in the skies soon becomes apparent.

DIET DURING INCUBATION

For male Buzzards, behavioural changes result in a sharp fall in their daily energy (food) requirements from the high values needed to sustain their vigorous activities earlier in spring. In females, energy requirements remain the same. Any savings from the reduction in flying are offset by the energetic costs of egg production and the subsequent start of the body feather moult. According to the Swedish study, egg production costs an average 19 kcal/day during a two-week period in April. In May the onset of the female's annual moult of body feathers requires a further 24 kcal/day (Sylvén 1982). By comparison, body heat lost through her brood patch to incubate the clutch at 35°C is small (3–4 kcal/day), thanks to good insulation from the thick and well-lined nest (Sylvén 1982).

The male Buzzard brings food each day to his mate at or near the nest. He now needs to catch at least 200 g of prey daily, the equivalent of 10 Short-tailed Voles or one very young Rabbit. Fortunately, the latter are starting to become available, at least in some territories for, as noted previously, small mammals are now in short supply. On occasion one might hear a hungry female Buzzard calling loudly and demandingly for food, or her excited juvenile-like squeals as the male approaches with a kill. Small Rabbits are usually shared. First, at or near the kill site, the male may partially eviscerate the kill before eating the fore-quarters, including part or all of the head, and taking the rest to his mate. Small kills, and occasionally a very small Rabbit, may be brought onto the nest itself. However, most young Rabbit kills, weighing just 150–350 g, and birds are taken to 'plucking stations', such as a prominent tree stump or mossy boulder, where piles of fur and feathers may later be found. In steep woodlands they are always uphill from, and within about 25–30 m of, the nest.

The range of prey species taken by Buzzards on Dartmoor during these weeks probably differs little from that of early spring but their relative proportions in a population's diet may change. Pellet collecting was restricted by the need to minimise disturbance in nest woods where the males also roosted. Instead, dietary information for May was limited to a small number (49) of pellets, and mainly from non-breeding Buzzards. The 59 prey items identified showed that, in weight terms, Rabbit had increased in importance from 40% to 70%. It seemed that Buzzards were now concentrating even more on the first spring 'flush' of unwary young Rabbits. In contrast, though not unexpected, Short-tailed Voles and the other small mammals had declined further in importance (to 10%); whereas reptiles, chiefly Adders, were now (at 13 %) a prominent prey. Two pellets were composed entirely of Adder and Common Lizard scales bound together with grass. Frogs apparently had become minor preys, making up only 1% of the food compared to 21% in early spring, most having dispersed from their spawning assemblies.

It was also evident that some Dartmoor Buzzards still occasionally foraged intensively on the usual invertebrate fare, presumably in poor weather. Of particular interest, however, were two pellets made of caterpillar skins entwined in grassy material that were found in a semi-heath territory. They contained 63 and 45 noctuid moth caterpillars, up to 4 cm long, of species that feed on heather and rough grasses; as well as a few tipulid grubs ('leatherjackets') and beetles. A further two pellets, from nearby moorland localities, each contained a large caterpillar of the Emperor Moth *Lasiocampa pavonina* and a grasshopper (Orthoptera, Acridae).

Elsewhere in Devon during May, the bird reports contain four records of Buzzards killing snakes including two Adders, another bird seizing food from a Carrion Crow, one stooping repeatedly at a Brown Hare, while an opportunist caught three 'mice' in rapid succession that were flushed by a farm worker clearing scrub – another example of Buzzards exploiting human activities. On Exmoor, one Buzzard took a female Cuckoo from a bush top while she was preoccupied with watching nesting Meadow Pipits (Davis & Seel 1983). Not only unsuspecting Cuckoos, but also unwary Buzzards can come to grief when hunting, as was observed in Devon one May (DBR 1974). In this curious incident, at a Rabbit warren, a Fox was observed eating a Buzzard while Rabbits looked on from close by. One may surmise that the Buzzard had dived at a Rabbit, missed and then itself been pounced upon by the Fox which was hiding in cover waiting to snatch a Rabbit.

Buzzard-Peregrine interactions

Buzzards and Peregrines not uncommonly nest close to one another (and to Ravens) on extensive cliffs and crags in mountainous parts of Britain. In such locations the Peregrines at times harass both their neighbours, in encounters enthralling for the observer, but they rarely strike either species. Harassment of Buzzards may not be without good reason, for Buzzards have been known to steal and scavenge kills from Peregrines. Lakeland Buzzards have twice been seen to take freshly caught Feral Pigeons from these falcons (Kinley & Thexton 1985). In each case, the female Peregrine dropped her kill near the eyrie while stooping to join her mate in mobbing the hawk. One Buzzard skilfully caught the first pigeon in mid-air, the other pirated the pigeon where it fell. Despite much buffeting on the ground from the angry falcons, this opportunistic and tenacious Buzzard did not relinquish its spoils and the Peregrines eventually made off. Occasional scavenging from the remains of Peregrine kills was recorded by Ratcliffe (1980). In Snowdonia the remains of large gulls and feral pigeons found at Buzzard nests in my study area suggested similar scavenging behaviour (Chapter 6).

Buzzards have been killed by Peregrines on rare occasions, perhaps by accident during aerial jousts; and they then might be treated as food (Ratcliffe 1980). Such scenarios could explain the death of a Buzzard that was watched being eaten on the ground by a Peregrine in Wales, and the remains of two others found at eyries in Lakeland (Ratcliffe *loc. cit.*). More remarkable are the numbers of Buzzards observed being attacked and killed by urban-nesting Peregrines in southern Britain during the last five years. At Exeter, an exceptionally aggressive pair of church-nesting falcons that were rearing young have regularly attacked any Buzzard unfortunate enough to pass across the city 'in their air space' from June into autumn. In 2012 the female Peregrine, in tandem with her mate, was seen to kill two Buzzards on the same day and to strike down another two that could not be recovered (Dixon 2013). The death toll was even higher in 2013, with at least six Buzzards being killed (N. Dixon, *in litt.*). Similar attacks were reported elsewhere in these years, involving cathedral-nesting Peregrines in Chichester (where one Buzzard was knocked down and injured) and Derby (where a Buzzard was chased away). The victims would most likely have been non-breeding immature (1–3 years old) Buzzards that were crossing urban areas devoid of breeding Buzzards, which would still be rearing broods in their rural territories during June to August.

NESTS & NESTING SITES

The best Buzzard territories provide the most secure and sheltered tree or rock sites and often with more than one option. Some Snowdonia pairs have both tree and rock sites in their territories. Tree-nesting pairs prefer large trees with stout branching forks in quiet locations which also afford shelter from bad weather and concealment from people and predatory crows, a wide field of view over the nest approaches, and unhindered access to and egress from the nest sites. If a nest site possesses all or most of these features then the species of tree and nest height above ground seem largely immaterial. Buzzards nesting on rock faces are naturally safer from human interference but there they also seek the more sheltered niches and aspects, preferably with some vegetation cover.

Many long-established territories will have several alternative nests surviving from earlier years. Those in woods may be in a loose cluster within a 200 m radius, while others may be 400 m or more apart. Many pairs in my areas had two or three alternative sites, a few had four or five. Nest re-usage is highly variable regardless of success or failure in the previous year. Some pairs switch frequently between alternatives. On Dartmoor some changes were enforced by Carrion Crows either starting to nest very close to or usurping the Buzzard nest. Tawny Owls have twice taken over nests for roosting or breeding. However, many Buzzard pairs keep to the same tree or rock nest for three or more years in succession. Exceptionally, two Snowdonia tree nests were re-used for remarkable sequences of 13 and 14 years, and another nest is known to have been used almost every year for at least 36 years (J. Driver, *in litt.*). Likewise, one Devon nest was used intermittently (by different tenants) for at least 30 years (DBR 1970). Such nests can reach an impressive size. A similar pattern of nest usage was reported among Buzzards in the New Forest but there, however, one territory held six old nests and another had an astonishing 14 nests within a relatively close grouping (Tubbs 1974).

The spacing between occupied nests of adjacent Buzzard pairs (nearest-neighbour distance) varies with the local population density which in turn will reflect topography, habitats and nest site availability as well as prey abundance. Across a large study area, nests tend to be more or less regularly spaced (Dare & Barry 1990). In most of our upland regions, pairs' nests are often 800 –1300 m apart; but they may be as far as 3 km in the mountains or as close as 300–350 m in wooded valleys. Exceptionally, two nests in north-east Wales were a mere 150 m apart and close to the pairs' common territorial boundary (Roberts & Jones 2009). Two instances of extraordinarily close nesting in woods have been reported. In lowland Devon four pairs nested in a 2 ha wood (DBR 1985). In central Wales three occupied nests were found in one small wood. The possibility exists that two unusually close nests might belong to two female Buzzards mated with a single male. Such bigamous pairings have been confirmed in three regions, as described above.

Tree nests

The selected nest tree may be in a large wood, upland shelterbelt, small spinney, field hedgerow or even in a lone tree on a moorland hillside (Figure 5.1a–f, 5.2d). Roadside trees are sometimes used in upland areas and confiding pairs have nested within 50–75 m of occupied dwellings on Dartmoor. Even more remarkable was the North Wales coastal pair that bred successfully in a tall garden pine tree not more than 20–25 m from an occupied house (J. Driver, *in litt.*). One successful Dartmoor nest was in a large beech some 30 m from a caravan that was inhabited intermittently through the nesting season. In extensive conifer plantations the nest sites are usually very close to broad rides or clearings and where mature trees are sufficiently spaced to permit easy access to the nest. In the steep valley oak woods of Snowdonia, most nests are found about one third of the way down from the upper edge, and often accessed by the adults gliding down between the trees, almost Goshawk-like, to reach the nest.

Most tree nests in the uplands are placed about 10-15 m above ground level, rarely above 20 m or below 5 m. The position in a deciduous tree depends upon the species and size of tree as well as its branching structure (Figure 5.2a–d). In large deciduous trees the nests typically are built against the trunk in a stout central fork but some can be well out along horizontal boughs or high in the canopy. In tall Sitka spruces and larch, they are placed in Sparrowhawk fashion high against the trunk and supported by the radial branches (Figure 5.3). In Scots pines many are out on high branches, sometimes beneath a protective umbrella canopy (Figure 5.3d). However, Buzzard pairs are extremely flexible and individual with regard to nest positioning and they may take advantage of any favourable branching layout, natural or abnormal, irrespective of tree size and shape. Some pairs take over old nests of Carrion Crows built in tall deciduous trees or in isolated hillside hawthorns and rowans (Figure 5.2d).

Figure 5.1 Tree-nesting Buzzards in Snowdonia use a wide range of sites: in valley woods. (© a: Steve Culley, b and c: Julian Driver)

Figure 5.1 Tree-nesting Buzzards on Dartmoor use a wide range of sites: in hedgerows, spinneys and shelterbelts on hill farms and moorlands.

Figure 5.2 Buzzard tree nests in North Wales. In steep deciduous woods the nests can be low down (b, c). Remote moorland pairs re-use old crow nests in isolated trees. (© a–c: Julian Driver)

The Buzzards on Dartmoor, like those on lower ground, nest in a wide variety of deciduous and coniferous trees, though often in the most plentiful and widespread species. Of eight species used here, mature conifers and old beeches are most favoured. Thus, of 93 different occupied nests, 29% were in Sitka spruce plantations, 24% in Scots pine, 26% in beech, 7% in larch, 6% in sycamore, 5% in oak and single nests were in rowan and hawthorn. Two more

Figure 5.3 Buzzard nests in conifers are built high against the trunks and often become very large, through frequent re-use. Note the sheep wool (from carrion) and a nearly-fledged young Buzzard standing on nest (b). (© Julian Driver)

d

hawthorn nests and an exceptional one, barely 3.5 m off the ground in a bog willow, were fully prepared but then abandoned (Dare 1999). On southern Dartmoor a nest with eggs was reported to be less than 4 m up in a holly tree (DBR 1960).

On hill farms and moorland country in the North Wales study areas, the Buzzards use twelve tree species, mostly sessile oak, birch, sycamore and spruce but occasionally they build in alder, ash, rowan and (once) in holly (Dare 1989). In Snowdonia, by contrast, only about 60% of Buzzards nest in trees, the rest being rock nesters (Dare 1989). More than half of the nests were in sessile oaks, often in thickly ivy-covered trees, 22% were in conifers, and very small numbers were in other deciduous species including single nests in holly and wild apple *Prunus*. It is evident from these lists that when searching for Buzzard nests one must never discount the unlikely. In the Lake District the majority of tree nests are either in sessile oaks (39%) or conifers (39%), mainly larches and Scots pines (Fryer 1986).

Rock nests

Among the hills and mountains of Snowdonia, the Lake District, northern Pennines and Scottish Highlands, many Buzzards build their nests on various types of rock formation. In Snowdonia, where 40% of pairs were rock-nesters, the great majority (32 of 37 pairs) used natural crags up to at least 575 m in elevation, while the remaining few were on disused quarry faces (Dare 1989, Figure 5.4c). Spectacular views can be obtained from those nests placed 50m and higher above the bases of formidable cliffs, where Peregrines and Ravens may be close neighbours. An extraordinarily high nest with young was located at 875–900 m on a towering cliff face. Beneath it, the ground was littered each spring with carcasses of sheep that had fallen from high ledges, doubtless serving as a convenient and well stocked larder! (J. Driver *in litt.*). Some Buzzards may use low rock outcrops found in some high *cwms* (Figure 5.4b). However, most nest sites (Figure 5.4d) are hidden on ledges of well vegetated crags or knolls on steep slopes (Figure 5.4e). Low (3–10 m high) rock outcrops on very steep slopes, and hidden within the edges of mature conifer forests, are also used (Figure 5.5d). Such unexpected nest sites may be only 3–4.5 m up on a small ledge or even beneath the exposed roots of an overhanging tree. Those pairs perhaps are maintaining a traditional trait pre-dating the planting of these forests during the period 1920–70. Among the Lake District mountains and the fells of the north-western Pennines the crag-nesting Buzzards have chosen similar rocky locations between 168 m to 640 m above sea level (Blezard 1946, Fryer 1986).

Quarry nests in Snowdonia were less exposed to the elements than many on crags. They are placed on vegetated ledges, sometimes tucked behind a rowan sapling, though one nest was on an exposed bare ledge among slabs of slate debris. At the other extreme, on my adjoining moorland study area, two Buzzard pairs nested 'below ground level' on ledges in narrow river gorges or gullies. On Dartmoor, in the 1940s, a similar site was used amid heather moor in the north of my study area. That nest was on a granite ledge in an ancient tin-mining gully, where Ravens subsequently nested annually for many years (DBR 1949).

In very remote areas devoid of trees or rocky sites, Buzzards have nested in the most unlikely places. Moorland Buzzards in central Wales have nested on the ground. The photographer

Figure 5.4 Mountain Buzzards in Snowdonia nest on rock ledges in barren high surroundings (© Julian Driver)

Figure 5.4 Mountain Buzzards in Snowdonia also nest on rock ledges in disused quarries and on small outcrops. (© Julian Driver)

Arthur Brook (1920) described seeing two such nests 'on more or less level ground.' One nest was in heather (a typical Merlin site); the other, containing two eggs, was in a patch of rushes 'eminently suitable for a Curlew'. This nest was constructed of rushes, heather sprigs and a small leafy branch from a Rowan tree. In remote parts of northern Scotland such as Easter Ross, exceptional Buzzards have nested on, or virtually on, the ground: on the roof of deserted buildings, under a gorse bush on a low wall, the edge of drainage ditches, on sand dunes, and – most extraordinarily – even on seaweed on a beach. (Hardey *et al.* 2006, Scottish Raptor Study Group website).

Sea cliffs can provide good nesting places for a few pairs of Buzzards in Devon, Cornwall and West Wales. Some are set in dramatic locations. One nest that I saw was on a broad ledge far down a sheer cliff on the Pembrokeshire island of Skomer. It faced out westwards, over a gully with a noisy Guillemot colony, to the distant Gannet colony on Grassholm with the Celtic Sea and Atlantic Ocean beyond.

Nest structure

Nest construction is usually a prolonged and covert business, as noted previously, but in the New Forest one new nest was built in only two days (Tubbs 1974) though its size and whether it was also fully lined is unclear. Tree nests (Figures 5.2 & 5.3) are built with a base of large sticks of different thickness, up to about 50 cm long, and then a new superstructure of thinner and more flexible fresh sticks, all roughly interlaced and giving an untidy outline as seen from below. Most materials are freshly broken off from nearby trees. Where available, larch is much favoured and such nests often have the slender stick ends projecting and curving down from around the nest sides. Repaired nests have a noticeable new rim added to the old structure. Finally, the nest cup is lined with soft, dry plant materials collected from trees and ground nearby, and thus varies with location. Many upland nests are lined with a mix of fine dead moor grasses, tussocks of sedge, a few dead bracken fronds and soft birch leaf sprays. Pairs using old crow nests usually add a few sticks and a lining of dry grassy materials. Woodland nests are lined with sprays of fresh green foliage, clumps of wood rush and sometimes a few green ivy leaves. Most unusually, in one North Wales nest photographed by Julian Driver, the eggs lay upon scraps of white paper. Most Buzzards add further fresh foliage to the cup and nest rim sporadically during incubation; the so-called 'decoration' of many writers. Nests in conifer forests in Snowdonia are often well padded with fragrant sprays of spruce or pine which, with a full clutch of eggs or newly-hatched chicks, presents an especially pleasing picture.

Buzzard nests in trees vary greatly in size and appearance according to their age and location. The smallest are about the size of a crow nest and, indeed, may be an adopted nest of that corvid. Others may be newly-built by first-time breeding pairs settling into a new area. Typical tree nests in well-established territories measure from 50–60 cm across (roughly a Buzzard's body length) while 'traditional' nests, re-used and enlarged regularly by successive occupants over the years, become very bulky and can easily span a metre (Figure 5.3d). A depth or thickness of 20–25 cm is normal with the largest nearer 75 cm. An enormous nest built in a New Forest oak was about 1.5 m across, 75 cm deep and had been used for 13 years in succession (Tubbs 1974). These are broad platform nests with a relatively shallow central cup for the eggs. In shape, as viewed from below, many nests are elliptical and, as the season progresses, tend to have one side extended to form a landing area for parents bringing prey to the young.

The nests of crag-nesting Buzzards, by contrast, are shaped to fit the ledge space available and are generally much less substantial. Those in Snowdonia are often necessarily rather spartan affairs (Figure 5.5a–b): typically, a depression on a grassy, heathery or bilberry ledge and well-lined with whatever dry plant materials are available, such as dead moor grasses, wood rush and sedge tussocks and protected by a frontal rampart of thin heather or rowan sticks. In an extreme case, one of my nests, containing just one egg and sited on a high and exposed barren ledge, was little better than a Peregrine nest scrape. At the opposite extreme, some Snowdonia pairs build substantial nests on lower rocks that are closer to woods (Figure 5.5c–d) while a few sometimes occupy disused but still sturdy old stick nests of Ravens in more formidable locations. Many nests on large rugged crags in Snowdonia are very difficult to find in the egg stage. Most of these become apparent only well after hatching, when viewing from a distance may reveal accumulations of sheep wool (from carrion) and streaks of droppings ('whitewash') at the site, or when the wailing calls of hungry large youngsters may be heard. On some nests the wool hangs over the side in large wefts, as it does also on some tree nests

Figure 5.5 Buzzard nests in rocky terrain vary greatly in size and structure depending on altitude and proximity to woods. (© a–c: Julian Driver)

(Figure 5.3b). Inevitably, as the broods grow some wool becomes trampled in to the nest cup. An occasional length of discarded red binder twine may be added by a few Snowdonia pairs (J. Driver, *in litt.*), an increasing habit among the local Carrion Crows.

On the Lake District and Pennine crags the Buzzards incorporate small amounts of sheep wool into the nest lining and one nest was fully wool-lined (Blezard 1946, Fryer 1986). Rudimentary nests are fairly common in both areas where some may be no more than a natural hollow on a grassy ledge (Blezard 1946, Fryer 1986). An exceptional nest on a sloping rock outcrop was described as being virtually on the ground (Blezard 1946).

Buzzards that nest on sea cliffs make do with whatever vegetation is available, including green and red seaweeds (Witherby *et al.* 1943) and a few pairs may use novel materials. A pair on Skomer 'decorated' their nest with wings and skeletons of Manx Shearwaters that had been killed by Great Black-backed Gulls! (Davis & Saunders 1965).

EGGS

In shape, Buzzard eggs are rounded oval and in the nest appear to be almost spherical (Figure 5.6). The average length and breadth of 481 eggs measured in Wales were 56.2 x 44.3 mm (Roberts & Jones 2009), virtually identical to the 55 x 44 mm given in a standard reference (Cramp & Simmons 1980). Many eggs are completely white but not glossy and look more like large Tawny Owl eggs. Others are variably marked with reddish-brown, usually just a few markings, but occasional eggs are handsomely patterned with large red blotches around the wider end. The average weight of five freshly laid eggs in my Dartmoor area was 63 g (range 54–73 g); identical with that of a much larger sample laid by Buzzards in southern Sweden (Sylvén 1982) and similar to the 60 g reported in Germany (Melde 1956). Egg shells weigh 4.5–5.7 g (Melde 1956). A freshly laid egg is estimated to be equivalent to about 5–8% of a female's spring body weight (Melde 1956, Newton 1979, this study); and thus similar to that (6.5 %) calculated for the Red-tailed Hawk in North America (Soltz 1984).

The interval between laying each egg in a clutch has been difficult to measure exactly without risking undue disturbance at this critical time. Nowadays, it could be measured by installing modern camera recording equipment ('nest-cam') to view the nest cup. Although an average of 2 days is given for various studies combined (Cramp & Simmons 1980), Melde (1956) quoted individual values of up to 6 days, the interval increasing between successive eggs.

Clutch sizes

Buzzards in Britain can produce clutches of up to 6 eggs but the great majority in our uplands, and most places elsewhere, lay just 2 or 3 eggs, with occasional single eggs but seldom 4 and rarely more. Data from 17 studies and 1,794 clutches in western, mainly upland, Britain (see Appendix 6) show an average clutch size of 2.64 eggs; but with regional differences from 1.86 to 3.03 eggs. Overall, 45.6% of clutches were of 3 eggs, 42.0% of 2 eggs, 6.4% were single eggs, and 5.6% were of 4 eggs. There have been only four documented cases of five eggs and one of six eggs in Britain. The number of eggs laid by an individual Buzzard each spring can vary. This perhaps largely reflects annual differences in food availability during the preceding winter and early spring (Chapter 12) and thus the female's success in finding sufficient food to attain prime breeding condition. Population density changes, affecting territory sizes, could also limit food availability. Other factors possibly involved might be the age of the female (in particular) and whether the pair is experienced or only newly formed.

In my Dartmoor and North Wales areas 80–95% of 106 completed clutches were of two or three eggs, the rest being single eggs (Dare 1995, 1999). More recent detailed work in Snowdonia has failed to find a 4-egg clutch among 184 inspected by 2009 (J. Driver, *in litt.*). Buzzards in the mid-Wales hills likewise laid no more than 3 eggs (Newton *et al.* 1982). In north-east Wales, however, 1.6% of 229 clutches comprised 4 eggs and only 6% were single eggs (Roberts & Jones 2009). Overall, therefore, upland buzzards in Devon and Wales seldom lay 4-egg clutches.

Further north, where hill and mountain Buzzard densities are lower than in Wales and on Dartmoor, larger clutches have been more prevalent. In the Lake District, where Buzzards

Figure 5.6 Buzzards usually lay two or three eggs, with few or no markings, in nests lined with dry plant materials, to which 'decorative' sprays of fresh green foliage may be added. (© a, b: Julian Driver; c: Colin Whittle)

on the fells also fed extensively upon sheep carrion, they usually laid 3- and 4-egg clutches but only one or two eggs after mild winters with low sheep mortalities (E. Blezard, in Bannerman 1956). Not far away, on the fells and sheep farms of the north-west Pennines, 4-egg clutches were frequent (18%) in the years between 1937–67, and 5-egg sets were noted once (Holdsworth 1971). More recently, in Scotland, two Buzzard populations in areas with plentiful Rabbits have laid large clutches. On Speyside they frequently laid 4-egg clutches (24%) while in nearby Moray 20% did so, the highest proportions recorded in Britain since myxomatosis (Picozzi & Weir 1974, Swann & Etheridge 1995).

The influence of abundant food upon clutch size is also apparent in older records from south-west England before myxomatosis had severely reduced Rabbit numbers. There, exceptional clutches of five and even six eggs were found in both Somerset (Pring 1947) and Devon (Mayo 1948) and a truly exceptional brood of five young was noted in Cornwall (Lewis 1934). During the 1930s an 'especially prolific bird' in Devon laid 27 eggs over seven successive years, an average clutch size of 3.86 eggs. These comprised two of 5, two of 4, and three of 3 eggs. Information for Continental Buzzards is presented later (Chapter 13).

Annual variations in average clutch size of a Buzzard population may be comparable with the differences between regions or between habitats within a region. Typically, the annual variability in a population average falls between 2.1 and 2.8 eggs, depending mainly on the relative proportions of 2- to 3-egg clutches. However, in mid-Wales, annual mean clutch sizes were persistently low (2.0–2.3) throughout the five-year study (Newton *et al.* 1989). Unfortunately, differences have been difficult to confirm statistically because of problems with finding enough clutches in the same year(s) for each of the populations and habitats.

Buzzards rarely replace a clutch lost to predation or other causes unless this happens soon after incubation has started, but this is often difficult to prove. The replacement clutch may be the same size or smaller. Replacements were not suspected in my areas but four, at least one proving successful, have been confirmed in north-east Wales (Roberts & Jones 2009) and on Speyside, with five cases, four of them successful (Picozzi & Weir 1974). It is evident, from earlier discussions, that the energetic costs of replacing eggs are likely to be met only where food is plentiful and the female is in top condition. Prior to myxomatosis when Rabbits were abundant, one Welsh pair astonishingly produced two repeat clutches in the same season, using three different nests. This event was attributed to persecution and was recorded by the renowned photographer Arthur Brook (Brook 1949).

Laying dates

In general, upland Buzzards across western and northern Britain start clutches during mid- to late April (Appendix 7). But, as with clutch size, the first-egg and average dates vary from year to year and with locality, again presumably reflecting local fluctuations in food available to the individual pairs during the previous winter and early spring. That, in part, may have been influenced by cold weather. Unfortunately, exact first-egg dates are difficult to obtain without repeated disturbance and risk of desertion or predation. Instead, dates often are estimated, by assuming a value of two days for the laying interval between eggs, and then back-dating from when a freshly completed clutch is found. Given these difficulties, it should be sufficient for practical purposes to determine first-egg dates, and the pattern of laying within a population, by grouping estimates into 5-day periods.

On Dartmoor, at least half of clutches are started during the 10-day period from 16–25 April but the laying period for the whole population could exceed a month in some years. For example, in 1957, and following a very mild winter, the first clutch was started on 6 April and the last on 10 May. The timing of laying also varied between successive years for the same pair or territory by as much as three weeks. Similar laying periods were reported from Buzzards elsewhere in Devon and in Somerset in the era before myxomatosis (Mayo 1948, Pring 1948) while in Cornwall the peak laying period was nearly a week earlier, 9–20 April (Ryves 1948). The earliest first-egg date for Devon appears to be 3 April, based on a clutch of 3 eggs found on 7 April (DBR 1950). Among Buzzards in North Wales most clutches were started during the period 15–20 April but ranging from near 1 April to 26 April. However, extreme dates of around 27 March and 8 May were considered possible, by back-dating from the earliest and latest observed fledging dates (Dare 1989). A more recent study in north-east Wales reported 15 April as the (median) date by when one half of all first-eggs had been laid (Roberts & Jones 2009). For Pennine Buzzards a median date of 21 April was reported, with extreme first-egg dates of 8 April and 9 May (Holdsworth 1971), and thus similar to those on Dartmoor.

Incubation

The incubation period for Buzzards can be measured accurately, for each egg, only by repeated inspections of the nest during both the laying and hatching of a clutch. Such an intrusive procedure would risk excessively disturbing the birds and be impractical in most cases; although nowadays one might use remotely operated video cameras. Instead, most data are based on opportunistic observations. Published values range from 33 to 38 days per egg for Buzzards in this country (Cramp & Simmons 1980). In North Wales the periods for the first eggs in three clutches were: 34–35, 35–36 and 35–36 days, giving an average of 35 days (Dare 1989). Female Buzzards start incubating from the first or second egg (Cramp & Simmons 1980) and this leads to asynchronous hatching of the chicks which in turn often strongly affects their growth and survival in the nest, as will be described in Chapter 7.

The female, prior to laying, has already been restricting her activities to the vicinity of the nest for two weeks. Now, she will be confined to incubation duties for the next five weeks and will depend utterly upon her mate for food. Sylvén (1982) reported, from lengthy field observations, that she spends the night and 98% of each day in the nest, leaving only to eat prey at plucking places, to exercise briefly or to defaecate. However, two Dartmoor females were seen to leave eggs briefly to support their mates in protesting at intruding Buzzards. In both instances they flew about near the nest site for a few minutes and had only recently completed clutches. I have twice flushed males off eggs when the females were engaged elsewhere and suspect that they were simply covering the clutch, and partly to protect it from chance discovery by marauding Carrion Crows. More than 100 pairs of these egg thieves nested in this Dartmoor area and were the major threat to all Buzzard nests (Dare 1961). As many as eight pairs of crows nested in some Buzzard territories.

Female Buzzards sit low in the nest cup as they watch their surroundings. On many occasions, the male detects an approaching observer and gives alarm calls. In the early days of incubation a tree-nesting female is readily flushed, typically slipping off the nest and sneaking away out fairly low through the trees and into the open before rising 100 m or more off to circle either silently or with a few weak calls. She will drift back slowly towards the nest area but not return before the intruding person has retreated several hundred metres. At such times the eggs are vulnerable to crows which are bolder and may raid an unguarded nest. Where a Buzzard nest is suspected in a well-wooded location a flushed female can easily be overlooked at first. As the weeks pass, however, they sit ever tighter and some will not leave the nest until the observer is beneath and makes a noise or knocks the tree itself. In windy weather, and if her mate is away hunting, a female in a high nest may even be unaware of one's presence if approached up-wind from behind. Sitting Buzzards get used to routine farm activities nearby as well as to vehicles passing beneath roadside nests, but in conifer plantations they may desert should major forestry operations encroach to within 200 m. Close to hatching time, females become very reluctant to leave eggs but, once off the nest, they will circle nearer than before and call more loudly, thereby often attracting the attention of the male even if he is hunting far off. Females may now return with little delay to the nest as the intruder retreats to a safe distance.

Egg losses

Buzzard clutches are lost every year to a variety of natural and human causes, though in most cases the reasons can only be surmised. Very few succumb to normal bad weather, even in high exposed sites, except soon after laying. Several new-laid clutches were lost following a very heavy snowfall in North Wales in late April 1981. Instead, crow predation and human disturbance are the usual causes of failure. On Dartmoor during the first years after myxomatosis, 29% of 27 full clutches (39% of all eggs) were lost. At six accessible nests where causes could be determined, three clutches had been taken by crows and the others had disappeared, due probably also to crow predation facilitated by unintentional disturbance from farming and road works, or by the general public, keeping females off their nests (Dare 1961). Chilling of unattended eggs then could be a potential hazard, especially in uplands and for well-incubated eggs. The statement that Buzzard eggs may withstand chilling for up to five hours (Melde 1956, citing von Schweppenburg) clearly should not be tested.

On Dartmoor in the late 1950s and 1960s, when Rabbit numbers were still low, a period of food shortage each spring may also have been implicated. Crow predation risks would have increased should a hungry female Buzzard have been tempted to seek food herself. Unusually, females were sometimes heard food-begging loudly from their nests. The influence of food supply is supported by later nest monitoring in the early 1990s. By then, and after Rabbits had become appreciably more plentiful, the loss rate (16%) of full clutches had almost halved.

Buzzards in North Wales experienced similar clutch mortality with nearly one third being lost, single-egg clutches being especially vulnerable (Dare 1995). Again, causes could not be determined but, in this sparsely inhabited region, they were probably mainly 'natural', including the collapse of a flimsily-sited plantation nest. Only two losses were related to excessive human disturbance during logging operations in conifer woodlands. In upper Speyside, an even higher (45%) rate of breeding failure was recorded but there, unlike in the other areas, at least two-thirds of the failures were due to persecution and other kinds of human disturbance (Picozzi & Weir 1974). The absence of predation by Hooded Crows on Speyside reflected the low corvid numbers due to constant persecution.

Infertile or addled Buzzard eggs, found in nests after the others have hatched, are uncommon in all areas. They amounted to 4.5% of eggs on Dartmoor and 6% in North Wales, including a 'dwarf egg'. Only three unhatched eggs were found during the five-year study in mid-Wales (Newton *et al.* 1982) and three single-egg clutches failed to hatch in Cornwall (Ryves 1948). Failed eggs may remain undamaged at the back of a nest holding half-grown chicks (Figure 7.3a). Exceptionally, a whole clutch may be infertile, as was reported once in Devon when the three eggs failed to hatch after being incubated for six weeks (DBR 1949). In other parts of Britain, the failure of some Buzzard clutches to hatch during the 1960–70s was linked to chemical contamination during that pesticide era (Chapter 15).

Hatching imminent

And so, after nearly six weeks devoted to laying, incubating and closely guarding her clutch, the female Buzzard should begin hearing the faint sounds of a chick stirring within the first egg that is about to hatch. The uplands have been transformed during this time into verdant landscapes with increasing numbers of young Rabbits and small mammals appearing above ground, while at high elevations fresh mutton becomes available thanks to spring lambing losses. It is a good time now for Buzzards to start rearing their broods.

6

BREEDING SEASON
II. Brood care and food

A period of about eight weeks, from mid-May into early July, spans the time when Buzzards in an area are caring for their broods in nests. Every day brings fresh events which the keen raptor ecologist will be eager to observe and record. Field work can last from dawn to dusk almost irrespective of daily weather conditions. Prime tasks now are to follow the growth and survival of the young in each brood while simultaneously logging their diet in terms of the amounts and types of prey brought to feed them. This should result, at the end of the season, in a good measure of the breeding success of the study population, together with likely factors influencing the outcome.

PARENTAL ROLES

This account describes – with reference to Buzzards on Dartmoor, but doubtless applicable elsewhere – the different roles of the sexes in raising their young, and shows just how vital it is that their efforts are coordinated. The development and survival of the broods themselves, the ultimate indicator of parental success, will be described in the next chapter.

Female Buzzard

Her main responsibilities are the care of the young and of the nest. These duties are clearly illustrated by sample observations from a nest log (Appendix 8 and Figure 6.1). She alone feeds and shelters the brood and looks after nest hygiene. For at least the first two weeks after the chicks have hatched, the female seldom leaves the nest other than briefly to 'stretch her wings' at a nearby lookout perch. As during incubation, she is still fully dependent upon her mate for food. Protecting the young from marauding Carrion Crows or other possible nest raiders is a high priority. Her loud calls in response to any perceived threat, especially human presence, may bring the male hurrying back from hunting to assist. In the early weeks it is virtually impossible to approach an active nest without being detected; her anxious and persistent cries are a sure sign of a brood nearby. When the young are about three weeks old, and in fine weather, the female can at last start hunting again, though only in the nest vicinity. It is not until the young are well-feathered on their upperparts, and large enough to deter crows, that the female finally is free to participate more fully in satisfying the ever-growing food demands of the brood. As fledging time nears, she is away from the nest for long periods during the day.

Observations from hides at nests with young broods provide fascinating insights into the behaviour of the female and chicks, and of the processes that determine the survival chances of each sibling (Chapter 7). As often described for other raptors, first by nest photographers and nowadays in wildlife films, the female Buzzard tends her young brood with great care and moves around the nest very cautiously with her claws tucked under her feet. Initially, the very small chicks are fed tiny prime morsels of flesh offered in her bill tip and held with great patience. At the end of a feeding session the chicks are brooded or the female may stand and preen quietly beside them. After two weeks the young are given progressively larger pieces of prey mixed with fur or small feather 'roughage'. Feeding is much reduced when they are big enough to swallow entire small mammals in a few gulps or to tear a meal from larger kills.

Figure 6.1 a–c Female Buzzard beside her 3-week-old chick before feeding it on a Red Squirrel kill; the chick is the lone survivor from a 3-egg clutch. (Lake District, 1977, © Colin Whittle)

b

c

For the first three weeks, the female Buzzard also covers her small young during rain and cold weather as well as (presumably) through the night. For a few weeks she keeps the nest clean by rummaging in the bottom for food scraps, which are swallowed, together with furry pellet debris from the brood's first castings. The chicks may be pushed aside as the female digs vigorously beneath them. During their time in the nest, the young defaecate at first on the nest rim and, later, over the side or against the tree trunk or rock surface behind the nest.

In southern France, broadly similar female behavioural patterns at two nests were confirmed and analysed from video camera recordings (Hubert & Gallo 1995). There were small differences in the timing of events, perhaps reflecting a climate warmer than on Dartmoor. Females reduced their brooding efforts and started hunting sooner and for long periods. They spent little time on the nest once the young were 30 days old and could feed themselves. The females' behaviour at the nest now suggested that they were increasingly avoiding contact with the ever more active, and sometimes aggressively begging, youngsters.

In addition, the female (mainly) adds green foliage sprays to the nest cup and rim at irregular intervals during the first few weeks, and these serve as fresh bedding. In the final weeks, as the young become well-feathered and spend much time standing, preening and exercising on the nest, the female now spends longer periods in hunting, and nest hygiene becomes increasingly lax. Just before fledging, Buzzard nests may have become a sodden trampled platform of pellet debris and discarded prey remains such as Rabbit fur, large feathers and perhaps sheep wool, all mixed with occasional skeletal fragments.

Male Buzzard

The success of rearing the brood depends critically upon the male's prowess as a hunter, most vitally during the first 2–3 weeks after the eggs have hatched and when his mate is still tied to the nest. He usually begins to bring in kills as soon as the first chick has emerged. For example, at one woodland nest in Snowdonia, a freshly-killed Bank Vole had been delivered by 06.50 BST while the first chick was still wet with its egg shells beside it. The rear half of a young Rabbit and another vole were brought in a few hours later (Figure 6.2).

At another nest containing two recently-hatched chicks and a 'chipping' third egg, the male already had provided six small kills – four Field Voles, a Common Shrew and an adult Meadow Pipit (Figure 6.3).

Now, the male must continue to catch enough prey to feed both his mate and the brood (Appendix 8) as well as to maintain his own fitness. Large kills enable him first to eat his share. For example, the head and some of the fore-quarters of a young Rabbit are usually eaten before the remainder is taken to the nest. En route, he may be harried by crows attempting (unsuccessfully) to rob him (Figure 6.4). Later, even though the female has resumed hunting, the male must still take the major role in satisfying the increasing food requirements of at least one youngster as it rapidly nears his own body weight.

Observations of Dartmoor Buzzards indicated the amount of hunting effort that the males expended when Rabbits were scarce. In effect, they spent almost every hour of daylight hunting, subject to interruptions by spells of stormy weather. In North Wales, where Rabbits also were not plentiful, similar conclusions were reached. Hide observations in both study

Above: Figure 6.4 Male Buzzards usually eat the head of small Rabbits before delivering the prey to their mate. (© R. & M. Battell/ www.moorhen.me.uk)

Above laft: Figure 6.2 Male Buzzards rapidly bring food to newly-hatched chicks here dwarfed by the hind quarters of a young Rabbit.

Left: Figure 6.3 A hatching brood with four Field Voles, a Common Shrew and a Meadow Pipit. Note the 'chipping' third egg. (Snowdonia © Julian Driver) areas showed that male Buzzards spent no more than a few minutes in total each day at the nest. Their fleeting visits with kills lasted seconds only; other kills might be brought to a nearby plucking station to which the female would be called by her incoming mate. With Rabbits and other large kills she could take a share before carrying the rest to her brood. Very occasionally, a male might bring a spray of green foliage to the nest.

As broods near fledging time, both parents, but especially the female, become increasingly noisy and demonstrative overhead when nests are being inspected. Some Buzzards then will swoop low above a person crossing open ground or skim within 1–2 metres over a tree-top nest during an inspection. By this stage, and having invested so much effort in raising a brood, Buzzards are tenacious in caring for any youngster that accidentally becomes 'grounded', as the following two events testify. In my North Wales moorland area, a large sycamore tree holding one of my study nests with young was found to have been felled just before an inspection visit. Amazingly, the two five-week old youngsters were unharmed and had been left standing in their battered nest on the ground. With my wife's assistance, the nest core and young were relocated to a low fork (only 3 m off the ground) in a smaller sycamore 30 m away. There, the parent Buzzards continued to feed their rescued offspring daily until both youngsters fledged safely two weeks later (Dare 2006). Many years before, in Pembrokeshire, Allen (1930) had found a fledged Buzzard on the ground in a wood. He then tethered the bird to the base of a nearby tree and recorded subsequent events. Over the next 19 days the parents brought food daily, amounting in all to 75 kills. These included 39 Rabbits, 23 Moles, a Weasel and 10 birds; after which the bird was released unharmed.

PROVIDING FOOD FOR BROODS

For at least the first few weeks after hatching, the fate of a Buzzard brood depends solely upon the hunting skills of the male and his ability to provide enough food regularly. How he, and later the pair, perform can be monitored by assessing the daily rate and amount of food delivery to (provisioning) the brood, and how hunting success is affected by weather conditions. Three methods were employed for the Buzzards on Dartmoor: directly observing the catch rates of hunting birds; using hides to record how frequently kills were delivered to nests; and inspecting nest contents four times a day to record prey species, weights and other data. The results, documented more fully later (Chapter 12), are summarised here.

The male Buzzards on Dartmoor were active from dawn to dusk throughout the long days of the nestling period. They searched their territories thoroughly by hovering and static (perch) hunting according to habitat and weather conditions. Males seemed to be more persistent and successful hunters than females. The latter spent less time hunting even when young were more than a month old. As a result, males caught probably some 70% of all food brought to broods. Each pair showed differences in the numbers, species composition and weight of kills from day to day and at different times of day. Rabbits, for example (Figure 6.2), were brought mainly in the evenings and early mornings, but none were taken on 30–40% of days at the two territories where they were the main prey. Capture rates, for all preys combined, varied between 0.1 and 1.1 kills per hour, being lowest when Rabbits were taken, and highest when catching small mammals and similar size preys. Comparable provisioning rates were observed for Buzzards

Figure 6.5 A Buzzard brings a young Rabbit to its brood in South Wales; a stunning action shot by Arthur Brook in 1952. (© National Museum of Wales)

feeding on small mammals in my North Wales area. Before myxomatosis Buzzards could capture Rabbits at very high rates. In South Wales seven were brought in by the parents of two large young in a single afternoon (Brook 1952). One of his superb photographs, taken using a hand-made focal plane shutter, has set a standard yet to be matched for this raptor (Figure 6.5).

The erratic hunting success of Dartmoor pairs in the 1950s, immediately after the myxomatosis-induced rabbit 'crash', led to wide daily fluctuations in the weight of food provided – from zero up to 1 kg. In general, however, broods of one or two young were reared in those places where the parents managed to provide a daily average of 200–350 g of food. These amounts were lower than the averages of 540 g and 250–450 g per day that were observed for Buzzards rearing broods on ample supplies of small mammals in Finland and Poland respectively (Suomus 1958, Czarnecki & Foksowicz 1954).

On Dartmoor, the strong impression gained from all field and nest observations was that the Buzzards were operating at maximum hunting effort in those years. The low prey amounts then brought to nests reflected the impoverished food resources remaining not long after myxomatosis. Food limitations clearly were responsible for the brood reductions at one nest where the entire brood came perilously close to disaster, as will be described in the next chapter.

DIETS OF BUZZARD BROODS

Frequent inspections of nests throughout the 7–8 weeks of brood rearing provide prime opportunities to collect better quality information on Buzzard diets than can be obtained at any other time of year. Details of prey species composition and of the size, weight, age and sex of preys can be gathered from freshly-caught whole animals, or from the remains (body parts, fur, feathers) of previous meals that may be scattered about, with pellets, on or under the nests. Nest visits are the highlights of the year for the field worker and can afford many insights into aspects of Buzzard predation. These benefits, together with caveats concerning biases with the interpretation of nest prey remains, will be discussed in later chapters. A fully representative sampling of dietary variations through a two-month period is labour intensive and difficult to achieve in practice. Continuous observations of nests from hides can provide valuable supplementary records of prey species and capture rates on particular days, but is not sustainable for long on a daily basis. The recently introduced use of video recording cameras at nests provides a wealth of information, and could supplement (or replace) hide observations, despite camera positioning requirements and time consuming tape analyses.

Dartmoor

In the Dartmoor study, 1–4 nest inspections were made daily during which 215 nestlings' pellets were collected for analysis. A total of 508 prey animals were recorded at ten nests. Four nests (with 347 kills) were in territories with moor and scrub land where Rabbits were available, albeit in small numbers. The remaining six nests (161 kills) were in territories on enclosed valley farms where Rabbits were much scarcer or absent. The estimated total biomass of prey represented by the 508 kills amounted to 36.7 kg and 7.5 kg for the with-Rabbits and Rabbit-scarce territories respectively. The species composition of brood diets comprised eight mammals, at least 23 birds, three reptiles and two amphibians.

Mammals

Brood diets in the aftermath of myxomatosis clearly reflected local differences in Rabbit availability (Figure 6.6). Rabbits comprised one third of kills where pairs could hunt at small colonies, but only 4% elsewhere. Conversely, small mammals collectively were less frequent (35%) kills in Rabbit territories than in Rabbit-scarce territories (64%). Short-tailed Voles made up a fifth of all preys in both territory groupings. Moles were a prominent prey at some nests. Birds and Frogs both made up 14% of prey items found at nests across the study area.

On a weight basis, Rabbits constituted 76% of prey taken where they were available, and 23% in Rabbit-scarce territories, thus again showing the importance of even occasional captures. A good idea of the relative sizes of Rabbit kills and Buzzards are very apparent in Figures 6.4 and 6.5. In territories with Rabbits, the remaining 23% of prey weight was divided fairly evenly between the various small mammals and birds, but amphibians and reptiles were insignificant. In Rabbit-scarce territories, small mammals made up half of the total prey weight, with more Moles (28%) than Short-tailed Voles (9% only). Birds (13%) were well represented and reptiles (Adders) featured locally. Thus, a scarcity of Rabbits was off-set by Moles and birds rather than by voles and Frogs. This suggested that the last two preys were themselves less readily available at this season in those territories (see also Chapter 11). Miscellaneous preys were: Brown Rat (7 kills) of which three were adults, Wood Mouse (4), Bank Vole (17), Water Vole (7) (mainly juveniles) and Common Shrew (35).

Birds

The 69 bird kills on Dartmoor, taken from one wildfowl and 11 passerine families, were mainly thrushes (15) and finches (12), although by weight the crows and pigeons would have been prized kills. Almost one third of bird prey was unidentifiable feather debris from small

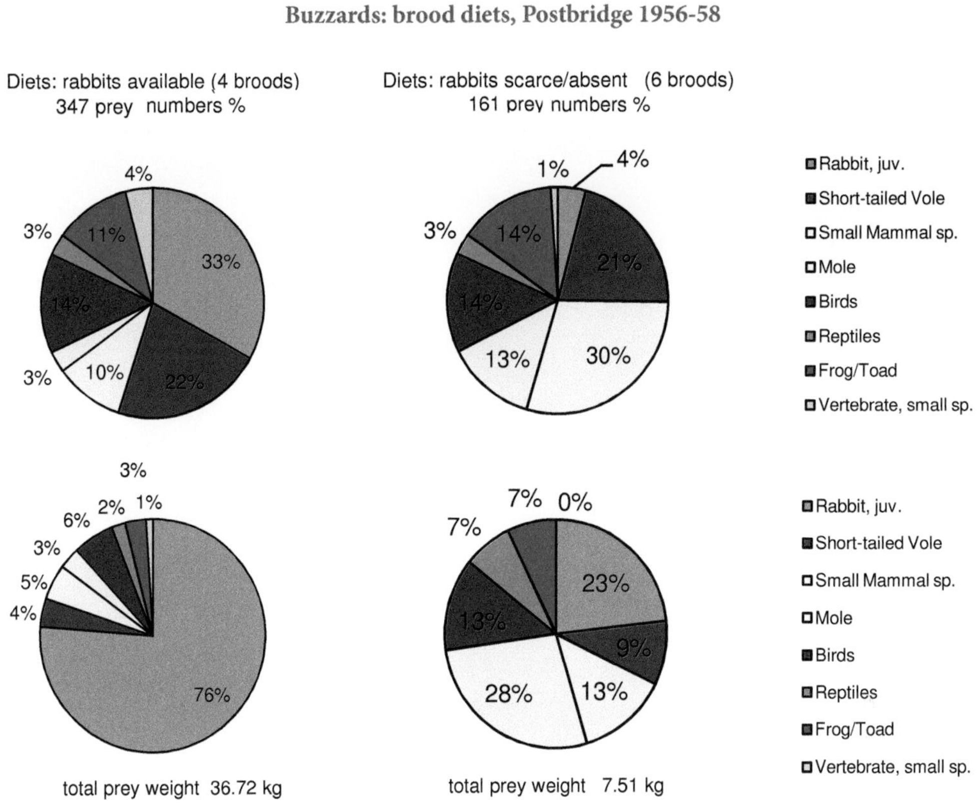

Figure 6.6 The diets of Buzzard broods at Postbridge, Dartmoor, in relation to Rabbit availability soon after myxomatosis. Pie charts compare the proportions of Rabbit in diets in territories where Rabbits were seen either often (left hand charts) or were absent or seldom seen (right hand charts). Prey species importance is shown by numbers brought to nests (upper row) and by weight (lower row).

passerines. Chaffinch (8) and Blackbird (5) were the commonest species. Victims ranged in size from Wren (1) and Dunnock (1) up to adults of Carrion Crow (2) and Wood Pigeon (1). The Buzzards caught birds opportunistically in all habitats. Thus, there were species from woodland (Robin, Song Thrush, Wren), scrub (Garden Warbler, Whitethroat, Linnet), fields and hedgerows (Blackbird, Chaffinch), open moor (Skylark, Meadow Pipit, Wheatear) and from bogs or riversides (Mallard duckling, Grasshopper Warbler). Elsewhere on Dartmoor, feathers from a Cuckoo have been found below a Buzzard nest (DBR), and predation of Wood Warbler nests there has been recorded (see below). Also in Devon, a brood of two fully-feathered young Wood Pigeons were taken from their nest.

The ages of 33 bird kills on nests could be determined from plumages. Most (51.5%) were fledglings, 24.3% were adults (including Carrion Crow and Wood Pigeon) while, surprisingly, the remaining 24.3% were nestlings of finch and thrush species, Skylark, Carrion Crow (1) as well as a small Mallard duckling. A group of three nestling chats, probably Whinchats, was found on one nest. Evidently, Buzzards occasionally found and robbed nests in woodland and also those of ground-nesting birds on moorland, presumably when hunting, respectively, from perches and by hovering. Oddly enough, catching Mallard ducklings may not be without risk, as the following unusual incident observed in Wales attests. A Buzzard that was attacking a Mallard brood on a Pembrokeshire pond was itself struck by the female duck and forced into and under the water. The exhausted Buzzard managed to struggle ashore after the duck had been frightened off by the intervention of the observer (Lockley 1955).

Amphibia and reptiles

Of the 60 amphibians found on Dartmoor nests, 50 were Common Frogs and 10 were Common Toads. Five of the toads, one with hind parts removed, were still alive, while one frog leapt out of the nest. The 15 reptiles, all identified from pellet traces, were mainly Adders (13) with single Common Lizard and Slow-worm. Several years later, a partly eaten small Adder was found beside one brood. Other observers on Dartmoor have seen Buzzards carrying snakes at this season on at least fifteen occasions. Nine of them were in my study area in recent years – 3 with Adders (one on a nest), 9 with probable Adders and three with Grass Snakes. One Buzzard was seen to capture a Grass Snake in a cut grass field in one of the territories (DBRs). Another Dartmoor bird took a young Moorhen. Elsewhere in Devon, other unusual prey seen on nests has included Grey Squirrel and, remarkably, Herring Gull chicks that were brought regularly by an enterprising coastal pair of Buzzards (DBRs).

Invertebrates

Invertebrate items were found in pellets of nestling Buzzards collected from at least seven Dartmoor nests. Some records were of exceptional interest since the items could only have been brought to the nests by the parents. Most unexpected were the six earthworms, some 6–8 cm long and still alive, found on one nest; and a part-eaten 15 mm black slug (*Arion ater*) at a neighbouring nest during the same period. Five dung-beetles (*Geotrupes* sp.) at a third nest were almost certainly adult captures, as were two 1–2 cm long dead millipedes (Julidae). All of these occurrences were in 1958, in a breeding season of prevailing bad weather and often poor hunting success. It appeared that, exceptionally, invertebrates were brought to broods in response to the generally adverse conditions. There are no comparable records in the British literature.

Insects and other invertebrates were found fairly often in the pellets of Buzzard chicks, usually first appearing when broods were about 16–24 days old. Their food value was negligible. A total of 150 items was noted, with all but seven mainly arboreal beetles. Five ants (Formicidae) were of a small species often observed in the tops of the conifers holding the nests. Other species may have wandered onto nests, e.g. many small flying beetles, a small spider and an unidentified moth caterpillar. It is likely that most of these unexpected records referred to insects snapped up casually by the young Buzzards either out of curiosity, in irritation, or incidentally with vertebrate kills. Nestlings were seen to catch and swallow small beetles on several occasions and it is interesting that invertebrate pellet records first appeared from the time that broods began to explore and investigate all objects on and around the nest.

The diets of the adult Buzzards themselves are not so easy to assess during this period because their pellets were difficult to find among the dense ground vegetation. On Dartmoor the food of parents could be deduced in part from preys brought to broods, since the adults normally took a share of Rabbits and the females also ate odd scraps from smaller kills. For non-breeders and failed breeders, pellet analyses (88 prey items from 77 pellets) enabled some comparison to be made between territories with differing Rabbit availability. Perhaps not surprisingly, the diets of Buzzards without broods differed little from the preys brought to broods (Figure 6.6).

North Wales

In my two areas during 1977–85 prey remains were generally scarce at nests, only 370 kills being noted on or beneath nests during 290 inspections in 93 territories (Dare 1989). Rabbits, still subject to recurring outbreaks of disease, were generally scarce and localised. They nonetheless comprised one third of all the 193 mammalian preys, though they were seldom noted on mountain nests. The Buzzards brought not only all the mammal species seen on Dartmoor nests but also five Weasels and a Grey Squirrel. Sheep carrion was noted on 50 occasions (35 territories), being most frequently brought by mountain and moorland Buzzards. One foot and wool from a feral mountain Goat kid was found at one crag site, and a Hedgehog elsewhere was probably scavenged from the nearby main road.

Bird kills, with 170 records, were noted in all districts, though most frequently at woodland and moorland nests. The most prominent and widespread victims were corvids, recorded in more than one third of territories, most being newly-fledged Magpies (47 records) and Carrion Crows (20). Species not recorded on Dartmoor were Jackdaw (1), Jay (4) and, unusually, a Kestrel (fledgling) as well as Pheasant (1) and Herring Gull (2 immatures). The gulls and some of the eight feral/racing pigeons might have been scavenged remains from Peregrine kills (see Ratcliffe 1980). Four Meadow Pipit nestlings provided further evidence of moorland nest robbing. Ten Starlings were all juveniles taken from the flocks that foraged on grass moors soon after fledging. There were only seven amphibian kills (4 Frogs and 3 Toads) on nests and no reptiles.

Further confirmation that small preys are under-recorded by casual inspections of Buzzard nests in North Wales was provided by the 54 hours spent directly observing kills brought to three nests at various stages of brood growth. A total of 27 small mammals, small birds and Frogs were delivered but no large preys, whereas 20 (50%) of the 40 food items noted from 31 visits to these same nests were large species, mainly Rabbits, corvids and Sheep carrion.

Many of the Snowdonia territories continued to be monitored during the following 25 years by a fellow enthusiast, Julian Driver, who found a broadly similar range and frequency of prey items. As before, few kill remains were seen at nests apart from numerous items of Sheep carrion. These comprised wool, bones and, once, a fresh leg of small lamb 'that would have made a tasty tea'! Only 86 other prey items were noted during hundreds of nest inspections. Of these, 19% were Rabbits and 31% corvids. Unusual preys were Weasel (1), Stoat (2 fully grown), Grey Squirrel (2), Chough (2 juveniles), Jackdaw (2), Jay (3) and an adult Cuckoo. Eight feral or racing pigeons had perhaps been taken from Peregrine kills. Other carrion records were of Goat (2), Otter (tail of a juvenile) and Hedgehog, while Domestic Fowl remains may also have been scavenged. The Otter and Hedgehog remains were thought most likely to have been scavenged from nearby road-kills.

In the North Wales uplands, therefore, no single food resource appears to be of outstanding importance, with the clear exception of carrion Sheep for some Buzzards living high in the mountains. That resource evidently was utilised by Buzzards nesting in the higher and more desolate mountain territories and on the wilder moorlands (Driver & Dare 2009). Rabbits, as ever, should contribute prominently in certain districts and in their 'better' years between recurrent myxomatosis outbreaks.

Other regions

Buzzard nest prey records have been published from six other specific breeding and food studies in various parts of Britain: the New Forest in southern England (Tubbs 1974), mid-Wales (Newton *et al.* 1982), the West Midlands of England (Sim *et al.* 2001) and for three upland regions in Scotland (Graham *et al.* 1995, Swann & Etheridge 1995). These provide interesting contrasts with my study areas. They are collated below, together with those from a further five smaller-scale studies and with anecdotal records in the national and regional bird literature. Comparisons between studies are complicated by the use of different data collection methods. In some areas only nest data were collected, while in others these were supplemented by pellet information. Only the main features, therefore, are presented here. The limited dietary information from Ireland is given separately.

Buzzards in Britain are known to have brought to nests at least 93 species of vertebrate preys although relatively few are of widespread dietary importance. The list comprises 16 mammals with a further 5 taken as carrion, 4 reptiles, 2 amphibians, and an astonishing 69 bird species belonging to 25 families. The most diverse diet appears to have been in Glen Urquhart, west of Loch Ness, where 62 species, 47 of them birds, were found at nests during a 13-year study (Swann & Etheridge 1995).

Mammals

Rabbits dominated the lists of nest preys in all areas. Short-tailed Voles were taken in most, but other rodents and Moles were seldom noted. Unusual preys were: Weasel (a few in six areas), Stoat (3), Brown Hare (occasional leverets in several places), Red Squirrel (a few at one northern Scottish site and one in the Lake District), Pygmy Shrew (1) and an unidentified Bat (Chiroptera). Sheep carrion was brought to nests in most uplands, but especially in central Wales and in Glen Urquhart, and dead Roe Deer calves were scavenged in northern Scotland.

Amphibians and reptiles

Of the cold-blooded (poikilotherm) preys found on nests, Common Frogs and Adders were the only species to achieve some significance, albeit locally. The frogs were taken widely, but mainly on Dartmoor, while Common Toads were noted occasionally in all the uplands. Among reptiles, Slow-worm kills were rare but widely noted in both lowlands and uplands. Adder kills were found most often at Dartmoor nests and in two of the Scottish areas. Grass Snake and Common Lizard were reported only from the New Forest and Dartmoor.

Snakes, however, can easily be under-recorded unless one undertakes pellet analyses, direct observations from hides or (better still) deploys video recording cameras to monitor activities at nests. For example, a camera at a Buzzard nest in mid-Wales revealed that Grass Snakes were captured surprisingly often (BBC TV, *Springwatch*, 2011).

Birds

Although Buzzards are not recognized as bird hunters, when they have young to feed they can catch a surprising variety of species in different habitats by using perches, hovering and pursuit flight, or chance encounters. Most kills found on nests were of passerines – at least 43 species from 15 families – including many fledglings, juveniles and even some nestlings. They have also captured: the young of 3 duck species, 6 game birds (and domestic fowl) and 7 waders; in addition to full-grown individuals of 4 gull species, an auk, 3 pigeons, 2 woodpeckers, a falcon and (though mainly fledglings) an owl.

Buzzards in Britain are not normally forest dwellers but instead prefer small woodlands in open landscapes. An exception is the population inhabiting the ancient New Forest with its 3,200 ha of continuous unenclosed deciduous tree cover, from where prey records were collected at 81 Buzzard nests during a nine-year study by Colin Tubbs (1974). These indicated that Buzzards hunted frequently within the forest as well as on the heaths and farmland beyond. Kills of seven forest bird species that were identified were predominantly Stock Doves (on 52% of nests) and Jays (62%) together with a few Green Woodpeckers (17%, adults and juveniles), Great Spotted Woodpeckers (7%), Woodcock (12%, mainly chicks), Tawny Owl (5%, fledglings) and Redstart (1%, nestling).

Of exceptional interest is the predation of nestling Osprey and Wood Warblers that was recorded recently, quite by chance, on nest surveillance video cameras. In the first incident, an opportunist Buzzard swooped down on and snatched one of the two small Osprey chicks from a momentarily unguarded nest in north-east Scotland (E. Webster, BBC News, June 2012). In central Wales, Buzzards were filmed raiding and taking nestlings from five well-hidden ground nests of Wood Warblers (Mallord *et al.* 2012). This unexpected behaviour has also been recorded in Dartmoor woodlands during current intensive studies of Wood Warblers (Burgess 2013). In these instances it seems clear that the Buzzards had been observing, from within the woodland canopy, the regular nest visits of the parent warblers.

Kestrels have occasionally been taken by Buzzards in Scotland and Wales. In Ayrshire, several adult Kestrels were killed, one being taken to a Buzzard nest (Riddle 2011). The remains of a recently-fledged Kestrel were found on one of my Snowdonia nests, and similar cases were reported earlier from Buzzard nests in mid-Wales (P.E. Davis, *in litt.*). Kestrels could be vulnerable to surprise attacks when they are hovering and peering intently at the ground. These two raptors hovered over the same rough hillsides in my Dartmoor study area, often at the same time, while searching for the same small preys (Dare 1961). However, they kept well apart and no interactions were observed. Nonetheless, the recent sharp declines in Kestrel numbers in the uplands of Wales and Ayrshire have been linked, at least in part, to increasing Buzzard populations (Dare 1986, Shrubb 1993, Riddle 2011).

Game-birds

Raptors that hunt where game-birds are reared for sport shooting still can be a contentious issue. It is worth stressing, therefore, that all records noted here, except those for the Red-legged Partridge, some Pheasants and one Red Grouse were from Scotland, and were spread over 13 years and three large areas. Thus, the annual predation by Buzzards during one breeding season would be much less than the figures might suggest. In one locality, two Red Grouse chicks were taken by a Buzzard only after a Hen Harrier had twice disturbed a brood and caused them to scatter. The opportunist Buzzard, hunting elsewhere but witnessing the incidents, soon arrived on the scene and took a grouse chick away, then returned to repeat the process. Buzzard pellets from its nearby nest revealed the diet to be mainly of Rabbits and voles, with no traces of grouse. The Buzzards were not observed to seek out grouse here during a detailed study of grouse predators (Redpath 1990). In the Highlands, a Capercaillie chick that was found in a Buzzard nest was known to have been killed by a Fox (D. N. Weir, cited by Brown 1976). The same writer had observed a Buzzard eating a Red Grouse at the side of a road.

In southern Britain, occasional Pheasant chicks were found at Buzzard nests in the New Forest (Tubbs 1974) and at a 1966 nest in lowland Devon (DBR). In the West Midlands, Buzzards have been suspected of scavenging from carcasses of full-grown Pheasants that had died from other causes (Sim *et al.* 2000). On estates where Pheasant chicks are reared in outdoor open-topped pens for release in large numbers, there is a risk of small losses to individual Buzzards in late June and July. This is the time when Buzzards are feeding large young or fledglings. However, a thorough two-year study in southern England, by respected raptor ecologists and working with gamekeepers, showed that losses could be minimised or avoided by relocating vulnerable pens away from Buzzard hunting perches or to sites with adequate protective shrub cover (Kenward *et al.* 2001). The relationship between Buzzards and released Pheasant stocks will be discussed further in Chapter 12.

Finally, it is worth stressing that these prey analyses may give the impression that Buzzards in many areas have a wide spectrum of prey species and choices available for them to exploit during the breeding season. This is true to some degree, although prey diversity alone can be a misleading measure of their food supply; and the nest prey remains can give a biased picture of diet. Furthermore, as the Dartmoor studies revealed, it is the total daily available biomass of key species, especially of Rabbits and small mammals, throughout the entire 7–8 weeks nestling period, which is of crucial importance for Buzzards to breed successfully (Chapter 13).

All records of unusual bird species, together with ages (if given) and the numbers of sites in Britain where each species was reported, are listed opposite.

Ireland

Buzzards have only recently been re-establishing themselves on this large island, with the first birds arriving in the north-east after crossing from Scotland. Their subsequent spread south has been rapid in recent years (Chapter 15). It will be interesting, therefore, to determine how they fare in a landscape which has an impoverished small mammal fauna – Short-tailed (Field)

Teal (1)
Goldeneye (1)
Red Grouse (75, 1 adult, otherwise probably chicks or fledglings, 4 sites)
Black Grouse (3, 1 site)
Capercaillie (4 fledglings, 2 sites)
Grey Partridge (4, 1 site)
Red-legged Partridge (1 chick)
Pheasant (95, mainly chicks or fledglings, 6 sites)
Kestrel (1 juvenile)
Osprey (1 small nestling)
Oystercatcher (2, 1 adult, 2 sites)
Golden Plover (2, 1 fledgling, 2 sites)
Lapwing (7, 1 fledgling, 1 site)
Common Sandpiper (1 fledgling)
Curlew (5, 4 fledglings, 2 sites)
Woodcock (21, 2 adults, 8 chicks or fledglings, 3 sites)
Common Snipe (4, 2 fledglings, 2 sites)
Puffin ('common', Skomer)
Stock Dove (at 52% of nests, 1 site)
Cuckoo (3, 1 fledgling, 3 sites)
Tawny Owl (15, 7 fledglings, 6 sites)
Green Woodpecker (8, 5 adults, 3 juveniles, New Forest)
Great Spotted Woodpecker (12, 3 fledglings, 3 sites)
Pied Wagtail (6, 4 fledglings, 1 site)
Dunnock (8, 2 fledglings, 2 sites)
Willow Warbler (8, 2 fledglings, 1 site)
Wood Warbler (5 broods, >1 site),
Whitethroat (1 fledgling)
Garden Warbler (1 adult)
Grasshopper Warbler (1 adult)
Goldcrest (1 fledgling)
Whinchat (5, 4 fledglings, 1 site)
Wheatear (14, 10 fledglings, 3 sites)
Redstart (1 nestling)
Robin (2, 1 fledgling, 1 site)
Ring Ouzel (1 nestling or fledgling)
Mistle Thrush (1)
Song Thrush (3, 1 site)
Coal Tit (1 fledgling)
Blue Tit (3, 1 fledgling, 1 site)
Great Tit (8, 5 fledglings, 3 sites)
Tree Creeper (1)
Wren (12, 2 fledglings, 3 sites)
Dipper (1 fledgling)
Reed Bunting (1 fledgling)
Yellowhammer (7, 1 fledgling, 1 site)
Goldfinch (1)
Siskin (2, 1 site)
Redpoll (1)
Crossbill (3, 2 fledglings, 1 site)
House Sparrow (1 fledgling)
Chough (2 juveniles, 1 site)
Also: Domestic Fowl (4, 3 sites)

Vole, Mole and Common Shrew are all, like snakes, absent. Only two endemic small mammal species are found – Wood Mouse and Pygmy Shrew. Two non-native species, however, have recently been found in southern counties of Ireland following accidental introductions – the Bank Vole and the continental Greater White-toothed Shrew (*Crocidura russula*). Both are spreading north from the south coast.

The limited information on Buzzard diets in Ireland is from a recent 3-year study in the north-east where the combined prey remains and pellet material from 61 nests on Antrim farmlands and heathy areas were examined (Rooney & Montgomery 2013). Despite the inherent biases in the analyses, it was clear that, in the absence of normally important small mammal preys, the breeding season diet is comprised mainly of Rabbits (with a few Brown Hares), Brown Rats, and medium–large birds (notably Magpies and Hooded Crows, with some pigeons and adult Pheasants). The two lagomorphs together made up 27% of the 987 vertebrate prey items identified, and 37% of prey biomass; Brown Rats were 9% and 12%, and medium–large birds 25% and 38%. Small mammals were far less important (10% of kills and 0.6% by weight), though they would have been under-represented by the method adopted. Small birds were more conspicuous among remains (19%) but also were unimportant (5%) by weight. Only six amphibians (presumably Common Frogs) were identified. The introduced Bank Vole has not yet reached this northern study area but when it does, it will doubtless be added to the Buzzards' dietary range, as has happened already further south in Ireland (Rooney & Montgomery 2013).

7

BREEDING SEASON
III. Brood growth and survival

These weeks are the busy pinnacle of a raptor enthusiast's year. As the Buzzard broods develop rapidly, there is so much to observe and record, particularly the food and other factors determining brood survival, and culminating in the breeding success assessment for the population. Although this account draws heavily from Buzzards observed closely on Dartmoor and in North Wales, it should be applicable, with minor deviations, to Buzzards in other regions of Britain.

HATCHING PROCESS

Most Buzzards in this country hatch their clutches in the last ten days of May, some in early June. The eggs hatch in their laying sequence and, assuming that incubation starts with the first egg, they should hatch at intervals of about two days (Cramp & Simmons 1980) though longer periods can occur. Thus, in a brood that has hatched from a clutch of three eggs, the last chick should be 3–5 days younger than its oldest sibling which, by then, may be at least twice as heavy. This hatching schedule is not invariable, however. At one Snowdonia nest the first two chicks emerged about seven hours apart (Figure 7.1), and same-day hatching of two eggs probably happened at some other nests. This suggests that the female did not start incubating fully until the second egg had been laid. This asynchronous strategy has profound consequences for the growth and survival chances of individual nestlings within a brood, as will become evident shortly.

One or two days before it hatches, the chick can be heard tapping inside the egg. Emergence from the egg (Figure 7.1a) is a slow process following the first puncture hole in the shell. Such a 'chipping' egg can be seen at another nest in Figure 6.3. The newly-hatched chick is covered with a damp, whitish and silky-light down. A few hours later, it is dry and can just raise its head, cheep feebly and stare with weak eyes at the observer (Figure 7.1b, c). The female closely broods her young and any as-yet unhatched eggs, and she usually protests noisily when disturbed. Meanwhile, the male responds rapidly by providing food (Figure 6.3, 7.1b). The egg shells soon disappear and presumably are eaten by the female in order to recover their calcium content.

Figure 7.1 Buzzard chicks hatching in two nests in Snowdonia. In (a), the first chick emerges at 07.00 BST and the second chick (in b, c) 7 hours later; the third egg hatched 1–2 days later; note the feet of a young rabbit. In the other nest (d) a day-old chick with its egg shell remnants; the second egg hatched a day or so afterwards. (© d: Julian Driver)

PHYSICAL DEVELOPMENT OF NESTLINGS

The Buzzard chicks pass through different phases of plumage, physical and behavioural development during their seven weeks in the nest. These phases can provide a useful guide to the approximate age of the chicks although development rates can vary with brood size and their nutrition.

Growth in weight

Newly-hatched Buzzard chicks on Dartmoor weighed around 40 g, compared with newly-laid egg weights of 65–70 g. The lowest value for a day-old chick was 39 g, but Heinroth (in Melde 1956) gave a figure of ~36 g. Given ample food, the chicks then increase in body weight very rapidly until about the fifth week, when the growth rate starts to slow progressively (Figure 7.2). This is around the time when the plumage begins developing quickly. Food requirements at this stage increase further, presumably to provide the energy needed for feather growth and for more strenuous physical activities such as wing exercises, exploratory behaviour and the tearing apart of large preys. Few weight data could be obtained in later weeks because, of the original ten chicks, only two (in different nests) survived beyond the third week. Later, these became increasingly difficult to weigh in the nest (with only one hand free). At fledging, these two young Buzzards weighed 850–1,000 g, which is within the range of adult weights. This represents a 20 to 25-fold increase in weight during about 7.5 weeks. The difference of about 150 g between these two birds could have been sex-related, with the heavier bird being a female. These growth data appear to have been the first obtained for Common Buzzard, and are very similar to those published for two broods of Rough-legged Buzzard in Norway (Olstad 1934, Barth 1952).

Plumage development

The sequential development of the various feather tracts can give a useful guide for estimating the ages of Buzzard chicks when inspecting a newly-found nest containing a part-grown brood. Individual development rates are likely to vary within and between different broods according to local food abundance. Information from Dartmoor broods is summarized in Appendix 9. Their changing appearance with age is illustrated for Buzzard broods in Snowdonia in Figure 7.3. The thin, silky down coat of the hatchling remains for 5–6 days and then becomes denser

Figure 7.3a Buzzard broods showing stages of plumage development during their seven weeks in the nest. The largest of these three chicks was 13 days old and the only survivor. Snowdonia (© Julian Driver)

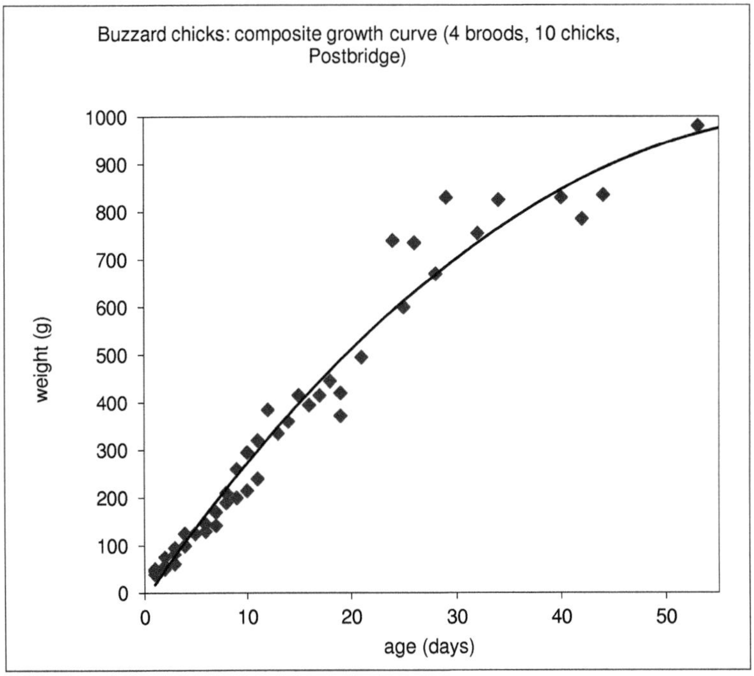

Figure 7.2 Growth curve of nestling Buzzards, on Dartmoor, until near fledging; composite curve for 10 chicks (four broods), of which only two fledged.

until, during days 11–15, it turns greyish-white, thick, coarser and 'woolly' in texture (Figure 7.3a). The first signs of flight feather growth are apparent when the quills of the primary flight feathers start showing, around days 12 or 13, followed soon by those of the secondaries. The first body feather tracts appear on the mantle and scapulars at around days 18–20. By this time a healthy chick should weigh about 300–350 g. The primary quills begin opening to show the feather tips around day 17, and the tail quills about a day later.

Wing measurements can be used to estimate the ages of Buzzard chicks in newly-found nests. In Scotland, the length (mm) of the longest (5th) primary feather was found to be a good indicator of most nestlings' ages, with an error of just one day (Austin & Houston 1997). An alternative method, using the standard wing length method of ringers, also has only small errors (Bijlsma 1999). The sex of individual birds in Dorset was assessed, with a high degree of accuracy, by measuring the width of the tarsal leg bone (Walls & Kenward 1995).

In the fourth week, feathers are appearing on the upper body, rump and wing coverts but the breast and head, except for the ear coverts, are still downy (Figure 7.3c). At a month old, the first crown, breast side and flank tracts are showing and plumage development has now entered a rapid phase. By the end of the fifth week (Figure 7.3d), the upper parts are completely covered and thus 'weatherproof,' while the breast, belly and flanks are well feathered and the ear and cheek coverts are more visible. During the sixth week (Figure 7.3e), the remaining gaps are filled, although some down persists on the face and around the bill as well as under

Figure 7.3 (cont.) Buzzard chicks showing plumages at ages of approximately: (b) 25 days, with an addled egg; (c) 35 days; (d) 40 days. Snowdonia (© Julian Driver)

Figure 7.3 (cont.) Two older chicks, close to fledging, aged about (e) 45 days, (f) 7 weeks and with immaculate plumage and ready to fledge. Snowdonia (© Julian Driver)

the wings and over the crop or upper breast area. The last downy wisps disappear from the head about day 46 (Figure 7.3f). The youngster is now in immaculate plumage and ready to leave the nest, although many will stay a few days longer.

BEHAVIOURAL DEVELOPMENT

Interactions and voice

In their first two days of life, Buzzard chicks appear to be too weak to do other than take a little food and sleep. Three days later, they can peck quite firmly at one's fingers and follow the movements of the parents circling low overhead. From the third day on, their cheeping calls can be heard from the ground if the female is flushed during a meal. They also cheep softly and contentedly just before falling asleep after a large meal. In a different context, louder distress cheeping is uttered in response to aggressive pecking by a larger sibling, and that can be audible 25 m from the nest. This aspect will be described separately below.

At two weeks old, the young will sit up alertly but still sleep for long periods, and the voice changes from cheeping to soft hunger whistles which soon take on a mellow or querulous fluty tone. Contentment is now expressed by soft clucking notes. They are now voiding their droppings onto the nest rim by cautiously backing part-way out of the nest cup. A very hungry 15-day old chick is able to swallow a shrew or small vole, head-first, in a few gulps. At some point in the third week, one begins to find the chicks' first small fur pellets. They respond to parental alarm calls by crouching quietly with eyes 'glazed', an effect perhaps caused by the nictitating membrane being drawn across the eyes. This behaviour continues until near fledging time.

During the fourth week the beak and feet grow rapidly, and the chicks spend time sitting up on their haunches with legs and feet extended in front as they flex their toes. From day 24 the more advanced chicks also begin to tear up small mammals and to dispute food items with nest mates. Very hungry young start to give shrill squealing calls, particularly when being fed by the female. They are increasingly active and curious about their immediate surroundings. They can stand briefly to shake their downy plumage and arch their backs with tiny wings extended.

From the start of the fifth week, they preen frequently, stand briefly and move carefully about the nest. Hunger calls can be at times strident and insistent, and more like those of fledglings. Droppings are now copious and voided powerfully as a viscous stream clear of the nest onto the tree trunk and branches, or onto the rock face behind a crag nest (Figure 7.4c). The ground and herbage below tree nests becomes well spattered with 'whitewash' (Figure 7.4d), always a good sign that all is well with the brood. In a dry summer this evidence may last for two weeks or longer after the fledglings have moved off, but it may be washed away at any time by heavy rain.

From 35 days old, a hungry youngster, now weighing some 750 g, may 'mantle' with spread wings over a Rabbit or other large prey, so as to exclude siblings, once they have learnt to tear flesh from an opened carcass (7.4a). They stand for long periods and start to utter loud juvinile hunger calls. In the sixth week, much time each day is devoted to wing flapping exercises (Figure 7.4b), feather preening and moving around the nest. They still crouch upon

Figure 7.4 Five-week-old Buzzards can tear up large food items (a) and expend much effort on wing exercises (b) and other activities. Droppings are voided in a powerful jet (c) and spatter ground and herbage below with copious 'whitewash' (d). (a: Lake District © Colin Whittle)

Figure 7.5 Fledging imminent: this young Buzzard, now in immaculate plumage, spent much time spreading its wings and exploring outside its nest in North Wales.

hearing parental alarms at a human approach. They are very alert and inquisitive, scanning the sky for signs of a parent bringing food, watching small birds and insects moving in the tree top, and snapping up and eating beetles that have strayed onto the nest.

Fully-feathered young Buzzards in their final week can now hold down a young Rabbit firmly and tear off flesh and pelt from the carcass. They rest by squatting on the tarsi and, when hungry, may call loudly in tones starting to resemble those of the adults. As fledging time becomes imminent, the youngsters are increasingly restless and active between meals as they indulge in frequent bouts of vigorous wing-flapping on the nest rim, bouncing up and down while gripping the nest sticks strongly. Brief exploratory forays out onto adjoining branches are also undertaken (Figure 7.5). When alarmed by a person at the nest they may utter '*pee-ee-ee-ou*' calls resembling those of the parents.

The young Buzzard's first flight is usually a short flap and glide with a clumsy landing in a nearby tree a few metres away, and from which it can return to the nest when the next prey is brought. Both parents protest angrily above the site at intruding people, thereby inadvertently drawing attention to their young. Viewing the nest from below, after a cautious approach, should be sufficient to check whether the young are still present. Actual nest inspections are inadvisable at this stage, to avoid any premature leaps from the nest. These could end in a youngster crash-landing into low bushes or on to the ground, from where it cannot return to the nest for food and may become vulnerable to predators. Even so, the parents do not abandon fallen young but will bring kills to them for some days, as was described in the previous chapter.

Threat display

Young Buzzards from their third week on, and particularly single birds, may adopt a threatening posture towards a human intruder on their first visit to the nest. Most of my Dartmoor study broods, however, were accustomed to me from an early age and did not display. In North Wales, however, infrequent visits could provoke defensive responses, typically by single youngsters. Even downy chicks, only about 14 days old, sometimes performed an incipient threat display (Figure 7.6a). Later, if the female was alarm-calling nearby, they usually crouched, head up, beak open and directed at the intruder, but they did not try to strike when touched. Others, however, might instead recoil and hiss softly (Figure 7.6b). In the next stage (Figure 7.6c) a lone large chick would stand in a silent threat posture, backing to the far side of the nest with wings spread and the open bill threatening, but again not striking at the hand. These reactions gradually cease as a chick becomes accustomed to more frequent visits.

A full threat display by a well-feathered youngster is quite impressive. It stands in the nest cup stiffly erect, wings well spread and its head, with open beak, inclined slightly downwards to show the 'hackles' raised on its nape. An 'icy' expression of the eyes and a piercing scream complete a pose charged with hostility. If further threatened more closely, however, the youngster does not strike but adopts a defensive attitude by retreating to the far side of the nest, where it reclines on tarsi with wings spread for balance, beak open and talons raised as if to lash out at an unwary intruder. The whole display is probably effective against avian

Above and following page: Figure 7.6 Buzzard chicks begin threat displays when 2 weeks old (a) and, from 3 weeks onwards, some displays may be quite impressive (b). Threat postures continue after fledging (d). (Snowdonia © Julian Driver)

predators, such as crows, where the talons presumably would be used, but against humans it is all bluff. Newly-fledged juveniles standing on perches may threaten in a similar fashion (Figure 7.6d). This display seems to be the origin of the 'angel' posture (Weir & Picozzi 1975) that is deployed more aggressively by immature and adult Buzzards during disputes over food, and particularly at carrion in severe wintry weather (Figure 3.6).

Figure 7.6b

NESTLING SURVIVAL

Buzzard parents may lose nestlings in two main ways. One is the simultaneous loss of all the young from predation or from human disturbance, although causal attribution is often not possible where nests are visited infrequently. The other is by brood size reduction, in which younger nestlings die in the competition for food when it becomes scarce. Nearly all deaths of young Buzzards occur during their first 2–3 weeks of life irrespective of cause.

Competition for food

The asynchronous hatching system of raptors is acknowledged to be an adaptation to fluctuating food resources. In the event of temporary prey shortages, it increases the chances of a pair to raise at least one youngster from a brood rather than lose all to starvation. Brood members are fed according to seniority (strength). As a result, the younger and therefore weaker members can fail progressively in competition and then are eliminated, one by one, through starvation. Often only the oldest youngster survives and fledges from this sequential process of brood size reduction.

Competition for food was frequently observed, and at times became severe, among the Buzzard broods on Dartmoor in the early years after myxomatosis. In two broods, the deaths from starvation of the weaker (younger) nestlings were confirmed (in 1956–58) by daily nest inspections. Both broods were reduced from three chicks to single survivors, in one case over a span of just 48 hours. In a third nest, only one of the two chicks was reared. At five inaccessible nests, from all of which only singletons were reared, the same process was strongly suspected, single-egg clutches being rare. Since then, many similar brood size reductions have been observed or inferred in all three of my study areas (Dare 1995, 1998). This adaptive process has since been reported from studies elsewhere in Britain and Europe.

Within the Dartmoor broods the eldest chicks began to compete actively with younger siblings for food from around their fifth day. At three days, the first-hatched chick may start to peck at surrounding objects including its nest mates. By the fifth day, when it can peck quite strongly, frequent bouts of one-sided aggression may occur, in which the advantage is clearly with the older and heavier chick. Sometimes an assaulted nestling cheeped loudly in distress. A 'pecking order' then becomes established among brood members and results in a hierarchical division of food based on seniority.

Under favourable conditions this aggressiveness waned after the first week, as nest-mates adjusted to one another and established a pecking order for the remaining 6 weeks in the nest. Thus, if all goes well, a stronger youngster, if hungry, would command a superior position to be fed first by the female. When older, it would be big enough to seize a small kill and to effectively ward off hungry companions by turning away and 'mantling' over the prey with open wings. Its siblings would then await their turn to be fed. This mild dominant behaviour is illustrated by observations of a 1957 Dartmoor brood (Appendix 8). Should, however, food became scarce for several days during the second and third weeks, the assertive behaviour of older chicks could become extreme. This was a critical period for brood survival for then the elder (or eldest) chick sometimes grew extraordinarily aggressive. At this stage, not only are there large relative weight differences between nest mates, but the absolute strength of the dominant chick may be sufficient to kill a smaller and weaker companion. Such aggression and outcomes are well known in broods of eagles and other large hawks and eagles.

The events at a 1958 nest (Cator) were followed closely (Figure 7.7). Upon food suddenly becoming scarce during the second week, the youngest of the three chicks soon ailed, and then died (disappeared) when it was 7 days old. At this point, the second chick had stopped growing. Four days later, after 24 hours apparently without any food at all, the 13-day oldest chick (weight 382 g) was calling hungrily, and it began to attack its much lighter (220 g) and downy companion quite aggressively. The latter's distress cries were audible at 25 m. Blows were directed mainly at the nape, where blood had already been drawn, and at the back. For the next few days of food shortage, and despite having had some food, the first-born chick continued its assault on its defenceless nest mate. The younger chick started to lose weight and by day 14 it was scarcely half the weight of its assailant, whose own growth rate had now slowed. The younger bird's skin had been severely lacerated across the nape and, within 24 hours, it was dead and being fed by the female Buzzard to the lone survivor. The food shortage was further reflected in the much reduced growth rate of the survivor throughout

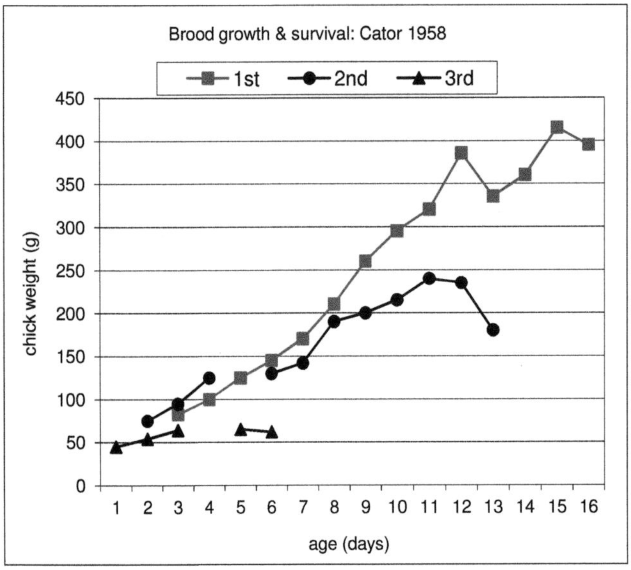

Figure 7.7 Growth of Buzzard chicks in a brood in which the two youngest died during periods of food shortage. On day 3 they were 1, 2 and 3 days old. The survivor fledged, after 7 weeks, at c. 980 g.

the following week. Finally, as soon as hunting success improved in the fourth week, the youngster resumed normal rapid growth and it fledged weighing about 980 g (Figure 7.2). Other Dartmoor nestlings that vanished without trace were presumably also cannibalised. In Germany, such incidents were proved in two populations (Schmaus 1938; Wendland 1952). Indeed, the latter author found the leg rings from vanished chicks in the pellets of surviving youngsters.

The Dartmoor study confirmed Wendland's view that the second and third weeks in the nest are the most critical period in brood life; four of five observed chick deaths from starvation in my area occurred during this fortnight. After three weeks, chick mortality from food shortage is unusual, because by then the siblings differ much less in size and strength, and they are also more companionable. Further, they are then becoming feathered and more capable of withstanding 2–3 day periods of poor hunting and bad weather, and the female parent at last is providing food.

Brood losses

In the Dartmoor area during 1956–58, one third of the 22 broods failed to reach fledging and two thirds of the 15 successful broods had experienced the loss of one or two chicks. Interestingly, and as Rabbit numbers thereafter slowly increased, complete brood failures fell to only 10% during 1961–69 and to zero in 1990–93. Brood reductions still occurred but, nevertheless, more (41% of 22) pairs reared two young in the 1960s and 60% (of 20) did so in the early 1990s, when also two pairs reared three young (Dare 1998). Despite the small samples of broods, the positive influence of Rabbit availability upon breeding success is once again evident. This factor will be assessed in more detail in Chapter 12.

Excluding deaths from starvation, one fifth of complete broods losses on Dartmoor during 1956–58 were attributable directly to Carrion Crow predation, and another fifth to exposure resulting from people (farmers and public) unknowingly keeping female Buzzards from returning in time to prevent fatal chilling or, perhaps more likely, attacks by opportunist crows taking advantage of her absence. Undoubtedly, marauding crows were directly responsible for many other total breeding failures, accounting for perhaps a half of clutches and a quarter of all broods lost. Crows were numerous throughout the study area. Some Buzzard territories were patrolled ceaselessly by up to eight pairs. Under these conditions, constant vigilance by the Buzzards was essential. Furthermore, it was conceivable that, in the earlier years after myxomatosis, some females might have become so hungry that they left the nest unguarded so as to hunt for themselves. Well-feathered young Buzzards appear not to be attacked and later, when six weeks old, they can withstand frequent human disturbance. A youngster in one Dartmoor nest in a tall pine, below which a camper had pitched his tent one foggy weekend, was unharmed; its assiduous parents delivered food in the early morning! When, on rare occasions, a large youngster is found dead beneath its nest (Figure 7.8) the cause of death seldom can be determined.

Disease does not appear to have been reported previously as causing nestling deaths in the Common Buzzard, but one case was confirmed. In 1958, the solitary chick in one Dartmoor nest died suddenly when about five weeks old. A post-mortem examination, at the Department of Animal Pathology in the University of Cambridge, found that death was attributable to the bacillus *Pasteurella pseudotuberculosis*. This pathogen probably had been contracted by eating infected prey, perhaps Short-tailed Voles. This vole sometimes carries high levels of infection with tuberculosis *Myzobacterium tuberculosis* (Chitty 1954). Prior to this Buzzard chick's death, the weather had been unusually cold and wet, and little food was being brought to the nest. It seems likely that such adverse conditions contributed to its death by lowering the chick's fitness and resistance to the infection.

Figure 7.8 An unusual event: a large youngster dead beneath its nest. North Wales.

Elsewhere in Britain, human disturbance, both accidental and deliberate, is the most frequently reported cause of clutch and brood losses, as it is also in Germany. There, Wendland (1952) noted that 53 (31%) of his 170 breeding pairs failed totally, primarily due to human interventions, either accidental disturbance or deliberate persecution. Starvation, presumably meaning brood size reductions, has been widely recorded among Buzzard broods both in Britain and on the Continent.

FLEDGED BROOD SIZES

There appears to be no information concerning the breeding success of Buzzards in Britain in the era when Rabbits were abundant prior to the advent of myxomatosis in the mid-1950s. Following the Dartmoor study, researchers elsewhere in Britain, over the past 50 years, have assessed the breeding outputs of other populations in various regions with contrasting habitats and diets (Chapter 12, Appendix 23). On Dartmoor, as in Wales and the New Forest, the most frequent (modal) brood size was one fledgling, whereas it was two fledglings in mid-Argyll, Glen Urquhart and the West Midlands of England, and even three in West Moray and in upper Speyside. In terms of average brood sizes, successful pairs in most areas reared between one and two fledglings. Only Buzzards in upper Speyside and West Moray produced more than two young, with averages of 2.64 and 2.54 young respectively. Average values, however, can mask considerable yearly variation. In Devon, for example, where a population of 14–21 pairs of Buzzards was monitored for 12 years (1989–2000), the long-term average size of successful broods was 1.57 whereas annual averages ranged, for reasons unknown, between 1.00 and 2.14 fledglings per pair (DBRs).

There is considerable evidence from these studies that food abundance plays a dominant role in determining the number of young that Buzzards are able to rear (Chapter 12). In upper Speyside and nearby West Moray, where Rabbits were especially plentiful, the Buzzards bred with notably high success. More than half (57%) of fledged broods in Speyside comprised three young and a further 15% had four. In West Moray, successful broods included 41% of three and 11% of four fledglings. These two regions recorded the highest productivities anywhere since myxomatosis, and thus give an indication of likely Buzzard breeding performances in many regions before the 1954 Rabbit 'crash'. Elsewhere in Britain, reported broods of four are

Figure 7.9 A recently-vacated nest with all signs of the brood having fledged successfully; also seen in Figure 5.4 at hatching time. (Snowdonia)

rare, with just single records in mid-Argyll and the West Midlands of England. Threesomes are likewise uncommon or unknown in many areas. In 1986, a Devon pair reared four fledglings (DBR), apparently the first such record in that county for more than 30 years.

Population breeding success

The annual success of a local Buzzard population of known size is assessed by determining the number of pairs which: (i) laid eggs, (ii) hatched eggs, (iii) fledged one (or more) young, and (iv) by determining the average size of fledged broods. These figures can then be used to express the population's success in terms of the number of young reared: (a) per successful pair, (b) per breeding pair, and (c) per territorial pair of the population. From these data the total number of fledglings (population productivity) is easily derived. This value is the ultimate measure of how well Buzzards are performing in a specific district. In our intensively-managed British countryside, the above studies have shown that local populations, when averaged over several years, have managed to rear annually between 0.5 and 1.5 young per territorial pair that was present in spring (Dare 1995). This aspect will be examined in detail in Chapter 12.

Once the fledglings have cut the final ties with their nests, they leave behind a trampled, flattened platform upon which there may be scattered prey and pellet debris (Figure 7.9). These signs remain for weeks to provide late confirmation of successful breeding. The juvenile Buzzards now embark, with parental support, upon rapidly developing their flying abilities and hunting skills as they explore their natal territories.

8

BUZZARDS IN SUMMER
(July and August)

By mid-July the breeding season effectively is over for the Buzzards. Their broods have fledged, apart from those of occasional very late breeders whose young may not fly until early August; the latest Devon date is 12 August (DBR 1954). High summer is then a time for the successful breeders to recuperate after the strenuous demands of the past three or four months. The juveniles, still in the care of their parents, start a lengthy process of learning to hunt and become independent. This is also the season when adults begin to moult their flight feathers. Fortunately, summer time is when prey is most abundant 'and the living is easy'. Adult Buzzards now become less conspicuous, retiring more into cover, with little need to exert themselves on territorial matters. The breeding season has now finished as well for most other bird species and the songsters have long since fallen quiet. In a now almost silent countryside, the wailing cries of hungry juvenile Buzzards carry far. These are, to my mind, one of the most evocative of summer bird sounds in Buzzard country.

POPULATION FEATURES

At the end of the breeding season a local Buzzard population is now at peak numbers and maximum stability, with no significant immigration or emigration. By mid-July, after a good breeding season, there could be roughly one juvenile per territorial pair of Buzzards. This results in a sudden 50% increase in total numbers. This peak is short-lived, however, because a few juveniles may come to grief and others begin leaving the area in late August. Immigrant youngsters from adjacent areas might then be expected but this has not yet been confirmed.

Juvenile deaths in natal territories are seldom recorded or explained. Two instances in Wales are particularly noteworthy: two fledglings were found either dying or suffering from severe malnutrition caused by heavy ectoparasitic infestations. Found at different places during their first month after fledging, both birds were in poor condition and found to be heavily infested with the blood-sucking hippoboscid flat-fly *Ornithomya avicularia,* a very common bird parasite. The more emaciated (490 g) youngster, was close to death and carried at least 80 flies. The other bird (610 g) was also well under weight and hosted more than 35 of the parasites (Jones 1985).

Parental care

Both parent Buzzards are now even more protective of their brood. They become increasingly demonstrative and noisy when their young are about to fledge and for several weeks thereafter. They respond to people nearing their young by calling aggressively while circling repeatedly low over the tree tops or above a person approaching across open land. One Buzzard on Dartmoor regularly swooped low over my head. Such protest displays can be taken as proof of successful breeding. Rarely, individual Buzzards become extremely aggressive and swoop past with talons outstretched to within 1–2 m of a person's head. The first recorded instance of such aggression appears to have been that by Brook (1920) in central Wales. That Buzzard swooped to within a foot (30 cm) of his head and followed him for nearly two miles (3 km) across open country. Another particularly aggressive Buzzard in Wales was encountered by Fenn (1957) in Breconshire. There, a bird which was said to have been present for ten years suddenly began attacking the local postman delivering mail to a farm and went on to draw blood from a photographer's head as it knocked off his cap!

Several female Buzzards in Snowdonia have remained aggressive, even intensifying their behaviour, over a number of years (Driver 2004). One of them drove home its attack and gashed this observer's forehead, in the process displaying unexpected aerial agility in dense woodland by weaving between trees at surprising speed, rather like a Goshawk. At two other locations in North Wales several Buzzard observers have described in detail how they were struck on the head with sufficient force as to draw blood (Williams & Coan 1973). On the Lake District fells several particularly aggressive females even left their eggs in order to strike observers vigorously (Brewster 1973, Fryer 1974). In recent years, aggressive Buzzards have become an almost annual summer 'drama' for local press reporters in southern counties, a likely consequence of greater public access to Buzzard nesting places at a time when Buzzard numbers are increasing.

JUVENILES: POST-FLEDGING BEHAVIOUR

Our knowledge of juvenile Buzzard behaviour soon after fledging is limited to young from tree-nests, where dense foliage usually impedes observations. On Dartmoor during July, after spending the first few days near the nest, to which they return to receive food, the youngsters finally move away through the trees. Typically, they cover up to 150 m during the next five days. Siblings tend to stay close to one another (Figure 8.1) and to move in the directions from which parents bring in food, and they stay within the tree canopy.

Their days are spent mainly waiting on perches for parents to bring food to them. Their whereabouts in cover frequently are indicated by the noisy responses of the parent Buzzards to human intrusion. The young are still often reluctant to fly but, if alarmed, may flap away heavily between the trees, or across an open space, or down a slope for 50–100 m and then land clumsily. Such flights usually are not attempted voluntarily until at least a week later.

After a further 2–3 weeks, by late July or early August, the first tentative flights above the canopy and over the nest area may be witnessed. Normally, these are brief and unsteady sorties on 'soft', not yet stiff, wings as the young Buzzard feels breezes and air turbulence for the first time. Soon the flights become more confident, lengthier and frequent as the parental

Figure 8.1 Young Buzzards just out of the nest. (Postbridge, Dartmoor, 1957)

Figure 8.2 A recently-fledged juvenile Buzzard showing the typical breast and underwing pattern. (Devon © Mark Darlaston)

territory is explored. The immaculately plumaged juveniles now may be seen circling low with one or both parents. Some observers (Prytherch 2009) comment that juveniles may circle with wings held flat, as do Honey-Buzzards, rather than with the characteristic up-tilt of adults. This could be just a temporary phase before their wing muscles are fully developed.

The juvenile Buzzards continue to be fed by their parents throughout July and August, some for longer. It is not known how and when they begin to learn hunting skills because they remain so unobtrusive. Most likely they start by August, using low hunting perches to drop onto insects and small mammals. For example, one Dartmoor juvenile was watched chasing beetles and other insects in a meadow in mid-August. When hungry, however, they still call for food, at first softly but on some days more stridently and persistently, presumably when parents are experiencing poor hunting success. Their basic begging call develops from the whistling notes used by large nestlings when being fed by the female. It is uttered fairly quietly at first, but very hungry juveniles yell an emphatic drawn-out '*pweee-eee-uk*' wail as they wait perched or, by August, even in low flight. Their loud demands are audible for at least 400 m. In difficult terrain, they can be invaluable in helping one to count the fledgling Buzzards or to locate nests that may have been missed earlier in the season.

Similar post-fledging behaviour of Buzzards in summer has been observed elsewhere. In the New Forest the young Buzzards stayed within about 300 m of the nest for some weeks (Tubbs 1974). Far more detailed information has been obtained by a recent Dorset study in which young Buzzards were fitted with radio tags just before fledging (Tyack *et al.* 1998). It was found that few birds moved 500 m until growth and 'hardening' of the flight and tail feathers had been completed, 65 days after hatching. This timing corresponds to late July, which would be some 2–3 weeks after leaving the nest. Thereafter, the exploratory distances in Dorset increased abruptly, reaching 1 km within the next five days and 2 km ten days later; that is some 4–5 weeks after leaving the nest. At these distances in mid- to late August, the most mobile young Buzzards may have almost left the parental territory. Indeed, further evidence from radio tagging, and from ring recoveries, has confirmed that the most advanced juveniles have left home by the end of August. Their subsequent movements and survival through their critical first months of independence will be described in the next chapter.

ANNUAL MOULT OF ADULTS

Adult Buzzards in western Europe moult and replace their feathers each year, a process spread over a 5–6 month period during the warm months from spring to early autumn (Cramp & Simmons 1980, Sylvén 1982). Although no specific studies have been made of British birds, one may assume that our birds differ little in timing from those breeding at similar latitudes in southern Sweden that were studied by Magnus Sylvén. This prolonged replacement process, which had started for females in May (with down feathers) and for males in June, is not completed until September and October, respectively. In the field, moult is first noticeable in early summer when circling adult Buzzards, after breeding, typically show some missing flight and tail feathers.

The flight and tail feathers are renewed progressively over a long period; as a result, flying and hunting performance are not obviously impaired. The primaries (remiges) start to be moulted first from the innermost primary outwards towards the wing tip, but in a seemingly irregular sequence caused by overlap of different moult cycles (Cramp & Simmons 1980). The secondaries moult begins a little later, in reverse order, from the outermost feather inwards towards the body. This is followed by the tail feathers (rectrices) which are shed from the centre outwards in an irregular and asymmetrical fashion. Soon, the moults of all three feather groups are in progress at the same time, at which stage replacement of the body contour feathers and other main tracts such as the coverts then commences.

The annual moult in Buzzards is such a complex process that individual variations in its timing, rate and extent, particularly of flight feathers, are probably not uncommon. Evidence for this can be deduced from detailed studies of the similar-sized Goshawk in northern Europe (Kenward 2006). Nutritional state appears to be one important factor. Wild Goshawks required around 160 days in which to replace all their primaries, very much longer than that for well-fed captive birds. Furthermore, hawks rearing young stopped moulting flight feathers completely and were presumed to have finished their moult later.

Among adult Buzzards and later in the breeding season, the state and timing of wing moult can be a useful, though not infallible, guide as to whether a pair is breeding successfully. In my areas, those Buzzards rearing broods showed few signs of wing or tail moult before late June or early July. The first dropped primaries and secondaries were usually noticed beneath or near nests at around the time of fledging. Buzzards with one or two missing flight feathers in each wing then became apparent when birds circled above nest areas. Unusually, one breeding female (with a juvenile) was seen to be in heavy wing and tail moult by 11 July, as was a non-breeding adult.

The important point to note is that by the end of winter the territorial adults are equipped with complete sets of wing and tail feathers with which to begin their aerial displays. In contrast, non-breeding adults, and failed breeders – that had lost clutches or recently-hatched broods – by early June generally showed signs of earlier wing moult. Immature (first-year) Buzzards moulted before adults in my areas. Several individuals passing rapidly through the Dartmoor area in May showed very ragged wings due to several dropped flight feathers on each side.

DAILY ENERGY EXPENDITURE

Adult Buzzards in summer experience favourable conditions of warm weather, usually ample food, and have less need for strenuous aerial displays and defence of territories. Their estimated daily energy expenditure (DEE), though, remains high. Two main factors account for this: the first is that the successful breeders must still continue to catch food for their fledged offspring throughout summer. The second, though less demanding, is the annual moult which is undergone by all adults whether or not they have bred (see below). In the Swedish study of breeding Buzzards, the sexes differed somewhat in the timing of events in summer. In males, the DEE fell gradually from a maximum in June, as their aerial activities declined, whereas the DEE of females peaked in July (Sylvén 1982, Chapter 11).

For a Buzzard pair still sharing the effort of feeding two juveniles, the daily costs for each parent probably amount to around 210 kcal (Sylvén 1982). Theoretically, this energy demand could be more difficult to achieve by pairs limited to a diet of small mammals and similar size preys than by those pairs able to feed regularly on small Rabbits. Foraging for small animals requires greater hunting effort, often including intensive hovering, and the catches are too small to be shared between family members. In those circumstances, each parent would need daily to capture and eat 140 g of food (equivalent to seven adult voles) for its own maintenance, in addition to catching others for its offspring. Catching young Rabbits weighing 250–500g, on the other hand, should markedly reduce energy expenditure. A Buzzard pair then should be able to catch one or two Rabbits on many days, by low-cost hunting from perches, for the family to share, and supplemented if need be by small prey species. Targeting young Rabbits would seem to be a profitable strategy, even where they are not plentiful.

Figure 8.3 Buzzard Diet: summer (July-August), Postbridge 1956-58

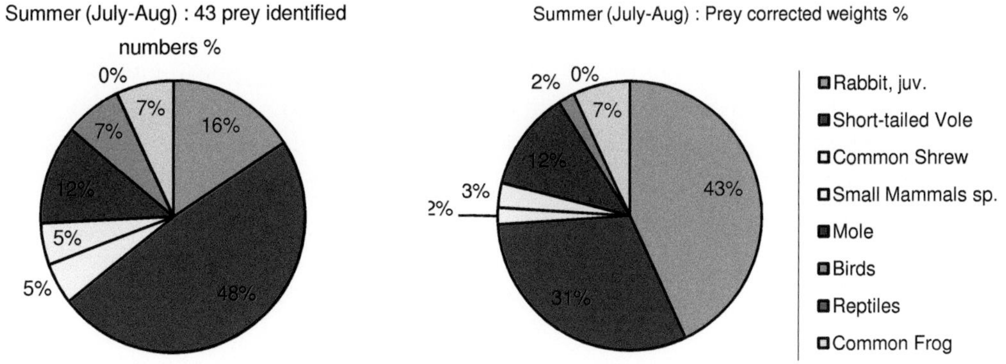

Figure 8.3 Summer (July–August) diet of Buzzards at Postbridge, Dartmoor, 1956–58. Charts show, as proportions: left – the numbers of prey animals identified in pellets; right – their estimated biomass contributions after correcting for differential digestion. [Colour codes to be read from the top of each chart]

A complete plumage moult requires an additional daily expenditure of energy for all bird species. The implications for Buzzards have been assessed indirectly (Sylvén 1982) based on physiological studies of moulting in other groups of birds. He calculated first that the average weight of a Buzzard's plumage is 51 g in males and 63 g in females, which is equivalent to 6–7% of their body weight. The energy expenditure required to synthesise from the food all the protein materials needed to replace the plumage was estimated to be 57 kcal per gram of feathers. The total demand of moulting thus should amount to about 2,900 and 3,590 kcal for male and female Buzzards, respectively. Spread over the entire moult period these values equate on average to an extra 19 and 24 kcal per day or, say, the energy content of one or two shrews. Thus, the extended moult strategy requires little extra hunting effort in these months when food is most available.

SUMMER DIETS

Assessing Buzzard food habits from pellets now becomes even more difficult because of dense ground vegetation. Thus, only 27 pellets from six Dartmoor territories were found, and these yielded 43 prey items (Figure 8.3).

As expected, the principal diet was similar to that in the previous few months. Short-tailed Voles were again the commonest prey (48%) followed by Rabbits (16%), Moles (12%) and a few other small mammals, small birds and Frogs. On a weight basis, and after the usual adjustments, Rabbits were the most important food (43%) followed by Short-tailed Voles (31%) and Moles (12%). The opportunistic nature of Buzzard predation is again evident from a study area farmer's reliable reports of two Buzzards seen catching voles flushed, in the first instance, by a silage-cutting machine and, in the other, by an inexperienced young fox! Visiting observers to this Dartmoor area in July and August have seen Buzzards carrying Common Lizard, an Adder, and a Grass Snake captured in a cut grass field (DBRs).

Some of these Buzzards still occasionally took beetles and earthworms. One breeding pair was observed ground-foraging in a ploughed field for more than 20 minutes on a warm and dry July day. Elsewhere, one Buzzard foraging in a pasture field in Somerset was seen to catch and eat 36 large dung beetles *Typhaeus typhoeus* in 27 minutes (Briggs 1983). Given the date, 31 August, it is quite possible that this was a juvenile Buzzard.

In other parts of Devon in summer, Buzzards have been reported feeding on a Stoat, killing Moorhen chicks (three out of five in two days), snatching a juvenile Jay from atop a telegraph pole, and striking down a flying Redshank (only to lose it to a Great Black-backed Gull). Carrion is still eaten in summer. For example, a gathering of 9 or 10 Buzzards, evidently non-breeders, fed with Ravens and Carrion Crows on livestock remains at an abattoir dump in August; and another Buzzard was feeding with two Ravens at a sheep carcass. A Buzzard tearing at a Rainbow Trout beside a lake was a most unusual sight. Finally, an especially agile Buzzard was watched catching Large White butterflies (*Pieris brassicae*) on the wing! (DBRs). On the Welsh island of Skomer in late July a Buzzard was flushed from a freshly-dead Little Owl (Saunders 1960).

By late August the most precocious of the juvenile Buzzards begin to drift away from the parental territories. Their subsequent movements and fates during their first autumn of independence will be followed in the next chapter.

9

BUZZARDS IN AUTUMN
(September–November)

This is the season when adult Buzzards complete their annual moult and the successful breeders finish recuperating from the breeding season. All must then prepare for winter by accumulating fat reserves. Food is still plentiful at first, with small mammals and Rabbits at or just past their peaks of abundance, although other and more seasonal small preys are declining rapidly or disappear (hibernate or migrate) as autumn progresses. Meanwhile, the juvenile Buzzards are leaving home, equipped with some basic hunting abilities. Consequently, this is a time of population turnover as juveniles disperse, while some adult losses may be replaced by new recruits. Charting these population changes and behavioural adjustments becomes a focus for attention during these three months, in addition to continuing the food studies.

POPULATION STRUCTURE

Autumn is a period of considerable population flux. In early September most young Buzzards are still with their parents while others are moving away to find their own niches elsewhere. After a very good breeding season, there can be almost equal numbers of juveniles and adults at the start of autumn. The proportion of young birds then decreases as the season progresses. At the same time a few older immatures are still wandering about and seeking opportunities either to refill any territory vacancies arising from deaths of previous adult owners, or to establish new territories.

All these Buzzard movements were evident in the small Dartmoor study area where this was an important time for replacement of lost adults. In the first year (1956) following myxomatosis, four Buzzard pairs disappeared (died or emigrated) from the area soon after breeding attempts had failed. Three were replaced quickly by new pairs in October and the fourth by birds arriving separately in November and late winter. All of these new pairs bred or attempted breeding in the next spring. A fifth pair settled in November, established a new temporary territory and attempted to breed, but failed and disappeared.

A few new Buzzards that appeared in the area were only temporary visitors to different territories that were occupied by pairs without young of their own. The intruders' presence clearly was resented, judging by the calls of owners, although no overt aggression was apparent. From their unobtrusive behaviour and sleek fresh-looking plumage the visitors were considered to be wandering juveniles from beyond the study area. The first two of six such visitors were seen on 5 September and 10 October, and they were followed by four others in early November, including an almost all-white individual. Two of the November birds stayed, for five weeks and at least four days respectively, in very limited parts of two territories. No high-flying transient Buzzards were observed, but a third bird heading west fairly low across two territories in early November was clearly passing through.

Unusual autumn movements of Buzzards that have been observed recently in Devon were most likely to be dispersing juveniles forming into the mobile groups that increasingly are being reported foraging in fields at this season (DBRs, and see below). Two notable examples of visible 'migration' across southern Dartmoor, and not far from my study area, were documented in late September 1980 (DBR). One comprised a passage of 27 Buzzards drifting south-westwards at great height off the moor edge; the other was of six birds heading south-east across open moor. In that same autumn, but well east from Dartmoor, an 'exceptional' total of 54 Buzzards was logged flying south-east above the 250 m-high Haldon Ridge between mid-August and early October.

Territorial behaviour

Adult Buzzards continue to maintain their territories, though with ever decreasing aerial or overt activities, as the autumn fades into winter. There is, however, usually a brief resurgence of soaring, calling, and perhaps even display-diving, in any spells of fine weather between mid-September and mid-October. Thereafter, and with rapidly shortening day length, the pairs once again settle down into their energy-conserving winter routine. The adults generally remain rather quiet unless provoked by trespassers. Wandering juveniles, keeping a low profile, seem to be recognised and tolerated as they pass through or stay briefly.

YOUNG BUZZARDS DISPERSE

The previous chapter described the life of Buzzard fledglings in their first 6–8 weeks out of the nest, when they were still fully dependent upon their parents. How these juveniles fare after cutting ties to their natal territories, and how far they subsequently travel before finding somewhere to settle, is now fairly well known – thanks to ringing, colour marking and radio-tracking studies in various parts of Britain.

Each of these three methods has its advantages and disadvantages. The 500–600 recoveries from more than 9,000 nestling Buzzards ringed nationally provide data on potential longevity and causes of death, and coarse-scale information about movement distances and directions. They may, however, give a biased picture in some regions because many deaths resulted from persecution. Far more detailed information can be obtained, albeit only for small local populations, from field observations of fledgling Buzzards marked with coloured leg rings or, better still, with numbered wing (patagial) tags. This method enables individual Buzzards from a local population to be identified repeatedly in the field over months, or for several years, but requires considerable searching effort. Results also may reveal the age(s) at which Buzzards first breed. Modern technologies, however, now can reveal in even greater detail the movements made by young Buzzards throughout their first few years. Fledglings fitted with back-pack radio-transmitting tags have been tracked across country, either from a vehicle on the ground or from a light aircraft. In due course, satellite tracking probably will be the next step.

The small-scale Dartmoor study, which provided the first data on the timing of juvenile dispersal (Dare 1961), was followed by Institute of Terrestrial Ecology projects in Scotland and Wales that both used more than 100 colour-marked fledgling Buzzards. These projects were located on Speyside (Picozzi & Weir 1976) and in central Wales (Davis & Davis 1992). More recently, in Dorset, radio-tagged fledglings have been monitored at frequent intervals and for several years during research by the Centre for Ecology and Hydrology (Walls & Kenward 1995). This study revealed a wealth of new and intriguing information about this critical phase in a Buzzard's life.

Leaving home

Juvenile Buzzards vary greatly in the length of time for which they remain dependent upon, or are tolerated by, their parents. This phase can be very protracted for the upland Buzzards of Dartmoor and Speyside, and for those in the lowland Dorset population, as the monthly patterns of numbers remaining 'at home' show (Figure 9.1).

The monthly decreases in numbers are thought largely to reflect emigration, though some disappearances will have been deaths (see below). These plots nevertheless show that most juveniles departed in August and September, leaving some 20–40% behind in their natal territories by October. A variable proportion (10–25%) then stayed on over the winter before eventually leaving as spring, and the parents' next breeding season, drew near.

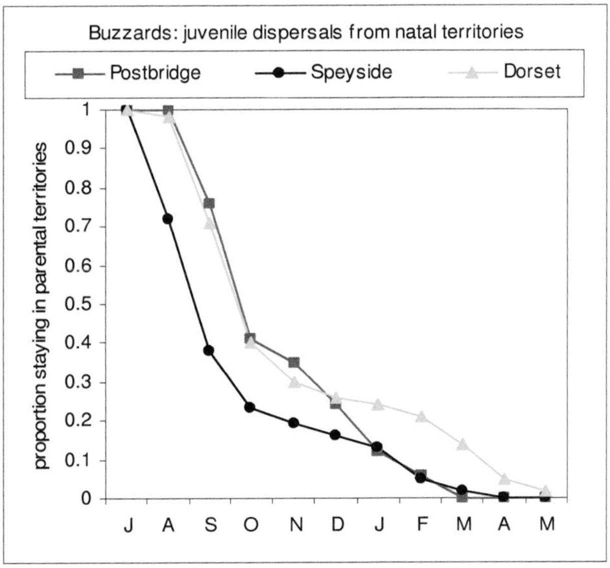

Figure 9.1 Juvenile dispersal patterns of Buzzards in three study areas, shown by the proportions of birds remaining each month with their parents. Based on individuals identified by: plumages (Postbridge), colour tags (Speyside) and radio tags (Dorset)

For New Forest youngsters, which were difficult to observe in thick cover, the less frequent observations nevertheless conformed to the above pattern. Juveniles did not venture more than 300 m from the nest for several weeks (Tubbs 1974). They were fed by the parents only sporadically after mid-August and occasionally into late September. Most had gone by mid-November and none was seen after mid-December.

Movements: ring recoveries

How far do the juveniles move away from familiar home ground and how many survive the critical first months of a fully independent lifestyle? The ringing data indicate that most young Buzzards move a surprisingly short way, whereas a few may travel significant distances. Until quite recently, analyses relied upon the 559 records of birds ringed in western and northern Britain that had been reported as 'found dead' in their first three years. Most had died within 50 km of their birthplace but several had moved much further (Kenward & Walls, in Wernham *et al.* 2002). Juveniles that were recovered in their first autumn tended to be found further away (median distance 21 km) than those that had survived until the following summer (median distance 13 km). These data included three Dartmoor Buzzards: one from my study area found dead near the coast 38 km to SSE at the end of its first winter; one that died in October before dispersing; and a bird from near my area which died in November, 91 km WSW near the north Cornwall coast.

Notable long distance movements, including sea crossings to the near Continent, have been undertaken by some juvenile Buzzards. The farthest recovery distances were by an emigrant from northern Scotland that had travelled more than 1,300 km to reach the Belgian-German border area, and by another moving nearly 500 km from north-west England to southern England. Two New Forest youngsters were also adventurous, for one of the seven recovered had gone 345 km NNE to Yorkshire, and the other 430 km ESE into north-east France, by their first September, only about 2–3 months after fledging (Tubbs 1974). Three Welsh birds dispersed up to 200 km: NNE to Cumbria, SE to Hampshire, and SSE to Dorset (Davis & Davis 1992); whereas three Speyside birds travelled no further than 100 km (Picozzi & Weir 1976).

Movements: colour marking

A finer-scale resolution picture of juvenile Buzzard movements and behaviour was obtained from the colour-marking projects. Among the hills in central Wales, 215 nearly-fledged young from 40 territories were fitted with wing tags (Davis & Davis 1992). Follow-up observations showed that the juveniles varied greatly in mobility. During their first winter some stayed within 1 km of parental territories but most had moved off to varying distances around the region during a protracted dispersal period. Some juveniles went quickly to about 40 km by the end of August while two dispersed up to 200 km, as noted above, and others soon settled in places on the borders of occupied breeding territories. Repeated sightings of some individuals indicated nomadic or wandering behaviour during which they sometimes met and collected into loose groupings to scavenge from carrion (see below).

The Speyside juveniles were more difficult to follow since most quickly dispersed away from the study area or otherwise 'disappeared' (Figure 9.1). Subsequently many were reported as 'found dead' before they had travelled 20 km and 69% of these had been shot, trapped or poisoned on nearby game estates. Despite such intense persecution, 11% of the tagged youngsters eventually survived to occupy nesting territories within this study area, where two of them had remained all the time.

Movements: radio-tracking

Among Buzzards in the Dorset lowlands, the radio-tracking work revealed complex patterns of dispersal behaviour but, significantly, with birds displaying a high degree of fidelity (philopatry) to the natal area. Only the main findings can be given here. The majority (71%) of juveniles dispersed in autumn, usually for only 5–20 km although some travelled much further and settled about 100 km away. In the spring, however, most of these youngsters moved back part-way towards their birth places, some to reside just 1–7 km from their natal nests (Walls & Kenward 1995). The remaining birds (29%) had remained sedentary over their first autumn and winter, keeping within 1 km of their nests, although many had made brief excursions in August and September of about 5 km on average (maximum 20 km) before returning home for their first winter.

In the spring, and with very few exceptions, the sedentary wintering juveniles departed, or were evicted from, parental territories. Interestingly, although these late departers did not move as far as the autumn dispersers, they were able to settle in better quality habitats; places with less arable land. There, the young Buzzards survived better than the autumn-dispersing birds that had gone further away (Walls *et al.* 1999). There was thus a clear advantage to staying over winter with parents. Those pairs with over-wintering youngsters evidently occupied good quality territories. Also, presumably, parents had used individual plumage and behavioural features to distinguish between their own offspring and any intruding juveniles. Exceptionally, in both Dorset and North Somerset (Prytherch 2009), a juvenile might stay with its parents beyond spring and well into its second calendar year, though whether the adults bred in such instances is not mentioned. The subsequent movements of immature Buzzards in later years, and their recruitment into the breeding population, will be described later (Chapter 14).

AUTUMN DIET OF JUVENILE BUZZARDS

Dependent juveniles

Little has been gleaned about the food of juvenile Buzzards, and how they develop hunting skills, while remaining in parental territories. They are so unobtrusive on many days that direct field observations yield sparse information. It might be assumed that the parents provide much of their diet though in steadily diminishing amounts. However, even the parental diet of Dartmoor birds was difficult to assess in autumn (see below).

In his detailed observations in the New Forest, Tubbs (1974) saw juveniles being fed very occasionally into late September but apparently did not witness juveniles themselves making kills. On Dartmoor, single juveniles occasionally were seen ground-foraging for invertebrates but the first observed kill of a small mammal was not until early December. Very likely, other kills would have been made, from hunting perches, before winter set in.

Some lingering youngsters still managed to obtain kills from parents though, presumably, less and less frequently as autumn progressed, as the following Dartmoor incident illustrates:

> *On a cool day in early October with a strong north-west wind bringing showers, two calling Buzzards, an adult and a juvenile, are flying towards me across boggy moorland after a hunting trip to a young conifer plantation. The youngster is calling loudly for food and 'tailing' its parent very closely although the latter is not carrying prey. When the youngster suddenly swerves up with talons outstretched too near its parent, the latter responds by extending its own legs whereupon both birds nearly tangle talons. The parent quickly lands on a bush and then moves onto a fence post, at the base of which the juvenile settles and continues to pester. Finally, the parent flies off alone.*

Independent juveniles

How juvenile Buzzards that have dispersed initially manage to obtain food has for long remained something of a mystery. Now, however, there is good evidence of them feeding on dead animals and picking up invertebrates but conclusive instances of juveniles making kills still appear not to have been documented.

Scavenging carrion

Juvenile Buzzards may occasionally chance upon and be able to scavenge from carrion, as was observed in a semi-moorland territory in my Dartmoor area one day in November:

> *An exceptionally pale Buzzard gliding along a high heathery hill side is being harassed by four Carrion Crows. This is a stranger to the study area. The hawk glides down across the valley to land on a hawthorn bush and then drops onto a sheep carcass lower down the slope. As it starts to feed, the resident pair of Buzzards arrive and proceed to protest noisily at the intruder. They fly to and fro along the hill side, but (surprisingly) they do not land at the carcass. Instead, they drift away down the valley, leaving the intruder to feed unmolested for at least 15 minutes. This bird is by far the palest I have ever encountered, having a pale sandy buff head, white body, and a few pale fawn areas on the otherwise white upper wings and tail. Only the primary tips and under wing patterns are near normal. In low flight it resembles a very large Barn Owl. The behaviour of the local pair, and the date, suggest that this is a wandering juvenile from beyond the study area. [It was not seen again.]*

In mid-Wales, carrion provides an important resource for juvenile Buzzards. Colour-marked juveniles were found to group together to feed at sheep carcasses, refuse tips and abattoir waste dumps (Davis & Davis 1992). Single birds have been drawn in autumn to Rabbit or other carrion baits laid out by bird photographers. Many are also readily attracted to gather for meat scraps at recently-established raptor feeding stations in Powys (Figure 9.2).

Figure 9.2 Many immature Buzzards are attracted to raptor feeding stations in mid-Wales. This juvenile/first-winter shows the typical pale eye and streaked throat. Powys, February. (© Steven Round)

Ground foraging

In Devon and Wales, searching for soil invertebrates is now an important strategy that is being adopted increasingly by juvenile Buzzards for surviving the first months of independence. Instead of leading a solitary lifestyle, as might be supposed, many youngsters congregate to forage for extended periods in fields of newly-reseeded leys and autumn-sown crops. Such assemblages afford protection from otherwise dominant territorial adult Buzzards while presumably reducing the risk of Fox predation.

In lowland Devon, the first anecdotal records were of up to 8–14 Buzzards feeding together in pastures and arable fields in autumn (DBRs 1952–79, Hayman 1970). These probably involved small groups mainly or exclusively of juveniles that were bred locally. Since 1980, however, a dramatic increase and spread of this social behaviour is reported from Devon and parts of Wales. By 1999, there had been 15 Devon records of 10–40 Buzzards foraging communally between late August and early November, with a distinct peak in late September and early October (Dare 1999). Exceptionally, one autumn gathering of up to 44 Buzzards fed for a month on hatching crane-flies (*Tipulidae)* along a hillside on the southern edge of Dartmoor.

In my Dartmoor area the first instance of group foraging occurred in September 1989, when a farmer reported seeing up to 23 Buzzards feeding in a newly reseeded pasture; about 14 birds then stayed there over the winter. This field was near the border of a small territory in which Buzzards had bred intermittently for more than 30 years. The following year, in late August, I saw the resident pair and their two juveniles feeding in an adjacent reseeded field where later, in October, I watched 15 feeding. Many, perhaps all, of these Buzzards were in juvenile plumages, scattered about and feeding with no sign of competitive interactions.

Since 2000, the number and average size of autumn gatherings in Devon have increased still further. In some localities, feeding assemblages of 12–27 Buzzards have continued into the early spring; with one instance in March of 19 birds feeding among farm slurry freshly spread on a field. Following-the-plough, by up to five Buzzards, is also now a more frequent sight. Even in June there were records of 12 and 27 hawks on freshly ploughed fields, and of 25 feeding in a cut silage field. At this date, however, the current breeding season would have still been in progress. Such gatherings thus would most likely have involved older, immature birds that were in their second or third calendar years.

In North Somerset, as in Devon, recently independent juvenile Buzzards seldom settle in defended territories, but apparently wander over a large area until they find, and join, other juveniles at a plentiful food supply (Prytherch 2009). In his farmland study area, autumn gatherings of mostly non-breeding Buzzards have been observed closely. In 2004, at least 60 birds fed upon the abundant earthworms present in two large autumn-sown fields. These were situated partly within an occupied Buzzard territory but the resident pair was unable to evict so many intruders despite frequently attacking them. Much smaller assemblies were present in subsequent years. The juvenile Buzzards fed often within 20 m of each other without disputes, except when a bird might fly low towards and then try to displace another from its feeding place. Some individuals did not submit, however, but instead turned to confront and even counter-attack the intruder. There then might follow a contest in which talons could be locked briefly or both birds stood erect and close together with wings spread in 'angel' postures. The subordinate individual would then fall back into a 'fallen angel' or submissive position to end the encounter (Figure 18, Prytherch 2009).

In Wales, foraging in fields by large groups of Buzzards has become a conspicuous activity since 1993 in some west coast and central districts (James 2000, Green 2002, Welsh Bird Report 2007). These authors list seven gatherings of between 14 and 57 Buzzards feeding ('worming') in reseeded leys or winter barley fields. Most were in October with some in winter and March. At one well-watched location Buzzard numbers varied through the winter with the weather and time of day, the largest numbers being present in the morning (James 2000). In another district, as many as 55 Buzzards fed at 'slaughterhouse slurry' – waste animal material spread on fields after anaerobic treatment (Green 2002). In north-east Wales, Buzzards have recently begun to adopt similar habits. Since 2006, up to 16 birds have gathered each autumn on arable fields beside the River Dee, and stayed from November into February (J. L. Roberts, *in litt.*). There are no comparable records, as yet, from Snowdonia or other north-western areas of Wales (J. Driver, *in litt.*).

The recent spectacle of these large and unexpected raptor assemblies appears not to be related to any seasonal change in the timing of agricultural operations nor to a shift in crop management (M. J. Shrubb, pers. comm.). A more likely explanation is that they reflect increased annual productivity of these western populations, now breeding at high densities in an era of much reduced persecution. The foraging strategies and daily food consumption of juvenile Buzzards would provide a rewarding field for studies by using, for example, techniques developed for shorebird feeding investigations.

AUTUMN DIET OF ADULT BUZZARDS

This proved to be another difficult season for assessing what Dartmoor Buzzards were eating. Pellets still were well hidden in thick ground vegetation and, with hover-hunting ceasing in September, the Buzzards resorted to static hunting from perches.

Analysis was restricted to the 46 prey items found in 37 pellets that were collected from five territories (Figure 9.3). These show that Short-tailed Voles again were the most numerous prey, comprising one half of all kills and 38% of the weight eaten. These voles are most numerous in early autumn having produced three or four litters of young since April.

Figure 9.3 Buzzard diets : autumn, Postbridge 1956-58

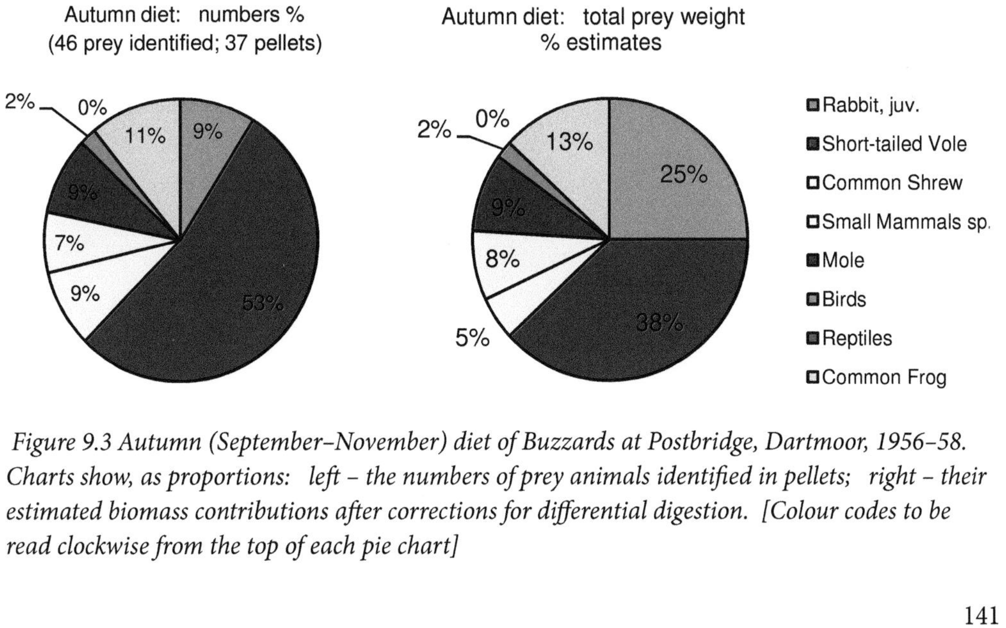

Figure 9.3 Autumn (September–November) diet of Buzzards at Postbridge, Dartmoor, 1956–58. Charts show, as proportions: left – the numbers of prey animals identified in pellets; right – their estimated biomass contributions after corrections for differential digestion. [Colour codes to be read clockwise from the top of each pie chart]

The five other species of small mammals together contributed 22% by weight. Rabbits, with fewer small young now available, declined in numerical importance though still making up a quarter by weight of the food eaten. Frogs were still being found and, unexpectedly, they formed as much as 13% by weight. One Frog was seen being captured as late as 6 November. Birds were unimportant, many having left the area after breeding. Reptiles were absent, possibly because of the onset of hibernation and the small sample of pellets. There was little evidence of adult Buzzards resorting to invertebrates during autumn in this area. Earthworm remains were present in only 6% of the pellets together with a few (mostly) ground- and dung-beetles and a single cranefly (leather-jacket) larva.

Field observations in November included an adult Buzzard that had just killed a Weasel and taken it up to a bare horizontal bough. There, it uttered short 'gruff' notes as it prepared to eat its unusual victim. In a nearby territory, during October, the farmer reported having seen three Buzzards at a sheep carcass, with attendant Carrion Crows and Magpies. Although only one small bird was found in the autumn pellets, an adult Buzzard was watched as it made a premeditated attack on feeding Starlings. This hawk dropped from its thorn bush hunting perch then, in the manner of a Sparrowhawk, beat rapidly very low across intervening heathy ground towards the flock 50–100 m away. It was hidden in a slight depression for part of the way. However, it was detected when only 10 m from the nearest birds and, as the Starlings rose in alarm, the Buzzard made an incomplete feint at them but missed, then carried on to another hunting perch. Such opportunistic tactics can be effective, however (see below).

Buzzards in Cornwall have been seen to catch birds by means of ground-level attacks, an amazing instance of which was witnessed, and photographed, at the Hayle Estuary one recent autumn. There, an adult Buzzard launched a ground-level attack on, and snatched, a storm-blown Grey Phalarope as it swam and fed in an estuarine saltmarsh (Figure 9.4). These remarkable images were taken late one afternoon in dull light at the Hayle Estuary in Cornwall in September 2008.

Cornish Buzzards, in October, also have been seen to catch and kill (after a struggle) a roosting Tawny Owl and, even more surprisingly, a hunting Short-eared Owl (Wooltorton 1985, Barnard 1981). In the same county and month, another Buzzard caught a 30–35 cm long eel which it subdued only with some difficulty (Madge 1992).

In Devon during autumn, Buzzards have been recorded utilising a surprising range of food sources (DBRs). Some were found on kills of Wood Pigeon, Little Owl, Stoat and Grey Squirrel, and another Buzzard was seen attempting to catch a Grey Squirrel in an oak tree. Others have scavenged from a Tawny Owl road-kill and hunted Starlings at a roost. Even more unusual were sightings of five Buzzards (evidently a family) peacefully sharing a Rabbit kill in mid-September; and of a single bird feeding on a Brown Hare carcass while encircled by 14 other Buzzards! The latter incident, in early October, could have concerned an adult dominating a collection of subordinate juveniles. Another gathering of 10 Buzzards that were 'waiting on' a linseed harvesting operation in September were observed dropping down and trying to catch fleeing small mammals. These Buzzards, too, were likely to have been mainly or entirely inexperienced youngsters. Another Buzzard, watched while foraging among

Figure 9.4 Buzzards are great opportunist hunters. This adult is seizing a Grey Phalarope on a Cornish saltmarsh. (© Paul Freestone/ SWNS.com)

seaweed on the seashore, had perhaps been attracted by crustacean sandhoppers. Bird tables have been visited by at least two enterprising Buzzards in recent years. A Devon bird took away fat lumps in autumn, and a Welsh bird (apparently sub-adult) in Ceredigion regularly came for chicken portions (Figure 9.5).

Figure 9.5 This Buzzard, probably a sub-adult, regularly visited a bird table for meat scraps. (Ceredigion © John Davis)

Buzzards hunting from roadside telegraph poles along the quieter country routes have long been a familiar sight throughout the year in Devon and other western counties. In recent years, some birds have taken to scavenging from road-kills along new fast highways, often with fatal results (DBRs). One casualty was noted lying beside a Rabbit corpse. In North Wales, a few Buzzards hunt, in calm weather, from atop the metal lighting structures beside a busy dual carriageway (J. Driver, *in litt.*). Birds were seen to fly across between fast moving traffic to drop onto the opposite grass verge, as if onto small prey. Not surprisingly, several Buzzards have been killed. Active birds have even been observed several hours after dusk on autumn and winter evenings, and again at first light, perhaps on the watch for fresh road-kills.

Preparing for winter

During autumn the adult Buzzards' energy demands fall gradually as hunting to feed offspring and territorial soaring flight activities are greatly reduced or cease. The annual moult is completed, in September for females and October for males (Sylvén 1982). The average daily energy need is now 12–13% less than it was from June to August (Chapter 11). In prey biomass terms, a Buzzard in autumn should need to catch each day about five well-grown Short-tailed Voles or an equivalent amount of other preys.

During this season all Buzzards now need to prepare for winter by building up at least 100–200 g of body fat reserves, as described in the winter section (Chapter 3). To do so will require higher daily prey capture rates, and presumably greater hunting effort. Fortunately, small mammal and Rabbit biomass and availability are still near their annual peaks in September. On the other hand, many of the other prey species have now either left or are departing the uplands (small birds) or are disappearing rapidly into hibernation (amphibians and reptiles). After September, the Buzzards are faced with a steadily diminishing food supply coupled with reduced hunting time as day length shortens, by around one-third (4 hours) between September and December. Adult Buzzards in good quality territories cope with this situation in normal years. For the juveniles, on the other hand, their chances of surviving their first winter will depend on how soon they become effective hunters of small mammals. Those in the uplands may also be able to find occasional sheep carrion. Juveniles living on productive farmland in the West Country and lowland Wales evidently can subsist, largely or in part, by 'grubbing' communally for earthworms and other soil invertebrates. Many Devon juveniles clearly have succeeded, so far, with the latter strategy during the recent (1980s–1990s) prolonged sequence of predominantly mild winters. How well the young Buzzards will cope during future cold winters remains to be seen.

10

TERRITORY

The primary advantage of holding a territory, though difficult to measure for any bird species, is to ensure an adequate food supply for adults to rear young in a secure nest site (reviews by Hinde, 1956, Thomson 1964). For a given raptor species, food is the main factor driving territoriality and almost every aspect of its population ecology (Newton 1979). Lack (1954) noted an absence of supporting evidence that the territory contains that minimum quantity of food required to breed successfully. This is not surprising. Whereas measuring the amount of food that would be needed by Buzzards has been achieved (Chapter 11), it would be a formidable task to estimate the available biomass of even one major prey species in territories with diverse habitats. Territorial behaviour is usually considered also to facilitate pair formation and maintenance of the pair bond by preventing interference from others, males especially, during courtship, copulation and nest building phases, notably where good nest sites may be scarce.

In many birds of prey, territorial behaviour involves the active defence, by a male or pair, of an area, generally termed a home range, from which others of the same species are excluded. This area contains the hunting grounds, nesting sites and other habitat resources necessary for survival and breeding of the pair. Territoriality results in the dispersion of a population across suitable habitats. It thus influences population density, although in terms of natural selection, this result is incidental to ensuring the needs of the individual pair (Newton 1979). Territories may be temporary or permanent; the latter type, classically seen in Robins, is defended constantly and provides all the requirements for breeding and survival throughout the year.

Large raptors with relatively low population densities, such as eagles, defend strongly an exclusive home range (or territory), containing the nest sites and main hunting areas, but share hunting grounds beyond its limits (Newton 1979). The great mobility of such raptors across wide expanses of often rugged terrain poses problems for the amateur enthusiast lacking access to modern tracking technology. On the other hand, some of the smaller and commoner birds of prey can be more amenable for study. In Britain, the first such work was a long-term investigation of Tawny Owls in woodland near Oxford. This sedentary and nocturnal, but vocal, species was found to be extremely territorial throughout the year, thereby enabling individual territory sizes to be mapped (Southern 1954).

Sixty years ago, Buzzards in Britain were considered to be non-territorial, away from the immediate vicinity of the nest, although no specific studies had been undertaken. When, therefore, in 1956 I noticed that Dartmoor Buzzards were strongly territorial, a major effort was made to investigate this seemingly 'novel' behaviour (Dare 1961). Coincidentally, at around the same time, territorial Buzzards were also 'discovered' at two places in Germany (Melde, 1956, Warncke & Wittenburg, 1959). Subsequently, similar behaviour was described for Buzzards in the New Forest, in southern England (Tubbs 1974), and in the hill farming country of upper Strathspey, Scotland (Weir & Picozzi 1983) and from further studies in well-wooded farmlands in Germany and Sweden (Sylvén 1982).

Until recently, the spectrum of social behaviours shown by Buzzards had been neglected for dedicated study, possibly because of problems with recognizing individuals in the field. Sightings tend to be of birds in flight, and often at a distance or silhouetted at height against the light. However, the advent of coloured wing (patagial) tags and electronic imaging techniques should now enable advances to be made. Our current knowledge of interactions within breeding Buzzard populations has been collected mainly during the course of ecological studies by non-behaviourists. All have relied heavily upon individual variations in plumage patterns, voice and mannerisms. Following on from the basic Dartmoor work (Dare 1961), summarized below, there have been notable studies of Buzzard behaviour in Strathspey (Weir & Picozzi 1975) and in North Somerset (Prytherch 2009). These are essential reading for an introduction to the population structure and dynamics of Buzzard populations.

WHAT IS A BUZZARD TERRITORY?

A Buzzard territory, as seen on Dartmoor, is an area of countryside that is defended by an occupying pair against other Buzzards throughout the year. Its primary purposes are to provide an adequate food supply for survival of the pair and favourable conditions for breeding. This definition applies to all populations so far studied in this country. The exclusive territory comprises a variety of habitats suitable for hunting in different seasons. Acquiring an intimate knowledge of the terrain, and of prey distribution and behaviour, could have considerable survival value, especially when rearing young and during periods of food shortage in cold winter weather. A good territory also contains safe nest sites and sheltered roosting places and is free from excessive human disturbance and harmful activities. These requirements have been noted in tree- and crag-nesting Buzzards in the mountains of Snowdonia as also in my other study areas, and doubtless will be similar in other populations.

Territorial behaviour

There are two basic categories of territorial behavior: advertisement and defence. A Buzzard pair, but particularly the male, advertises the extent of its claim to an area by both passive and active methods, as fully described previously (Chapter 4). Passive advertisement occurs throughout the year. It involves frequent, perhaps daily, use of conspicuous resting and hunting perches near the periphery of its territory. Active advertisement comprises two contrasting and familiar forms of aerial manoeuvring – soaring and display-diving – both accompanied by loud and far-carrying calls. These conspicuous displays are seasonal, reaching a peak in spring, when they also serve a courtship function (see also Witherby *et al.* 1943; Melde 1956). Fine descriptions of these and related behaviour have been given for Buzzards resident in the New Forest (Tubbs 1974), Strathspey (Weir & Picozzi 1975, 1983) and Somerset (Prytherch 2009).

It is rare that the early stages in the establishment of, and development of territorial behaviour by, a new Buzzard population can be followed. In north-east Suffolk, during its current re-colonisation by Buzzards, breeding began again in 2005 after an absence of about 100 years (Dare 2009). At first, the newly-settling pairs were scattered at low densities, their potential hunting ranges large and with ill-defined boundaries. Overt territorial behaviour in the first 3–4 years was less frequent and intense than in densely populated western regions. Since then, however, as their numbers have increased, Buzzards have become more assertive in spring towards neighbours, while clear territory boundaries are evident among some pairs.

HABITAT COMPOSITIONS OF TERRITORIES

Buzzards are widely associated with a countryside mosaic of woodlands, for nesting, mixed with open areas of scrub, rough grassland and agricultural land for hunting. This hawk, unlike Goshawk and Sparrowhawk, is not a woodland specialist. On the contrary, many Buzzards can be equally at home in some of the wildest uplands or on treeless islands. Recent studies have examined the extent to which Buzzards may select (or avoid) certain habitat features and how territory size and associated breeding success may vary between different habitats.

Dartmoor

Territory boundaries frequently followed topographical features such as hill tops and ridges, which generate up-currents for soaring, gliding and hovering, and also allow commanding views of other territories. Such features were regular rendezvous places for soaring contests and boundary encounters between neighbours. In general, pairs occupied cross-sections of valleys, thereby giving them hill slopes (some steep, others shallow) on each side. On more featureless terrain, such as wide commons, the Buzzards used isolated and prominent trees, bushes, and even rows of fence posts as boundary markers. There was little overlap between adjacent pairs. Indeed, several territories were separated by unclaimed expanses of moorland and conifer plantations. Buzzards seldom hunted over these strips of 'no-man's-land'.

In this study area, most Buzzard territories contain five broad habitat types – fields, heath/grass moorland, scrub, including young conifer plantings, old woodland and bogs – thus potentially providing a wide range of preys (Figures 10.1, 10.2, 10.3, Appendix 27a). Naturally, however, the amount and proportion of each type of habitat in a territory varied greatly according to territory location and size, with attendant consequences for prey diversity and availability. The total ground occupied by territories amounted to about 1,840 ha and on average the territories comprised 47% fields, 32% open heath/moor (rough grazing) and about 6–8% each of wet bog, mature woodland and scrub including thicket stage conifer plantings. Within the individual territories the proportions of the two major habitats varied inversely and that affected the breeding performances of Buzzard pairs (see below).

Figure 10.1 Four Buzzard territories on Dartmoor with contrasting habitats and breeding productivities. Pairs in adjoining territories A and B, on valley farmland, were more successful than those in C and D with mostly open moorland sheepwalk.

North Wales

Similar characteristics were evident in many territories in the North Wales uplands. In both survey regions, the habitats within a 1 km foraging radius of Buzzard nests likewise varied greatly between territories; and also differed from the overall land-use pattern in each region (Dare 1995). The range of habitats has been illustrated in Chapter 2. The Migneint-Hiraethog uplands (Figures 2.7–2.9) are dominated equally by open sheepwalk or rough grazing. Here, two-thirds of the 62 Buzzard pairs favoured farms. Their territories, on average, were made up overwhelmingly of fields with hedgerow trees (91%) but very little woodland (4%) or open sheepwalk (5%). Another 29% of pairs were on marginal farmland with fewer fields (59%) and trees (2%) but more extensive rough grazing (39%). The remaining three pairs bred, successfully, in isolated trees or groups of trees on otherwise treeless moors.

In Snowdonia (Figures 2.10–2.14), nearly two-thirds of the 93 territories likewise were classed as hill sheep farms, where Buzzards nested mainly in valley woods but foraged higher up scrub and rough grazing slopes to around the tree limit (*c.*450 m). On average, their territories contained 31% fields, 26% open sheepwalk and 40% woodland. The remaining 32 territories were on higher ground dominated by montane and sub-montane sheepwalk. Montane territories, with 89% sheepwalk, often were treeless, and Buzzards there foraged up to the 970 m contour. The (intermediate) sub-montane territories also were predominantly sheepwalk (68%) but usually were partly afforested (16%) with conifers at lower levels, and held some enclosed fields (15%). Buzzards nested exclusively on crags in both of these groupings.

Central Wales

The topography, habitats and land use of this 425 km^2 area in the Cambrian Mountains was very similar to that of the Migneint-Hiraethog and eastern Snowdonia study areas farther north. Open sheepwalk grassland and large conifer plantations on higher ground (above 250–330 m) gave way at lower levels to enclosed farmland pastures (for sheep and cattle) and valley woodlands (Newton *et al.* 1982). Many Buzzards bred throughout the area, wherever there were suitable trees, crags or slopes for nesting. Most pairs appeared to reside in territories all year, but some of those on higher ground left for periods in winter. Although detailed data are not given, the habitat compositions of Buzzard territories probably differed little from those of many pairs in the North Wales study areas.

Strathspey

The habitats in the 173 km^2 highland area, between 220–380 m elevation, comprised a mixture of rough pastures on valley farmland, birch and oak woods, mature conifer woods and young plantations at lower levels. The upper slopes which were predominantly heather moor partly afforested with young conifers, were little visited by Buzzards (Weir & Picozzi 1983). A later and detailed analysis of this population (Halley 1993) found that habitat compositions in Buzzard territories were not representative of the habitat structure of the area as a whole. Instead, the breeding pairs favoured places with a mosaic of mature woods (birch, oak and pine) and farmland with rough grazing and a little cultivation. They avoided young thicket-stage pine plantations, treeless moorland, marshes, open waters and built-up areas.

These regional studies collectively indicate that upland Buzzards prefer a range of habitats within their territories, including a large component of livestock farmland, the most productive habitat for prey through the year.

TERRITORY SIZE

Buzzard population densities vary greatly within and between study areas (Appendix 26). Size reflects the spacing between pairs, which in turn determines locally the population density that can be established in different landscapes. In my areas, the territory boundaries that were mapped all delineated the observed regular activity area of each Buzzard pair. In the small Dartmoor area it was possible so to map all defended territories, whereas in North Wales only a sample of pairs could be followed in sufficient detail during 1977–84. Further information was collected in 2003–04 for Buzzards on the Carneddau range of northern Snowdonia (J. Driver, *in litt.*).

Figure 10.2 The Dartmoor study area, showing the original 13 territories occupied in 1956–58 (within dashed lines), the nest locations during 1956–69 (red) and new sites (yellow circles) used in 1990–93. By 1990 the population had been augmented by three new breeding pairs (P). (© Google Earth)

Dartmoor

Buzzards held 13 'permanent' territories during the 14-year period of 1956–69, including six on or centred on valley farms, and four predominantly on or around moorland (Table 27a). These are displayed on a Google Earth image (Figure 10.2). They ranged in size (Appendix 26b) from 53–223 ha, averaging 142 ha; of which 47% was fields, 32% grass or heather moor, 8% bogs, 7% woodland (mostly dense conifer plantations) and 6% natural scrub or early stage plantations. Farmland territories on average were 95 ha in size and were predominantly pasture fields (60–80%) with 5–23% moorland. Most were in the eastern half of the study area, where they abutted one another, and boundaries were defended at all times. Moorland territories (185 ha) were twice as large and predominantly open moorland (50–80%) with smaller proportions (10–40%) of fields. The diversity of habitats within two moorland edge territories, as would be viewed by a Buzzard circling 300 m above, is shown in Figure 10.3.

North Wales

In North Wales, around the Migneint-Hiraethog moors, the 17 Buzzard territories that were assessed (1977–84) were larger than those on Dartmoor, ranging between 60–340 ha, with an

Figure 10.3 Buzzards' eye views (from 300 m) of the core areas of two Dartmoor territories (a) Archerton, (b) Runnage, showing habitat diversity; open moor beyond northern boundaries.

average of 220 ha. An isolated breeding pair on open moorland (with fewer than ten trees) ranged over not less than 450 ha. Even larger territories were found in Snowdonia during the same period. Those of the 25 most studied pairs, in the Carneddau range, varied from 150–630 ha (Dare 1995). Territories were smaller in wooded valleys and on other lower ground, where they averaged 260 ha, than at higher levels on the more exposed mountainsides (440 ha). These values are likely to be underestimates, for in such landscapes these territories also had a vertical dimension so that many pairs hunted up steep hill and mountain slopes spanning 200–790 m of altitudinal range.

A subsequent doubling of Buzzard numbers in Snowdonia by 2008 (Driver & Dare 2010) resulted in very much smaller territories. This was most evident on the 250 km^2 Carneddau range where numbers had risen by 168% during 20 years. Territories, mapped from observed activity ranges of pairs, were found now to be much smaller. Territory size increased with elevation. The smallest, on the wooded slopes below 200 m, usually covered 50–100 ha, whereas pairs above 500 m typically had territories of 300–400 ha.

Further east in North Wales, 20 Buzzard territories on hill farms with woods, and abutting onto higher moorland, have also been assessed from direct observations (Roberts & Jones 2009). Their average size of 125 ha (range of 60–260 ha) was comparable with the Dartmoor territories but smaller than many on the Migneint-Hiraethog uplands.

Welsh Border

In Powys, a 1994–95 survey of Buzzards in one 10-km square (SO37) of hill farmland, unimproved grazing and woods, located 81 territorial pairs, the highest density yet reported in Europe (Sim *et al.* 2001). Territory sizes were calculated by a geometrical method in which a polygon is drawn around each occupied nest by linking the mid-points between it and its nearest-neighbour nests. This procedure estimated a mean territory size of 120 ha, range 39–221 ha; and thus was close to values for hill farmland Buzzards in north-east Wales and on Dartmoor.

Strathspey

Here, there were 38 Buzzard breeding territories of 75–355 ha extent, average 175 ha. They occupied 61% of the ground, the rest being mainly open moor. Some contiguous territories overlapped one another but overall the boundaries remained virtually unchanged between years (Weir & Picozzi 1983). A repeat survey of one half of the area 17 years later (Halley 1993) found that territory sizes had not changed significantly despite a 57% increase in the population. This had been achieved by new pairs settling on previously unclaimed low ground. He also found that territories which included young, thicket-stage conifer plantations were significantly larger than the others, as was noted on Dartmoor. Most Buzzards in Strathspey, however, selected places with birch and other mature woodland, rough pastures and cultivated fields. Their territory sizes were not related to habitat composition.

This research also provided fascinating new information on how young Buzzards squeeze themselves into, and thus recruit to, an established breeding population (see also Chapter 14). First-year or juvenile (unpaired) Buzzards in Strathspey occupied, and some defended, small winter home ranges. These were mainly on farmland in open country, and did not overlap the adults' territories. The ranges of 11 colour-marked, or otherwise recognizable, juveniles varied from 24–45 ha, average 35 ha. They were thus much smaller than those of resident pairs in winter. A few birds subsisted partly or wholly within adult-occupied territories and even defended a home range against intruders, but not against the owners which presumably were their parents.

Interestingly, in colder winters the paired Buzzards retreated to lower parts of their territories on the valley floor where they defended smaller areas of 45–200 ha, average 105 ha. On Dartmoor, likewise, some pairs with larger territories were seldom seen in winter on the higher slopes and commons; but instead confined their hunting to core parts with ample perches in the valleys. Only in severe conditions did the Dartmoor birds appear to move down, temporarily, to sheltered lower districts outside the study area.

North Somerset

Buzzards breed now at very high densities in the farmed lowlands of a 75 km^2 area studied by Prytherch (2013). The undulating pastoral landscape – of valleys separated by ridges up to 200 m in altitude – is fairly typical of much of south-west England. The land use is predominantly (66%) enclosed grass fields of various kinds, including flower-rich meadows. There is little arable land (12%). The many woods and spinneys (17%) are mainly deciduous, with scattered conifers. Most of the Buzzards here nest in hillside woods, the rest in trees along the broad valley bottoms. Villages and other man-made constructions make up the remaining 5%. Buzzard territories have become much smaller during a five-fold rise in Buzzard numbers between 1988 and 2010. Mean size more than halved, from 139 ha to 56 ha, during these 23 years. Territories of individual pairs ranged in size from 233 ha (in 1994) to only 18 ha (in 2007). By the end of the study, territories occupied virtually the entire habitable countryside.

New Forest

The Buzzards of this ancient 292 km^2 forest appear to be unusual because, as noted earlier, they defend combined nesting and hunting territories wholly within mature woodland and along its edges. These boundaries could not be determined by direct observations (Tubbs 1974). Instead, the average sizes of defended areas around nests were estimated indirectly, using the average distance (1.4 km) between neighbouring nests. It was then assumed that each pair defended an area enclosed within a circle of a radius equal to half the average nearest-neighbour distance. The resultant population average value was approximately 225 ha. However, most pairs also hunted over large, but ill-defined and undefended, areas stretching for up to 3–5 km across adjoining farmlands (Tubbs 1974).

Germany

A similar indirect method was used in southern and western regions of Germany, where Buzzards likewise nested in large forests and woods surrounded by farmland (Melde 1956). As in the New Forest, it was particularly difficult to assess the sizes of entire (nesting plus foraging) territories in the extensive woodlands, where pairs were well scattered. Most total territory sizes do not seem to have been measured by direct observations. Rather, the nesting areas, which were vigorously defended, were mapped as roughly circular or elliptical home ranges around each woodland nest. One such pair was never seen outside a wooded area of 1300 m by 550 m, or 72 ha. Melde further noted that where good numbers of Buzzards inhabited more open country the nesting territories typically had radii of 600 m, equivalent to 110 ha. It is not clear, however, if birds ever hunted outside these defended areas. In another and similar region, 18 territories were estimated to occupy 80–180 ha, with an average of 130 ha (Mebs 1964). Unlike Buzzards in Britain, the German populations were not resident all year. Only a few birds remained during winter, and they were then joined by immigrants from elsewhere (Melde 1956).

Sweden

Buzzards remain in and defend their nesting territories all year in the southernmost lowlands of Sweden, at the latitude of southern Scotland (Sylvén 1982). The well-wooded farmland habitats support a diversity of prey species. Nesting territories appear to have varied in size between approximately 50 and 125 ha with minimal overlaps and often small gaps between them. In winter, however, these Swedish pairs also had to defend their territories against both immigrant Common Buzzards and Rough-legged Buzzards arriving from northern regions. Careful mapping of bird movements showed that winter territories were somewhat smaller but largely discrete from those taken up by the winter visitors.

Other Buteo hawks

In California, breeding Red-tailed Hawks also strongly defend a defined hunting and breeding territory (Fitch *et al.* 1946). They show behaviours very similar to those of Buzzards on Dartmoor. Their territory sizes and shapes depend on the food supply, the number and distribution of perches, local topography and population pressure. In this American study, an average land area of 130 ha was available per pair of hawks. Defended territory sizes –

as enclosed by defended perches only – were quite small, 30-80 ha, and in effect were core ranges. The discrepancy was due to the presence of 'shared' peripheral areas around each defended territory. This particular population exhibited constant territorial friction, and was believed to be near saturation density.

TERRITORY PERMANENCE

On Dartmoor, the number and spatial pattern of Buzzard territories and nests sites have remained more or less constant for at least the past 50 years (Fig. 10.2). The dispersion of nest sites remained little changed throughout the 45 years, suggesting few changes in the basic territory pattern. In fact, five of those in the western sector existed, based on the same pattern of nest distribution, back in the early 1940s (Robinson 1945, Dare 2013). Most territories in this study area were still recognizable in 2009, apart from relatively small local boundary adjustments. These were made when incorporating two additional pairs that had appeared as Rabbits slowly increased. These settled along the northern moorland margins.

During this study, any territory that fell vacant was not immediately annexed by the neighbours but remained empty until new birds arrived. Consequently, a consistently productive Dartmoor territory (as doubtless elsewhere) is a valuable resource, or 'real estate', to be inherited and defended vigorously by a succession of Buzzard pairs. According to some recent ideas, these are thought most likely to be 'high quality' individuals, whereas least productive territories become occupied by lower status birds, such as prospecting immature Buzzards. That notion might explain why even poorly performing territories continued to be occupied within the local dispersion pattern.

On Dartmoor, where the long-established Buzzard population has been quasi-stable for decades, the territorial pattern has seemed virtually immutable. Nevertheless, territories do appear to have been flexible to some extent over time, to a limited degree, in response to changing population pressures arising from new pairs attempting to settle peripherally, some perhaps temporarily. This had happened there sometime in the period 1970–1990 (Fig. 10.2). Similar events were noted in Strathspey (Halley 1993).

Clues about how additional Buzzard territories become established among an existing pattern can be provided by observing the expansion of an already established population. In Snowdonia, for example, a formerly slow increase in breeding numbers has recently accelerated and led to a doubling within 20 years (Driver & Dare 2009). The increase was achieved in part by settling on higher mountain slopes, but mainly by in-filling. Newcomers either took over the spaces between existing lower altitude territories, or they usurped part of larger holdings (J. Driver, *in litt.*).

TERRITORY QUALITY

The quality of a Buzzard territory may be inferred from its ability to sustain a successful breeding pair over a sequence of years. A combination of factors evidently is involved, particularly habitat composition and land use, which together determine the variety of available prey biomass and potential breeding productivity. Particular resource factors are likely to be: the local distributions of productive habitats, adequate hunting perches, safe and secluded nesting sites, and lack of undue human disturbance. Habitat diversity provides scope for Buzzards to exploit a greater range of preys that become plentiful at different times of year. On Dartmoor, for example: Frogs appear in early spring in bogs, young Rabbits on farmland and heaths from mid-spring into autumn, voles and other small mammals on rough grassland from early summer through autumn, and earthworms on pastures during wet autumn and winter conditions. Size of a Buzzard territory in itself is not necessarily a reliable predictor of breeding success, as the Dartmoor study showed (Appendix 10). There, for example, Buzzards with a compact 73 ha farmland territory regularly bred just as successfully as others occupying far larger semi-moorland territories; and occasionally successful breeding occurred in the even smaller (53 ha) neighbouring territory.

Breeding success on Dartmoor was monitored for 17 years, from 1956–69 and 1990–93. This revealed three persistent territory groups (A–C) of differing quality, as measured by (a) annual occupancy rate, (b) frequency of breeding attempts, and (c) fledgling production (Appendix 10, also 27b). During the 221 nest-years, an average 86% of the 13 territories were occupied by pairs each spring, eggs were laid in 71% and young were fledged in 65%. The average annual production of fledglings amounted to 0.57 per territory, 0.71 per breeding pair and 1.43 per successful pair. However, although most territories were occupied every year, there were consistent disparities between the breeding success of their occupants. Over all years, in the five best territories (A group) annual occupancy was very high (96%), most pairs laid eggs (87%) and reared young (76%). By contrast, in the four poorest performing territories (group C), while most (79%) also were occupied each year, far fewer pairs (33%) attempted to breed and only 24% were successful. The average sizes of successful broods varied little (1.30-1.50) between groups.

Most strikingly, nearly two-thirds (65%) of all young fledged in this area were reared by pairs in just 38% of territories. Good and poor territories sometimes abutted one another. These differences were consistent between both study periods, despite annual variations in general success. They suggest that, over the long-term, even 'permanent' Buzzard territories within a small area can retain wide individual differences in the quality of their habitats and reproductive potential.

This disparate breeding performance of Buzzard pairs at the local level is probably not uncommon, for similar evidence is accumulating from 35 years of observations in Snowdonia (J. Driver, *in litt.*). A few territories there have been occupied annually by pairs for more than 30 years and with a high frequency of breeding success. In others, both occupancy and performance have been more intermittent and erratic. The best territory, sited on lower slopes, now has been occupied continuously for 32 years (since 1981) and probably had been established in the late 1970s. Annual monitoring of breeding performance here showed that eggs were laid in 19 of the last 21 years, 18 broods were reared, from which 30 young fledged at an average of 1.43 each year. In an adjoining territory that has been occupied annually for 34 years, Buzzards bred in at least 25 years and were successful in 22 of those years.

In North Somerset, land use on rich farmlands was found to affect the breeding productivity of Buzzards (Prytherch 2013). Pairs inhabiting territories in which more than half of the land was made up of arable fields fledged significantly fewer young than pairs in territories with less than 20% arable. The annual average differences varied between 0.25–1.5 young fledged per pair. The reasons for this have not been investigated but quite likely reflect, in part, the impoverished prey fauna normally associated with intensive cultivation of cereal and other crops. This finding could have implications for Buzzards that are presently recolonising many eastern counties where arable farming dominates the landscape.

For Buzzards in Germany, a sign of territory quality is considered to be occupancy rate, which was positively related to breeding success (Kostrzewa 1996). In Finland, during years of low vole abundance, Buzzards bred successfully only where habitat (and presumably prey) diversity was high (Löhmus 2003). Recent detailed studies of other raptors have produced similar findings. In a migratory population of the related Red-shouldered Hawk of North America, studied for more than nine years, 44% of the young were produced in just 25% of the nest areas (nesting territories), whereas the least productive 25% produced only 7% of all young hawks (Dykstra *et al.* 2009). The authors concluded that such contrasts were likely indicators of differences in habitat qualities between individual territories. Among Sparrowhawks in southern Scotland, a long-term study found that the most productive 50% of nesting territories produced 83% of all young (Newton 1991); an output virtually identical to that of Black Kites in northern Italy (Sergio & Newton 2003). The equivalent value for the most productive 50% of Buzzard territories on Dartmoor was 74% of fledglings. In all these other raptor studies the most productive territories were those most frequently occupied. This has led to the proposal to use territory occupancy frequency as a reliable indicator, or a quick practical guide, for the initial evaluation of territory, and hence habitat quality, at the landscape scale. However, this was not the case among Buzzards on Dartmoor where occupancy rate was high (79%) even in the least productive territories. This difference could be a result of the Buzzard's highly sedentary and territorial lifestyle in Britain, features not displayed by the other Buzzard and raptor populations studied, cited above.

Future challenges for raptor workers will be to find methods for estimating the available prey biomass in different Buzzard territories, and to discover how Buzzards themselves appraise the prey resources of an area and its suitability as a breeding territory.

SUMMARY

- Buzzard pairs in Britain remain throughout the year in combined hunting and breeding territories. These are advertised by frequent use of conspicuous boundary perches and soaring flights; and are defended by vocal and aerial displays backed, if need be, by the males aggressively chasing intruders.

- Territory sizes reflect population density, land use, habitat composition and (presumably) prey availability, but sizes can be highly variable even between adjacent pairs. Upland territories may range from 50 ha to 630 ha in extent; lowland territories from about 20–230 ha. Some pairs breed successfully in territories as small as 50–70 ha on hill farms, whereas others in large territories with more moorland may succeed only intermittently.

- In a long-established Dartmoor population, Buzzard territories are well-defined entities that have been inherited by a succession of occupants for at least 45 years. Minor boundary adjustments were made to accommodate a few new pairs mainly around the margins of the study population. Some territories in Snowdonia are known to have been occupied continuously, and have sustained a high level of breeding success, for 30–35 years.
- Territories vary greatly in quality, defined as the capacity to sustain successful breeding pairs over a run of years. Size alone is not a reliable indicator of reproductive potential. In the quasi-stable Dartmoor population most territories were occupied by pairs each year, but 65% of all young fledged were produced from only 38% of territories; a result in line with recent findings from other raptor studies.

11

ENERGY AND FOOD NEEDS

The amounts of food required by a bird of prey to survive each year and enable it to breed successfully, or to estimate its potential predation impacts upon particular prey species, are key questions underlying many ecological studies. Fundamentally, however, all are governed by the amount of energy required to sustain essential life cycle functions. Whether results are expressed in terms of prey numbers, prey biomass or energy units consumed, all are difficult to assess for wild raptors. This chapter summarises prey consumption information for the Common Buzzard obtained during my research project on Dartmoor, at Postbridge (Dare 1961). These results then can be compared with the theoretical energy requirements of Swedish Buzzards (Sylvén 1982). This aspect is presented first. These remain the only two studies of a *Buteo* species in Europe, whereas several related *Buteo* species in North America have been investigated (Glading *et al.* 1943, Fitch *et al.* 1946, Olendorff 1975).

ENERGETIC CONSIDERATIONS

Adult energy requirements

The energy that a Buzzard expends each day performing activities essential for its survival, and with seasonal additions when breeding, together determine the amount of food which a hawk needs to catch and eat daily at different times of the year. Information is available for Common Buzzards from a pioneering, yet little known, study in southern Sweden (Sylvén 1982). There, as in Britain, adult Buzzards are sedentary and remain in territories all year. The time spent by Buzzards on their daily and seasonal activities (time budgets) was constructed for each sex from field observations over two years. The energetic costs of each activity were estimated by applying published physiological data, and then combining them with the field data to calculate a total energy budget. This daily energy expenditure (DEE) is expressed in kilocalorie (kcal) units. The aim was to get a satisfactory picture of the relative costs of various seasonal activities additional to those of maintaining a bird's life support functions, its daily basal metabolism.

The basal metabolic rate (BMR) differs between the sexes, being higher (81 kcal/day/kg body weight) in the smaller male than in the larger female (75 kcal/day/kg). It also varies with seasonal changes in ambient temperature (and thus thermoregulation costs) and as body weight fluctuates, especially its gradual winter decline as fat stores are consumed. The estimated combined cost of these vital processes (termed 'resting' by Sylvén) ranges seasonally between 113–130 kcal/day for males and 131–147 kcal/day for females. Efficient plumage insulation keeps temperature regulation costs low, at 20 kcal/day in winter and less in the warmer seasons. Passive hunting from perches is regarded as a form of resting with no extra costs. To these daily energy requirements are added the activity costs of: gliding and soaring flight (10 kcal/hr), flapping flight (36 kcal/hr), egg production (88 kcal per egg), incubation and brooding (probably negligible), and the annual moult which lasts five months (19 kcal/day for males, 24 kcal/day for females).

Sylven (1982) found marked seasonal changes in the daily energy expenditure of Buzzards that were breeding and rearing two young in southern Sweden (Figure 11.1). DEE is lowest in winter then rises rapidly in males through spring as aerial activities increase linked to territory defence, courtship and hunting. In early April male Buzzards spent 20% of daytime in the air: 17% soaring or gliding around, and 3% in active flapping flight. Their aerial display activities then fell back to 1% or less in May, once the females were incubating. However, these reduced flight energy costs were offset by the increased hunting effort necessary to feed the female and, later in May, also the newly-hatched brood. In contrast, females flew less actively and for a shorter period in spring prior to laying eggs. For both sexes, peak DEE was reached in June (males) or in July (females) when feeding their broods. The later peak of the female is a result of her initial brood care duties which delay her participating in hunting. At the peak, male Buzzards spent 3–4 times more energy each day than they did in winter, but females only doubled their winter costs.

The large increase in DEE needed for successful breeding is achievable because of the longer daylight now available for hunting, which increases with latitude. In southern Sweden, the Buzzards were active for 18 hours a day in June. In Britain, day length (officially, sunrise to sunset) in south-west England doubles, from 8 hours in December to around 16.5 hours in June; and it nearly trebles in the Scottish Highlands, from 6.5 hours to about 18 hours in June. Thus, compared with Buzzards in the south-west, Scottish birds have 1.5 hours (11%) more daylight available in June but, and perhaps more importantly, 1.5 hours (19%) less time in mid-winter. Buzzards are great twilight hunters, especially of Rabbits. Taking twilight periods into account could lengthen available hunting time in June by at least a further two hours in Scotland though by less in south-west England. From August onwards, and with the gradual departure of their youngsters, the DEE of adult Buzzards returns steadily to lower winter levels by October or November.

It is instructive to compare the averages of DEE during the seasons when Buzzards are least and most active. The DEE estimates, averaged for both sexes, are 149 kcal in winter (November–February) and 278 kcal when breeding (April–July). For an entire year, the total energy costs amount to some 56,300 kcal for males and 61,300 kcal for females. The average requirement for an adult Buzzard is some 58,800 kcal, equivalent to the energy value of about 39 kg of food.

Energy content of preys

Estimates of annual energy requirements can be converted to the equivalent weight (biomass),

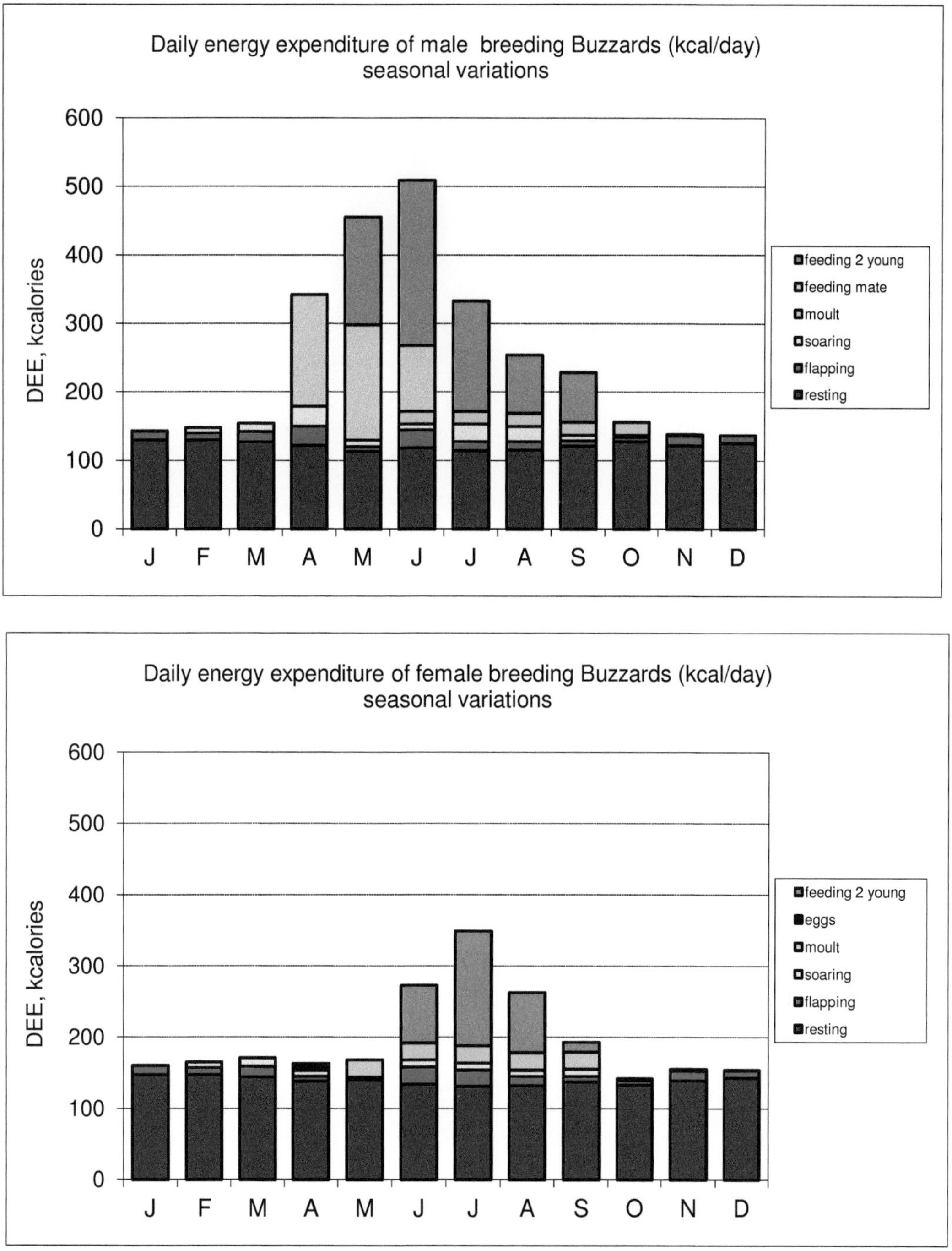

Figure 11.1 Seasonal variations in daily energy expenditure (DEE) for a breeding pair of Common Buzzards rearing young, showing the energetic costs of each essential activity (redrawn from Sylvén 1982)

and hence numbers, of any prey species that a Buzzard would need to eat. That depends on the energy (caloric) value of the main prey animals. In small rodents, Rabbits and bird preys the energy value of their flesh (muscle) ranges between 1.4–1.5 kcal/g when fresh (Appendix 3). For practical purposes, 1.5 kcal/g is a reasonable value to use when estimating the energy content of these foods. Values for other small mammals probably are similar. That of frogs, however, is much lower, 0.75 kcal/g, and similar values are assumed for snakes and other reptiles. No allowance is made here for the proportion (82%) of the food intake that a Buzzard actually absorbs, its 'apparent digestive efficiency' (Barton & Houston 1993), the remainder being ejected after digestion as faecal and pellet materials.

The caloric values of invertebrates (Appendix 3), sometimes eaten by Buzzards in considerable amounts, show that they are, perhaps surprisingly, more nutritious than Frogs. For example, the energy value of earthworms (Lumbricidae) is 0.81 kcal/g fresh weight, caterpillars (Lepidoptera) 1.33 kcal/g, and leatherjacket larvae (Tipulidae) 0.98 kcal/g.

The two most important preys of Buzzards on Dartmoor were Short-tailed (Field) Voles and young Rabbits, with approximate mean weights of 20 g and 250 g. Their energy value should amount to 30 kcal and 375 kcal per animal. Frogs, an important spring food of some Buzzards, should provide about 20 kcal for an average 25 g individual. On this basis, the winter DEE (149 kcal) of Swedish Buzzards is equivalent to 100 g of food, or five voles, which matches some consumption estimates also of Dartmoor birds (see below). However, in colder Swedish winters the Buzzards probably relied upon body fat stores and reducing activities when prey was in short supply. The estimated annual energy requirement of 58,800 kcal for a breeding Buzzard thus can now be expressed in prey equivalents as: 1,960 Short-tailed Voles or 157 young Rabbits. The additional needs of a growing Buzzard brood are described below.

ASSESSING FOOD CONSUMPTION

The amount of food required by wild Buzzards on Dartmoor during the year was estimated from two sources: prey remains in the pellets of adults, and the fresh kills brought for nestlings. It is well known that correctly interpreting hawk diets from pellet remains is fraught with difficulties. The two main ones are: (a) unknown pellet production rates, and (b) the extents to which different key small prey species are digested (differential digestion) and subsequently are identifiable in pellets. Combining results from studying these two processes should provide more reliable measures of prey composition and then, by using prey biomass data, of the daily food intake rates. Feeding experiments with captive hawks are therefore necessary. Such a programme of feeding experiments was carried out with two fledgling Buzzards taken from nests not far from the study area. They were maintained in healthy condition in outdoor aviaries and were fed entirely on natural prey species. After nine months, the Buzzards were 'hacked back' into the wild in the early spring (and near their birthplace) by a falconer (full details in Dare 1961).

Pellet production

This is a complex and variable process, as the experiments revealed. The frequency of pellet production relative to the number of days when food was eaten ('food days'), and to the size and type of prey, was measured during eight feeding experiments spanning 51 days. The diets were varied so as to simulate prey conditions experienced by Buzzards on this moor. Pellet dimensions and weights are given in Appendix 4. Fresh pellets were equivalent to 8%, and dried pellets to 3%, of the daily weight of food eaten. Each Buzzard produced on average close to one pellet per day (Appendix 16). However, significantly more pellets (1.06 per day) were ejected when eating only Short-tailed Voles, and similar size prey (such as Frogs), than when eating a mixed diet including occasional larger preys such as Rabbit, Brown Rat or thrush-size birds (0.76 pellets per day).

A switch to feeding only on large preys usually interrupted an otherwise regular sequence of daily pellet production. Where Rabbits were taken regularly, the corresponding fur pellets were large and of two types. Approximately one half contained bone and tooth remains, sometimes in quantity, whereas little more than bone traces occurred in the others. These observations suggested that two pellets were normally produced from a large meal of Rabbit, and that only the first contained many bones. The captive birds would usually eject pellets 20–22 hours after consuming a large prey such as Grey Squirrel. In one Dartmoor territory, where Rabbit figured prominently in the diet, a Buzzard was seen to cast two large pellets within five minutes during the afternoon. Wild Buzzards cast pellets at various times of day, for while many were found beneath known overnight roost trees, others were under their scattered hunting perches.

When the captive Buzzards ate Rabbits or Grey Squirrels fairly frequently, the associated pellets were delayed ('held over') by one day on 10–20% of the food days (Appendix 15). For this reason, wherever practical, the pellet data were separated into those from Buzzards with, and those without, a regular supply of Rabbits in their territories. Holding-over was a feature also of a captive adult Red-tailed Hawk (Fitch *et al.* 1946). The rate of pellet production by my two Buzzards was higher than that of the Red-tailed Hawk. However, that bird, which produced on average only 0.38 pellets per day (over 61 days), was given a diet of large rodents. It occasionally dropped pellets on successive days. Wild Red-tails often do not feed daily, according to the authors. The influence of meal size upon pellet frequency was also shown by a captive Short-eared Owl, a major predator of Short-tailed Voles in Wales (Chitty 1938). For that bird, the length of time that a pellet was retained appeared to increase logarithmically with meal size.

Differential digestion of prey species

The differential digestion of the main Buzzard preys is the greatest single source of error for the interpretation of pellet data. The identification and counting of vertebrate remains in pellets relies on the resistance of diagnostic skeletal structures and other hard parts to powerful gastric action. Most identifications depend upon the preservation of bones and teeth, the resistance of which to digestion is likely to be affected by several factors – prey species, individual age/size, the variety of preys eaten during a day, and time spent in the stomach prior to a pellet being regurgitated. The last factor applies especially to the last items to be eaten in the day. For example, occasional Dartmoor pellets contained small preys with some undigested flesh still adhering to bones. Food retention time and digestive efficiency are governed by the length of the small intestine, where food absorption takes place. This organ is relatively much longer in Buzzards, Red Kites and other generalist feeding birds of prey than that in bird-hunting specialists such as Peregrine and Sparrowhawk (Barton & Houston 1993). This feature enables Buzzards to digest efficiently a wide variety of foods including low-quality decomposing carrion, but poses problems for ecologists.

The captive Buzzards were fed the three commonest small prey species (Short-tailed Vole, Common Shrew and Frog) in order to compare the ratios of numbers of animals identifiable in pellets with the known numbers eaten. Diets were either entirely of voles or of voles mixed with other small rodents and shrews. The ratios provide a correction factor or 'recovery conversion factor' (RCF) for each species. The RCFs could then be applied to estimate the true numbers of animals represented by remains in pellets of wild Buzzards. Details of the eight experiments (spanning 56 days) are given elsewhere (Dare 1961). The nature of pellet prey remains of each species is given in Appendix 11. Results from the two Buzzards were almost identical.

Short-tailed Vole: Only one third (104) of the 312 voles eaten could be identified in pellets (Appendix 12a). This proportion was not constant, however, but varied with the daily numbers eaten (Appendix 13). Thus, pellet contents became increasingly inaccurate indicators when vole consumption increased from one to three voles per day. When 4-9 voles were eaten daily, however, as might be expected in the wild at times, roughly 30% were identifiable. Taking all data into consideration, the average identification rate is equivalent to a recovery conversion factor (RCF) of x3. This value was applied to estimate vole consumption from the monthly collections of pellet remains of wild Buzzards.

Shrews: Common Shrews and a few Pygmy Shrews were mixed with other small mammals, although the numbers available and eaten (53) were rather small (Appendix 12a). The combined recovery rate of 20.8%, considerably lower than that for voles, provided an RCF of x5.

Common Frog: To provide roughage for pellet formation, a vole was added to the amphibian meals. All 33 Frogs were eaten avidly. The combined data (Appendix 12a) show that only 24.8% of Frogs eaten were traceable in pellet remains, thus giving an indicated x4 RCF.

Comparing pellet contents with a known diet

Finally, the combined digestive effects when the Buzzards ate a simulated natural diet of mixed preys were assessed (Appendix 12b). In a further four experiments, the captives were given mostly Short-tailed Voles and other small mammals varied with a few larger mammals, birds, frogs and reptiles. When RCFs were applied to the pellet remains, a reasonable reconstruction of the original diet was achieved, notably for the rodents, shrews and birds. The over-representation in pellets of birds, and under-representation of shrews, were corrected as was, to a lesser degree, that of Frogs. The results thus validated the use of recovery factors to obtain more realistic assessments of wild Buzzard diets from pellet material. This study apparently remains the only one of its kind.

DAILY FOOD CONSUMPTION

The daily amount of food that Buzzards eat has been assessed both directly, for the two captive birds which were fed natural preys in large outdoor aviaries, and indirectly, from the prey remains in pellets of wild Buzzards on Dartmoor.

CAPTIVE IMMATURE BUZZARDS

The feeding trials provided many insights into feeding behaviour and consumption patterns when Buzzards have ample and reliable amounts of prey, as would have been the case (pre-1954) when Rabbits were super-abundant throughout Britain. Initially, when the fledglings were six to eight weeks old, and fed mainly Rabbits for 17 days, they ate a daily average of 150 g per bird. With body weights at the start of 870 g and 875 g, their mean daily consumption represented 17% of body weight. Very large meals were sometimes eaten: 265 g (30.5% of body weight) on the first day, and 235 g (*c.*26%) on the penultimate day. Two further feeding trials, on a basic diet of Grey Squirrels offered in excess, were conducted in autumn (29 days) and the early spring (15 days). By then, and just before their release to the wild, the hawks' body weights had risen to 1,053 g and 1,075 g, values typical for female Common Buzzards.

In the autumn trial (Figure 11.2), food intakes varied greatly from day-to-day between fasting and gorging, but the two patterns were not synchronised. Consistent differences in consumption were shown, however, with hawk 'B' having both an absolute and a proportionally greater daily consumption. Whereas 'A' ate no more than 25% of its body weight in a day, 'B'

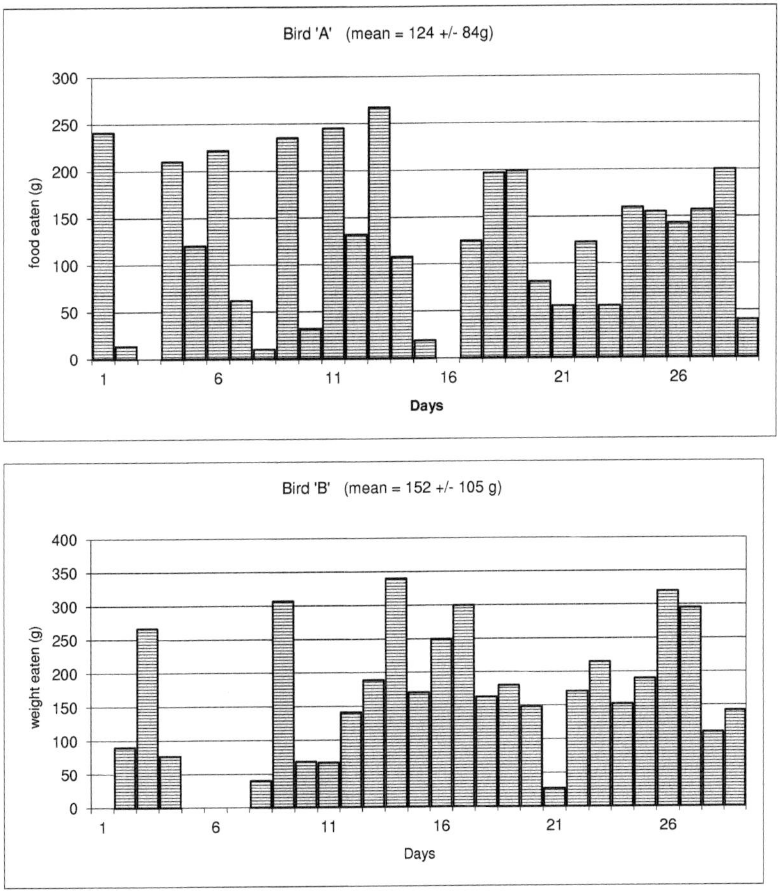

Figure 11.2 Daily food consumption patterns in autumn of two juvenile Devon Buzzards held in outdoor enclosures and fed a diet of Grey Squirrels (Dare 1961)

exceeded this intake on six days and reached a maximum of 31.6%. Overall, their mean daily food consumptions were 124 +/– 84g and 152 +/– 105g, equivalent to 11.8% and 14.1% of body weights (Appendix 14).

The spring feeding trial, in early March, again produced highly variable daily consumption rates. This time, the birds' mean daily intakes (142 g and 143 g) were identical (Appendix 14) and, being equivalent to 13.0% and 13.5% of their body weights, were close to the autumn values. Both birds also performed major feats of gorging, eating 340 g and 378 g in one day, or 32.4% and 34.4% of their body weights. Combining results for all 44 days (Appendix 14) gives a value for the two full-grown juvenile or first-winter Buzzards of 140 g daily food consumption, equivalent to 13% of body weight. In energy terms, these Buzzards consumed 210 kcal/day, some 50% more than that estimated for wild Swedish Buzzards in winter. For the latter birds, food would not have been as plentiful, and they would have needed to draw upon their fat reserves (Chapter 3).

The experimental findings are useful indicators of the amount of food needed to maintain a captive Buzzard's weight over the winter. For more active wild Buzzards, however, these values could be minimal requirements, although probably seldom achievable in winter. Then, available food resources and hunting time are constrained, and critically so during prolonged severe weather (Chapter 3). In Sweden the Buzzards lose weight, by 13% in males and 10% in females, as they do also in Germany. In such conditions, the ability of a Buzzard to consume huge meals (of up to one third of its own weight), when an opportunity arises, is clearly an adaptation to an uncertain food supply. It also highlights the need for each Buzzard to have deposited adequate fat reserves before winter.

There appears to be no comparable detailed information for Common Buzzards elsewhere in Europe. However, in Germany, Eylert (1986) noted that his captive birds could eat up to 420 g in a day, 'three times their daily requirements' (i.e. around 140 g and thus similar to my vales). These daily intake rates of fresh food also match values for the ecologically comparable Red-tailed Hawk in North America. In two experimental studies there, adult hawks were estimated to require daily 140 g of food, or 17% of body weight (Fitch et al. 1946), and from 117–136 g or 10–11% of body weight (Craighead & Craighead 1956).

Adult Buzzards in the wild

Estimating just how much wild Buzzards manage to eat poses many problems. On Dartmoor, the average daily food intake (DFI) was assessed from the prey remains in pellets of individual pairs that were collected each month. This approach assumes that each pellet is the product of a single day's food consumption. The numbers of small preys identified in each pellet were first corrected for digestion effects (see above), then converted to weights, from which the total prey biomass represented in each pellet was calculated. This should provide a guide to the average daily amount of food that was eaten on those days. However, the frequency of pellet production in the wild is not known but could be irregular owing to inevitable weather-related vagaries in prey availability and hunting success. Little or no food might be eaten on some days, particularly in winter. For example, a wild Red-tailed Hawk that was watched on 21 days in autumn and winter made only five large rodent kills. From these, it fed for eight

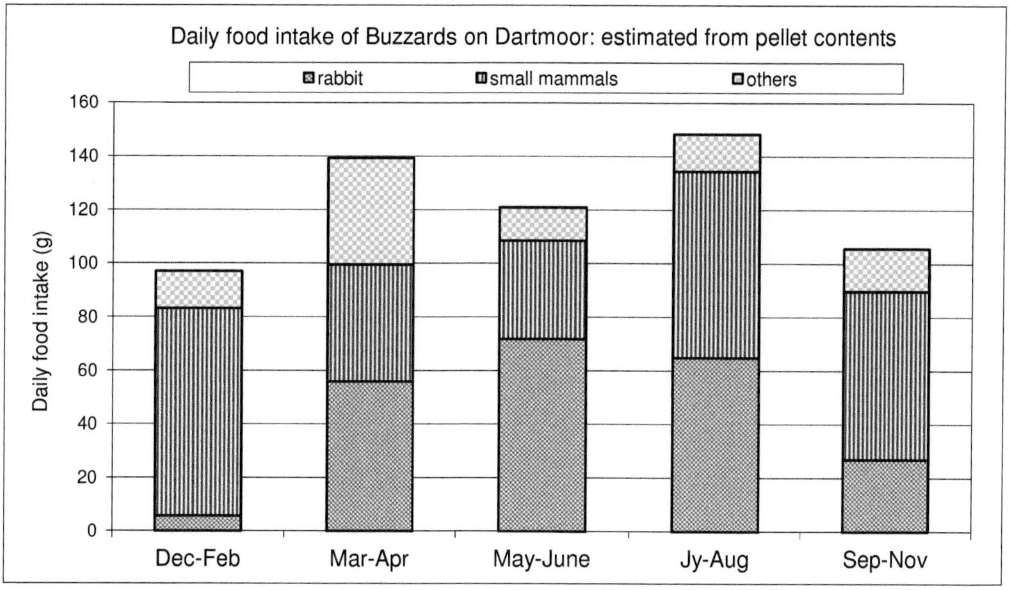

Figure 11.3 Daily food intake rates of Buzzards in the Dartmoor study area (1956–58) estimated from pellet contents after correcting for differential digestion effects.

days. Its average daily food intake was below 100 g and probably less than half its needs (Fitch *et al.* 1976).

The seasonal results for all the Buzzard territories (Fig. 11.3) indicate that daily food intakes (DFI) were lower in autumn and winter (95–106 g, or 140–160 kcal) than from March to August (120–150 g, or 180–225 kcal). The former values are close to the Swedish (theoretical) estimates whereas the latter are similar to the consumption rates of the captive Buzzards. Within this overall picture, however, there is evidence that the amount of food eaten differed according to whether or not Rabbits were available in a territory (Appendix 17).

During March–June, in three territories where Rabbits were taken regularly, they comprised 74% of the 135 g/day food intake; whereas in five Rabbit-scarce territories, where small mammals were the staple food in all seasons, the estimated DFIs were lower – 105 g/day of which Rabbits formed only 20%. During November–February, when Rabbits generally were less available, the respective intake estimates were 104 g/day (41% Rabbits) and 85 g/day (9% Rabbits).

The contributions made by Rabbits are not always straightforward to measure, because two pellets can be produced from one such large meal (see above). Buzzard pairs occasionally, perhaps regularly, share Rabbit kills and each then casts a pellet or pellets for the same kill. Sharing of Rabbit kills on the ground was noted in the area. Days of voluntary fasting after large meals might also introduce errors. In those territories where Rabbits were available, only 58 kills could be identified in 94 pellets, i.e. 0.62 Rabbits per pellet or

1.6 pellets per Rabbit meal, which is equivalent to an average consumption of 143 g (210 kcal) on such days.

FOOD REQUIREMENTS OF BROODS

Few field measurements have been made of the food consumption of raptor broods through the complete nestling period (Newton 1979). The only work in Britain was on the Sparrowhawk (Newton 1978) and no comparable information has been found for the Common Buzzard in Europe. Previously unpublished data for Buzzards on Dartmoor (Dare 1961) therefore form the basis for this assessment.

Although the amounts of food brought to Buzzard broods can be estimated from nest prey observations, not all is fed to the young. The actual proportions consumed by nestlings increase with their age and ability to feed themselves, and as the female spends increasing time away hunting (Chapter 6). In particular, amounts eaten during the first three weeks are more difficult to determine. Later, as young become more proficient at feeding themselves, a better idea of prey weights consumed daily may be inferred from the kills brought to them. For young close to fledging, the data from the two captive youngsters also can be used.

A proposed scheme of the likely food requirements of developing nestling Buzzards has been constructed (Table 11.1). For 1–5-day-old chicks (Stage I), a mean daily food intake of 30 g is assumed. Body temperature control then is inefficient and insulation poor due to the thin down covering, so that a high food intake is needed. Similarly high rates were reported for very young Snowy Owls (Watson 1957a).

From 6–14 days (Stage II) the daily food requirement is assessed at 75–100 g. The observations at the Cator nest (Chapter 7) showed that at least 75 g/day is needed. There, a mean daily weight of *c.*225g of prey was insufficient to maintain three chicks of between 4–9 days old. During the next six days (ages 10–15 days), when an average of *c.*130 g/day was brought for the two survivors, the next younger nestling also died of starvation, when 14 days old. From 15–21 days (Stage III) the daily consumption is estimated at 125–150 g of food. When the single Cator survivor received *c.*133 g/day at this age, its growth rate slowed markedly (Fig. 6.3, Chapter 7). Throughout the fourth and fifth weeks of life (Stage IV), body growth and plumage development both proceed very rapidly, and young begin wing-flapping exercises (Chapter 7). These processes require high food consumptions. A higher food intake, 150–175 g/day, is indicated then, and could exceed that of fledglings (juveniles) and adults. The captive juveniles, ate 150 g/day when weighing *c.*870 g, a weight that can be attained by day 36 (Chapter 7). It seems likely, therefore, that each nestling requires at least 150 g/day during these three weeks of fastest development. The two Stage IV youngsters in one nest (Bellever) were almost continually hungry, even when an average of more than 350 g/day of prey was brought to them. They would consume around 250 g in a day when hunting had been good and still be hungry the next day. At another nest, the 34-day old chick ate *c.*250 g of small mammals in one day.

From 6 weeks onwards until fledging (Stage V), growth and feather development has virtually finished, but wing-exercising and other activities reach a peak. It is reasonable to assume slightly lower food needs then – at *c.*150g/day – similar to that measured for the

Table 11.1 Probable food requirements of Buzzard nestlings at different ages

Stage	Age (days)	Body Weights (g) (average range) *	Daily Food Needs (g)	Total each Stage (g **)
I	1-5	40-100	30	150
II	6-14	100-300	75-100	765
III	15-21	300-475	125-150	910
IV	22-42	475-850	150-175	3,465
V	43-52	850-	150	1,500
				6,790

[*from growth curves (Fig. 7.2) ** from mid-range values of daily food needs]

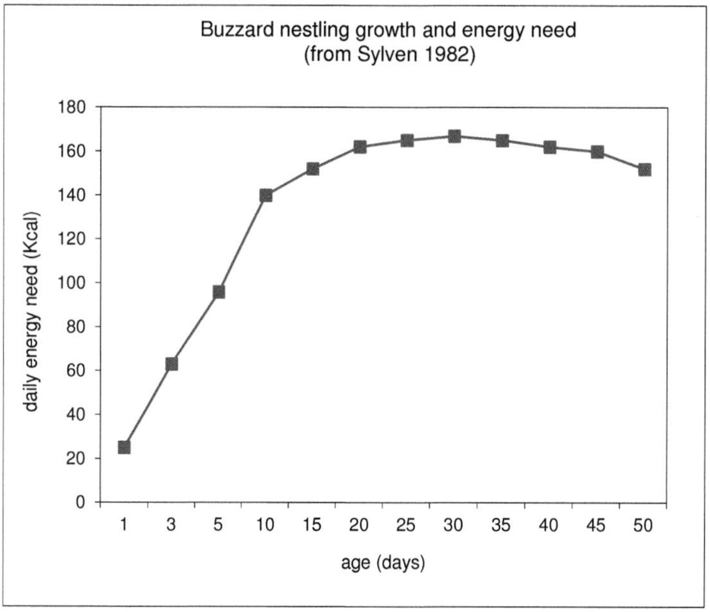

Figure 11.4 The estimated daily energy needs of a growing nestling Common Buzzard (replotted from Sylvén 1982). Note: 150 kcals is approximately the energy content of 100 g of natural prey.

captive juveniles. Indeed, growth studies of some young nestling eagles and owls found that they may eat less towards the close of the nestling stage (Sumner 1933).

A pair of Buzzards would need to provide some 7 kg of food to rear one chick to fledging; the equivalent of 350 adult Short-tailed Voles (of 20 g mean weight) or 28 young Rabbits (250 g mean weight). This amount agrees with the recorded 14.26 kg of prey brought to two young reared in 53 days by one pair (Bellever, Appendix 18); and with the 15.85 kg actually recorded at that nest over 58 days, which included the first five days after fledging. Most of the food delivered to this nest was fed to the brood. At another nest (Cator), however, where only one of three chicks survived, an estimated 12.6 kg of prey were brought to the nest, of which probably 1.6 kg was fed to the other two chicks in the first 1–2 weeks before they died (Appendix 18). The hen Buzzard is known to have eaten from the larger kills, especially Rabbits, whenever hunting was good.

The Dartmoor field data can be compared with theoretical estimates derived from the Swedish energetics study of nestling growth (Sylvén 1982). He constructed a growth path curve of the daily energy intake (Figure 11.4), based in part on a Red-tailed Hawk study (Olendorff 1974). Those young hawks attained maximum food consumption (energy demand) in their fourth week, after which it declined slightly. By then, the extra needs for increasing activities were offset by a slowing in body growth and more efficient plumage insulation. Overall, a Red-tail chick consumed 4.7 g (range 4.2–5.4 g) of food for every gram it increased in body weight through the 45-day growth period. If this conversion ratio is applied to Common Buzzard nestlings, which fledge at 850-1,000 g weight (Chapter 7), then their total food consumption should amount to only 4.0–4.7 kg for each youngster.

This assessment showed that the total energy intake of a young Buzzard reached a maximum of 165 kcal/day when young were around 25–30 days old, and that the total during 50 days in the nest amounted to about 7,200 kcal, though this was thought perhaps to be an underestimate. Such a need would equate to about 4.8 kg of prey, which is considerably lower than that observed for the Buzzards on Dartmoor. The discrepancy between field and experimental methods arises partly because the Dartmoor nest data are 'whole prey' weights, including bone and essential roughage, and of which unknown proportions were eaten by the female parents, particularly in the first two weeks. Energy figures, on the other hand, are based on flesh alone (see below) and thus will be less. Nonetheless, it seems clear that to rear one Common Buzzard youngster requires in the order of 5–7 kg of freshly caught prey, or about 5–6 times the young Buzzard's body weight at fledging.

These are not excessive amounts of prey when compared with those brought by Goshawks, which are roughly comparable in size to Common Buzzards. In Finland, broods of 2–4 young received food totals of 34–43 kg over their 45-day period in the nest, with up to 950 g in a day (Kenward 2007). Even much smaller Sparrowhawks can bring 5.9–18 kg of (mainly bird) kills to their broods of 3–4 young during their 32 days in the nest (Newton 1974).

WEIGHT LOSSES IN WINTER

Many Common Buzzards on the Continent starve to death during prolonged periods of very cold weather, as happened in Germany during the severe winters of 1939–40 (Melde 1956) and 1953–54 (Piechocki 1955). Although extreme conditions are less frequent or prolonged in Britain, they do occur; on Dartmoor 2–3 weeks of snow-cover and frost are not unusual (Chapter 2). In early 1947 and again in 1963, deep snow with severe frosts lasted at least six weeks on the moor. Prompted by the incidence of cold weather in the study area, it was decided to examine the initial effects of a short period without food upon body weight during one week in January 1958 (Appendix 19).

Throughout the previous month, the two Buzzards had been kept in good health on their basic squirrel diet. Their weights, with empty crops, immediately before the experiment started were: 1,016 g ('A') and 1,132 g ('B'). For the next seven days no food was provided and the birds were re-weighed (with minimal disturbance) at noon on alternate days until

23 January. Fortuitously, the weather suddenly turned cold with snow after the third day, thus reproducing conditions which many Buzzards may experience. The experiment was terminated after the fifth successive very cold day.

Weight losses were identical in trends and the proportional amounts lost (Fig.11.5). The birds lost 13.4% and 13.3% of their initial weight at a mean daily rate of 1.9%. The gradually decreasing rate of loss is noteworthy, and was perhaps due, in part, to reduced activity. Recovery of weight lost was rapid once normal feeding was resumed. Although feeding was hindered by the squirrel carcasses freezing during continuing night frost, both Buzzards had made up over half their weight loss by noon the next day. Their crops by then were empty at weighing, and little food had been eaten on that frosty morning. Hawk 'A' had eaten 180g and increased weight by 70 g, while 'B' had eaten 255 g and regained 108 g.

In the warmer climate of southern Spain the metabolic responses of captive Common Buzzards to an experimental 13-day fasting period, followed by 15 days of 're-feeding', have been studied (Garcia-Rodriguez *et al.* 1987). Body weight decreased linearly during the first 10 days and by day 13 had fallen on average by 26%, or 2% per day, a similar rate to that of birds in the much colder Devon winter. Blood biochemistry analyses suggested that tissue catabolism ('breakdown' of proteins) had strongly increased during fasting. This is a wasting process that ultimately would lead to emaciation, as previously found in German winter casualties. Captive healthy Buzzards in that country, as in Devon, were able to withstand 8–10 days privation 'without harm' (Eylert 1986).

For how long Buzzards can survive without food in severe winters is not known. For obvious reasons, the captive birds were not starved to anywhere near the critical point. However, weight data (Piechocki 1953) for healthy and emaciated Buzzards examined in German cold winters, show the large weight losses that may be incurred before death ensues (Appendix 20). Emaciated male Buzzards were 33% (261 g) lighter than healthy birds, and the

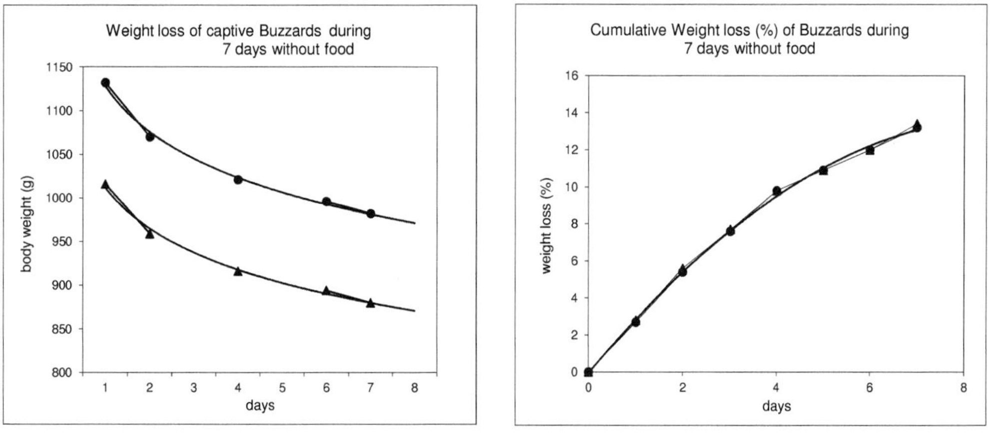

Figure 11.5 Weight losses of two captive Buzzards in winter during seven days without food in cold weather (Dare 1961)

females 43% (470 g) lighter. Incredibly, the emaciated birds' weights were similar to those of 3–4 week old Dartmoor nestlings!

The experimental results can be used to estimate the likely minimum time needed for healthy Buzzards to lose body weight to a critical extent. At a continuing daily loss rate of 1.9%, it could take approximately 17 days for males and 23 days for females to starve to death. In the wild, however, the true time to death is probably longer because the loss rate slows progressively (Fig. 11.5). Moreover, even in a very severe winter, starvation is likely to be a more protracted process because occasional carrion and live prey will be obtained by the more fortunate or fitter birds, the survivors. Buzzards starting winter with large body fat reserves should survive longer. In Germany, Piechocki (1953) measured the amount of visceral fat deposits found in healthy Buzzards that were shot between November and January in a mild winter (1951–52). Some birds carried 105–158 g of visible visceral fat, or as much as 10–14% of their body weight, whereas others had only 5-8%.

In Devon, large fat deposits were found in a female Buzzard, killed by road traffic in January 1956, which I was able to examine (Chapter 3). That bird was very heavy, at 1,220 g, and contained large visible fat deposits, the major part of which weighed 63 g or 5% of total body weight. A similar distribution of fat was reported by Piechocki (1953), who noted an extreme case where a single huge mass of fat covered the viscera (Appendix 20).

With an ability to lay down such reserves during late summer and autumn, amounting at times to 10–15% of total weight, the Common Buzzard clearly is well adapted to withstand long periods with little or no food during extreme Continental winters. In our usually shorter and less severe cold periods, most Buzzards should be able to cope for two weeks and then, upon the return of milder conditions, recover lost weight fairly quickly.

SUMMARY

- Practical and theoretical problems encountered when attempting to assess a raptor's food requirements are highlighted.
- Buzzard daily food requirements, depending on sex and seasonal activities, are estimated to range between 100 g of prey in winter and 150 g in the breeding season and in autumn. These amounts equate to 10–15% of the average body weight, and to the weight of 4 and 6 adult Short-tailed Voles.
- In a full year, an adult Buzzard requires around 39 kg of food. Breeding pairs need to provide an additional 5–7 kg of prey to rear each chick to fledging.
- For full-grown Buzzards, food intake can vary greatly from day to day and between seasons. Short-term variations are caused by weather fluctuations affecting prey behaviour and hunting conditions.
- Buzzards, like other predators, compensate for poor feeding periods by eating large meals (up to one third of body weight) when hunting is good.
- Seasonal differences in food consumption reflect within-year natural cycles in prey availability (abundance and behaviour) combined with increased energy

demands when breeding, and in autumn when laying down body fat reserves to buffer against reduced winter food resupplies.

- Most Buzzards in Britain should be able to cope without food for two weeks in severe weather, and then recover weight losses fairly quickly upon the return of milder conditions.

12

FACETS OF PREDATION

Common Buzzards are versatile or generalist predators capable of taking a wide range of preys as opportunities afford. Their food habits therefore could be expected to change continuously through the year as the main prey species fluctuate seasonally in abundance. Buzzard diets could also differ between territories and sometimes even between individuals of a pair. Several aspects of predation are explored below using data from Buzzards in the Dartmoor study area. This information should improve our understanding of the extent to which Buzzard diets and breeding success may reflect, and be controlled by, changes in prey abundance and availability. Conversely, the extent to which Buzzard predation might limit prey numbers also will be examined.

SEASONAL PREY AVAILABILITY

References have been made earlier to varying availabilities of different prey species. Here, prey availability at any given time is defined as the product of its numerical abundance combined with its exposure or vulnerability to hunting Buzzards. Among the small mammals, for example, vulnerability increases or decreases with seasonal changes in their behaviour and the extents of protecting ground vegetation and snow cover.

On Dartmoor, this approach helped to interpret prey data from pellets and nests, and to set Buzzard predation in a wider context. For this, notional monthly availability indices for key preys or prey groups were derived by combining field observations and literature information. Factors to be considered each month included: the stage in a species' annual cycle between peak and low abundance, the timing and duration of the breeding season and resultant productivity, any relevant seasonal behaviour changes (aggregations, dispersal, other movements, weather responses, hibernation), as well as vegetation cover. The availability index is scaled for each prey from 0–100 but is not numerically comparable between species or years. Instead, it provides a theoretical view of the ever-changing seasonal prey compositions, thereby identifying likely periods of highest and lowest profitability for Buzzards hunting each species (Figure 12.1a, b).

Rabbits, Short-tailed (Field) Voles and other small mammals (Figure 12.1a), including shrews (not shown), have closely similar annual cycles. From relative scarcity in winter or early spring, their numbers and availability reach summer or autumn peaks at the ends of their breeding seasons. However, catching small mammals then may be hampered increasingly by the dense new growth of ground vegetation. Thereafter, their availability declines through autumn and winter, due to mortality, until lowest numbers are reached – just at the start of the Buzzard breeding season. On the other hand, Short-tailed Voles then become increasingly vulnerable, as vegetation cover dies back, so that their decreasing abundance is offset by greater exposure to Buzzards, except when snow cover provides temporary protection. Rabbits, by contrast, spend most of the winter day in burrows, especially in cold or very wet weather. They are now all fully-grown and less easy to catch. It is not until the first young Rabbits appear above ground later in spring that their availability rises rapidly, in time for Buzzards to start feeding them to their newly-hatched brood.

Of the other three prey groups (Figure 12.1b), birds show a similar cycle to mammalian preys, but differ in that many species are totally or partly migratory to uplands, and thus absent or scarce from early autumn until their spring return. Birds reach peak availability for Buzzards in June–July when the more easily caught nestlings and fledglings of both small and large species are present in all habitats. Amphibians and reptiles differ from all other Buzzard preys in being most vulnerable to predation in the early spring, soon after emerging from hibernation. Frogs, which re-appear usually in February and early March, are easily taken where large numbers

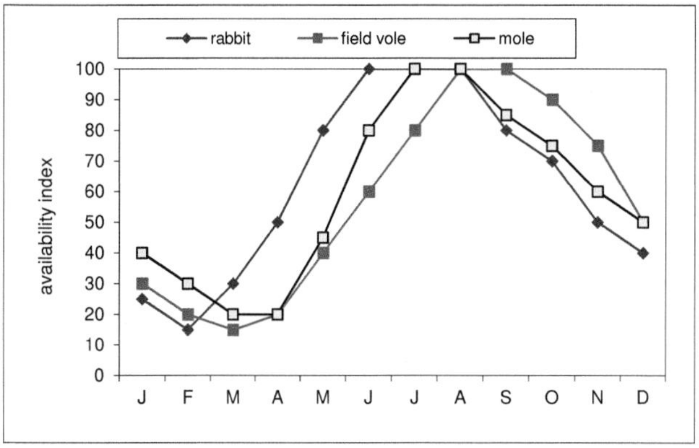

Figure 12.1a Schematic diagram of the annual cycles in the notional availabilities of mammal preys on Dartmoor. Note: the actual numerical abundance scale differs between species.

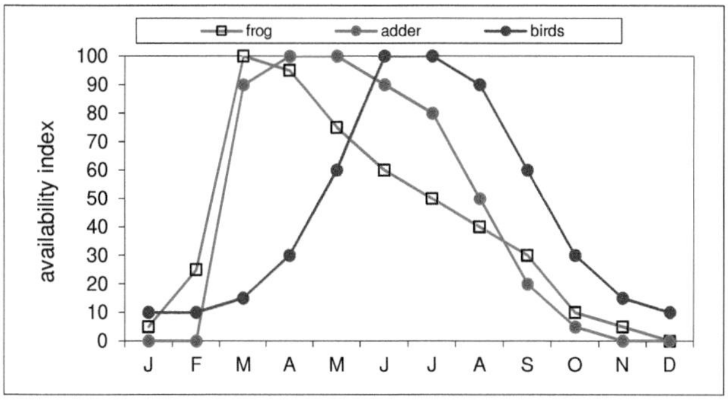

Figure 12.1b Schematic diagram of the annual cycles in the notional availabilities of bird, Frog and Adder preys on Dartmoor.

assemble at spawning sites. Afterwards, they disperse widely and become less visible in ground vegetation until they re-enter hibernation in the autumn. Adders, emerging a little later, spend much time, often in small groups, basking on dry open ground on sunny days through March and April. They are lethargic and less aggressive at this time (Prestt 1971). Later, the Adders disperse into wetter habitats and most have retired into hibernation by October.

SEASONAL PREDATION PATTERNS

The extent to which the seasonal food habits of Buzzards on Dartmoor may reflect annual cycles of prey availability can be shown in two ways, using pellet material.

Changes in prey proportions

Seasonal patterns of diet become apparent when the pie-chart data for successive two- or three-month periods (used in earlier chapters) are plotted as time series to show trends more clearly (Figure 12.2). Here, prey species' importance is expressed by relative weight, based on pellet material after adjusting for differential digestion effects. In particular, one can see that the relative proportions of Rabbits and Short-tailed Voles, with other small mammals, show clear but opposite annual cycles. Rabbits were the most important food from spring to early summer whereas small mammals, mainly Short-tailed Voles, dominated the diet in autumn and winter when few Rabbits were taken. Of the other prey groups, Frogs were important from autumn to early spring; and small but notable contributions were made by reptiles (almost entirely Adders) from March to June. Birds were taken mainly between May and August but, even then, they contributed little to the amount of food at any season.

The results for the main breeding period, May–June, are composites for adult Buzzards living in territories of contrasting Rabbit availability. As was described in Chapter 6 (Figure 6.6), the diets of these two groups differed accordingly. Not surprisingly, where Rabbits were more available, the prey composition was dominated by Rabbits (36% of captures and 68% by weight), with Short-tailed Voles and other small mammals of secondary importance. Where Rabbits were scarce, small mammals were the main food but the few Rabbits that were taken still constituted one third of the biomass of food eaten. Reptiles (Adders), unexpectedly, were the next most important prey in Rabbit-scarce territories.

Changes in predation indices

This index is the average number of animals of a species identified per pellet during given periods (Appendix 21). In the 380 intact pellets from adult Buzzards that were examined, a total of 516 vertebrate preys were identified and then grouped by two-month periods. The indices reveal seasonal changes in predation patterns of each species. Direct comparisons between index values of disparate species or groups are not valid, however, unless corrections are made for differential digestion effects (Chapter 11).

Predation on Rabbits (Figure 12.3) was greatest during spring and summer, reaching a peak in May–June, followed by decline through autumn to a late winter minimum. This pattern closely reflected availability (Figure 12.1a) and matched the seasonal and timely appearance of young Rabbit litters. Predation was heaviest when the hawks had rapidly-growing broods; young Rabbits being a crucial source of sizeable yet portable and easily captured prey. The

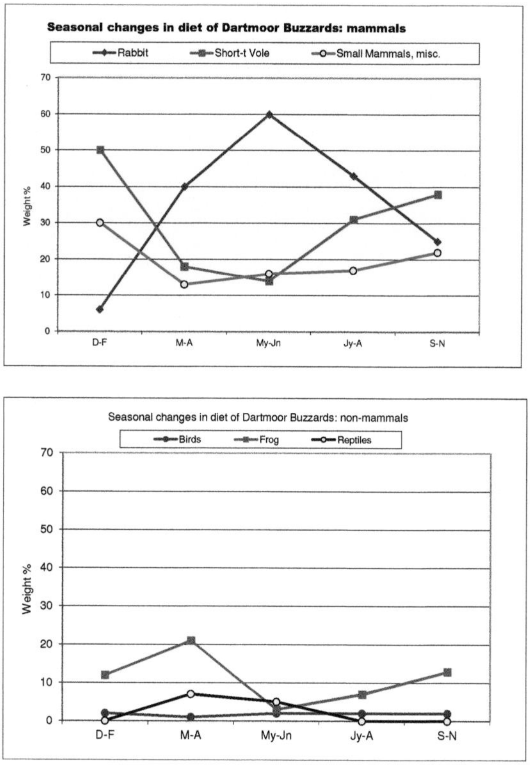

Figure 12.2 Seasonal diets of Buzzards on Dartmoor, 1956–58, by weight. From pellet material adjusted for differential digestion effects.

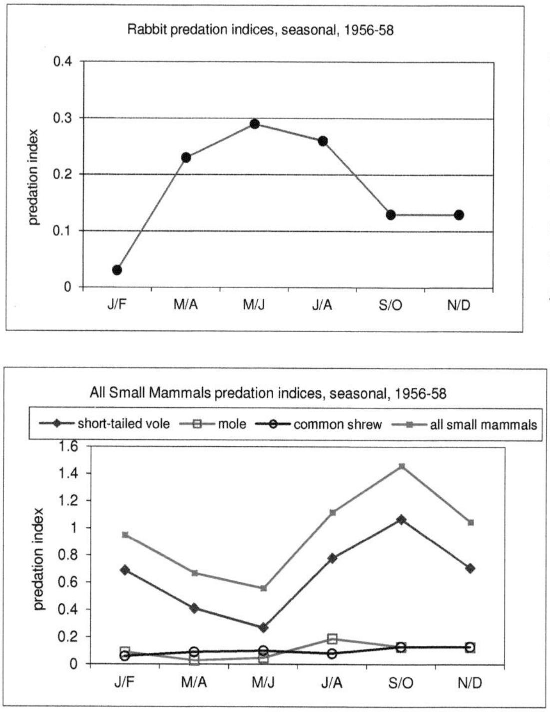

Figure 12.3 Seasonal changes in the predation indices of the main mammalian prey species eaten by Buzzards at Postbridge, Dartmoor, during 1956–58. left: Rabbit; below left: Short-tailed Vole, Common Shrew, Mole, and for all small mammals combined.

nest prey records confirmed that over 95% of all Rabbits fed to broods were only 3–6 months old. In winter, the Buzzards appeared to concentrate upon small mammals rather than wait for those few wary adult Rabbits that surfaced before nightfall.

Peak predation on Short-tailed Voles occurred in autumn (Figure 12.3). During winter and spring, the predation index fell steadily to a low level in May–June before recovering during summer. This pattern agreed well with the vole's annual cycle of availability. An apparent time lag could have been caused by growing vegetation cover and the increasing availabilities of Rabbits and other preys. This may explain why minimum vole predation was not reached until May–June, despite the appearance already of the first litters of young voles, for by then the ground cover was dense and young Rabbits would have been available. By autumn, the reduction of meadow grass cover by hay-cutting in July–August, and the subsequent die-back of coarse herbage, exposed the augmented vole population to increased predation.

Predation on Common Shrews showed little seasonal variation and was far less intense than that on Short-tailed Voles. The index was least in winter, when low temperatures perhaps drove the shrews deeper under cover, and highest in autumn, when they were most numerous and likely to be taken more often, as the Buzzards were switching to a mainly small mammal diet. Since Moles are subterranean insectivores, any changes in their vulnerability to predation will probably be related to fluctuations in earthworm numbers and soil conditions (temperatures and moisture content) in addition to the annual cycle of Mole abundance. Predation on them was always low but still showed a pattern. The index was lowest from March to June, when adult numbers were low and the young still underground, but then increased five-fold in summer, when young and some adult Moles use shallow tunnels. Some Moles in summer may disperse or even forage above ground, thereby risking detection by Buzzards. For example, Moles have been seen by day leaving their tunnels in pursuit of carabid beetles (Godfrey 1955), and another mole was watched feeding voraciously on banded snails (*Cepea* sp.) in a hedge bottom during very dry summer weather (I. J. Linn, *pers. comm.*). On Dartmoor, however, it seems certain that Mole kills were made by Buzzards from hunting perches or when, while ground- foraging in Mole-infested fields, they saw soil movements during the casting of molehills.

For birds (Figure 12.4), the seasonal predation pattern showed a minimum in winter (November–February) and a steady increase through early spring to a peak in late spring and summer (May–August) followed by decline to the winter level. From May to August birds were more numerous, diverse and available than at any other time. Fledgling and juvenile birds were brought to Buzzard nests, but the ages of bird preys in pellets could not be determined.

The reptile predation index (Figure 12.4) shows good agreement, until summer, with the availability of Adders (Figure 12.1b) and probably also with that of Common Lizards in the area. The few winter records were kills of very early emerged Common Lizards during mild weather in late February. The index was highest in spring, March–April, shortly after both reptiles had emerged from hibernation. It fell in May–June, when Adders dispersed from basking places, and to zero thereafter. The absence of summer and early autumn records

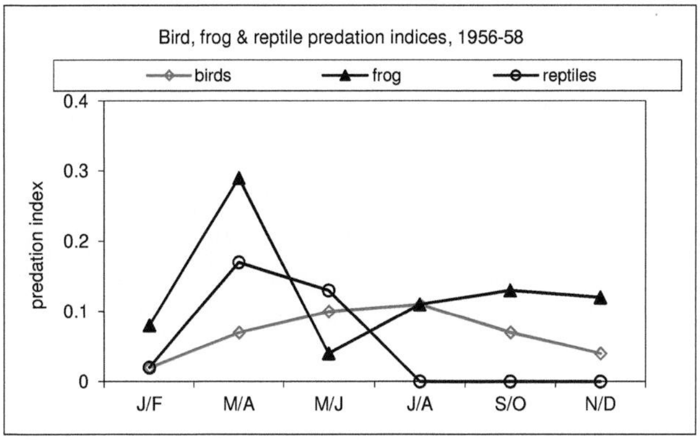

Figure 12.4 Seasonal changes in the predation indices of birds, amphibian and reptile preys eaten by Buzzards at Postbridge, Dartmoor, 1956–58.

might have been due to Adders dispersing into cover in damper habitats (Prestt 1971) and to inadequate pellet samples at this season.

The spring 'flush' of Frogs was reflected in March–April by a higher predation index (Figure 12.4) and it also corresponded with Buzzards being seen eating Frogs at the communal spawning sites. Frogs then became almost as important a prey as Short-tailed Voles, appearing just as voles were becoming scarce. The very sharp fall in the index for May–June may reflect the post-breeding dispersal by Frogs into damp and thicker cover. The reason for a secondary index rise during summer and autumn, when small mammals are most plentiful, is not clear. Some behavioural change then seems to have made Frogs more vulnerable again, perhaps by gathering once more in bogs and other wet places before retiring into hibernation. The few winter Frog records were during very mild interludes in February when several were observed.

Thus, the pellet analyses revealed seasonal variations in Buzzard food habits. These largely could be explained as the interplay between asynchronous cycles in abundance and behaviour of several main preys which, together with seasonal vegetation changes, determined their availabilities for Buzzards.

HUNTING EFFORT AND SUCCESS

How Buzzards collect enough food for their broods, and the problems they encounter due to variations in prey abundance and weather conditions, were investigated during my initial Dartmoor study, at the time when Rabbits had been almost exterminated by myxomatosis. Information was gathered in three ways: by directly observing hunting strategies and measuring prey catch rates; by using hides to record how frequently kills were delivered to nests; and by inspecting nest contents to record prey amounts and other details.

Field observations of hunting Buzzards

Buzzards were active from dawn to dusk throughout the long (16.5 hour) days of the nestling period. For example, on 20 June 1956, a pair (Soussons territory) with four-week-old young, began hunting at 05.20 BST, which was 25 minutes before sunrise. On 11 June 1958, both parents from a neighbouring nest (Cator territory) were still hunting Rabbits at 22.15 BST, when it was nearly dark. Frequent inspections of that nest each day showed that Rabbits were brought seven times more frequently in the early mornings and evenings than in the late mornings, and almost twice as often as in the afternoons. Voles and Frogs also were brought most often in early mornings. Frogs are likely to be most active in the open at night and in cool, dewy dawn conditions in summer. Normally, late hunters were males, while their mates tended the young, but as broods became well-feathered the females were also able to participate in twilight hunting.

In Finland, a similarly long working day of about 15 hours was recorded for Buzzards feeding on an ample supply of small mammals and other small preys (Suomus 1953).

In southern Sweden, the male Buzzards studied by Sylvén (1982) were active daily for 17 hours during the incubation stage, and for nearly 18 hours when feeding broods in June and July. Their daily energy expenditure rose accordingly, by 32% from the May level, to 172 kcal/day, as high as during the spring display season. The females showed a similar pattern once they had resumed hunting. The energetic cost of feeding young peaked for males in June, at 13 kcal/hour, but was later and lower for females, whose cost was 9.4 kcal/hour (details in Chapter 11).

Marked differences between partners in effort expended may occur even when month-old young are large enough to allow the female to hunt part-time. One such pair (Soussons) was watched from dawn for 14.5 hours in fine June weather with a north-westerly breeze until rain with deteriorating visibility set in (Appendix 22). Unusually, the topography of this territory and the nest site, in a broad open basin, enabled the Buzzards to be kept in view almost continuously (Figure 12.5). Rabbits were very scarce here at the time (1956). The male was a much more persistent and successful hunter, searching widely across his territory and making 11 kills of vole/shrew-size animals. He hunted for 86% (11.5 hours) of the time, including one spell of 5 hours, with only two rest periods. The female hunted in six short spells amounting to 50–60% (6.5–8 hours) and caught only two small preys. She spent almost half of her time at the nest or perhaps hunting from perches nearby.

Their searching pattern on that day covered about two-thirds of their territory (Soussons), only the lee (south-east facing) ground not being utilized. Hunting was concentrated on seven distinct areas of fields, scrub, bog and rough hillside. From these, 13 small kills, four from one area in 2.5 hours, were made and carried in the talons to the nest. Although hovering at up to 30 m was the main hunting method, some use was also made of hunting perches and ground foraging, notably in the early morning light airs before hovering was possible, and again when the weather deteriorated in late afternoon. Invertebrate prey were caught from low hovers and eaten *in situ* by the adults. The pair showed that all three hunting methods could be interchanged quickly to enhance operational flexibility.

In all, these two Buzzards were watched on four days when their brood was between 2–7 weeks old. During 25.75 hours, 23 small kills were seen being captured and brought to this nest, 87% being by the male, at an average rate of 0.9 kills an hour. Such observations thus can provide a measure of absolute success or hunting efficiency of a pair.

Figure 12.5 Part of the Buzzard territory on Dartmoor where a hunting pair was observed for 14 hours on one day in June. (See text and Appendix 22)

Hide observations: food deliveries and parental roles

Dartmoor

The rate at which prey is delivered to the brood during a closer watch from a nest hide provides a more convenient index of a pair's hunting success during that period. On Dartmoor it provided a satisfactory measure for Buzzards feeding mainly on rodents and other small animals but was less suitable where they hunted scarce Rabbits. This prey was caught outside the watch periods, mostly in late evening or early morning. For example, in one territory (Bellever) with some Rabbits, the nest was watched for 51 hours over nine days spanning the period when the two chicks were 4–27 days old. On the first five watches, when a small Rabbit had already been brought, 10 small kills were delivered, at a low frequency of 0.3 kills per hour; 60% of them by the male. On the last four watches (14 hours), when no Rabbit was on the nest, 10 small preys were brought, at 0.7 per hour, 40% by the male. The highest rates during watches lasting more than four hours were: 6 kills in 8 hours and 5 kills in 4.5 hours. It is possible that pressure to hunt was eased on days when Rabbit already was available on the nest.

Hunting success also could vary dramatically during the course of a day as was noted for the Bellever pair on 20 May, just four days after the chicks had hatched. Over a period of 10 hours (05.00–15.00 BST), the male was away and presumably hunting for all but a 2.5-hour rest period. This interlude was spent near the nest in the early afternoon, soon after rain and thick mist had arrived. By then, only one small kill had been brought to the nest and it seemed that hunting was badly affected. However, when the poor weather cleared in the early evening, the male's hunting soon became successful. Then, a late evening nest inspection at 20.30 BST revealed four fresh kills: a young Rabbit, two Short-tailed Voles and a Common Shrew. The female brooded and tended the chicks throughout in the very cool and damp air, apart from a brief absence for a few minutes. In later weeks, she was seen hunting successfully for the brood.

The observed intervals between prey deliveries to nests varied greatly, from rare simultaneous arrivals by both parents carrying kills up to an observed maximum of 8 hours. A 3–4 hour interval was not uncommon at any stage, although longer gaps were often linked with feeding on large preys. On the other hand, where Dartmoor brood diets contained more large preys (usually young Rabbits) the combined delivery rates for all preys, not surprisingly, were low, at around 0.1–0.2 kills per hour, and they also varied with time of day. There were even occasional days when no prey was brought (see below).

Finally, estimates could be made of the prey numbers and equivalent weight of food brought to nests on those days. For example, assuming a mean weight for small vertebrates (voles, Frogs and small passerine birds) of 20 g, a hunting day of 16.5 hours (as above), and an average delivery rate of 0.9 kills per hour, then: total kills = 14.8 (0.9 x 16.5) and total prey weight = 296 g (14.8 x 20 g); or (rounded to) 15 kills weighing 300 g.

North Wales

In Snowdonia, twenty years later, I observed similar prey delivery rates by Buzzard pairs in territories where, likewise, Rabbits generally were scarce. Three broods in tree nests were watched from hides on nine days for a total of 54.5 hours. The broods of one or two young were from 2–6 weeks old and at times both parents were hunting. Twenty-seven small kills (mainly Short-tailed Voles, shrews, small birds and Frogs) were brought at average rates of 0.5–0.6 kills per hour. Males brought 81% of kills. Only one Rabbit was found on a nest during these nine days. Elsewhere in Wales, a moorland Buzzard pair was watched for 32 hours by the renowned photographer Arthur Brook. They brought an average of 0.9 small kills per hour during watches, initially when feeding two young aged 3 weeks and then, after one chick had fallen from the nest, the single 5-week-old survivor (Brook 1920). Foods here comprised Moles, voles, shrews, Frogs and Mallard ducklings.

Europe

Similar success rates have been logged in some countries on the Continent. At Buzzard nests in Finland, comparable delivery rates of small kills have been recorded. Four Buzzard pairs feeding on small animals, and hunting for about 15 hours a day, brought a combined total of 358 kills in 337 hours. Their average hunting success amounted to 16.5 kills daily brought to the brood at a delivery rate of 1.1 kills per hour, and with little variation through the day

(Suomus 1953). In Poland, where Buzzards also take mainly small mammals, two pairs on average brought 6.7 and 9.7 kills, mainly moles, per day for a period of 3–4 weeks (Czarnecki & Foksowicz 1954). By contrast, in southern France, only 0.1–0.4 kills per hour were brought to two broods (video camera records) irrespective of the age of the brood (Hubert & Gallo 1995). Video recordings also have been used in Norway where the Buzzards were observed to bring 0.57 small preys an hour on average to six nests (Selås *et al.* 2007).

Nest inspections: long-term fluctuations in hunting success

On Dartmoor, intensive observations at two nests tracked the day-to-day variations in hunting fortunes by measuring the amounts of prey brought daily during seven weeks (Figure 12.6). Another two nests that were followed for only two weeks gave similar results. Nest inspections were reduced, from four to one a day, in the final 4–5 days before fledging in order to minimise the risk of causing the young to depart prematurely. At one nest (Bellever 1957), the full brood of two fledged successfully. At the other nest (Cator 1958), an initial brood of three chicks was reduced to just one fledgling. Nests were under daily observation (hides or inspections) for 72% of the time at Bellever and for 94% at Cator. Probably 90–95% of kills brought to both nests were recorded, with only some small items being undetected. In both territories Rabbits were available in small numbers, but the habitats were very different. Cator territory (72 ha) was in a farmed area with mainly pasture fields and a few small woods, whereas the larger Bellever territory (190 ha) comprised extensive and diverse conifer plantations, heaths and bog interspersed with some hill pastures.

Hunting success was erratic throughout the brood periods (Figure 12.6) with not more than 8 kills being brought in a day. Average daily delivery rates were 4.1 (Bellever) and just 1.8 (Cator), a reflection in part of the important role of Rabbits in the diets. Although average daily Rabbit captures were low (0.8 and 0.9) they comprised, respectively, 66% and 84% by weight of all food brought. Even so, no Rabbits were caught on 30% and 38% of days. The Bellever pair was able to bring, on average, more food (355 g/day) than could the Cator birds (242 g/day). Indeed, a food shortage at Cator, during very wet and cold weather, led to the deaths of the two youngest chicks when 9 and 14 days old (as described in Chapter 7). At Bellever food appeared to run very short during the fourth week despite both parents hunting but, by then, the two well-feathered chicks were strong enough to withstand a short period of privation.

The Bellever territory also was larger with more varied habitats, especially for Short-tailed Voles. This rodent comprised 40% of all captures, while a further 5% were Bank Voles. By weight, however, these voles contributed only 11% to the diet. In contrast, at Cator where vole habitats were very limited, they were 11% of kills and only 2% by weight. At both nests, other mammals provided only 6% by weight. Birds made up 10% of kills and 11% by weight at Bellever; and 18% of kills and 8% of weight at Cator. Occasional Frogs, Toads and Adders were taken, mainly at Bellever.

Immediately after myxomatosis, in my area, any residual Rabbits clearly were a valuable resource and, wherever even a few were available, it was profitable, indeed vital, for Buzzards to hunt them. The smallest Rabbits found on nests weighed 150 g (equivalent to 7 mature Short-tailed Voles) and the largest was 700 g, or more than half the body weight of an adult

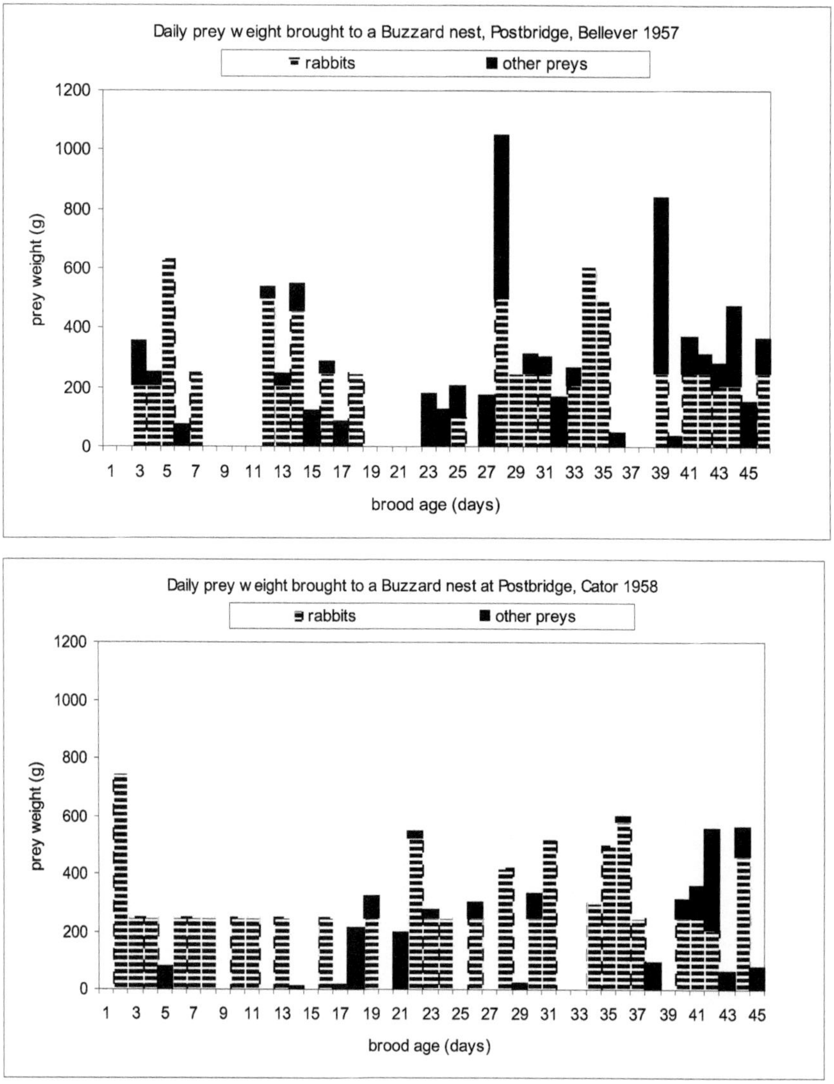

Figure 12.6. Fluctuations in the daily amounts of food brought to two Buzzard broods at Postbridge during 7 weeks in the nests. Bellever pair (left) reared its 2 young; Cator pair reared only one of three. No food was brought to Cator nest on days 9 and 12; other gaps show days of no nest inspections. Males provided all food in the first two weeks.

Buzzard. Furthermore, when chicks were small, one Rabbit kill could sustain the brood and the female parent for perhaps two days. With few exceptions the Rabbits were headless, and sometimes also missing the forelegs (Figure 6.4), the hunter having eaten them before delivering the catch.

The overwhelming impression gained, from all these field and nest prey observations, was that the Buzzards were operating at maximum hunting effort, and that the low prey amounts brought to nests reflected impoverished food resources soon after myxomatosis. Food limitations clearly were responsible for the brood reductions at Cator where the entire brood came perilously close to disaster (Chapter 7). Later monitoring of this Buzzard population indicated that the depleted food resource persisted for at least ten more years.

The Dartmoor food situation during this study was a far cry from the pre-myxomatosis era when Rabbits here and throughout Devon had been 'super-abundant'. Before 1955, some Buzzards amassed large caches of young Rabbits on their nests; 14 on one nest and 8 headless kills beside a lone chick on another! (DBRs). Further afield, in South Wales, seven Rabbits were brought to three young Buzzards during a single 11-hour photographic session (Brook 1952).

Europe

In northern countries, where small mammals often are more abundant than in our uplands, measured long-term catch rates by Buzzards are higher than any reported in British study areas. In Finland, for example, a Buzzard pair brought 668 kills, of mainly voles and other small mammals, to its brood over 42 days at an estimated average weight of 540 g/day (Suomus 1952). In Poland, where two broods were reared on a staple diet of Moles, one brood was brought an average 448 g/day for 20 days, and the other 254g /day during 26 days (Czarnecki & Foksowicz 1954).

ANNUAL CONSUMPTION OF PREYS

Information on daily food consumption rates is particularly important since it can be applied to estimate the food requirements of Buzzards. As a first step, the annual amount of food required by a pair of Dartmoor Buzzards in order to survive and breed successfully is calculated (Table 12.1) by combining the needs of adults and nestlings (Chapter 11) with those of their juveniles until they disperse from the parental territory. The total requirements

Table 12.1 Annual food consumption estimates for Postbridge Buzzard pairs and broods

No. of Buzzards in Territory	Food Required per Annum		
	Weight (kg)	Equivalent No. of	
		Voles (adult)	Rabbits (juv.)
Pair of adults	102	5,110	409
Pair rearing 1 young to dispersal	126	6,300	500
2 young to dispersal	150	7,500	600
3 young to dispersal	174	8,700	700
4 young to dispersal	198	9,900	800

note: 1. 1-2 young is the normal breeding success in Britain; 3 may be reared if food is plentiful, and 4 only where Rabbits are abundant. The 24 kg allowance per youngster allows 6 kg for nestling stage (Chapter 11) and 3 months at 140 g/day as a juvenile until dispersal from territory.

are expressed both as absolute biomass and as the equivalent numbers of either adult Short-tailed Voles (20 g mean weight) or of young (250 g) Rabbits. Ultimately, potential predation pressures on these preys can be estimated if prey abundances themselves could be assessed.

The calculations show that a pair of Buzzards resident in a territory for a year, and rearing one youngster to dispersal three months later, thus need to catch some 126 kg of food, equivalent to some 6,300 adult voles or 500 optimum-size young Rabbits. For each additional youngster reared, an extra 24 kg of food would be needed. A small additional amount should be allowed for nestlings that die in the nest.

These prey requirements are the minimum annual amount of food that a territory needs to provide and to be available at the appropriate times for the Buzzards, irrespective of the size of the territory. In my Dartmoor area, average territory sizes ranged from about 65 ha for the smallest to 210 ha for the largest. For successful breeding, therefore, Buzzards in small territories would need on average to catch about 2 kg of prey per hectare of territory, equivalent to 100 voles or 8 young Rabbits per hectare during the course of the year. In the large territories, the corresponding figures would be around 30 voles or 2–3 Rabbits per hectare. In reality, the fragmented habitat patterns within most territories resulted in patchy or clumped prey distributions. Observed Buzzard predation then tends to be concentrated on areas of rough grass (for voles), bogs (for Frogs) and around hedge banks or on heaths wherever Rabbit colonies were present.

Predation effects on prey numbers

Rabbits

The extent to which birds of prey may control the numbers of particular prey species, or *vice versa*, has long been a controversial topic among ecologists, farmers and the wider rural communities. One question that arose from the Dartmoor study was the extent to which Buzzard predation might contribute to limiting recovery rates of Rabbit populations following a myxomatosis outbreak. Before 1954 the relatively low numbers of still-persecuted Buzzards clearly had no discernible impact upon the Rabbits that then swarmed across the British countryside. Indeed, the converse was evident (Chapter 13).

Although Rabbit abundance and size composition data are lacking, the estimated potential maximum consumption of this prey by the local Buzzards (given above) suggested that only pairs in small territories might be able to help retard the initial recovery phase. In the first few years following myxomatosis on Dartmoor, the Buzzards would have been operating in conjunction with the numerous Foxes, and scarcer mammal predators. The pre-myxomatosis reports of 14 young Rabbits cached on one nest, and of seven brought in one afternoon to another nest, are striking examples of intense predation when Rabbits had been extraordinarily abundant.

A similar view is provided by a more recent assessment of factors that could limit Rabbit populations in England and Wales (Trout & Tittensor 1989). Their review of (mainly anecdotal) field evidence found that Rabbits were significantly more abundant and widespread where predators were removed, or at low densities, than where predators were undisturbed or at high densities. Predation also was reported to prolong the time that Rabbit numbers remained low following a significant reduction by some other cause. The authors concluded that predation is more likely to be a limiting factor at low Rabbit densities.

Short-tailed Voles

To calculate the proportion of a vole population that Buzzards are capable of removing in one year from a territory requires good information about: (a) the annual food requirements of breeding Buzzards, and (b) the constantly changing numbers, densities, size/age structure and dynamics of this rodent through its annual cycle. Such information is available for Buzzards on Dartmoor (Table 12.1) but, as ever, not for the voles. The wide spectrum of alternative preys that Buzzards can exploit during the breeding season introduces further complexity into any assessment. Nevertheless, it is feasible to estimate potential predation pressures during winter when voles are a staple food, they are not breeding (thus only full-grown animals are present) and they are most exposed to predation because of thinner ground cover.

For this exercise, several assumptions are necessary: (a) predation by a Buzzard pair is exclusively upon Short-tailed Voles; (b) food requirements are met, i.e. seven 20 g voles per bird per day; (c) the vole population is comprised of full-grown (20 g) and non-breeding animals; (d) voles are distributed more or less evenly through all favourable vole habitats in a territory. Three size ranges of Dartmoor territory with corresponding mean areas of vole habitats are chosen. The proportion of vole habitat increases with territory size: a mean of 25% in small, 60% in medium, and 75% in large territories. A range of vole densities is selected (from British studies) to represent low (50/ha), medium (200/ha) and high (500/ha) population levels. On the Scottish border, 240–480 voles/ha were considered a high density (Elton 1942). The two lower densities are arbitrary values. Dartmoor does not have a history of widely fluctuating or cyclic vole populations.

This exercise (Table 12.2) suggests that Buzzards on Dartmoor in winter theoretically could have measurable effects on vole numbers, but only at low to medium vole densities

Table 12.2 Maximum theoretical predation pressures of a Buzzard pair in winter (December–February) upon Short-tailed Voles, relative to territory size, area of vole habitat, and vole population density. (Proportions of voles taken are shown in parentheses)

	Territory Size (ha)		
	Small (65)	**Medium (145)**	**Large (210)**
Mean size of vole habitats (ha)	16	87	157
No. of voles in December at densities (voles/ha) :			
High 500	8,000 (16%)	43,500 (3%)	78,500 (1.5%)
Medium 200	3,200 (34%)	17,400 (7%)	31,400 (4%)
Low 50	800 (100%)	4,350 (29%)	7,850 (16%)

(based on a mean daily consumption of 7 voles (140 g of food) per bird) in small territories, and at low densities in medium size territories. Under the most circumscribed circumstances, a Buzzard pair theoretically could remove all voles from a small territory. Clearly, this would be unattainable because the birds perforce would switch progressively to other preys as vole numbers and catch rates fell. In all other circumstances, predation rates would be negligible. Nonetheless, when voles are relatively scarce, possession of a large territory with more vole habitats could be an advantage; indeed, it could be an essential on moorland where few alternative preys are available in winter. It should not be forgotten, furthermore, that the Buzzard is but one of a suite of bird and mammal predators competing for voles on Dartmoor, as doubtless elsewhere. Their collective predation throughout winter could limit vole numbers significantly by the start of their breeding season.

In southern Sweden, some ecologists (Erlinge *et al.* 1983) have calculated that the annual predation of Field Voles and Wood Mice by all predators, including Common Buzzards, was comparable to the annual breeding production of these rodent populations. Such collective predation, by specialists and generalists combined, effectively stabilised populations and explained the absence of population cycles in both these rodents. Their falling abundance through winter into spring matched the numbers taken by predators. Subsequently, a high predation rate at the beginning of the rodents' breeding season delayed and reduced their annual recovery phase, thereby lowering the autumn peak in numbers. Another Fennoscandian group (Hanski *et al.* 1991), using computer models, likewise found that sufficiently large numbers of generalist predators, such as Common Buzzards and Foxes, could dampen cycles and stabilise rodent populations. The Swedish findings seem to reflect the situation found in my Dartmoor study area.

To summarise, there is circumstantial evidence that Buzzards living in small territories could help to delay a recovery in Rabbit numbers for a time, following a severe population 'crash' caused by myxomatosis. Similarly, predation pressures on Short-tailed (Field) Voles in winter theoretically could contribute to limiting the vole numbers by the start of their breeding season, though again only in small territories and at lower vole densities. Pressures are relaxed once both prey species begin reproducing rapidly and the voles become protected by dense ground cover. By then, however, the Buzzards are able to exploit alternative seasonal food resources.

SUMMARY

- The extent to which Buzzard predation reflects, or may be controlled by, changes in seasonal abundance and availability of their main prey species is explored using dietary data and prey information from a Dartmoor study area.
- Food habits correspond with seasonal cycles in prey numbers and according to their exposure to predation, the latter varying with behavioural factors and changes in protective ground vegetation cover.
- Rabbits, mainly young ones, were important food in the breeding season whereas few were taken in winter. Peak predation on voles and other small mammals was in autumn at the end of their breeding season, though they were

most vulnerable in spring when numbers were low and ground cover sparse. Frogs (spawning) and reptiles (sun-basking) after emerging from hibernation were important spring preys. Birds were taken, mostly as fledglings, to feed to broods, in late spring and early summer.

- Buzzards rearing broods, soon after myxomatosis, hunted intensively but often with erratic or low catch rates. On average, 300 g/day of food was brought to nests (range typically 150–600 g) but sometimes fell to zero in prolonged wet weather. Occasional captures of young Rabbits were vital for successful breeding.
- A pair of adult Buzzards requires annually 102 kg of prey, equivalent to about 400 young Rabbits or to 5,100 adult Short-tailed Voles. A further 24 kg of food is needed to rear each youngster until it disperses three months after fledging.
- There is circumstantial evidence that Buzzard predation on Rabbits could retard their recovery in numbers for a time after a severe population 'crash' caused by myxomatosis, but only in small territories and in conjunction with Foxes and other predators.
- Predation on Short-tailed Voles in winter theoretically could contribute (with other predators) to limiting vole numbers by the start of the rodent's breeding season, but only in small territories and at relatively low vole densities.

ADDENDUM

Predation on pheasants

This section has been added to inform all sides in the recently rekindled conflict between game-shooting interests and wildlife conservationists. It is based on reviews of raptor-game-bird interactions studies (e.g. Park *et al.* 2008), and the original official field research assessments of Buzzard predation on Pheasants. The latter's important findings and recommendations seem to have been ignored by the relevant government department in making its recent decisions, outlined below.

The intensive rearing and mass releases of Pheasants for organized shoots is a profitable business for landowners on many central and eastern estates in England. These are the very places from which Buzzards had been exterminated by game-preservers more than a century ago. Buzzards resettling these lands where Pheasant poults are reared and released each summer are therefore still liable to be viewed with suspicion, if not inherent hostility. Inevitably, the Buzzards are being perceived in some areas as endangering the commercial viability of the shooting 'industry'. By 2012, a strong lobbying campaign had been mounted in an attempt to have statutory protection status removed from Buzzards. In 2013, trial destruction of Buzzard nests and 'removal/translocation' of adults from several (undisclosed) estates was sanctioned by government. This controversial and ill-conceived policy has been examined and strongly rebutted on sound practical and ecological grounds (Lees *et al.* 2013). In particular, it is very likely that removed breeding Buzzards will be replaced quickly by others from the large 'floating' population of immature birds seeking vacated territories. It is stressed also that mortality from Buzzard predation is much lower than that from road traffic collisions involving adult Pheasants, for which the high economic costs of vehicle damage are not taken into account. Furthermore, the Pheasant is not a native species and the environmental impacts on food chains of releasing millions of birds at unsustainably high densities are unknown.

In my Suffolk study area, estate owners and farmers initially accepted having the first Buzzards settle on their land. Within five years, however, the first concerns about possible predation risks were being raised with me as Buzzard sightings rapidly increased. In fact, many of these sightings actually are of groups of transient birds that nowadays pass conspicuously across this district during March and April (Dare 2013). With game-birds being so plentiful in the region it remains to be seen whether Buzzards might attempt, or be able, to utilize such a widespread food resource. This is inevitably a contentious topic that requires urgent official field investigations so that appropriate information and advice can be provided to landowners and gamekeepers.

Predation of adult pheasants

There appear to be no confirmed and published records of Buzzards killing full-grown Pheasants, which match these hawks in weight and are – the cock birds in particular – quite powerful. On the other hand, Buzzards would be expected to (and do) scavenge from Pheasants and Red-legged Partridges injured by shoots or which had died from natural causes and accidental collisions with road traffic. More significantly, according to Game Conservancy Trust research reports, many adult Pheasants in spring are weakened by parasitic worm infestations, starvation or other natural factors. Further, I am reliably informed that males often die after their spring peak activity period. The poor physical condition of adult Pheasants in spring may well explain the otherwise unexpected finding of their remains at some Buzzard nests in two study areas.

In the West Midlands of England, breeding Buzzards were suspected of having found carcasses of Pheasants that had died from unknown causes (Sim *et al.* 2000). In the Southern Uplands of Scotland, the remains of 17 Pheasants and 40 Red Grouse (ages not given) were found on the nests of nineteen pairs of Buzzards, some of which had access to heather moorland. These game-birds comprised 56% of all bird kills and 15% of all prey remains, which included lagomorphs (Rabbits and/or Brown Hares) and small mammals (Graham *et al.* 1995). It was in this region that an opportunist Buzzard was seen to take two Red Grouse chicks from a brood that had been disturbed by a Hen Harrier (Chapter 5). In southern England, occasional Pheasant chicks, from 'wild' breeders, were found at a nest in lowland Devon (DBR 1966), and at just five of the 50 nests studied in the New Forest (Tubbs 1974).

There, the total of six Pheasant chicks was greatly exceeded by the Jay remains that were found on all 50 nests. Clearly, the Buzzards of the New Forest might have been regarded as beneficial predators by gamekeepers!

Buzzards and pheasant rearing

Buzzards are widely reported to take Pheasant poults being reared in open-top feeding and release pens placed within woodlands. This non-native species every summer is released as small poults into very large enclosures, from which they are eventually allowed to escape into the wild. Their unsustainably large numbers are then 'harvested' during the following autumn and winter shooting season. In a detailed radio-tracking study of the fate of 486 released Pheasants by the Game & Wildlife Conservation Trust, it was shown that the harvesting rate was low. Only 37.5% of birds were shot during the following season and 16% survived into the spring (Turner 2007, www.gwct.org.uk/research). Losses to other causes therefore were high. Predation and scavenging, mainly by Foxes, accounted for 23% of young Pheasants before the shooting started and a further 13% during the season. Another 7% were killed by road traffic, disease and various other causes, and the remaining 3% had died in the pens before release. It is not stated whether Buzzards were present in this study area.

Buzzard predation on Pheasant poults had been assessed a decade earlier, in 1997, by the British Association for Shooting and Conservation. Their report, based on a nationwide survey of gamekeepers (cited in Kenward *et al.* 2001), noted that losses attributable to Buzzards ranged from below 1% to more than 10%, the average loss rate being 3.2%. If applicable to the GWCT study area, this level of predation would have been but a small component of their reported 23% losses to all predators and scavengers before the shooting season.

The only fully scientific investigation of Buzzard predation on reared game birds in Britain all involved radio-tagged juvenile Buzzards that were implicated in taking poults from feeding and release pens. The pens were located on ten estates in a study area of 125 km^2 in Dorset in southern England (Kenward *et al.* 2001). The findings from this detailed research are both revealing and important. Breeding Buzzards themselves took few Pheasants, the remains of which were found on six (15%) of the 40 nests, and they formed 2.6% of all preys on nests. Pheasant remains were greatly outnumbered by each of the other prey groups: Rabbits (predominant), small mammals, small birds, corvids and pigeons. The adult Buzzards brought in twice as many corvids as Pheasants. An equally significant finding was that some Buzzard pairs nesting close to Pheasant pens, including one pair with its nest tree actually inside a pen (!), did not kill Pheasants.

Juvenile Buzzards were responsible for some losses of Pheasant poults in this Dorset area. Their fledging period more or less coincided with the time when the pens were first stocked, each with up to 1,000 small, 5–7-week-old poults. Radio-tracking showed that some young Buzzards became associated with pens for a few weeks or months until October, by which time the fully-fledged Pheasants had dispersed. However, only a minority (8) of the more than 100 tracked juvenile Buzzards were significantly associated with any of the 32 Pheasant pens monitored. For young naïve hawks learning to hunt, an open pen with abundant and vulnerable small birds would be a lure. Young Buzzards that had fledged nearby were the most likely to visit pens though it is important to note that many did not do so.

During the two study years, the Dorset gamekeepers estimated that 9.5% of the more than 20,000 poults were killed by predators. Of the 901 losses, 4.3% were attributed to Buzzards, a finding similar to that of the earlier BASC national enquiry. Losses to Buzzards in Dorset varied markedly between sites – from zero to more than 20% of poults – according to features of the pens themselves. Differences in their habitat, size, and the numbers of poults they contained influenced patterns of Buzzard behaviour. The juveniles were found to be attracted most often to pens that were sited in mature deciduous woodland where tree branches nearby provided convenient hunting perches. Pheasant poults in pens with only low ground herbage were more vulnerable than those with shrub cover; while poults stocked at low densities in large pens were more at risk than when being reared at high densities.

Other aspects of Buzzard behaviour also should be taken into account. The scale of potential predation by young Buzzards could be affected by the breeding productivity and territorial behaviour of the parent population. For example, most successful Buzzard pairs fledge only 1–2 young in a territory that could be large enough to accommodate a dozen or more large Pheasant pens holding thousands of poults. It is possible that the inexperienced young Buzzards take mainly the weaker poults. A further point for consideration is the number of poults, at different sizes (ages), which a juvenile Buzzard would need to eat to satisfy its (140 g) daily food requirement. Given basic data on Pheasant growth and their period of vulnerability in or near pens, one could estimate the maximum potential predation impact of individual Buzzards. Their effects upon final game bag 'harvests' have yet to be estimated, but are likely to be very small relative to other mortality factors among Pheasants released into the countryside at such unnaturally high densities.

The thorough Dorset study, by raptor ecologists at a government laboratory, and in conjunction with gamekeepers, concluded that losses could be minimized or avoided by relocating vulnerable pens away from Buzzard hunting perches or to sites with adequate protective shrub cover. These findings should be disseminated officially to, and acted upon by, all game managers and concerned interests.

13

FOOD AND BREEDING SUCCESS

A common thread throughout previous chapters has been the many ways, some obvious but others more subtle, in which prey availability continually affects the ability of Common Buzzards to survive and breed successfully in different environments in this country. These aspects will be explored here by drawing on British research findings and those from continental Europe, where this raptor's predator-prey interactions have been examined in greater depth.

The relationships between the numbers of a raptorial bird and those of its main or preferred prey species are still problematic despite decades of field studies in different ecological regions across northern Eurasia and North America. In Britain, notably, the effects of Sparrowhawks upon songbird numbers, and of Hen Harriers on Red Grouse stocks, are still contentious issues despite much thorough research effort. At Arctic latitudes, however, the relationship appears to be simpler to resolve in pristine tundra habitats. There, small rodent populations and their main avian predators both exhibit near-synchronous and cyclical fluctuations in abundance. Debates continue (especially among Fennoscandian ecologists) as to whether the prey cycles are driven by predation pressure, or arise when peak rodent numbers 'crash' after severely depleting their own food resources. The roles of other environmental factors, such as snow cover protection, and of changes in the intrinsic physiology of rodents under stress at high densities, also are not fully understood. Most attempts to unravel these predator-prey relationships have been undertaken for the Rough-legged Buzzard and other specialist predators that breed in the comparatively simple ecosystems on Arctic tundras. These classic studies have provided the clearest results and will be summarized first before moving to the lower latitudes, where Common Buzzards are components of more complex ecosystems.

In the tundra zone, Rough-legged Buzzards as well as the Snowy Owl, Pomarine Skua and, to a lesser extent, the Arctic Fox all depend largely upon lemmings (*Lemmus* and *Dicrostonyx* species) and microtine voles. These rodent populations exhibit frequent (3 or 4 year) cycles of abundance and scarcity, although the timings of peaks and lows generally are not synchronised between geographical regions. It has long been known that the numbers and breeding success of the three bird predators each year are closely linked to the large annual fluctuations in prey abundance, both on Eurasian and North American tundras (first documented by Elton 1942, Lack 1954).

These Arctic avian predators, which over-winter further south, have adapted their breeding strategies to cope with the unpredictable food supplies which they find upon returning to the tundra in spring. All their populations are nomadic to various degrees, concentrating to nest only in areas with adequate prey numbers. In good prey years, other adaptations are shown: earlier and extended breeding, laying larger clutches, and rearing large broods. Overall, a very high breeding success (fledglings per pair) is achieved. In poor years, however, immediately after a lemming population 'crash', the predators either do not attempt to breed or, if eggs are laid, few or no young are reared due to reduced clutch size and a high mortality of eggs and broods. Rough-legged Buzzards in the mountains of southern Norway show these graduated responses to changing vole abundance very clearly (Hagen 1969, cited in Newton 1979). No breeding was attempted in low vole years, whereas pairs laid 4–7 eggs and reared 4–5 young when voles were abundant. In Siberia, these relationships are less simple and can be affected by interactions with competing Snowy Owls (Potapov 1997). In Siberia and other regions, breeding success can be affected to some extent also by the variable timing of snow melt after the arrival of the predators.

Below the Arctic in Europe, similar population cycles of Common Voles and related species occur in the extensive boreal forests of mixed conifers in Fennoscandia between 70°N and 60°N. There is also a latitudinal gradient in cycle length, amplitude and synchronization between species (Hanski *et al.* 1991, Sundell *et al.* 2004). The gradient is thought largely to reflect the relative influence of specialist and generalist predators on vole dynamics (Lambin *et al.* 2006). The most northerly Common Buzzards (generalists) breed in the boreal forests together with some Rough-legged Buzzards (vole specialists). Here, the voles are major foods also for six owl species and four carnivorous mammals. Except for Common Buzzards in southernmost Sweden (south of 60°N), both of the hawks migrate south in autumn to avoid the harsh cold and permanent snow-cover of the long winters. South of 60°N, across temperate Europe, regular 3-year cycles of Common Voles also occur in agricultural areas of many countries (Lambin *et al.* 2006). These manipulated landscapes offer Common Buzzards a broad diversity of mammalian and other vertebrate preys throughout the year, many of which they exploit regularly. Common Buzzards may be partially migratory in Germany, Poland and other central and eastern countries often subject to very cold winters. They are sedentary in the milder western temperate regions, notably in the British Isles and France, as they are in the Mediterranean climatic zone.

Although the Common Buzzard (hereafter Buzzard) is a generalist predator, it is evident from many studies that small rodents and Rabbits are the staple preys across much of Europe. Moreover, for Buzzards in boreal and some temperate regions, relationships between their breeding success and the fluctuations in abundance of the preferred preys have been demonstrated. In his review of raptor ecology, Newton (1979) considered such evidence to be circumstantial. The effects of sudden prey depletions on Buzzard numbers, and the extent to which they may be offset (buffered) by switching to alternative preys, have been assessed in several countries. The findings from these studies form the basis of this chapter.

BUZZARDS AND SMALL RODENTS IN EUROPE

Fennoscandia

In Finland, Common Buzzards, of the *vulpinus* subspecies, show clear responses to cyclic vole populations, principally involving Common Voles and Field (Short-tailed) Voles. This seems to have been first reported by Suomus (1952) who observed, from hides, the food brought to four Buzzard broods. He found that when voles were unavailable the Buzzards switched to shrews and frogs. More recently, an 18-year study in western Finland (Reif *et al.* 2001, 2004) found that several species of 'forest grouse' were the alternative preys in years when voles, with a 3-year cycle, were scarce. The nesting success of Buzzards in good years averaged 1.7 fledglings per breeding attempt and 2.2 fledglings were reared by successful pairs. The proportion of territorial pairs that laid eggs and the success rate for all territories were positively correlated with the abundance of *Microtus* voles in the spring but not with grouse numbers. The results were considered to indicate that, by switching to grouse in the poor vole years, the Buzzard predation may dampen vole population cycles but amplify the grouse cycles.

In southern Norway, an 8-year study (Spidsø & Selås 1988) found, from prey remains at nests, that voles, especially the Field Vole, were the preferred prey. Breeding success was high in peak vole years, averaging 2.6 young fledged per successful pair. It was very poor, 0.3 fledglings per nest, in vole-crash years when many pairs failed. Maximum clutch size was typically 3 eggs, with 4 eggs noted only once. When voles were scarce, small birds (adults, fledglings and nestlings) became the dominant prey. The few 'woodland grouse' taken here were chicks of Hazel Grouse, Black Grouse and Capercaillie. Reptiles (Adders and Slow-worms) were taken every year with Adders mostly in vole-peak years. This unexpected finding was possibly because Buzzards concentrated their vole hunting in clear-cut forest areas where voles were numerous and when the snakes (also vole feeders) were basking in sunshine (Selas 2001). Breeding success also seemed to be affected adversely in years with a late spring snow melt.

In southern Sweden, where there is greater habitat diversity, the Field Vole populations are considered to be non-cyclic (Erlinge *et al.* 1983). This is a result partly of heavy predation by raptors and mammals during the vole breeding season. It also reflects the predators' ability to maintain their numbers by switching to plentiful alternative preys in winter, when vole numbers decline. In one such district (near 56°N) a resident population of 16–21 breeding pairs of Buzzards was studied for six years on 45 km^2 of grazing farmland, woods and marshes offering a wide range of preys (Sylvén 1982). Buzzards fed mainly on Rabbits, Field Voles, Water Voles, Moles and frog species. Field Voles, the main spring prey, showed no significant annual variation in spring abundance. Productivity of individual Buzzard pairs was positively related to the biomass of Rabbits and Field Voles within one kilometre of each nest. Where Rabbits were least available, the Buzzards compensated by taking a wider range of preys. The mean clutch size of 2.69 eggs was rather high and included clutches of 4 eggs. Annual breeding success also was high, with 83% of clutches, 72% of eggs and 61% of territorial pairs producing fledglings. The average productivity was 2.09 fledglings per successful pair, or 1.37 per territorial pair, and included four broods of four young.

Estonia

South of the Baltic, in the hemi-boreal vegetation zone of central Estonia, landscapes dominated by conifer forests give way to more diverse habitats and greater human alterations. Vole populations here still show regular 3-year fluctuations in abundance (Löhmus 2003). His 11-year study of Buzzard breeding performance was made in 112 territories across a 900 km^2 area predominantly of forests (40%) and farmlands (37%). He found that success rates varied not only with the phase of vole cycles but also with habitat diversity. Breeding success was twice as high (1.43 fledglings per pair) in peak vole years than in low and intermediate vole years (0.76), when the only successful Buzzard pairs were those in territories with more varied habitats.

Poland

The Common Buzzard population apparently contains birds that are intergrades between nominate *buteo* and the migratory eastern *vulpinus* subspecies or Steppe Buzzard. In eastern Poland, many breed in ancient forests at densities of around 5 km^2/pair (Jedrzejewski & Szymoura 1994). The breeding pairs on average lay 2.4 eggs and rear 1.3 fledglings. The breeding performance of pairs which have forest- edge territories was found to be positively correlated with the cyclic abundance of microtine voles in the open river valleys and meadows where these hawks hunted. Birds and moles were other important preys.

In a 105 km^2 study area in central Poland during 11 years, a stable population of Buzzards occupied a mosaic of woods and farmland at a density of 5.8 km^2 per pair (Goszczynski 1997). On average, 93% of pairs bred each year and productivity was high, averaging 1.78 fledglings per breeding pair and 2.34 fledglings per successful pair. Common Voles were an important prey and fluctuated in annual densities from fewer than 10/ha to nearly 80/ha. As further east, these Buzzards took a wide range of prey with birds again being the major component. Nevertheless, annual variations in breeding success were positively correlated only with the biomass of Common Voles and other small mammals in their diet.

Germany

In grassland habitats of eastern Germany the Common Vole (*Feldmaus*) exhibits regular and large cyclic fluctuations in numbers. These have reached 'plague' proportions at times (Frank 1957). Other rodents show irregular fluctuations. The breeding success of *Mäusebussards* is clearly linked to *Feldmaus* population cycles in regions dominated by a mosaic of rich farmlands, meadows and woods. Breeding Buzzards are numerous and mainly resident, and have long been known to take a wide spectrum of small mammals, birds and other preys. Earlier compilations of diet were derived from prey remains at nests and numerous analyses of stomach contents from birds shot, often in winter (Rörig 1903 and Uttendorfer 1939, 1952). Field studies of breeding populations have provided the most useful ecological insights, however. Initially, it was shown (Schmaus 1938, Wendland 1952) that Buzzard mean clutch sizes were larger than normal in outbreak years of Common Voles and related species (Table 13.1). In peak vole years, Buzzards laid proportionally more clutches of 3 and 4 eggs, from which broods of 3 or 4 young were fledged. When voles were less plentiful, 2 eggs were the normal clutch, 3 eggs were uncommon, and 4 eggs unknown. Few broods of 3 young then were fledged and none of 4 young.

Table 13.1 Clutch sizes of German Buzzards and variations in Vole abundance

Normal Vole Year Clutches						Peak Vole Year Clutches						
Year	No.	c/1	c/2	c/3	Mean	Year	No.	c/1	c/2	c/3	c/4	Mean
1932-36	14	0	13	1	2.07	1937	7	0	1	2	4	3.43
1951	13	3	9	1	1.85	1933	19	2	6	8	3	2.63
Totals	27	3	22	2	1.96		26	2	7	10	7	2.85
%		11.1	81.4	7.4				7.7	27.0	38.5	27.0	

(note: upper data row from Schmaus (1938), lower from Wendland (1952)

Wendland studied 28–30 breeding pairs for nine years in a 137 km² area of coniferous forest, farmland and wet ground in a northern district near Berlin. Buzzard broods ate a varied diet of voles and other small mammals, small birds and reptiles, as well as some Rabbits and Brown Hare leverets. Voles were not considered to be the staple prey, however, although their importance could have been underestimated in prey remains at nests; a common bias noted in previous chapters. Wendland also found that in peak vole years few nestlings died from starvation and more were fledged by successful pairs (Table 13.2). It was clear also that one third of breeding pairs failed to rear young in most years, irrespective of vole abundance, due mainly to human interference of various kinds. Overall, the population's annual productivity (potential replacement rate) averaged virtually one fledgling per breeding pair, and 1.41 young per successful pair. Wendland considered this level of success was probably sufficient to maintain a fairly stable population in his area.

In south-west Germany and similar countryside, the annual breeding performance of Buzzards also was found to be strongly associated with varying vole abundance. The most

Table 13.2. Fluctuations in breeding activity and success of a German Buzzard population, 1940–51 (after Wendland, 1952)

	1940	41	42	43*	44	47	48	50*	51	Totals
Pairs breeding	14	23	25	30	20	3	7	21	27	170
Pairs fledging	12	17	16	19	14	3	7	14	15	117
Total fledglings	15	24	20	29	17	6	9	25	20	165
Deaths to starvation	1	3	10	1	10	0	1	0	4	30
Fledglings per pair:										
Breeding	1.07	1.04	0.80	0.97	0.85	(2.0)	1.29	1.19	0.74	0.98
Successful	1.25	1.14	1.25	1.53	1.21	(2.0)	1.29	1.79	1.33	1.41

(Notes: * = 'mouse years' (1943, 1950)
Non-breeding pairs not given in original source
53 pairs (31%) failed to rear young, due mainly to human disturbance
Small 1947 sample is given in parentheses (severe winter in early 1947)

comprehensive research in the early years was the six-year study of Buzzards occupying 18 territories on 30 km² of farmland and woods in southern Bavaria (Mebs 1964). Broods had a diet mainly of Common and Field Voles varied with small birds, and occasional other small rodents, Moles, shrews, Red Squirrels, Brown Hare leverets, lizards, frogs and toads. Vole abundance was measured each season and expressed as numbers per 1000 m² (0.1 ha). Mebs found significant effects of vole abundance upon the breeding performance of the Buzzards. The mean date on which clutches were started was 12–20 days earlier in the peak vole year (1959) than in the other years. Clutch sizes and breeding success were strongly correlated with vole abundance (Figure 13.1). Increases in mean clutch size were due almost entirely to higher proportions of 3-egg clutches. Over the six years there were only seven clutches of 4 eggs (7%) six of them in the peak vole year. A rare 5-egg clutch, and one of 4 eggs, had been found in the previous good vole year of 1955. Single-egg clutches were also rare even at low vole levels. Hatching rates were higher and nestling mortalities were lower when voles were plentiful.

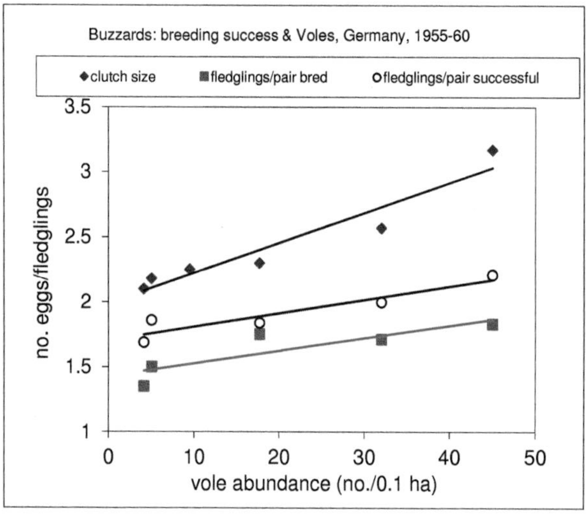

Figure 13.1 Relationships (all significant) between Buzzard breeding success and abundance of Common Voles in Bavaria (redrawn from Mebs 1964). [All correlations are significant]

Weather conditions could also have affected success in some years (Rockenbauch 1975). During a 12-year period, 110–180 Buzzard pairs occupied 400 km² of wooded farmland. The food at nests comprised mainly voles, other small mammals and small birds. Clutch size and vole abundance data are not given. In 'good' vole years, Buzzard population density, the proportion of pairs breeding, the number of young fledged and overall breeding success were all higher than in the years of lowest vole abundance (Figure 13.2). In the two peak vole years (1966, 1970) an average of 88% of pairs laid eggs and reared 2.04 fledglings per pair, whereas only 43% of pairs bred and reared just 0.43 young per pair in the three poorest vole years (1962, 1968, 1969). The successful pairs produced twice as many fledglings (2.26 per pair, including a brood of 3) in the good vole years than in the poorest years (1.0 fledgling per pair). In one year (1964) of intermediate vole abundance all Buzzard pairs laid eggs but fledging success was only about average.

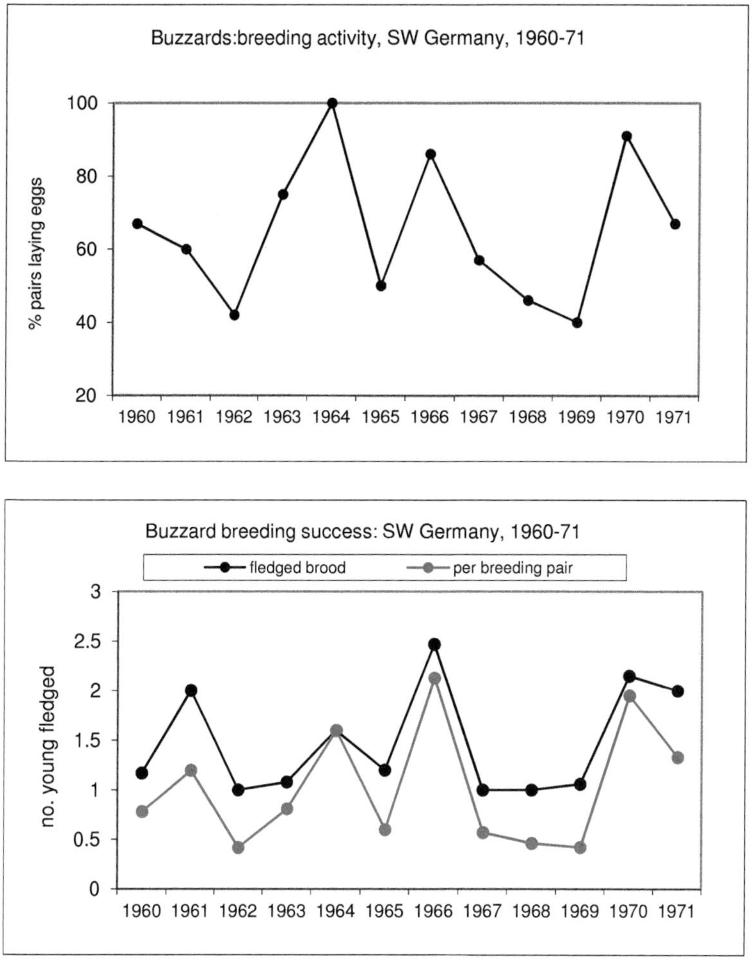

Figure 13.2 Annual breeding activity (left) and success of Buzzards in relation to fluctuations in vole abundance in south-west Germany (redrawn from Rockenbauch 1975). Peak vole years were in 1966 and 1970, the poorest years in 1962, 1968 and 1969.

For Buzzards in north-west Germany, Kruger (2004) found that much (78%) of the variance in population changes could be explained by the fluctuating abundance of Field Voles, their main food also here. Both population density of Buzzards and the size of fledged broods were positively related to the index of vole abundance. On the other hand, other measures of breeding performance, such as egg-laying date and hatching success, were not food related. Instead, other environmental factors – rain, human activities, and interference from hunting Goshawks (which even took some Buzzard chicks) collectively could have important influences. On average, one-fifth of breeding pairs (range 9–30%) failed each year. Success between years varied from 1.08–2.05 (mean 1.43) fledglings per pair, and only 14% of broods were of three young.

France

There appears to be very little information. Population cycles of the Common Vole are found in south-west parts of France (Lambin *et al.* 2006). Breeding of Buzzards in France may begin earlier than usual in years of abundance of the Bank Vole, according to an old source (Heim de Balsac, cited in Schmaus 1938). Bank Voles, however, are not known to be an important prey of Buzzards anywhere in Europe, and this statement requires verification.

Europe: Overview

The European studies reveal a widespread and positive correlation between the annual breeding success of Common Buzzard populations and the cyclical abundance of *Microtus* voles in both the temperate and boreal zones. This association is evident despite breeding Common Buzzards in these regions being generalist predators able to switch to alternative preys and to rear smaller broods on a broad diet consisting mainly of other small mammals and birds. Such versatility enables Common Buzzard populations, unlike specialist Rough-legged Buzzards, to produce some young every year. Common Buzzards can match breeding effort to a fluctuating food supply by a sequence of graduated responses. This is reflected initially by the proportion of pairs that attempt to breed (lay eggs) and by small adjustments of clutch size (ratio of 2-egg to 3-egg clutches). These are followed by variations in hatching rates, nestling survival and ultimately fledging success. For Common Buzzards in northern Europe, their success depends largely on the voles' own breeding productivities. Nonetheless, even when voles are scarce, a small proportion of Common Buzzards still can rear small broods by exploiting alternative preys. Rabbits, although widely distributed, were seldom recorded as prey whereas young Brown Hares were more important in some places.

BUZZARDS AND VOLES IN THE BRITISH ISLES

Short-tailed (Field) Voles and Rabbits are by far the two most important prey species for Buzzards in Britain; voles all year round but Rabbits principally in the breeding season (Chapter 12). Several studies have attempted to measure the effects of changes in abundance of these two preys upon Buzzard breeding productivity but with limited success, because assessing mammal numbers over large areas, often of mixed habitats, is fraught with practical and theoretical problems. Anecdotal accounts for voles and Rabbits may provide useful supporting evidence covering the last 80 years. The current state of our knowledge is summarised in the review of species research and the conservation status of British mammals commissioned by the Joint Nature Conservation Committee (Harris *et al.* 1995).

Short-tailed (Field) Vole populations

This species is widely distributed in Britain (but not Ireland) wherever rough grassland, heaths, grassy scrub and hay fields are found. However, it has always been most numerous on the extensive grass moors and in enclosed young coniferous plantations on western and northern uplands. In the agricultural lowlands, on the other hand, these voles are much less plentiful and have more fragmented distributions, especially in intensively farmed arable regions. There, most voles are restricted to strips and patches of unkempt grasses and herbage (Village 1990). For a while, they also colonised 'long-term' set-aside land until this scheme was phased out (Tattersall *et al.* 2000).

Vole populations have almost certainly been in substantial decline throughout the countryside since the early 1900s due to habitat changes and losses, and competition for food with increasing stocks of hill sheep. In the southern Pennines, for example, vole densities were greatly reduced by the intensive grazing of moor grasses and herbs by sheep (Wheeler 2008). In Snowdonia the exclusion of sheep enables Short-tailed Voles once more to become the dominant herbivores (Hill *et al.* 1992). These voles also compete for food with Rabbits, as became clear after the demise of the latter in the mid-1950s caused by myxomatosis (see below). Then, vole populations increased in many areas (Harris *et al.* 1995), even reaching plague levels through Wales in 1956–57. It seems likely that this recovery in vole numbers continued into the early 1970s, but subsequently fell again from the mid-1970s as Rabbit populations continued to recover from myxomatosis. On Dartmoor, however, vole increases were not reported after myxomatosis, perhaps because livestock grazing pressure remained heavy. During more than 25 years in my Dartmoor and North Wales study areas there were no indications, from observations or farmers' reports, of any noticeable changes in vole abundance.

Short-tailed Voles are prolific breeders; a female produces 5–6 litters, each of 4–5 young, which themselves become capable of breeding at six weeks. Each year, numbers rapidly increase and decline, with peak numbers being reached in September–October and the minimum in early spring. Autumn numbers can be more than ten times greater than those after the winter (Village 1990). Overwinter survival is higher in years with prolonged snow cover which enhances protection from many predators.

Upland vole populations, like others in northern Europe, undergo three- or four-year cycles in numbers (Lambin *et al.* 2000, Petty *et al.* 2000), although none has been observed on Dartmoor. On low farmlands, cycles are less pronounced or even may be suppressed owing to habitat degradation, fragmentation or loss caused by agricultural and urban changes in land use (Harris *et al.* 1995). There are no recent data on population densities from upland parts of Wales or Scotland, even though these regions probably contain the bulk of the British population. In some peak years, densities of about 700 voles/ha were estimated in favourable habitats in central Wales (Chitty 1952). In southern England, 100–300 voles/ha have been estimated in suitable grasslands (in Harris *et al.* 1995). Vole 'plagues' had been documented in the Scottish Border country during the late 1800s and early 1900s, after which they became increasingly intermittent. These evidently continue but perhaps usually on a smaller scale. For example, a regular three-year cycle in vole numbers was recorded, using a vole sign index (see below), on grass moors partly afforested with conifers in Ayrshire between 1987 and 2009 (Riddle 2011). Even more recently, 'exceptionally' high vole numbers were reported in the Southern Uplands and elsewhere in highland Scotland in May 2011 (BBC News Scotland).

Estimating Short-tailed Vole numbers is especially difficult because of their patchy distributions across broad tracts of land. Population density estimates, based on catch data, are labour- and time-intensive. Moreover, results should not be extrapolated over large areas (Harris *et al.* 1995), such as those covered by many upland Buzzard territories. An alternative but indirect method for comparing relative vole abundance between (for example) raptor territories is to use a visual indicator, a Vole Sign Index (VSI). This method records clear evidence of recent vole feeding activity, such as droppings and nibbled grass tips, at a series of randomly-located sampling points. Though still requiring considerable time, it enables large areas to be surveyed relatively quickly. Such a study in the Southern Uplands found no correlation between the vole index and the percentage of voles in pellets and food remains at nearby Buzzard nests (Graham *et al.* 1995). However, no allowance was made for biases in the nest data due to the well-known under-representation of small mammals in pellets and mixed prey remains on nests.

In conclusion: in many upland areas where Rabbits are scarce or absent, Short-tailed Voles usually become the most important alternative prey for Buzzards. Nevertheless, it is difficult to measure the influence of vole abundance on Buzzard breeding success, unlike the clear connection found for vole-eating Buzzards in central and northern Europe. The basic problem stems from the apparent absence of prominent vole cycles in the habitats where most Buzzard studies have been made. As a consequence of widespread habitat loss or degradation, coupled with predation pressure, vole populations may have become acyclic. In addition, the Buzzard is a generalist predator. Consequently, the potential effects of any vole fluctuations are likely to be dampened or masked by the Buzzard's ability to switch to alternative resources including sheep carrion. A further stabilizing factor in my study areas, as mentioned in Chapter 12, was the combined predation pressure exerted by five species of major vole predators: Kestrel, Buzzard, Tawny Owl, Fox and Weasel. In the other upland regions Short-eared Owl, Hen Harrier and, at lower elevations, Barn Owl are also significant vole consumers.

BUZZARDS AND RABBITS IN THE BRITISH ISLES

Buzzards in this country uniquely appear to be reliant upon Rabbits for maximum breeding success. In south-west England, more than 70 years ago, Buzzards were known, from anecdotal observations, to prey heavily upon Rabbits, particularly in the breeding season. The dramatic arrival of myxomatosis, and its rapid near-annihilation of Rabbit populations almost everywhere, had conspicuous effects on Buzzard populations (described below). These impacts stimulated the first ecological investigations into Buzzards and their food supplies. Such studies, together with scattered anecdotal information can be assessed here, by: (a) reviewing how clutch and brood sizes vary between regions with different prey compositions; and (b) taking a detailed look at the responses of Buzzards to the sudden depletion of this important prey resource.

Rabbit populations

The main information sources are the above JNCC mammal review, and the national game-book census report of the Game and Wildlife Conservation Trust (2010) which presents its estimated 1961–2009 trends in Rabbit populations in different regions of Britain. Following their introduction to this country by the Normans in the 12th century, Rabbits were for centuries protected in 'warrens' as a valuable resource of meat and fur, and were later introduced to remoter parts of Britain. Like rodents, Rabbits are prolific breeders; a female may rear up to seven litters, each of 3–7 young, from mid-winter until late summer. Wild populations became established and these had increased enormously by the 1950s. Despite permanent control measures killing some 40 million animals annually, Rabbits had become serious pests of agriculture everywhere by seriously reducing crop yields and over-grazing pastures. Their population densities vary with habitat but may reach 15/ha in winter and 40/ha in summer (Harris *et al.* 1995). In some places, as on Dartmoor, farm and roadside banks with hedgerows were undermined and often collapsed.

In 1953, the release of the extremely virulent and species-specific *myxoma* virus into Rabbit populations in southern England triggered a myxomatosis epizootic, vectored by fleas, which spread rapidly. It had killed over 99% of the British Rabbit population by 1956; locally, all died within weeks of the disease arriving. There were unforeseen, far-reaching and dramatic consequences (both positive and negative) for not only Rabbit predators but also for flora and fauna in various ecosystems (review by Sumption & Flowerdew 1985). After this sudden catastrophic decline, Rabbit numbers began to recover very slowly. Even by 1995, they were considered nationally still to be at only 30–50% of pre-myxomatosis levels (Harris *et al.* 1995). Recovery rates were retarded by further localised and sporadic outbreaks, supplemented by control measures in many places. By 1995, mortality rates had fallen to 40–60% as a result of Rabbit populations acquiring increasing levels of genetic resistance.

Trends in the national Rabbit population, as indicated by changes in the annual numbers shot per gun (game-bag index) since myxomatosis, are plotted in Figure 13.3. The changes are shown relative to the 1961 baseline year which has an index value of 1.

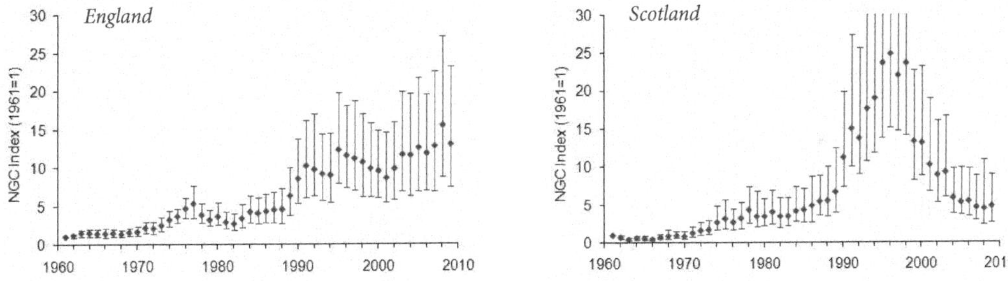

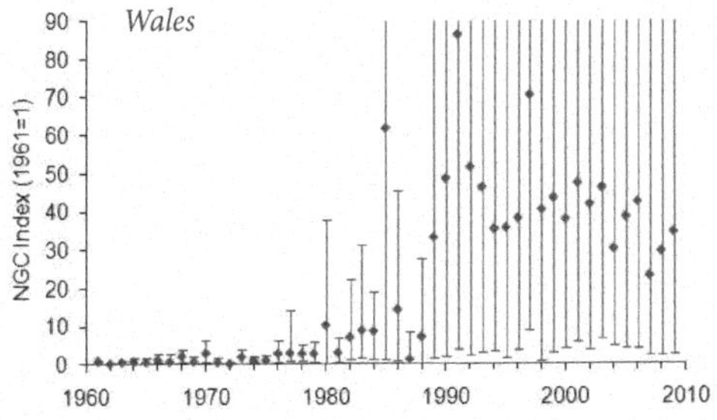

Figure 13.3 Trends in the Rabbit populations of Britain, 1961–2009; derived from annual game-bag census data. Error bars indicate 95% confidence intervals; inadequate sample sizes in Wales after 1990. (Source: Game and Wildlife Conservation Trust Report, 2010)

By 2009, Rabbits in Britain as a whole had increased about 10-fold since 1961, but marked contrasts were evident between countries: a 10–15 fold rise in England, possibly a 30-fold increase in Wales but only 5-fold in Scotland. Even so, bag sizes by 2009 were only roughly half of what they were in the early 1900s. A very slow recovery of Rabbit numbers had occurred in all three countries between 1961 and the late 1980s, followed by rapid increases until the mid-1990s. Even so, the mammal review panel concluded, in 1995, that Rabbit populations were still well below those recorded before myxomatosis. After the 1990s the Scottish population size fell rapidly back to 1980 levels. In England, however, the Rabbit index remained more or less stable after 1995, as possibly it did also in Wales, but small sample sizes there prevented firm conclusions. The declines in Scotland were possibly linked to the spread of the new viral haemorrhagic disease. The GWCT analysis also noted that changes in Rabbit population indices varied between different broad environmental zones. Over the 50 years, Rabbits had increased most in the upland regions of England and Wales and least in the lowlands. Conversely, the greatest declines since the 1990s were in the Scottish uplands, with unexpected lesser falls in some western lowlands of England and Wales. On the other hand, Rabbits continued to increase slowly in both the Welsh uplands and eastern lowlands of England.

Rabbits and Buzzard clutch sizes

Pre-myxomatosis: In south-west and north-west England, the normal clutch was probably 3 eggs while 4-egg clutches comprised only 5.7% of all clutches in the south-west and 1.6% in the north-west (Appendix 6). Exceptional clutches of five and even six eggs were found in both Somerset (Pring 1947) and Devon (Mayo 1948), and a brood of five young was noted in Cornwall (Lewis 1934). During the 1930s, an 'especially prolific bird' in Devon laid 27 eggs over seven successive years. Her average clutch size of 3.86 eggs comprised two 5-egg, two 4-egg and three 3-egg clutches. Only one other 5-egg clutch seems to have been recorded since then. That was on the north-west Pennines, although whether before or after myxomatosis was not made clear (Holdsworth 1971). Overall, however, the frequency of 4-egg clutches in Britain was far lower than in Germany, where 27 % of clutches were of four eggs in the 'mouse years' of Field Vole abundance (Schmaus 1938, Wendland 1952).

Post-myxomatosis: There is some evidence that Buzzards lay more eggs in areas where Rabbits are most available than where they are less plentiful, scarce or absent, as judged from Rabbit counts and (or) brood diets. The 13 studies (Appendix 6) found a scarcity (3.5%) of 4-egg clutches similar to that recorded before myxomatosis. All but four of the 39 records were in two areas of northern Scotland where Rabbits were very plentiful and were found frequently at nests. The tabulated data also show that mean clutch sizes were highest (2.60 to 3.03 eggs) in the four data sets collected where Rabbits were a main food. They were lower (1.86 to 2.40) where small mammals, birds and miscellaneous preys dominated diets. Differences in clutch size generally resulted from changing ratios of 2-egg and 3-egg clutches. The Buzzard population densities in these study areas (Appendix 26) do not seem to have influenced egg production.

In some hill areas, another factor that could affect Buzzard clutch size is the availability of sheep carrion. This has been thought to influence clutch size in the Lake District of England, where Blezard (in Bannerman 1956) noted that average clutch size was related to the abundance of dead sheep on the fells in the previous winter. The usual clutch was 3 or 4 eggs, but only 1 or 2 eggs after mild winters with low sheep mortality. Raven clutch size in some uplands likewise can be positively related to the abundance of dead sheep before egg-laying (Ratcliffe 1997). On the other hand, where carrion is not so available, a very severe winter conceivably may reduce the fitness of Buzzard females to produce any eggs (Chapter 3).

Rabbits and Buzzard brood sizes

Rabbit availability after hatching appears to be a strong determinant of the number of young that can be reared. The sizes of almost 1,400 successful broods recorded, in the 13 populations studied since 1954 (Appendix 23), show that 54% of pairs reared single fledglings, 33% had two, 11% had three, and 2 % were of four fledglings. The mean sizes of fledged broods in the different areas ranged between 1.2 and 2.84 youngsters.

In most parts of Britain, three fledglings appear to be the largest brood that normally can be reared. The most successful Buzzard pairs were in those areas, notably Speyside and Morayshire, where abundant Rabbits were considered to be the main food. The birds were able to rear more than twice as many young as those pairs which relied mainly on small mammals and birds. Almost all of the broods of four fledglings recorded in Britain since myxomatosis were in the above two Scottish areas. The remaining two areas were in Argyll and the West Midlands of England. The smallest broods were those raised mainly on small mammals and birds, as in the uplands of Wales and Dartmoor, and in the New Forest where birds were the main food resource.

Before myxomatosis, a rare brood of five healthy young Buzzards was reported from Somerset (Lewis 1934) and many young Rabbits were found on other nests beside broods. In Devon, for example, 14 such kills were seen laid out on one nest and eight at another while, in Wales, a nest photographer observed seven small Rabbits being brought to three large youngsters in one afternoon (Chapter 6).

Buzzards and myxomatosis

The initial impact of the disease on Buzzards was soon revealed by a national survey into the ecological effects of myxomatosis (Moore 1957). This showed that, in the first year (1955) after the 1953–54 epizootic had reached most areas and swiftly destroyed virtually all Rabbits, there was a great fall in Buzzard breeding activity and success. Indeed, many – perhaps most – pairs did not even attempt to breed in 1955. In 1956, breeding activity in affected districts was about double that in 1955, but still far below normal, and Buzzard numbers had fallen markedly since 1954. It was suggested that the Buzzard population was stabilising at lower densities. By contrast, where Rabbits locally had not yet been exposed to the disease, or where they had never been abundant, Buzzards continued to breed normally. The unfolding of events can be reconstructed in some detail from two local studies that were in progress at that time in small areas of south-west England and Wales.

Devon

The sequence of events closely followed the national pattern. Myxomatosis arrived in autumn 1954, after the Buzzard breeding season which thus was quite unaffected. The 1955 breeding season, however, was drastically affected and was probably the poorest on record (DBWPS Report 1955). Very few Buzzard pairs bred and fledglings were rarely recorded. In 1956, breeding by a few pairs was more widespread, though only small numbers of young were reared. The Buzzard population clearly had declined, by as much as one third in some districts (DBWPS Reports). Many birds, including adults, are known to have starved.

In the Avon Valley of south Devon, a Buzzard enthusiast (D. R. Edgecombe) observed the impact of myxomatosis upon his local birds. Soon afterwards, he kindly provided me with his detailed survey data (Appendix 28) which compare the breeding performance immediately before (1954) and after (1955–56) the disease reached his area. Before the outbreak, the 18 km^2 survey area had supported 21 pairs of Buzzards which, at 1.2 pairs/km^2, was one of the highest densities in Britain (Moore 1957). In 1954, while Rabbits were still abundant, 90% of Buzzards had bred and very successfully, rearing 1.48 fledglings per breeding pair, or 1.33 per pair of population. This compared favourably with that of German Buzzards in good mouse years (Table 13.2) and would appear to have been quite normal in Devon before myxomatosis. By spring 1955, however, Buzzard numbers in this valley had fallen by 33% and the breeding season was a total failure; only one of the 14 surviving pairs laid eggs, and those were lost. In 1956, despite losing two more adult pairs, there was a marked recovery in breeding success. Two-thirds (66%) of pairs bred and 42% were successful, rearing 0.88 fledglings per breeding pair and 0.58 per pair of population. This modest success, though near the poorest recorded in Germany (Table 13.2), suggested a rapid adaptation to the new Rabbit-less conditions in Devon. A population recovery had begun.

On Dartmoor, in my Postbridge study area, the Buzzards adapted even more quickly to the local Rabbit 'crash', which occurred there after the 1955 breeding season (local reports). There was no dramatic breeding failure in the following year (1956) but the number of pairs had fallen by some 25%. Nevertheless, 67% of surviving pairs laid eggs and half of them bred successfully, rearing 0.88 young per breeding pair, or 0.58/pair of population (Appendix 28). Their performance thus was identical to that of Avon Buzzards two years after myxomatosis had struck their area. However, the 1957 and (especially) 1958 seasons in my area were very poor despite a small increase in pairs. This was in part caused by higher clutch losses and adverse weather during the 1958 brood period. The subsequent recovery of this Buzzard population was slow (see below).

Wales

The only other place where detailed information was obtained was on the small (2.92 km^2) and treeless south-western island of Skomer, where up to eight pairs of cliff-nesting Buzzards bred annually during 1954–64, sometimes at the astonishingly high density of 2.7 pairs/km^2. Broods were fed mainly on an unusual mixed diet of abundant Rabbits, Manx Shearwaters and Puffins (Davis & Saunders 1965). Their observations spanned two 'crashes' in the Rabbit population, in 1956 and 1960. The first was induced by myxomatosis, arriving in autumn 1955; the second was caused by a severe outbreak of intestinal coccidiosis. In the two years before myxomatosis, 8 and 7 pairs had bred, rearing 11 and 6 young respectively. In the following year only two pairs of Buzzards remained and just one youngster fledged. In the year (1960) of the coccidiosis outbreak, four Buzzard pairs bred but all failed. Another total failure, in 1963, followed the severe 1962–1963 winter. In between these episodes the numbers of Buzzards partly recovered to 4 or 5 pairs, which together reared up to six young each year. Through the next 31 years (1965–95) the Skomer Buzzard population fluctuated between 2 and 6 pairs, usually 3–5 (Sutcliffe 1998). On average they fledged 0.8 young per pair despite Rabbits again being plentiful. Field observations suggested that, in these small (75 ha) and exposed territories, the Buzzards' hunting success was seriously reduced by constant mobbing by Carrion Crows and flocks of breeding large gulls.

In the Welsh Borders region, some measure of changes in Buzzard breeding performance either side of the myxomatosis event were revealed (retrospectively) by a recent analysis of the nest records database of the British Trust for Ornithology (Sim *et al.* 2000). These authors plotted the annual variations in the average number of young fledged per successful breeding pair between 1950 and 1995. They found that during 1950–53, just before the disease, successful pairs fledged 2.2 young, but that rate fell steeply to 1.5 in 1954 and to just 1.0 in 1955–56, immediately after the Rabbit 'crash'. Subsequently, performance recovered to 1.7 during the late 1950s, but thereafter it fluctuated widely around 1.5 fledglings. Unfortunately, though not surprisingly, the nest records excluded information about the proportions of territorial pairs breeding and the failure rates in those years.

Rabbits and Buzzard breeding productivity

Productivity data of Buzzard populations conventionally are aggregated as mean values for all pairs within each study area. This enables average breeding performance and success to be compared between regions of contrasting habitats and Rabbit abundance (Swann & Etheridge 1995, for example). A more detailed picture might be obtained for each area by comparing Buzzard performance with the Rabbit abundance in individual territories over (say) 5–10 consecutive years. An attempt at such fine-scale resolution is given here for my Dartmoor study population. In all cases, the effects of adverse 'confounding' factors on Buzzard breeding success, such as bad weather or nest failures caused by predators or human disturbance, should be made clear.

Dartmoor: a case study

The breeding activity and performance of Buzzards occupying twelve permanent territories were monitored annually during the first thirteen post-myxomatosis years, from 1956 to 1968, except in 1959–60. Rabbit abundance and availability to Buzzards was rated in six categories of a qualitative index, based on frequent personal observations and farmers' reports. These are expressed for each year as the proportion of territories with three different levels of abundance (Figure 13.4).

In all years Rabbits generally were scarce or absent except for clusters in a few territories in some years. Recovering numbers were depleted again in autumn 1961 by a recurrence of myxomatosis in three territories and by shooting. The severe 1962–63 winter further reduced numbers in 1963 to levels reportedly even lower than after the first disease outbreak. A

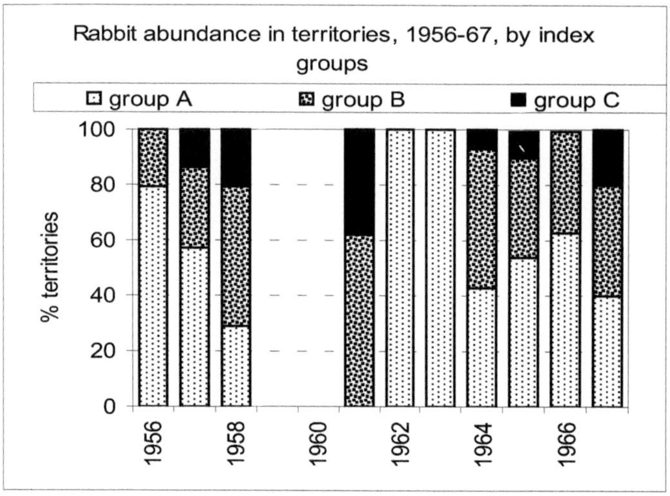

Figure 13.4 Fluctuations in the annual index of abundance of Rabbits in 12 Buzzard territories at Postbridge, Dartmoor, during 1956–67. Three classes of Rabbit index are used: A – absent/scarce: availability nil/rare. B – occasional small clusters: availability irregular; C – widespread: small number available, probably daily.

small recovery ensued but Rabbits continued to be scarce in most territories. In only a few were they judged likely to be available daily for Buzzards when rearing broods. Even in the best years Rabbit numbers everywhere were said to be still far below their pre-myxomatosis levels.

At the individual pair/territory level some associations between Rabbit abundance indices and Buzzard breeding performance were revealed (Figure 13.5). This approach takes better account of asynchronous and localized changes in Rabbit distributions within single or several neighbour territories. The breeding activity and productivity of Buzzards in each of the 12 territories improved with the availability of Rabbits (Figure 13.5, upper). In territories with more Rabbits (higher indices) Buzzards showed the highest pair-occupancy rate (*c.*90%), incidence of breeding attempts (*c.*85%) and success (*c.*80%) in rearing broods. Pairs without Rabbits nevertheless attempted to breed but less often and with lower success (see below).

The advantages of possessing a territory with more Rabbits were most evident in terms of ultimate breeding productivity and the numbers of young fledged annually by each Buzzard pair (Figure 13.5, lower). Thus, on average, territorial pairs with Rabbits fledged nearly three times as many young as pairs in rabbit-free territories. This was the result of less frequent nest failures combined with a higher proportion of successful broods of two fledglings. Fewer chicks died of starvation in territories with some Rabbits. Four of the above six relationships were strong, but increased Rabbit abundance did not appear to influence the proportions of pairs breeding or the average number of young reared by successful pairs.

Further monitoring in the early 1990s found that the breeding success of this population had been transformed by a major recovery in Rabbit numbers throughout most of the area. In nine of the 'old' territories they had increased markedly and, significantly, there were now 15 Buzzard pairs, three new pairs having established territories where Rabbits had become

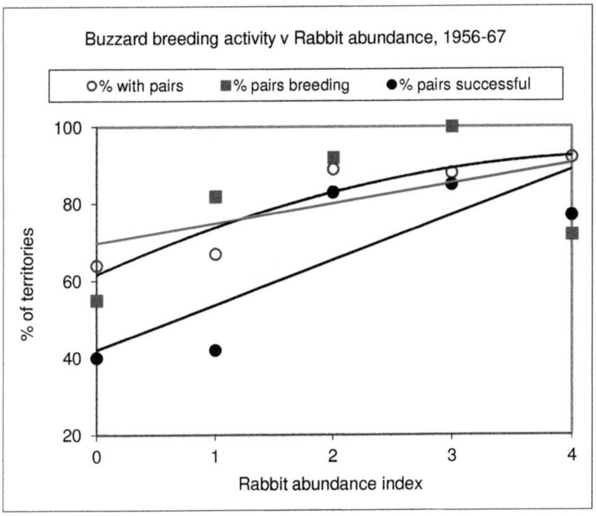

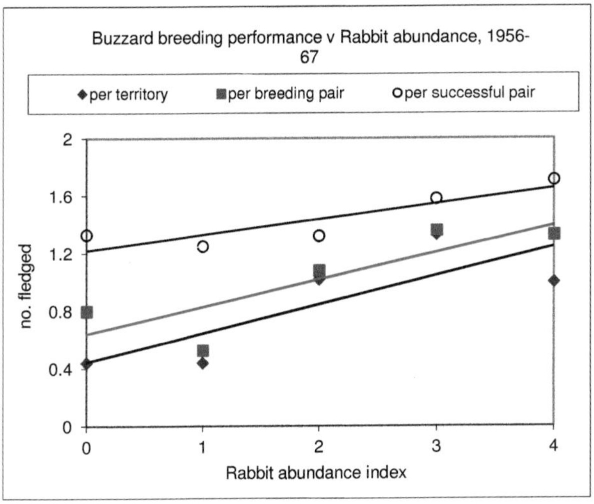

Figure 13.5 Relationships between Rabbit abundance and the breeding performance of Buzzards at Postbridge, Dartmoor, during 1956–67; soon after the 1954–55 myxomatosis outbreak. Upper: average frequencies of territory occupancy, breeding (eggs) and successful brood rearing; lower: average numbers of young fledged per territorial pair, breeding pair and successful pair. Rabbit indices as in previous figure.

common. Breeding success was good in both the nine old and three new territories containing many Rabbits, but was poor in those three old territories with fewer Rabbits. Of the Buzzard pairs in the 12 territories where Rabbits were plentiful, on average, 88% bred each year, 77% successfully, and they reared 1.65 fledglings per successful pair or 1.25 per territory. More pairs now fledged broods of two fledglings rather than singletons, and the first trio was recorded for this area. In all, there was a great improvement compared to 30 years before. By contrast, breeding success in the three poorer territories was reminiscent of the early years after myxomatosis. In this small sample, there were only 25% confirmed breeding attempts that produced around 0.2 fledglings per territorial pair. Nonetheless, across the entire study area, the increases in pair numbers and individual breeding success resulted in a doubling of the total of young fledged by the Buzzards in this part of Dartmoor.

Elsewhere, too, conclusive relationships between Rabbit abundance and Buzzard productivity have proved more difficult to demonstrate. Obtaining reliable data for Buzzards is straightforward whereas assessing Rabbit numbers, particularly for the sizes taken by Buzzards for their broods, poses major problems. These require considerable extra field effort, and are usually beyond the resources of one person. The pressing need is for a method to assess the numbers of small Rabbits available for Buzzards to hunt in given territories. Direct observation of warrens from hides and use of remote cameras would be necessary.

British Isles: Overview

This review provides evidence, confirming long-held impressions among naturalists, that abundance of Rabbits is the major natural factor determining the breeding success and productivity of Buzzard populations in this country. A close relationship was demonstrated most convincingly by the national myxomatosis 'crisis' of the mid-1950s. Since then, studies in many regions collectively have shown how Rabbits influence all stages of Buzzard breeding performance, except perhaps the start date of egg laying. That can be affected by other factors including weather and nest construction demands. Rabbit populations do not exhibit cyclic behaviour but nowadays may have irregular short-term local declines due to recurrent disease episodes. The responses of Buzzards to such temporary declines in Rabbit numbers have not been assessed.

Buzzards adapt quickly to Rabbit scarcity or absence by increasing their predation on Short-tailed Voles and many other small preys which, although previously often taken, had been of lesser importance. Short-tailed Voles typically become the staple year-round food in upland regions. However, Buzzard populations reliant upon these alternative preys generally have lower breeding performance and output of fledglings. Nonetheless, upland Buzzards breed successfully and maintain populations that are stable or, where sheep carrion becomes readily available, may even increase in numbers. On those extensive southern Scottish grass moors where cyclic vole populations still exist, rather few Buzzards breed owing to a shortage of nest sites. Elsewhere, occasional smaller fluctuations in vole numbers may be reported anecdotally, but lack of vole data precludes the chances of detecting effects on breeding Buzzards.

SUMMARY

- In European temperate and boreal zones, the annual breeding success of Common Buzzard populations is positively correlated with the cyclical abundance of *Microtus* voles. This association is evident despite Buzzards being generalist predators, able to switch to alternative preys and rear smaller broods when voles are scarce. Rabbits are not an important prey in these continental regions.
- Breeding effort is matched to the fluctuating availability of voles in early spring by varying the proportion of pairs that attempt to breed (lay eggs) and by small adjustments in clutch size. Vole abundance in late spring and summer then

determines hatching rates, nestling survival, fledged brood size, and hence overall breeding productivity.

- In Britain, however, availability of Rabbits is the major factor determining high breeding productivity of Buzzard populations. The national myxomatosis 'crisis' in the mid-1950s caused not only a sudden and near-extermination of Rabbits but triggered total breeding failures and high mortalities among adult Buzzards.
- Surviving Buzzards adapted quickly to Rabbit scarcity or absence by increasing their predation on Short-tailed Voles and many other small preys formerly of lesser importance. These voles became the staple year-round food in many upland regions.
- Buzzards reliant upon voles and other alternative preys generally have lower breeding productivity. This may be because Short-tailed Voles in Britain are normally acyclic and in long-term decline due to habitat loss and deterioration. Nonetheless, upland Buzzard populations remain stable and, where sheep carrion is readily available, they may even increase.
- Rabbit populations have slowly recovered but are still generally well below pre-myxomatosis levels, and also subject to irregular short-term local declines due to recurrent disease episodes. Buzzards in regions where Rabbit availability is again high have shown the highest breeding productivity.

14

DEMOGRAPHY AND POPULATION DYNAMICS

The processes by which a bird population maintains its numbers at a more or less stable level define its population dynamics, and these may differ between habitats and over time with changes in environmental conditions. Stability in a population is achieved when the reproductive rate and mortality rate are balanced, otherwise a population either increases or declines. In reality, a 'stable' population typically fluctuates annually around a certain value but without any trend in the number of its individuals.

Following their recent release in most regions from the restraints imposed by more than a century of persecution, Buzzard populations in Britain have increased and expanded their range at a remarkably rapid and unforeseen pace (Chapter 15). Population densities are very high, at around 1–2 km^2 per pair, in some areas (Appendix 26). However, although easing of persecution has been undoubtedly a trigger, the rapidity of the national population recovery requires further explanation. For example, by how much has survival improved and which age groups have benefitted most? Are Buzzards breeding more successfully, and at younger ages perhaps, aided by increasing food resources? Unfortunately, Buzzard population dynamics in this country have yet to be investigated. This should not be too surprising. Until the 1980s, few Buzzard populations had remained unaffected by persecution, pollution or myxomatosis (Chapter 15) for long enough to reach any semblance of stability.

This chapter summarises the demographic characteristics of Buzzards in Britain, particularly their survival rates, mortality causes, age at first breeding, and reproductive rates.

SURVIVAL AND LONGEVITY

Buzzards are potentially long-lived in the wild as befits a fairly large bird of prey with generalised food habits. This is confirmed by some recoveries of ringed nestlings which indicate that, where not persecuted, a large population is likely to contain some individuals of more than 20 years old. In Britain, the two oldest Buzzards died when in their 29th and 26th years respectively of living close to their natal sites in the uplands of Cumbria and North Wales (BTO online ringing report, 2014). In the lowlands of Somerset, a bird ringed when already adult lived a further 23.5 years before dying from natural causes. This Buzzard must have been at least 26 years old. In a North Somerset study area, recognisable individuals are known to have lived for up to 22 years in their territories (Prytherch 2013). In northern Britain, three birds that died in their 25th year – in Kintyre, Dumfries and Galloway, and in Cumbria – had all lived in relatively remote areas. In Devon, a leucistic Buzzard is known to have lived 21 years in its natal area (Hurrell 1974). In Europe, where a number of 15–25-year-old Buzzards have been recorded, the oldest bird was in its 29th year (Cramp & Simmons 1980, citing Rydzewski 1974).

The ring recovery data from the long-running BTO and European schemes have been used by analysts to estimate annual mortality and survival rates, and hence potential life spans (Table 14.1). Comparisons between studies are problematic due to geographical variations between populations, environmental conditions and migratory behaviour apart from the use of different analytical methods, sample sizes and periods.

Table 14.1 Annual survival rates (%) for Buzzards

	Annual survival rates (%) for Buzzards			
	Sweden	**Germany**	**Britain 1969–89**	**S. England**
Year of Life	**rings**	**rings**	**rings**	**radio tags**
	425		288	146
1	43.5	49	55+/−3	70+/−4
2	69.7	68	75+/−3	93+/−3
3	71.6	81?	75+/−4	88–91
4	79	81	88+/−3	88–91
5	80.5	81	88+/−3	
6	83.1	81		
7	85.0			
8	94.8			
9	81.3			
10	89.6			
	Olsson (1958)	Mebs (1964)	Kenward *et al.* 2000	

Nonetheless, it appears that first-year survival was lower in Sweden and Germany (43–49%) before 1964 than it was in Britain (55%) in later decades. Such a discrepancy, if real, could have resulted from heavier persecution (see below) combined with severe cold winter mortalities and migration losses among the continental Buzzards. The Britain estimate is close to the 60% estimated for first-year Buzzards in central France that was derived from twenty years of ringing, colour-marking and recent radio tagging (Nore 1999). Estimates of second-year survival were higher (probably significantly) in all these studies; 68–70% in

Sweden and Germany, and 75% in Britain. After their third year, when all Buzzards would have become adult, their annual survival in all populations exceeded 80%, averaging 85% in Sweden, 81% in Germany and 88% in Britain.

Even higher survival rates were found for radio-tagged juvenile Buzzards that were tracked after leaving nests in a Dorset study area in southern England (Table 14.1); thus, 70% in the first-year, 93% in the second-year, and around 90% thereafter. Most juvenile deaths occurred within four months of fledging whereas the spring months were the most critical time of year for older age classes. It was estimated that 49% or more of juveniles reached their fourth year and adulthood. This is a much higher proportion than in the ringing-derived estimates (31%) for Buzzards ringed in southern England, and 28% for the British population (Kenward et al. 2000).

The survival curves obtained from the above data sets show clearly how life spans and the age structure of populations are determined primarily by the first-year survival rate (Figure 14.1). When Buzzards in Britain become adult, with an annual survival rate then close to 90% (Table 14.1), the expectation is that 20–30% of them should still be alive 10 years later, and that 5–10% will reach 20 years. Consequently, where there exists, as in Devon and central Wales, a long-established and seldom-persecuted population of 500 or more pairs, a

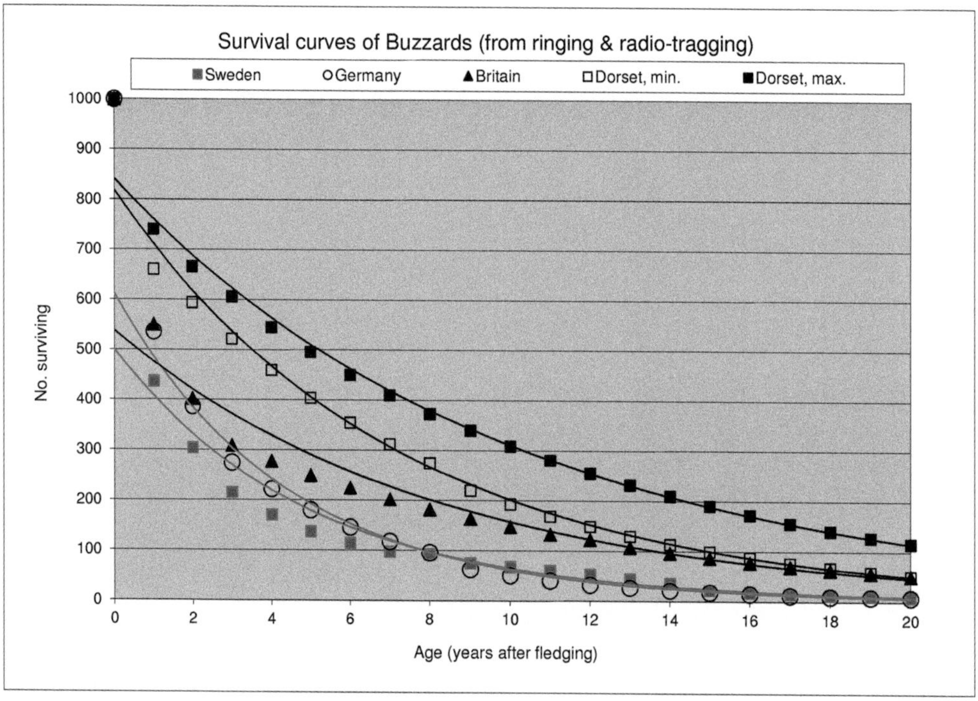

Figure 14.1 Survival curves of Buzzards fledged in Britain, Germany and Sweden; the lower three from ringing data, the top two from radio-tagging. [Curves refer to initial cohorts of 1,000 fledglings and have been extrapolated to span 20 years. (see Table 14.1)

substantial proportion of 10–19-year-old Buzzards, and a few aged 20 years and older should be present. There appears to be no information on the detailed age structure of any specific population in Britain or Europe.

The longevity data for adult Buzzards in Britain suggest that annual survival remains high and more or less constant. This might not be the case everywhere, however. In north-west Germany, by contrast, adult survival was found to peak at a certain age and to differ between the sexes (Kruger & Lindstrom 2001). These workers observed, for 11 years, 400 breeding Buzzards that could each be identified by individual plumage markings. These were birds newly recruited into the breeding population. Results showed that annual survival was highest (c.80%) for males when in their seventh year after starting to breed; but for females it peaked a year earlier and at a lower level (c.70%). Thereafter, survival rates of both sexes fell sharply to only 30% by their tenth breeding year. The absolute ages of individual Buzzards, or when they began to breed, were not known. A conservative assumption (see below) would be to add three pre-breeding years. This would estimate that survival peaked when these Buzzards were about 9–10 years old. Whether similar survival patterns are found elsewhere remains to be demonstrated.

Causes of mortality

British populations

Our knowledge stems predominantly from the recoveries of Buzzards that were ringed as nestlings (pulli) and subsequently reported as found dead, dying or fatally injured. Finders sometimes indicated known, or suspected human-related or natural causes. The recoveries have all been heavily biased by human factors (persecution) because most data were from the decades when persecution was rife. During that period, the recovery rates were high, especially for young Buzzards, and most reports reflected the prevailing persecution levels.

In upper Strathspey in the late 1970s, for example, almost one third of young Buzzards (52 from about 185 ringed) were recovered within 20 km of the study area, and 14 from further away (Picozzi & Weir 1976). Of the nearest birds, 64% died in their first year, and 54% of those had been poisoned, 15% trapped or shot, and 12% were injured or died from accidents. The remaining 20% were described as 'found dead', but many of these could have been killed. A different pattern was apparent in the more distant recoveries, of which only 7% had been killed, 14% were found injured and the rest had died from unknown causes.

There is strong post-mortem evidence that widespread persecution continued in Scotland, as well as in Wales and many English counties, during the 1970s and 1980s (Elliott & Avery 1991). Of 238 Buzzard casualties examined in 15 years, 89% had been poisoned and the others either shot or trapped. It is probable that many other such incidents were undetected. Most deaths, whether intentional or accidental, happened during the spring hill-lambing season when poisoned baits were set illegally to kill Foxes. Buzzard deaths peaked in March and April, and were fewest in June and July. On a regional basis, there were 101 incidents in Scotland (87 poisoned, 8 pole-trapped, 6 shot), and 26 cases in Wales (14 poisoned, 8 shot, 4 pole-trapped). Twelve of the poisoned Buzzards in Wales had died not far from my study areas. Even in Devon, 8 Buzzard shooting and 19 poisoning cases were confirmed. Similar deaths in my Dartmoor study area during the late 1950s have already been mentioned. The impacts of such persecution on national Buzzard numbers cannot be estimated, for the population was increasing at that time, though it might have retarded their spread back into some districts. The recovery data show also that juvenile Buzzards are especially vulnerable to poisoning because they are attracted more readily than adult Buzzards to baits (see also Chapter 9).

An updated analysis of the Buzzard recoveries from 8,967 Buzzards ringed in Britain over the past century can be found in the BTO Migration Atlas (R. Kenward, in Wernham *et al.* 2002). Of about 530 recoveries of birds ringed as nestlings, 98% were found dead. Causes of death had been attributed by finders for 49% (about 260) of the birds. For this sample, the overwhelming influence of humans upon the survival of young Buzzards was apparent. Thus, 21% had been deliberately killed, 49% died from 'other human-related accidents' (including pollution and accidental capture) while a further 12% died from unspecified human activities. Only 11% of the Buzzards had died from natural environmental factors. However, it is stressed that much of the data relate to decades (before 1981) when Buzzards were inadequately protected and, especially in northern areas, were routinely persecuted. A further check, using only the recoveries in southern Britain between 1970 and 2000, showed that little had changed.

An additional source of information concerning the fates of young Buzzards is that provided by the 50 recoveries of ringed and radio-tagged nestlings from a Dorset study population (Kenward *et al.* 2000). Again, a substantial proportion (24%) of birds had been deliberately killed (shot or poisoned). Many (40%), however, had died from natural causes (starvation, disease, other) while 36% had collided with human artefacts such as trains, cars, wires and power cables. It is notable that none of the sedentary adults died during the study period. On the other hand, the juvenile Buzzards dispersing from natal sites, some for considerable distances, became more exposed to human persecution and to risks of starvation. Most deaths occurred in March and April, a feature already noted.

European populations

Common Buzzards in Scandinavia and Germany have long been persecuted, and this was the predominant cause of death cited in the recoveries of ringed nestlings, and of breeding adults. Of 473 Scandinavian birds recovered, 42% had been shot and a further 20% died from 'other human-related causes' (Olsson 1958). These populations migrate to or through Germany, where Mebs (1964) considered that persecution caused 50–80% of all recorded deaths. It seemed to be a major and 'highly detrimental' factor in the population dynamics of the Common Buzzard. According to the Atlas of European Birds (Hagemeijer & Blair 1997), persecution was, and locally still is, a factor limiting this raptor's distribution and numbers, reducing breeding success and disrupting population turnover.

Common Buzzards in northern and central Europe die also from a wide range of natural causes. Many may starve to death during severe winters while others, especially juveniles, are accident prone. They strike road and rail traffic when hunting, or are electrocuted by power lines. Predation of incubating Common Buzzards, and of nestlings, by more powerful raptors – Goshawks and Eagle Owls – has been recorded in Scandinavia (Olsson 1958). The

European literature up to 1975 listed 65 records of Eagle Owls killing Common Buzzards, and of Goshawks taking 16 others (Newton 1979, citing Mikkola 1976 and Őttendorfer 1952).

AGE AT FIRST BREEDING

Reference books speculate on the age at which Buzzards first start to breed although many authors favour when birds are two or three years old. Only recently has direct evidence been obtained based on two field studies of individual birds that had been marked with patagial colour tags or with radio tags just before fledging. These showed a wide range of starting ages in both areas, where breeding density already was high. The limited observations suggest that Buzzards may experience problems with finding favourable territory vacancies under such conditions.

In central Wales, seven colour-marked males on average started breeding when 3.1 years old, one year ahead of four females that first bred at 4.0 years (Davis & Davis 1992). Of the males, one bred at two years, four at three years and two at four years. The first female did not breed until three years old, with two others at four years, and one not until it was five years old. It was thought that the sex difference possibly was due to wider dispersal by some young females to beyond the surveyed area; as has been found with female Sparrowhawks (Newton 1979). A similarly gradual recruitment process was a feature also in the Dorset study area. There, none of the radio-tagged Buzzards bred in their first year (second calendar year) and only 6% and 14% did so in their second and third years, respectively. The rest deferred breeding until later, and this led to a high proportion of non-breeders in the total population (Kenward *et al.* 2000). According to the ringing and radio-tracking estimates of juvenile survival (above), respectively 43% and 66% of birds should still be alive (potential recruits) at the end of their second year, and 32% and 59% at the end of the third year. During these 2–3 years before each year-class of juveniles can begin recruiting to its adult population, 21–29% of the parent Buzzards could have died.

In contrast, where Buzzards are re-colonising former haunts, as in my part of Suffolk, most of the new pairs are breeding successfully within twelve months of settling (Dare 2013). Precisely when new recruits first arrive is difficult to determine in this study area. However, two territories (only 1 km from my home) were claimed by new pairs of Buzzards that appeared suddenly in late February and early March. In North Somerset similarly, some newcomers also turn up already paired (R. Prytherch, pers. comm.).

REPRODUCTIVE RATES

The annual breeding success of a Buzzard population can be expressed variously as the number of young reared (fledged) per successful pair, breeding pair or territorial pair. The last value is probably the best indicator of a population's overall breeding performance. It is used to estimate the total number of young produced each year by a population of known size. More often, this measure of output is used to compare the breeding performance of Buzzards living at differing densities in other habitats or bio-geographical zones. All such performance values reflect the interplay of multiple factors that affect the proportions of pairs breeding and the survival of eggs and young in each Buzzard population.

Thirteen studies of breeding Buzzards in Britain have been made since 1956 (Appendix 24), the longest being for 20 successive years between 1988 and 2007 in North Somerset (Prytherch 2013). The first was on Dartmoor just after the initial 1954–55 myxomatosis outbreak, with further monitoring through the 1960s as the Buzzard population was readjusting to the depletion of their main food resource (Dare 1961, 1998). Productivity of the Dartmoor birds slowly improved from a very low level of 0.5 juveniles per territorial pair. The studies elsewhere were made just before or during different phases of the national population expansion (Chapter 15).

The annual productivity of populations has varied between 0.6 and 1.6 young per territorial pair. Lowest values were in three Welsh areas, on Dartmoor and in one Scottish area, Glen Urquhart, during or after the 1970s. The success of those Buzzards was little better than that of the Dartmoor birds in the 1960s post-myxomatosis period. Highest productivities, of 1.2–1.6 juveniles per territorial pair, were achieved in five areas, three of them with plentiful Rabbits. Scottish pairs in Speyside and West Moray produced 1.5 and 1.6 young per pair of population, as did Buzzards in North Somerset during 1988–90 (Prytherch 2013). These values probably represent the maximum achievable anywhere in our modified British countryside. Ten of the studies referred to well established populations. The increasing populations in north-east Wales and the West Midlands of England fledged 1.2–1.3 young per territorial pair on diets which included Rabbits. It is interesting, therefore, that productivity is also good (1.1 per territorial pair) in a new population that is currently re-occupying north Suffolk (Dare 2013). The productivity of actual breeding pairs, including failed attempts, was highest in the two areas of north-east Scotland where Rabbits were abundant, and in North Somerset (1998–90). Those Buzzards on average reared two fledglings per breeding attempt, and around 2.5 young from successful nests. In contrast, the average production of two Welsh upland populations failed to reach even one fledgling per territorial pair.

Productivity thus varied between populations by factors of two to three. Although it was low in Snowdonia, the total number of territorial pairs nonetheless doubled (102% increase) during the twenty years from 1984, at an annual average rate of 5% (Driver & Dare 2009). This doubling of population density did not affect productivity in the large Carneddau sub-region (Appendix 24). This increase was part of a general trend observed in adjacent regions of North Wales (and elsewhere) at that time (Chapter 15).

Productivity might be expected to decline over a long period should a Buzzard population increase to a high density. Such an event happened recently in North Somerset, during 1988–2007, and was closely monitored by Prytherch (2013). Buzzard numbers increased almost five-fold, from 19 to 92 territorial pairs, during those 20 years. By then, density was exceptionally high, at 0.8 km^2 per pair (123 pairs per 100 km^2). The mean territory size halved, from 137 ha in the first three years to 62 ha in the last three years. Although virtually all pairs continued to breed each year, breeding success progressively declined as more pairs failed to rear young to fledging. The proportion of successful pairs fell by a third, from around 70–80% to 50–55%, and they fledged 25% fewer young per pair on average. Fledged brood sizes also fell, from 2.06 young in the first three years to 1.5 in the last three years. This appeared to be due to higher losses of small chicks, since brood sizes at hatching remained unchanged. Chick mortality was significantly associated with high rainfall in May, when the small chicks (as noted on Dartmoor) are most vulnerable to chilling and especially to food shortages caused by poor hunting success. Conceivably, reduced territory sizes, affecting food supplies, could have been a contributory factor.

At the population level, these North Somerset values equated to a 43% reduction (from 1.4 to 0.8) in the annual number of young produced per territorial pair. Nevertheless, as Prytherch points out, the total number of young Buzzards produced by this population actually increased over time. High density, at least in this area, thus could be beneficial in nett population terms despite lowering the individual breeding success of territorial pairs. Food resources in this area, though not assessed, clearly were unusually favourable, as was the absence of persecution.

On the national scale, the productivity of Buzzards has been monitored yearly since 1968 by the British Trust for Ornithology, using small annual samples of aggregated nest record data (www.bto.org). Surprisingly, and *contra* the main North Somerset findings, there appears to have been no significant change in breeding performance over recent decades. The BTO analyses suggested that clutch size, brood size and the failure rates of nests had not changed over the past 40 years. This approach appears to be insufficient for detecting regional trends and differences in productivity (see also below).

Finally, it is instructive to compare productivities of Buzzard populations in areas of different land use or habitat compositions by taking the numbers of juveniles fledged per unit area. Thus, preliminary calculations show that Buzzards occupying rich agricultural farmland in North Somerset recently were fledging annually some 100 juveniles per 100 km^2. This would be about twice that achieved by upland Buzzards on Dartmoor in the 1990s, and five times the output of birds in the Snowdonia mountains region ten years ago.

ACCOUNTING FOR POPULATION CHANGES

An increase in Buzzard numbers can result only when the number of young birds recruiting each year to an adult population exceeds the adult annual death rate, here taken to be 12% for British birds (Table 14.1). The recruiting Buzzards may come either from within the population (the philopatry effect) or by immigration from elsewhere. Leaving aside immigration for the moment, increases can be achieved by higher survival rates of adults, and especially of returning offspring, that would follow a reduction in persecution. The number of juveniles produced by a population in a particular year depends initially upon both the proportion (70–85% typically) of territorial pairs that breed, and on the success of those attempts. The final breeding productivity (of undisturbed populations) is then governed largely by food availability.

The subsequent rate at which young Buzzards recruit to a particular population will depend critically upon their survival over the two or three years needed to reach maturity; which corresponds to their third or fourth calendar year. By then, ring recovery data (Table 14.1) indicate that, respectively, 43% and 32% should still be alive. However, a much higher survival (66% and 59%) is possible, according to the radio-tagging work. Recruitment, however, depends also upon the availability of vacant territories each year, as noted previously.

In areas of already high breeding density, as in Dorset and central Wales, the chance to start breeding can be delayed by several years. In contrast, pioneering Buzzards in eastern England currently face little or no competition when establishing new territories, and many of these newcomers are known to breed within a year of settling (Dare 2013).

Can these estimated values for general mortality/survival rates be applied, with the more specific data on breeding rates of individual small populations, to help explain the recent rapid and national increase in Buzzard numbers? Fortunately, this can be attempted here, thanks to a long-term (30-year) population study of Buzzards, free from persecution, in North Somerset by Prytherch (2013).

A case study: North Somerset, 1982–2012

In this unique endeavour, the annual productivity of each territorial pair was monitored for 20 of the years (1988–2007) spanning different phases of this population's 8-fold increase during the 30 years. Buzzard numbers followed a typical growth curve (Figure 14.2) from 13 up to 105 pairs, at which point numbers levelled out and were considered to be nearing saturation density. By then, the average breeding productivity had declined significantly. As territory sizes became nearly 50% smaller, density-dependent factors increasingly came into play. The percentage of successful pairs fell from 70–90% in the first five years to fluctuate around 50% in the second decade. The mean size of their successful broods declined from 2.1 to 1.5 fledglings between the first three and last three years, respectively. For the population as a whole, however, whereas the average individual productivity halved between these 3-year periods, from 1.4 to 0.8 fledglings per territorial pair, the collective output of juveniles by the population had tripled by the end of these 20 years.

The data provide insights into the extent to which this rapid population increase could have been sustained by self-recruiting young Buzzards from its own breeding success, or whether it stemmed in part from immigration. For this exercise, the estimated 12% mortality of the parent population in each year (y) is compared with the numbers of their juveniles that would have survived long enough to reach breeding age, when two (y + 2) or three (y + 3) years old. These survivors would then become potential recruits should they remain in or return to their birth area (Figure 14.3). Two sets of survival estimates are used, the first derived from national ringing recoveries, and the other from radio tagging (see above). These probably provide lower and upper survival limits for Buzzards in recent decades.

The outcomes, not surprisingly, are sensitive to the juvenile survival rates applied. Those based on ring recoveries suggest that enough young Buzzards should have been available to replace adult losses, but not to trigger the rapid trebling in numbers that was observed in the first ten years to 1998. That would seem to have been caused by immigration, presumably (as Prytherch suggested) from further west, where numbers were already high. In Devon, for example, Buzzards had been increasing for some time. After 1998 there would have been an increasing availability of potential recruits reared in the North Somerset study area itself to continue their rapid rise. Applying the radio-tagged survival rates suggests that potential recruits would have been sufficient to drive the population trend. Ultimately, in both cases, as saturation density neared, the over-production of young would lead to

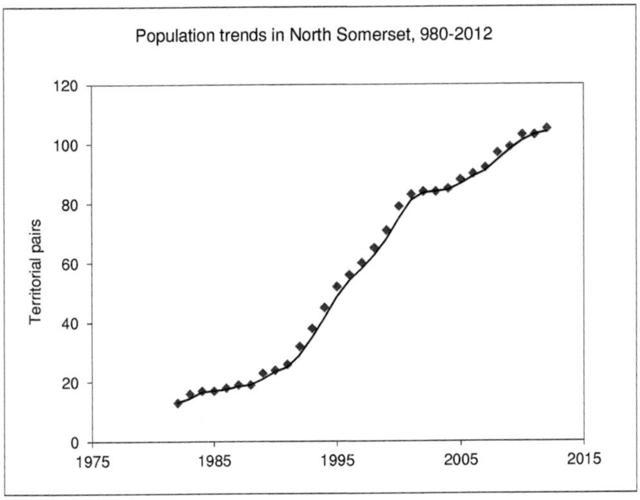

Figure 14.2 The long-term increase in the Buzzard population of a North Somerset study area during the 31 years, 1982–2012 (from Prytherch, in litt.)

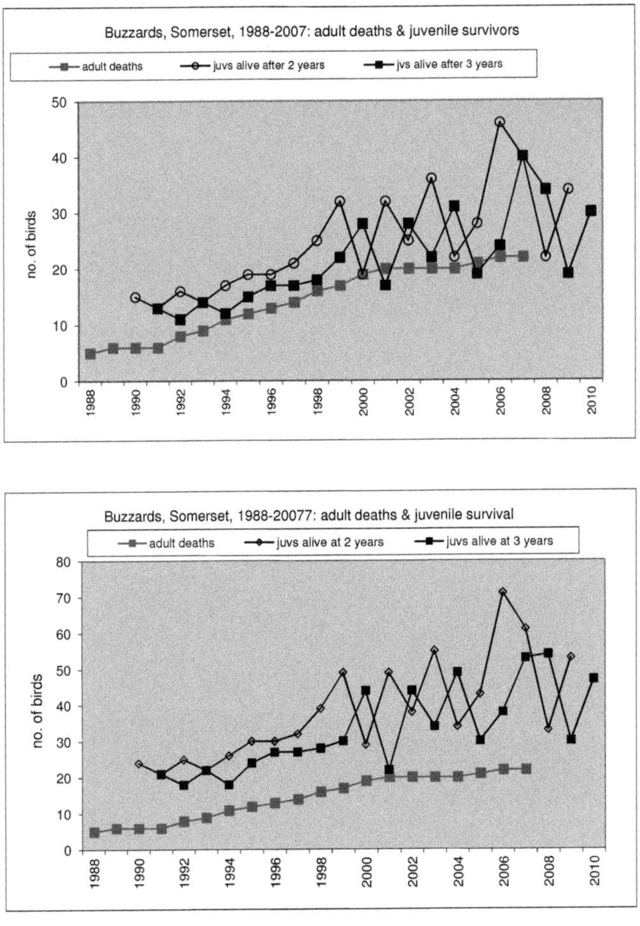

Figure 14.3 Estimated numbers of adult territorial Buzzards dying each year compared with the numbers of their offspring surviving to 2 or 3 years old, as potential recruits to the breeding population. Mortality/ survival values based on: upper – national ringing recovery estimates; lower – radio-tagging (Kenward et al. 2000). Data for North Somerset Buzzards (reworked from Prytherch 2013)

increasing numbers being unable to establish new territories and thus forced to emigrate instead.

Evidence of emigration from this North Somerset area is provided by 24 recoveries from the 322 nestling Buzzards ringed in the study area (Prytherch & Roberts 2012). Six juveniles had dispersed from the area for 46–117 km (average 81 km), mainly favouring directions between east and north. These distant recoveries were mostly of first-autumn or -winter birds. Two, however, had become adults that had died in the breeding season up to 46 km away eastwards, evidently having settled in those localities. Otherwise, as expected, most recoveries were within or close to the study area, and less than 10 km from natal places. Most birds had died in their first autumn or winter, the rest being sub-adults and adults that presumably were recruiting into, or close to, their parental breeding population. Deaths from persecution were unusual – one shot, after moving 46 km away – whereas accidental (collision) deaths were quite common.

This long-term population history helps to explain the processes behind the present expansion phase of Buzzards in Britain. It shows how a self-sustaining, productive and non-persecuted Buzzard population at a low density can be transformed rapidly, at first by nett immigration and self-recruitment, into a high density population that exports its surplus young birds to other areas. In this North Somerset area, immigration most likely was from the west, and emigration largely eastwards into under-populated areas previously kept Buzzard-free by persecution (Prytherch 2013). Repetition of this process in the new areas should then accelerate the further spread of Buzzards into eastern counties.

RECENT EXPANSION PHASE

The recent striking up-turn in our Buzzards' fortunes naturally has prompted much interest and speculation about its causes but few hard facts seem to have emerged concerning the processes involved, other than a preliminary assessment ten years ago (Walls *et al.* 2004). The primary 'trigger' is generally agreed to have been a widespread if gradual reduction in persecution coupled with the more positive attitudes of landowners and farming communities towards wildlife assets and conservation. Initially, Buzzard numbers and densities had increased steadily in their core western regions and edged slowly eastwards. With further easing of persecution through the 1980s, however, Buzzard populations began their unexpectedly rapid full recovery and range expansion phase. Precisely how Buzzard population dynamics may have changed in response to reduced persecution, however, is far from clear. Our limited knowledge of the suggested contributory factors, summarised below, is often inconclusive.

Improved survival

The ring recovery rates showed the high vulnerability of young Buzzards to persecution. However, this could depend in part upon the individual dispersal patterns of juveniles, and their philopatric tendency, so well demonstrated by the radio-tagging studies in Dorset. Juveniles were found to comprise two groups. The majority stay in or return close to their natal areas to breed, whereas others disperse quickly far and wide and attempt to settle in new areas. These 'pioneers' have a chance to establish territories with ample food and other resources, and with little or no competition from other Buzzards. There, they could begin breeding sooner than might have been possible in their more crowded natal areas (Walls *et al.* 2004). In the past, most ringed Buzzards were from core (stronghold) populations where persecution was low or absent. Any juveniles that formerly dispersed eastward into game-preserving areas were very likely to be killed, thereby preventing range expansion. Once persecution levels began to ease, however, more of these pioneer settlers could survive and re-colonise the new areas. Adult Buzzard survival similarly would be enhanced. As yet, unfortunately, survival rates of Buzzards over the last 30 years have not been published.

Population increases in source areas

There is good evidence from two census studies, and anecdotal county reports, that Buzzard numbers rose significantly in western populations after 1980. Repeat censuses in North Somerset and Snowdonia showed that territorial pairs had increased by, respectively, 600% and 150% between 1980 and the early 2000s, but most rapidly during the 1990s (Chapter 15). On regional scales, the BTO indices of Buzzard abundance increased between 1994 and 2007 in both the Lake District (by 111%) and south-west England (by 21%). The Wales population index rose by only 5%, and was deemed stable (www.bto.org), a conclusion at odds with the measured increases across north Wales and the views of experienced observers in other counties.

Enhanced breeding productivity

Evidence from all but two of the study areas (Appendix 24) is insufficient to show any trends, owing to the short-term nature of most projects. In North Somerset, an eight-fold increase in Buzzard numbers resulted in an extremely high population density but a halving of individual breeding success. Nonetheless, annual total output of young Buzzards in this defined area increased, as noted above (Prytherch 2013). In Snowdonia, on the other hand, the growing population maintained (but did not increase) its overall low individual productivity rate over the thirty-year period since the 1970s. In some western areas, notably Devon and west Wales, the increasing frequency of large autumn gatherings of juvenile Buzzards could reflect higher population (rather than individual) productivity in recent decades.

Food resources

Knowledge is insufficient for a meaningful assessment. Buzzard diets during their expansion phase have not been studied since the 1990s. Suggestions that they are now exploiting plentiful prey resources are not well supported by the findings from the national review of the status of British mammals (Chapter 13). Although Rabbits – the most important prey resource – are now plentiful locally, their numbers everywhere are kept far below the pre-1950 abundance level by the recurrent episodes of myxomatosis. Furthermore, the important small vertebrate preys of Buzzards have all become less numerous throughout lowland Britain during recent decades (Chapter 12). Short-tailed (Field) Voles probably have continued their long-term decline in lowlands, and their numbers may also have fallen in those uplands where over-grazed by high sheep densities. In some uplands, however, increasing amounts of sheep carrion perhaps have compensated for vole losses. Moles and shrews are both likely to have declined due to habitat loss and agricultural intensification, especially in arable regions. These land-use changes have also reduced populations of many once common small bird species. Frog populations have 'crashed', most notably in the lowlands, where high mortalities have been caused by the rapid spread of the ranavirus and chytrid fungus diseases.

The only birds likely to be of some importance as prey for lowland Buzzards are Magpies and fledgling Carrion Crows. These two corvids are taken widely to feed Buzzard broods in western counties. Their populations have doubled across much of central and eastern Britain during the last 40 years (www.bto.org) but now are stabilising, and they remain much less numerous than in the west. Magpies continue to be scarce in much of Scotland. There is no evidence that game-birds, which abound in many districts, have played an important part in the present success of Buzzards (Chapter 7).

In conclusion: The primary and most critical initiating factor undoubtedly has been the easing of persecution of Buzzards in most counties. This should have improved survival of all age groups, but more importantly that of juvenile Buzzards dispersing into the new areas. It will be some time, however, before new estimates of survival rates over the last 30 years are forthcoming. That recruitment rates to the new (colonising) populations have been greatly enhanced is evident from their rapid increases in numbers. Moreover, at present they face less intra-specific competition for key food resources than those Buzzards in densely populated western regions. On Suffolk farmland, the productivity of new settlers is impressive: with at least 78% breeding in the first years and fledging around 0.9 juveniles per territorial pair (Dare 2013).

Towards a model of Buzzard population dynamics

Ideally, an attempt should be made to construct a prototype model that could help to explain how Buzzard populations function; and to identify the relative importance of factors (including persecution) that have initiated and are driving the current significant changes. Buzzard dynamics are certain to be complex and fluid, varying between populations according to environments. One can almost envisage some Buzzards living even as 'communities' that are adapted to local circumstances and share local traits in social behaviour and reproductive performance. Annual productivity of a population depends in part upon the proportion of pairs breeding. In North Somerset, virtually every pair breeds each year even though at extremely high density. In contrast, some of the other populations studied have contained fairly high proportions of non-breeding territorial pairs every year. More importantly, regularly successful breeding in long-established populations can be restricted to rather few 'higher quality' territories. For example, on Dartmoor, approximately two-thirds of all juvenile Buzzards were raised in just one third of the permanent territories (Chapter 10). Similar disparities have been strongly suspected in Snowdonia. All of these aspects would need to be considered when attempting to construct a realistic computer model of Buzzard dynamics.

SUMMARY

- A population dynamics model for the Buzzard is needed, particularly to identify the main biological processes driving the ongoing rapid increase and range expansion of the national population. Meanwhile, the limited demographic information available is assessed.

- Annual survival estimates of fledgling Buzzards based on national ring recoveries are lower than those of radio-tagged birds from one study area. The two methods estimated first-year survival at 55% and 70%, second-year at 75% and 93%, third-year at 75% and 88%, and for adults 88% and 88– 91% thereafter.
- Buzzards potentially are long-lived in Britain; six ringed birds have lived for 21–26 years in western regions. Survival curves indicate that 28% of birds reaching adulthood could be alive 10 years later, and 7% after 20 years.
- Deliberate killing by gamekeepers and farmers has been the major cause of death stated in recoveries of ringed Buzzards, followed by collisions with human artefacts. A significant reduction in persecution since 1980 is probably the major factor enabling the re-colonisation of central and eastern England, though its specific effects on Buzzard demographics have not been measured.
- Buzzards probably start breeding when two or three years old but, in areas with high population densities, some wait 4–5 years for a vacant territory. The cumulative mortalities of young birds by the end of their second year are 57% and 34%, and by the end of the third year 63% and 41%, according to ringing and radio-tracking estimates, respectively. In the 2–3 year period before each year-class of juveniles can begin recruiting to its parental population, 21–29% of the adults from that year will have died.
- Average annual reproductive rates of nine established Buzzard populations ranged between 60–160 juveniles fledged per 100 territorial pairs, 80–220 per 100 breeding pairs, and 120–260 per 100 successful pairs.
- The ongoing national increase and range expansion of Buzzards is largely a response to greatly reduced persecution. The roles played by suggested increases in food resources and individual breeding productivity are yet to be confirmed.

15

POPULATION: DECLINE AND RECOVERY

The distribution and abundance of Buzzards in Britain have fluctuated dramatically over the last three centuries. Past changes in populations and their current status were assessed first in 1954 by a national enquiry set up by the then Nature Conservancy and the British Trust for Ornithology. This major project was triggered by serious concerns about the likely impacts upon Buzzards of the newly-arrived rabbit disease myxomatosis. The survey was accomplished in the 1954 breeding season, one year before the first effects on Buzzards became apparent. The detailed findings (Moore 1957) are the baseline with which all subsequent population assessments can be compared.

Unfortunately, estimating the total population size of Buzzards at county and regional scales is still fraught with sampling and interpretational problems. National surveys have used a variety of methods based on sample survey areas. The 1954 areas varied in size and were selected by observers familiar with the districts, and thus introduced risks of bias towards places where Buzzards were known to be plentiful. On the other hand, the 1954 observers provided more reliable data on the numbers of confirmed and potential breeding pairs than did subsequent surveys. The latter (BTO) surveys have been based on numerous, randomly allotted national grid squares of a standard size (either 100 km^2 or 4 km^2). Buzzard densities were estimated indirectly from birds seen during the breeding season or from soaring birds in spring. This approach achieves much wider geographical coverage of comparative abundances but provides less certain data on actual breeding numbers. The resultant estimates of total Buzzard numbers have wide error margins and thus are very approximate. Nevertheless, such estimates over the decades detect major trends in abundance and range since 1954. Of particular value are repeat smaller-scale surveys within study areas, or at county level, during the past 60 years.

Changes in the geographical range and relative abundance have been measured in considerable detail at 20-year intervals since the 1960s by three national mapping (atlas) surveys: in 1968–72, 1988–91 and 2008–11 (Sharrock 1976, Gibbons *et al.* 1993, Balmer *et al.* 2013. In addition, an index of recent trends in potentially breeding Buzzards, based on monitored areas, has been published annually since 1994 by the British Trust for Ornithology in conjunction with other organisations. The collated information from all of these sources provides a broad history of the changing fortunes of Buzzards during the past 250 years.

NATIONAL POPULATION CHANGES

From his thorough search of county archives, bird literature and other sources, Moore (1957) produced a sequence of maps showing changes in the geographical range of Buzzards prior to 1954 (Figure 15.1). Those for 1800–1900 were compiled from historical documents and that for 1954 from local field surveys (Moore 1957). Several periods of change were recognizable prior to 1954, since when further phases can be distinguished.

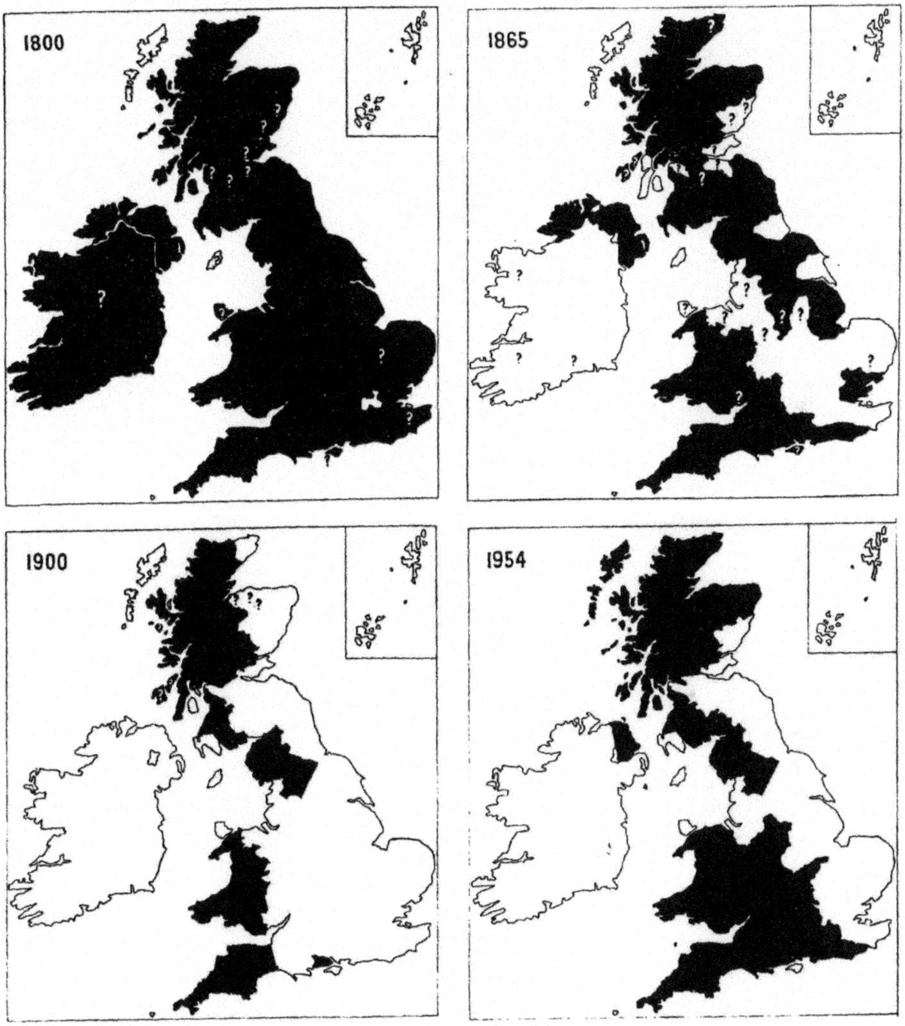

Figure 15.1 The changing breeding distribution of Buzzards in Britain and Ireland from 1800 to 1954 (reproduced with permission from British Birds). Map key: black denotes breeding proved, or good circumstantial evidence of breeding; white on black in 1800 and 1865 maps – circumstantial evidence of probable breeding; white – no evidence of breeding; black on white in 1865 and 1900 maps – inadequate evidence of breeding.

1700–1915: Persecution and decline

In the 1700s Buzzards were widely distributed and common across England, Wales and Scotland, and probably breeding in every county. From Ireland they were known only 'to occur'. Around 1775, however, game-bird preservation, and a wholesale campaign of shooting and trapping all raptors and other perceived 'vermin' then began. During the 1800s, game rearing became one of the principal activities in the British countryside. By 1865, Buzzards had been exterminated in many eastern and central counties of England. Growing concerns led in 1880 to Buzzards officially being declared a protected species, but to little or no effect. By 1900, the population had been reduced to its lowest level and in Ireland had been exterminated. In 1915, it was stated by the British Ornithologists' Union to have become confined to south-west England (Devon, Cornwall, westernmost Somerset), the western half of Wales, and north-west England (the Lake District, with a few on the adjoining north-west Pennines). In Scotland, Buzzards were restricted to the south-west uplands, the west and central Highlands, and the islands of the Hebrides. These regions of reduced game preservation effectively became refuges for remnant populations. Nonetheless, Buzzards there could still be persecuted, though less intensively, by farmers and warreners guarding their food stocks of Rabbits.

The refugia in south-west England, as in west and central Wales, were mainly the remoter moors and hill country with wooded valleys, and also along the rocky coasts. But, even there, Buzzards were at low densities (see below). The mountains of the Lake District and the remote parts of Scotland likewise became major refuges where Buzzard numbers remained relatively stable.

1915–1954: Slow recovery

From their safe havens, Buzzards later were able to begin recovering some of the lost ground as persecution by gamekeepers began to ease during and after the First World War. Statistics gathered by the Game and Wildlife Conservancy Trust (www.gwct.org.uk) show (Figure 15.2) that there had been some 23,000 gamekeepers during 1900–1910 but only about 13,000 by 1920, a 40% fall. Many keepers had perished on active service. By the end of that war, Buzzards had returned to much of their former range in southern England, the Welsh Border country and other places, though only to be exterminated again in some of these re-occupied districts as keeper numbers had recovered slightly to 15,000 by the 1930s. In that decade, however, Buzzards returned naturally to north-east Ireland, from Scotland, and maintained a foothold into the 1950s. Despite their initial setbacks in England, by 1940 Buzzards had spread back once more into Dorset, Somerset, Hampshire, Hereford and Shropshire; and they were then being described as numerous in their refuge areas. During the Second World War (1940–45) and for some years thereafter, game preservation again declined and keeper numbers fell steeply to around 3,000 in 1950. That trend continued slowly until 1980, since when their numbers have changed little.

A steady recovery of Buzzard numbers and range continued through the 1940s, and by 1949–54 in their core range they were thought to be probably more abundant than in the early 1800s. Buzzards had become a common sight across much of Wales and south-west England.

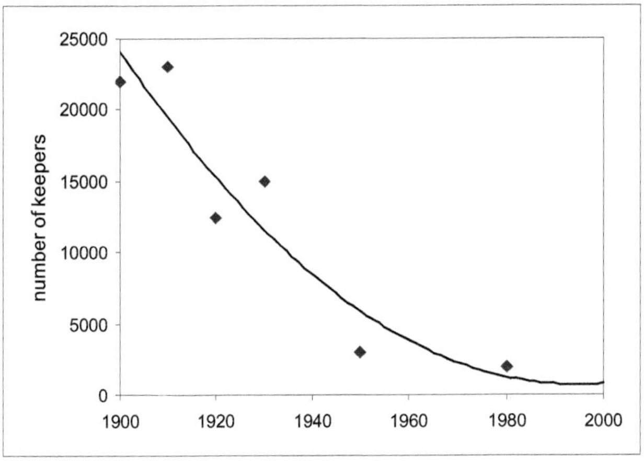

Figure 15.2 The changing numbers of gamekeepers between 1900 and 2000. [replotted from graph in a report of the Game and Wildlife Conservation Trust]

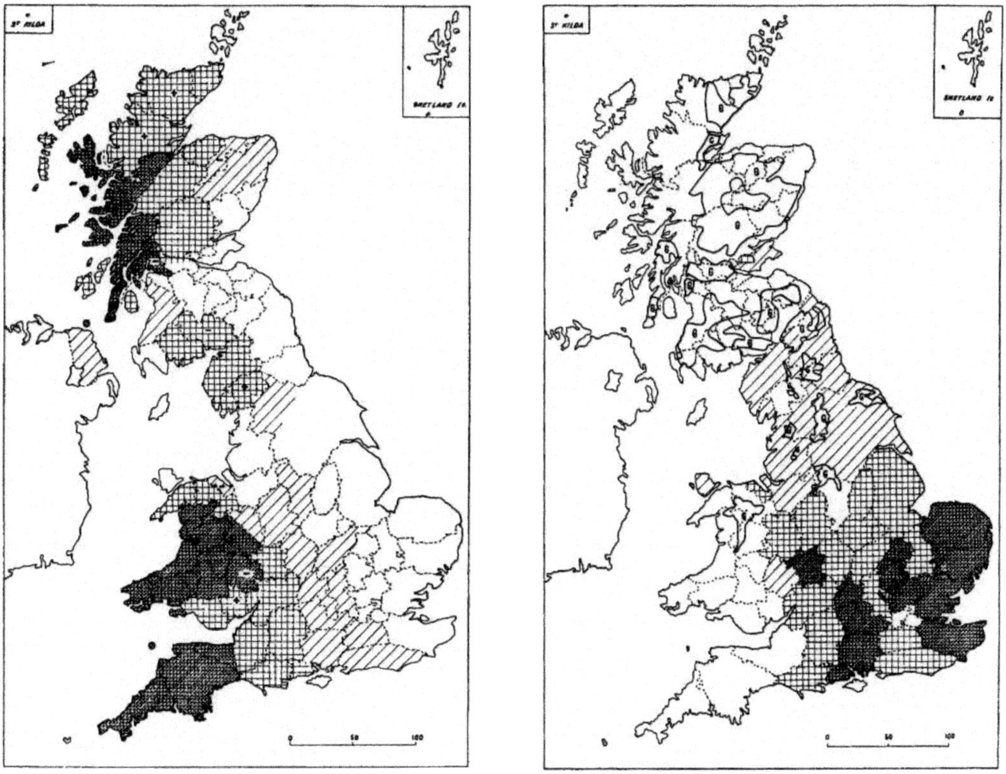

Figure 15.3 Maps showing in 1954: (left) The Buzzard breeding population density, and (right) Game preservation areas (Moore 1957)0 [reproduced with permission from British Birds]. Map key – (left) black – 10 or more breeding pairs per 100 square miles; cross-hatch – 1–9 pairs per 100 square miles; diagonal hatch – less than 1 pair per 100 square miles; white – 0. Map key (right) Numbers of gamekeepers per 100 square miles: black – 3-6; cross-hatch – 1–2; diagonal hatch – 0.5-0.9; white – less than 0.5. Red Grouse preserving areas denoted by 'G'.

The recovery coincided with declining levels of persecution on keepered lands. However, it is not known whether there were parallel falls in Buzzard deaths attributable to farmers shooting hawks suspected of taking poultry, or indirectly to them setting out poisoned baits for Foxes. In his national survey report, Moore also demonstrated with maps (Figure 15.3) that the distribution and relative abundance of Buzzards in 1954 was inversely correlated with the geographical pattern of intensive game preservation. The conclusion, from both this spatial pattern and the coincidence of Buzzards increasing as keeper numbers fell, was that population changes had been driven primarily by prolonged persecution. In 1954 statutory legislation finally granted full protection to Buzzards and other birds of prey.

The 1954 national survey showed (Figure 15.3) that Buzzards had reclaimed much lost ground in England and were now breeding, albeit at low densities, as far east as Sussex, central counties and the Peak District. In Wales, only Anglesey and the northeast corner, where persecution was still rife, had not been reoccupied. The gains in Scotland were more modest and confined to the south-west and parts of the north-east. The small Irish population had grown to about 10 pairs. The total Buzzard population in 1954 was estimated to be in the order of 8,000–12,000 territorial pairs (Moore 1957, Appendix 25). This value was extrapolated from densities observed in 104 census areas. Densities were highest in parts of Wales and Devon where 1–2 pairs per square mile (4–8 pairs per 10 km^2) were considered likely to be the normal maximum density. The nests of 45% of the pairs recorded were found in 1954.

1955–56: Population 'crash' and myxomatosis

Any further recovery process experienced a dramatic setback in the mid-1950s when the *myxoma* virus was introduced into Kent in 1954. From there, it (was) spread rapidly through Rabbit stocks, virtually annihilating this major Buzzard prey across Britain within the next two years. Buzzard numbers plummeted in 1955–56, widely by more than 20%. Falls of 25% and 33% were measured in two Devon localities (Dare 1961) and, reputedly, up to 50% died in some other areas of south-west England (Parslow 1967). As a result, and based on the above 1954 census figure, the national population of Buzzards might have fallen to around 6,000–8,000 pairs in the late 1950s. The few pairs in Ireland died out at this time. The impacts of myxomatosis upon Buzzards breeding on Dartmoor have already been described.

Buzzards were found dead or weakened by starvation, and widespread, sometimes total, failures to breed were recorded in local populations (Chapter 13). In addition, persecution by Devon poultry farmers and gamekeepers persisted throughout this period, quite possibly aggravated by alarmist local press claims of starving Buzzards attacking all kinds of livestock (Dare 1958). Moore (1957) was informed that more than 400 Buzzards had been shot in three quite small areas of Devon in winter during 1955.

1960–90: Recovery despite pesticide threats

A subsequent recovery in the Buzzard population was slow and lasted well into the1970s, even in the Devon heartlands. In the Dartmoor study area, breeding success remained low for more than ten years after myxomatosis had first appeared. The nett effects were confirmed when the first national atlas mapping survey during 1968–72 (Sharrock 1976) showed that the breeding range actually had contracted slightly since 1954 (Figures 15.4 and 15.1). It seems likely that this setback was caused in part, at least, by frequent recurrences of myxomatosis which had prevented any resurgence in Rabbit numbers in many areas. By 1980, myxomatosis clearly had become endemic in the greatly reduced national Rabbit population (Chapter 13).

By the end of the 1960s, however, a new and potentially more serious threat to recovery had become evident in certain areas. In the Lake District and the New Forest, Buzzard breeding success began falling again. Field evidence suggested a causal link: contamination of Buzzards by DDT and other persistent organochlorine pesticides then being used widely for crop protection and for sheep-dips. In particular, usage of dieldrin in dips posed clear risks for carrion-feeding hill Buzzards. In both these areas some freshly-laid eggs were found to be lightly contaminated with pesticide residues. Nonetheless, such levels were deemed sufficient for clutches to be lost due to egg-shell thinning and breakage, the diagnostic initial indicators of pesticides poisoning in raptors (Ratcliffe 1965, Tubbs 1974, Newton 1979). Buzzard numbers themselves appeared to be little affected directly, fortunately, but recruitment rates of young birds would have been depressed for some years. Their varied diet, chiefly of small mammals, saved them from the catastrophic mortalities suffered nationally (and internationally) by specialist bird-eating raptors such as Sparrowhawks and Peregrines. Small mammals, unlike birds, are able to metabolise and excrete organochlorines, and thus do not accumulate these chemicals in their bodies (Newton 2013). The remnant populations of bird-eating raptors (and others) began to recover fully from near-extinction only once usage of these pesticides had been restricted first and then phased out in the 1970s.

In the 1980s, and onwards, Buzzards began to benefit from stronger legal protection afforded to all raptors by the Wildlife and Countryside Act 1981. In Devon, Buzzard numbers were said to be more or less back to pre-myxomatosis levels by 1980 (DBRs). A national survey in 1983, based on spring counts of soaring birds, estimated the population at 12,000–17,000 pairs (Taylor *et al.* 1988, Appendix 25), a marked increase on the 1954 estimate. Extrapolations from field counts suggested that nearly one half (44%) of Buzzards were in Scotland, one third (31%) in England and a quarter (24%) in Wales; an unexpected outcome. Various major caveats were attached to this survey, as emphasized by the authors, however. Nonetheless, it is reasonable to accept that Buzzards had become noticeably more plentiful by then. The soaring survey was followed by the second national mapping survey during 1988–91 (Gibbons *et al.* 1993). The resultant map (Figure 15.4) showed few changes in distribution during the intervening 20 years. These involved in-filling and slight extensions of range eastwards in England and Scotland, but a more marked expansion in the northern counties of Ireland. Buzzard relative densities, as expected, were highest throughout most of Cornwall, Devon, Wales, and in scattered areas in western Scotland.

Post–1990: Increase and range expansion

From 1990 onwards, Buzzards unexpectedly began to increase rapidly in many areas. With more enlightened attitudes to wildlife conservation on the part of most farmers and

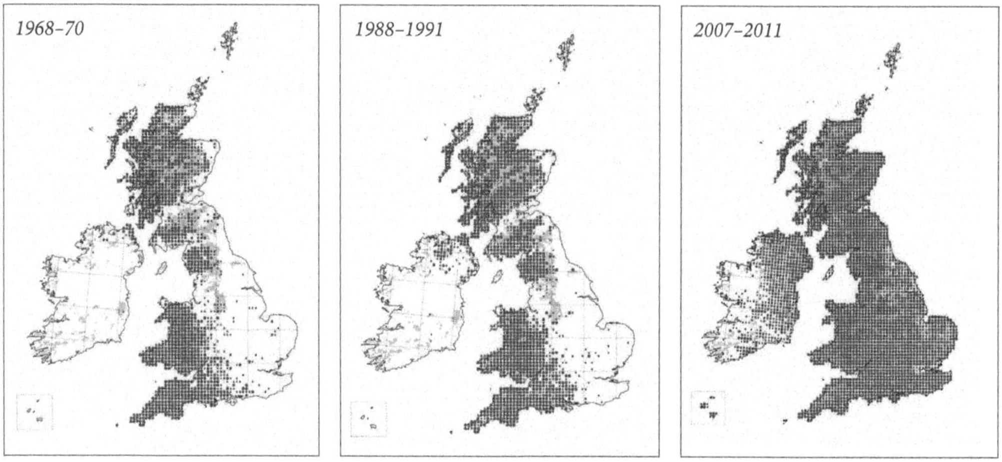

Figure 15.4 The expanding breeding range of Buzzards in Britain and Ireland since 1970, as revealed by national atlas surveys. Evidence of confirmed breeding is shown by largest dots, probable and possible breeding by smaller dots, in the 10 x 10-km squares of the Ordnance Survey grid. (Distribution maps from Bird Atlas 2007–11 which is a joint project between BTO, BirdWatch Ireland and the Scottish Ornithologists' Club. Maps reproduced with permission from the BTO)

landowners, and consequent further reductions in persecution, Buzzards began to spread steadily eastwards across southern and central England, many settling in places where Red Kites were released and now breed almost in loose 'colonies'. As in Wales, the two raptors coexist with few signs of competition, except perhaps at times for carrion, and they may even share the same woodland when nesting (Carter 2007). East of the Pennines and in eastern Scotland, however, the return of the Buzzard was slower. In these regions, continuing persecution, especially poisoning, by gamekeepers was still rife, particularly on some large estates (Elliott & Avery 1991, RSPB reports).

The 2008–2011 national atlas mapping survey has confirmed the impressive gains made by Buzzards over the last 20 years (Figure 15.4, Balmer *et al.* 2013). By 2012, Buzzards were virtually ubiquitous throughout England, Wales and Scotland, with breeding recorded in more than 70% of 10 km squares. They were now breeding also throughout the Outer Hebrides, on Orkney and had even made sea-crossings of more than 50 km to reach and breed for the first time on the Isle of Man, in the northern Irish Sea, and on the Isles of Scilly off west Cornwall. In Ireland, Buzzards spreading southwards had been retarded until the 1990s by the (then legal) use of strychnine on carrion baits set for Foxes but, inevitably, taken also by Buzzards. After 1991, when strychnine was banned, Buzzards expanded rapidly south through eastern and central counties (Hussey, http://countynaturetrust.com). By 2010, Buzzards had reached the south coast and were breeding in Co. Cork. They remain scarce or absent, so far, along the west coast of Ireland.

The total numbers of Buzzards breeding in Britain remain difficult to assess with much confidence. In 2000, they were estimated by the BTO (www.bto.org) to have reached 31,000–

44,000 territorial pairs (Appendix 25). The Wales population was considered to be 3,800 pairs around that time (Green 2002). An alternative assessment by Clements (2002, Appendix 25) used updated distribution and land use maps coupled with Buzzard densities measured in small sample survey areas across the range and in different habitat types. This comprehensive exercise led Clements to propose an even higher estimate, of between 44,000 and 61,000 territorial pairs. A much greater and coordinated national sampling effort will be needed to refine these two estimates. The latest (for 2009) BTO estimate, based on trends in transect counts, proposes the even higher total of 57,000–79,000 pairs (Musgrove *et al.* 2013). If so, that would equate to an average Buzzard density of around one pair for every 3–4 km^2 of non-urban land throughout England, Scotland and Wales; and thus comparable with measured densities in mid-Wales (Appendix 26) and north-east Suffolk (Dare 2013). Despite sampling deficiencies, these results do give some measure of the substantial scale of population growth achieved by Buzzards over recent decades.

LOCAL POPULATION CHANGES

The above account provides a broad-brush picture of historical and current changes at the national scale. Here, one can examine in finer detail changes in Buzzard populations within nine smaller areas (Appendix 25). These are either a county or study area, where populations have been re-assessed, in some places over several decades. The areas chosen (one county and six study areas) are those with which the writer is most familiar, or are well recorded in regional literature.

Devon

This large county was not only one of the main refuge areas but also has probably the best historical and detailed information, spanning some 120 years. At the end of the 19th century, near the climax of the persecution era, the county avifauna (D'Urban & Mathew 1892) described Buzzards as being 'not uncommon' about the sea cliffs and in wild uncultivated localities and wooded districts but, as a rule, rarely seen in cultivated parts. Even so, they were continually diminishing in number, primarily due to being easily trapped at rabbit warrens. A 'considerable' population recovery began during the 1914–18 war and continued in the 1920s (Hurrell 1929); although local persecution or interference and the severe 1928–29 winter caused a reduction in mid-Devon in 1929. Hurrell also noted that some keepers were well disposed towards Buzzards and prevented nest disturbance on their estates.

In 1929, a county-wide survey was carried out by the Devon Bird-Watching and Preservation Society (Hurrell 1929, 1952). The results indicated a total population in the breeding season of 900–1,200 adult Buzzards, i.e. a putative 450–600 pairs. A substantial proportion (63 pairs) nested on sea cliffs where nests were spaced on average 2–2.5 km apart. Densities inland were twice as high in the north (10 pr/100 km^2) than in the south (4 pr/100 km^2) of the county. In the latter region, Buzzards avoided agricultural land, being instead largely confined to the deep well-wooded valleys around the fringes of Dartmoor. It was not until the 1930s that Buzzards began to nest in hedgerow trees on farmland in south Devon (Hurrell 1954). There, in one area (34 km^2), where the first Buzzard was not seen until 1917, there were 9–11 pairs by 1946 and 15 pairs in 1954. The 1929 census, despite all the caveats attaching to such wide-scale endeavours (noted earlier), was the first to be attempted for Buzzards in Britain. It provided a useful reference point for the 1954 and three subsequent survey, listed in the Devon breeding birds atlas (Dare, in Sitters 1988).

The 1954 pre-myxomatosis survey (Moore 1957) provided sufficient data from the ten Devon sampling sites to roughly estimate Buzzard numbers in the county. The average density was 47 pr/100 km^2 with a maximum local density of 77 pr/100 km^2; but with wide error margins because of the small number of sites sampled and high local variations in observed Buzzard densities. There are about 5,700 km^2 of habitats probably suitable for breeding Buzzards. This suggested that between 1,700 and 3,650 (average 2,650) pairs of Buzzards were in Devon in 1954, assuming the above average density was typical, and allowing for sampling errors. If true, this would suggest at least a quadrupling of the population since 1929, which seems not unreasonable.

The first post-myxomatosis assessment of Buzzards across Devon, based on an extensive survey of almost 500 woodlands in 1966, estimated that at least 3,700 adult Buzzards (or about 1,850 putative pairs) were present during the breeding season (Moysey 1970). This estimate is lower than that for 1954 but not unexpected, given that Buzzard numbers had not then fully recovered from the Rabbit crash (DBRs). This interpretation is supported by annual census data from the Dartmoor study area (Figure 15.5) showing that Buzzard numbers remained low until 1969, possibly longer.

In some years a few territories were occupied only by single birds. Mortalities in the severe 1962–63 winter further reduced numbers in 1963, temporarily, to their lowest level. The population had recovered fully by 1990–93, when 16–17 pairs held territories each year (Dare 1999), though just when this was achieved is not known.

In spring 1974, a county-wide tetrad survey of flying (territorial) Buzzards, covering more than 400 km^2, was organized by the Devon Bird-Watching and Preservation Society.

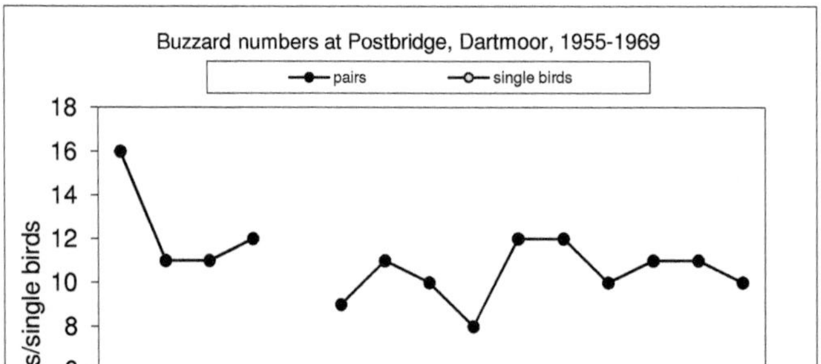

Figure 15.5 Changes in the numbers of Buzzards in a 33 km^2 Dartmoor study area during each breeding season 1955–69. The 1955 population had not yet been affected by myxomatosis. The low point in 1963 followed the severe winter. [No data for 1969]

The counts produced an estimated 1,380–1,450 pairs. By 1980 the Buzzard was reported to have become the commonest raptor with its breeding densities 'high in most areas'. A similar survey of soaring Buzzards in 1983, part of a national BTO exercise (Taylor *et al.* 1988), arrived at a broadly similar figure of 1,530–1,980 pairs. During the years 1977–85, Buzzards bred or probably bred in 75% of Devon tetrads (Sitters 1988). Despite several years of poor breeding success in the late 1980s, the Buzzard population remained stable, evidently having adjusted eventually to the changed food resources of the post-myxomatosis era. This stability has been maintained up to the present with little or no evident persecution. A new population assessment is overdue but should be possible from the field data gathered for the forthcoming 2008–11 breeding atlas. It would not be surprising if 2,500–3,000 pairs are reckoned to be holding territories in Devon. If so, this would confirm a return to the pre-myxomatosis level of abundance.

North Somerset

A lowland population of Buzzards occupying 75 km^2 of productive farmland has been studied intensively for more than 30 years by Robin Prytherch, who has kindly supplied the census data plotted in Figure 15.6. This is an area of meadows, some arable fields and woods on broad flat valley bottoms separated by low ridges; and thus not unlike many parts of Devon. During the period 1982–2007 there was a remarkable seven-fold increase in the numbers of territorial Buzzard pairs. The increase was exponential up to 2001, since when it has been slowing, presumably as resources become limiting near the carrying capacity of the environment. The average population density (Appendix 26), now exceeding one pair per square kilometre, appears to be the highest recorded anywhere in Britain, or continental Europe. Moreover, I am informed (*in litt.*) that high breeding success has been maintained on a diet predominantly of small mammals and birds. For how long this population level remains sustainable will be interesting to observe.

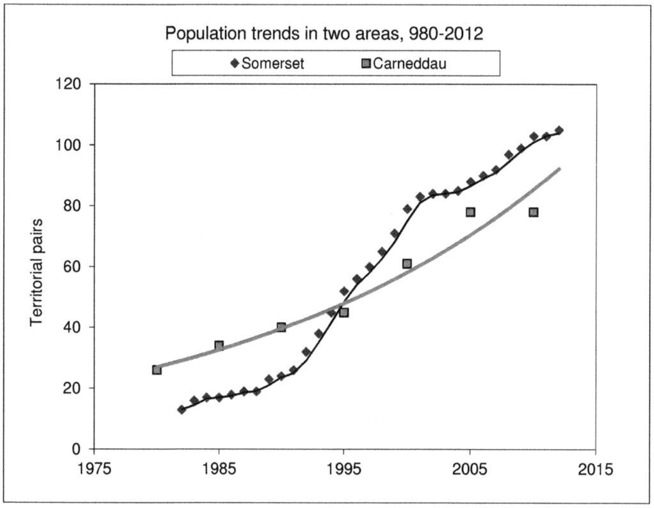

Figure 15.6 Changes in the numbers of territorial Buzzard pairs in North Somerset and Snowdonia during 30 years. [Note: the fitted trend lines have no predictive value.] Data: Somerset (R. Prytherch, in litt.); Snowdonia (Driver & Dare 2009)

A slower rate of increase is reported on 60 km^2 of mixed farms with good woodland cover in the more hilly part of north-east Somerset. The number of territorial Buzzard pairs there rose from 32 to 56 in the ten years from 1995 to 2004 (Holmes 2012). Population density thus almost doubled, from 1.9 per 1.1 km^2 per pair, but with no significant effects on breeding performance. The proportion of pairs breeding varied annually between 57–72%, and they fledged brood sizes averaging between 1.00 and 1.95 juveniles.

North Wales

This large region, comprising five counties, extends from Anglesey east to the River Dee and estuary border with England. By 1907, Buzzards survived in small numbers only among the mountain crags of Snowdonia and in remote uplands of Meirionydd to the south (Forrest 1907); areas where persecution from gamekeepers was virtually absent. The subsequent pattern of Buzzard recovery followed the national trend, being delayed longest in the game-preserving counties of Anglesey, Denbigh and Flint where persecution lasted into the 1990s on some estates (Lovegrove *et al.* 1994, Jones & Whalley 2004, Roberts & Jones 2009). In Anglesey, there were several 'exploratory' breeding attempts by Buzzards between 1964 and 1970 but it was not until 1991 that recolonisation at last began. Subsequent progress was rapid, so that by 1997 there may have been as many as 40 pairs on the island (Jones & Whalley 2004). By 2010, some 100–130 pairs were probably breeding, according to the BTO 2007–11 atlas survey; during which breeding was confirmed in 61 tetrads and probably occurred in 71 others (Brenchley *et al.* 2013). However, interpreting tetrad counts is not always straightforward when the survey period spans several years. For example, where a Buzzard territory overlaps the intersection of tetrad boundaries, the same pair could nest in adjoining tetrads in different years.

In their nearby mountain stronghold of Snowdonia, only a dozen pairs of Buzzards were known in the early 1920s, the highest nesting at about 750 m (K. Orton, in Carr & Lister 1924). Their numbers remained low into the 1950s, for the 1954 survey found only 7 pairs in 427 km^2 of the northern ranges. Throughout Snowdonia, however, the late Derek Ratcliffe informed me (*in litt.*) that he had come across 23 occupied Buzzard territories, seven with crag nests, during his annual wide-ranging surveys of breeding Peregrines and Ravens. Although some woodland nesting Buzzards would have been missed, it is clear that Buzzards were sparsely distributed and probably amounted to only 30–35 pairs in this region in the 1950s.

Subsequently, a slow increase took place in Snowdonia through the 1960s and into the 1970s, then followed by a rapid rise which was measured by two census surveys and regular monitoring studies. The first complete census of this 926 km^2 region was undertaken during 1977–84. A total of 96 territorial pairs of Buzzards were located; an average density of 10 pr/100 km^2 (Dare & Barry 1990). Locally, densities varied between sub-regions according to the terrain and habitat availability. By the time of the second census, in 1998–2004, there were 244 pairs, or 24 pr/100 km^2; a 154% increase in twenty years (Driver 2004). Numbers had risen in all parts but at different rates. The pattern of increase in the northernmost mountain block of 251 km^2, the Carneddau, is shown in Figure 15.6 (Driver & Dare 2009). Population growth was exponential in the middle period. Buzzard numbers had nearly quadrupled between 1975 and 2005 before levelling off as the present carrying capacity of the area is being reached. They have risen by processes of infilling at lower levels, generally, and by extension to higher altitudes where one pair has nested successfully at approximately 900 m. An increased availability of sheep carrion in the breeding seasons, resulting from over-stocking, is thought to have been the main causal factor. However, a recent reversal of agricultural policy has led to a reduction in sheep stocks and their removal from higher ground in winter. Any effects of this diminished food supply on the mountain Buzzards remain to be seen.

In neighbouring Denbighshire, Buzzards were still very scarce in 1954, when only 23 pairs could be found in 13,270 km^2 surveyed, i.e. 0.17/100 km^2 (Moore 1957). In one district in the east of that county, Roberts and Jones (2009) suggested that persecution had delayed the recovery and spread of Buzzards until the mid- to late- 1990s. Since then, a rapid rise in numbers has occurred in their area. In west Denbigh, by contrast, Buzzards were already common by the late 1970s. In a 440 km^2 area of hill farms and moorland, in roughly equal measure, the overall Buzzard density was 14 pr/100 km^2. In fact, because virtually all nested only on the enclosed farmlands, the densities there were probably 25–30 pr/100 km^2 (Dare & Barry 1990). Here, game preservation was restricted to two small areas where occasional persecution was suspected into the 1990s. Nowadays, throughout Denbighshire Buzzards are now numerous and breed in the majority of tetrads (BTO atlas survey). They have spread eastwards across Flintshire, reached the Dee Estuary and over-spilled the Welsh border into Cheshire.

Today, there are an estimated 900–1,200 territorial Buzzard pairs dispersed across all five counties of North Wales, according to the results from the fine-scale (tetrad) survey (Brenchley *et al.* 2013).

South Wales

In the uplands of north Breconshire, thorough surveys of soaring Buzzards in the early springs of 1983 and 1999 indicated that numbers had increased during the period by 115% in the 372 km^2 study area (Shrubb 2000). Numbers rose in all habitats but especially where the preferred enclosed farmlands abutted open hillside grazing and mature conifer forests that (by 1999) had been partly clear-felled, thereby providing better nesting opportunities. Reasons for an increase were not evident. Persecution had remained absent or insignificant in this predominantly sheep farming area, and the patchily distributed Rabbit stocks had perhaps declined, rather than increased, since 1980. Instead, the increase of Buzzards was considered partly to reflect a recovery from the effects of adverse weather that probably had reduced Buzzard numbers and breeding success just before the first survey. In particular, the 1981 summer had been very wet and the 1981–82 winter severe, especially on the higher ground at around 500 m elevation.

West Midlands

In lowland farming areas not far from the Welsh border, large increases in Buzzard numbers were recorded between 1983 and 1996, using counts of soaring birds in many 10 x 10 km squares (Sim *et al.* 2000). There were marked local differences. Increases (348%) were twice as great in eastern squares nearer the edge of the range, where Buzzards were colonising, than in more westerly squares (118%), where Buzzards already were well established. The overall average increase (231%) suggested a 9.5% annual rate of population growth. The increase and spread were attributed primarily to a combination of apparently reduced persecution since 1990 and increasing Rabbit abundance.

Upper Strathspey

Buzzard numbers here rose between 1972 and 1989, since when no further information appears to have been published. During 1988–89, a 94 km^2 section of the original (1968–72) study area of Weir & Picozzi (1974) was resurveyed by Halley (1993). He found that the territorial population had increased by 57% from 14 to 22 pairs. Persecution in this farming district apparently had become 'much reduced since 1972'.

East Anglia

In Suffolk the first Buzzards bred again in 1999, in the west of the county. Recolonisation was thought then to be a good possibility but would depend upon levels of persecution (Piotrowski 2003). Happily, this fear has not been realised. In fact, the re-establishment progressed at such a pace that by 2006 about 50 territorial pairs were reported, of which half were confirmed breeders (Gregory 2006). In 2010 probably between 120–150 pairs were present (Suffolk Bird Report 2010). Buzzards were breeding once more even in the most easterly woods of East Anglia (and Britain), from which they had been exterminated more than 100 years before (Dare 2008).

In part of my 82 km^2 study area in coastal north-east Suffolk, at least two pairs bred successfully in 2006 and four pairs in 2007. The first full census in 2008 found 10 pairs, rising to 17 pairs in 2010, and to 20 pairs in 2012 (Dare 2013), a doubling in four years. Some pairs are still well separated from neighbours and territorial behaviour in places is at low intensity, except when repelling intruding transients and prospectors in the spring. The density in 2012 of 4.1 km^2/pair (25 pr/100 km^2) is probably still below the carrying capacity of this productive and mainly arable farming area with its ample mature woodlands and many large hedgerow trees. The landowners and managers have been well disposed towards Buzzards in this district.

In neighbouring Norfolk, breeding occurred first in 1992 but, unfortunately, details of the initial stages of recolonisation were obscured as a result of breeding by Buzzards released in central Norfolk during the mid-1990s (Taylor *et al.* 1999). By 2005 there were probably 47 pairs, of which 25 certainly bred (Norfolk Bird and Mammal Report 2005). Numbers evidently have since risen rapidly, for in the early spring of 2012 a survey in north Norfolk located an estimated 79–90 potential breeding pairs of Buzzards soaring and displaying above woods within a 288 km^2 survey area (Porter & Abrams 2013). The population density in this rich farming area with its numerous woods amounted to about 3.3 km^2 per pair (33 pairs/100 km^2), or one third higher than in my Suffolk area. Repeated observations and woodland searches during the breeding season itself (May–August) would be needed to establish the true size of the resident territorial population. A further 50–70 'unattached' birds recorded in the Norfolk area were thought likely to have been passing through, as do so many Buzzards in Suffolk in spring.

The settlement of Buzzards to breed in coastal woodlands around East Anglia now raises the possibility of competition for food with the Marsh Harriers nesting in adjoining wetlands or in arable fields. Already, in north Norfolk two Buzzards have been observed seizing prey from harriers that were bringing food to their nests, while another Buzzard robbed a juvenile harrier in autumn (Bloomfield 2013). In my Suffolk area, Marsh Harriers hunt daily up to 8 km inland and across many Buzzard territories where they are known to catch very small Rabbits, small rodents and birds. Some Buzzard nests are within 500 m of Marsh Harrier nests in reed beds. At one such site, a Buzzard that approached too close to a harrier's nest was chased off by the female Marsh Harrier (A. Watson, *pers. comm.*). It will be interesting to observe how events unfold.

BUZZARDS IN THE 21ST CENTURY

With their rapid re-claiming of ancestral lands in eastern England, the fortunes of the Buzzard have now turned nearly full circle. Their return, however, is to a landscape and ecology much changed during the 100 intervening years or more of their absence. It remains to be seen how many Buzzards will fit in and cope with living in one of the most intensively farmed regions in Britain, where many wildlife habitats have disappeared and prey resources have been much depleted. In Suffolk at least, the portents so far appear favourable, with pioneering pairs showing good survival and breeding productivity. The ultimate distribution pattern of Buzzards will be determined by local availability of suitable woodland for nest sites, which varies greatly across Suffolk and the arable farming regions of England. In western haunts, where numbers are now at or near saturation level, little further change should be expected unless there is another major collapse in Rabbit stocks.

In their new areas, the food habits of Buzzards have yet to be ascertained. Consequently, one cannot predict the eventual population densities of this raptor. Nevertheless, some reasonable speculation of likely diets can be offered, based on the limited knowledge of potential prey resources. Compared with western areas, for example, some of the regular small preys are scarcer in the dominantly arable countryside. Intensive cultivation provides little small vertebrate, or even invertebrate fare, for Buzzards. Short-tailed Voles, other small mammals, the Common Frog, and many small bird species are all now much reduced in numbers in eastern landscapes (Chapters 12 and 13).

On the other hand, larger potential preys are widespread and reported to be increasing in many central and eastern parts of England. Most importantly, Rabbits are considered widely to be plentiful and still increasing, though locally still prone to irregular recurrence of myxomatosis. A greater potential threat to Buzzard food supplies everywhere would be posed by Rabbit viral haemorrhagic disease (RVHD). This pathogen has become endemic in Europe, and has caused large mortalities among wild Rabbits in Spain and many other countries. It was first reported in Britain in 1992 and was implicated in the subsequent large decline in Rabbit populations in Scotland during the 1990s. It seems likely, however, that a RVHD epizootic in this country would eventually follow the same path as myxomatosis, and become endemic in Rabbit populations, according to a Scottish Natural Heritage assessment.

A new supplementary rodent prey resource for Buzzards could be Grey Squirrels, a very plentiful pest, across much of central and eastern England. Buzzards occasionally catch them in western counties where they are less common generally. Young squirrels foraging on the ground could be especially vulnerable during the Buzzard breeding season.

West Country Buzzards usually take small numbers of medium-large birds such as Carrion Crows, Magpies and Wood Pigeons. Of these, the slow-flying Magpie is the most vulnerable to Buzzards. Wood Pigeons are far more numerous in eastern than in western regions, whereas the two corvids remain much less plentiful than in the west. It is interesting to note that some farm managers in Suffolk consider that Buzzards make most effective bird scarers, by frightening away Wood Pigeon flocks that are feeding upon young oilseed rape crops in winter (Barker 2010 and S. Allen, *pers. comm.*). In many central and eastern regions the intensive rearing and release of Pheasants and partridges for sport is widespread. With game birds being so plentiful it remains to be seen whether Buzzards might attempt, or be able, to utilise such a widespread resource (Chapter 13).

Overall, therefore, one may envisage a nett switch from a varied diet of Rabbits with smaller mammals, birds and carrion – as found in western regions - to one dominated more often by Rabbits and larger bird preys in those eastern lowlands where biodiversity has become impoverished. Rabbits will be vital for the continued breeding success of Buzzards everywhere, but especially in the lowlands. However, being vulnerable to disease outbreaks, Rabbit abundance may become subject to large fluctuations which, in turn, could affect Buzzard numbers. Where small vertebrates are in short supply, some common large birds (corvids and pigeons) could become more important during the breeding season than they have been in western Britain.

Raptors in Britain have been under heavy pressure from anthropogenic threats – persecution, environmental pollution, habitat loss or degradation - for many decades. Indeed, some species remain at high risk, even in these 'enlightened' times. Some with much reduced populations survive thanks to long-term conservation research and high profile public relations programmes. Meanwhile, and unremarked until recently, the Buzzard has made the most spectacular comeback of all, aided only by the 1981 protection legislation and a growing realization among most land-owners and rural communities that they pose little or no threat to their field sports interests. The Buzzard is now officially our most numerous diurnal bird of prey, having replaced the Kestrel whose numbers unexpectedly are now declining. Against this background, it seems somewhat ironic that the under-valued Buzzard has not only survived successive threats and setbacks but now is thriving in our ever-changing modern countryside. Today, it graces the skies above most of the British Isles. The Buzzard truly is the most versatile, adaptable, resourceful and resilient of raptors.

SUMMARY

- Buzzards were common and widespread in Britain and Ireland during the 18th century until the advent of game bird preservation for sport shooting. Since 1800, its abundance and distribution in all regions have fluctuated dramatically as populations underwent phases of decline and recovery. Declines resulted from periods of persecution, pollution, or disease induced food shortages.

- Phase 1 (1700–1915): *Severe decline nationally* caused by intense and prolonged persecution throughout the 1800s. By 1900, Buzzards in Britain were confined to refugia in western uplands with minimal game bird interests and persecution.
- Phase 2 (1915–1954): *Gradual recovery and some range expansion* eastwards in response to reducing persecution. Buzzard populations were again high in western counties, where sustained largely by abundant Rabbit stocks. A national survey estimated that 8,000–12,000 pairs were present in spring 1954.
- Phase 3 (1954–56): *Buzzard populations 'crash'* as their Rabbit food resource is almost exterminated by myxomatosis disease introduced to control Rabbits. Buzzard numbers everywhere fell rapidly, to perhaps 6,000–8,000 pairs. Elevated adult mortality and high breeding failure rates persisted for several years.
- Phase 4 (1960–90): *Gradual recovery despite pesticide pollution threats and recurring myxomatosis episodes.* Buzzard numbers increased slowly but with no significant range expansion. Recovery rates were retarded during the 1960–70s in some areas, where organochlorine contamination of eggs depressed hatching success; and more generally by further, but less potent, outbreaks of myxomatosis. By 1970, the national population may have recovered to 8,000–10,000 pairs. Persecution remained significant locally, especially along the eastern range limits, until full protection legislation came into operation from 1981. In 1983, a national estimate of 12,000–17,000 pairs was derived from a soaring Buzzard survey.
- Phase 5 (post-1990): *Rapid recovery and range extension.* Buzzard populations increased and spread eastwards at an accelerating and unexpected pace. By 2010, after an absence of more than a century, Buzzards recolonised much of eastern England and eastern Scotland, and were spreading south-westwards through Ireland. Causes are not well understood but higher survival of juvenile and adult Buzzards, resulting from marked reductions in persecution, are likely to be the prime driving factor.
- In 2000, the national Buzzard population was variously estimated at between 30,000–60,000 pairs, suggesting an approximate trebling in numbers as Buzzards spread eastwards. Their re-occupation of these intensive game-rearing regions, with consequent potential for renewed conflicts, calls for research to provide information on Buzzard and game-bird interactions.

BIBLIOGRAPHY

Akos, Z., Nagy, M. & Vicsek, T. (2008) Comparing bird and human soaring strategies. *Proceedings of the National Academy of Science USA,* **105** (11): 4139–4143.

Allen, G.S. (1930) Diet of young buzzard. *British Birds*, **24** (3): 79.

Alvarez, J.C., Meseguer, J., Meseguer, E. & Perez, A. (2001) On the role of the allula in the steady flight of birds. *Ardeola* **48** (2): 161–173.

Austin, G.E., Thomas, C.J., Houston, D.C. & Thompson, D.B.A. (1996) Predicting the spatial distribution of buzzard *Buteo buteo* nesting areas using a Geographical Information System and remote sensing. *Journal of Applied Ecology*, **33**: 1541–1550.

Austin, G.E. & Houston, D.C. (1997) The breeding performance of the Buzzard *Buteo buteo* in Argyll, Scotland and a comparison with other areas. *Bird Study*, **44**: 146–154.

Balmer, D., Gillings, S., Caffrey, B., Swann, B., Downie, I. & Fuller, R. (2013) *Bird Atlas 2007–11. The breeding and wintering birds of Britain and Ireland.* T. & A. D. Poyser.

Balmer, D., Gillings, S., Caffrey, B., Swann, R., Downie, I. & Fuller, R. (2013) *Bird Atlas 2007–11. The breeding and wintering birds of Britain and Ireland.* T. & A. D. Poyser.

Bamber, L.K. (1955) Buzzard seizing Barn Owl. *Nature in Wales*, **1**(2): 88.

Bannerman, D.A. (1956) *The Birds of the British Isles. Vol. 5.* Oliver & Boyd, Edinburgh.

Barker, P. (2010) Buzzards in Suffolk. *Nest Records News*, **26**:10. British Trust for Ornithology, Thetford.

Barnard, C.C. (1981) Buzzard preying on Short-eared Owl. *British Birds*, **74**: 226.

Barrett-Hamilton, G.E.H. & Hinton, M.A.C. (1910–21) *A History of British Mammals.* London.

Barth, E. K. (1952) Litt forplantningebiologie hos fjellväken, *Buteo lagopus*, og svingninger i bestanden 1938–52. *Papers of Game-Research, Helsingfors.* **8**: 127–138. (English summary).

Barton, N.W.H. & Houston, D. C. (1993) A comparison of digestive efficiency in birds of prey. *Ibis,* **135**: 363–371.

Blomert, A-M., Ens, B.J., Goss-Custard, J.G., Hulscher, J. & Zwarts, L. (eds) (1996) *Oystercatchers and their estuarine food supplies.* Ardea, **84A**, 538pp.

Both, C., van Asch, M., Bijlsma, R.G., van den Burg, A.B. & Visser, M.E. (1999) Sex determination of nestling common buzzards *Buteo buteo. Limosa,* **72**: 1–10.

Blezard, E. (1945) The Lakeland Pennines and their birds. *Lakeland Natural History*: 100–115.

Bloomfield, A. (2013) Common Buzzards robbing Marsh Harriers of prey. *British Birds*, **106**: 411–412.

Brenchley, A., Gibbs, G., Pritchard, R. & Spence, I.M. (2013) *The Breeding Birds of North Wales.* Liverpool University Press, Liverpool.

Brewster, K.W. (1973) Aggression by female Buzzard at nest. *British Birds*, **66**: 279.

Bright, G. (1955) Buzzard killing Tufted Duck. *British Birds*, **48**: 326.

Briggs, K.B. (1983) Buzzard feeding on dung beetles. *British Birds*, **76**: 135–136.

Brook, A. (1920) *The Buzzard at Home.* Witherby & Co., London.

Brook, A. (1952) How Buzzards feed their young. *The Field*, 355.

Brown, L. (1955) *Eagles.* Michael Joseph, London.

Brown, L. (1976) *British Birds of Prey.* Collins, London.

Brown, R.H. (1935) The food of certain birds of prey. *British Birds*, **28**: 257–258.

Brown, R.H. (1948) Nesting season of Common Buzzard. *British Birds*, **41**: 53–54.

Browne, K. & Browne, E. (1957) An analysis of the weights of birds trapped on Skomer. *British Birds*, **49**: 241–257.

Burgess, M. (2013) Investigating the decline of Wood Warblers in Devon. *Devon Birdwatching & Preservation Society, Harrier Newsletter*, 2013 (**2**): 8–9.

Burr, F. (1936) Ueber die jahreszeitliche Verbreitung des Mäusebussards (*Buteo b. buteo* L.) mit besonderem Vergleich einzelner Populationen. *Vogelzug*, **7** (1): 17–34.

Campbell, B. (1947) Nesting season of Common Buzzard. *British Birds*, **40**:182–183.

Carr, H.R.C. & Lister, G.A. (1924) *The Mountains of Snowdonia*. Crosby Lockwood, London.

Carter, I. (2007) *The Red Kite*. Arlequin Press, Upton Magna, Shrewsbury.

Chitty, D. (1938) A laboratory study of pellet formation in the Short-eared Owl (*Asion flammeus*). *Proceedings of the Zoological Society of London.*, **108 A**: 267–287.

Chitty, D. (1952) Mortality among voles (*Microtus agrestis*) at Lake Vyrnwy, Montgomeryshire in 1936–9. *Philosophical Transactions of the Royal Society*, **236 B**. 638: 508–552.

Christie, H.H.V. (1931) Buzzard killing Little Owl. *British Birds*, **24** (12).

Clements, R. (2000) Range expansion of the Common Buzzard in Britain. *British Birds*, **93**: 242–248.

Clements, R. (2002) The Common Buzzard in Britain: a new population estimate. *British Birds*, 377–383.

Clouet, M. & Wink, M. (2000) The buzzards of Cape Verde *Buteo (buteo) bannermani* and Socotra *Buteo* (*buteo*) spp: First results of a genetic analysis based on nucleotide sequences of the cytochrome b gene. *Alauda*, **68** (1): 55–58.

Coombes, R.A.H. (1948) Nesting season of Common Buzzard. *British Birds*, **41**:53.

Combridge, P. (2000) Common Buzzard soaring on flat wings. *British Birds*, **93**: 644.

Condry, W.M. (1955) Buzzard following the plough. *Nature in Wales*, **1** (3): 139.

Condry, W.M. (1957) [Buzzard unsuccessfully attacking incubating crow]. *Nature in Wales*, **3** (2): 444.

Condry, W.M. (1976) *The Snowdonia National Park*. Collins, London.

Craighead, F. C. & Craighead, J. J. (1956) *Hawks, Owls and Wildlife*. Washington, D.C.

Cramp, S. & Simmons, K.E.L. (eds.) (1980) *Handbook of the Birds of Europe, Middle East and North Afric: The Birds of the Western Palearctic. Vol.2*. Oxford University Press.

Czarnecki, Z. & Foksowicz, T. (1954) Observations and composition of the feed of Buzzard (*Buteo buteo* (L.)). *Ecologia Polska*, **2**: 477–484.

Dare, P.J. (1957) The post-myxomatosis diet of the Buzzard. *Devon Birds*, **10** (1): 2–6.

Dare, P.J. (1958) Myxomatosis and the Buzzard. *Country-side*, vol.18 (new series) **8**: 305–314.

Dare, P.J. (1961) Ecological observations on a breeding population of the Common Buzzard, *Buteo buteo* (L), with special reference to the diet and breeding habits. *PhD Thesis (unpubl.), University of Exeter.* Exeter.

Dare, P.J. (1986) Notes on the Kestrel population of Snowdonia, North Wales. *Naturalist*, **114**: 49–54.

Dare, P.J. (1986) Raven *Corvus corax* populations in two upland regions of North Wales. *Bird Study*, **33**: 179–189.

Dare, P.J. (1989) Aspects of the breeding biology of the Buzzard *Buteo buteo* in North Wales. *Naturalist*, **114**: 23–31.

Dare, P.J. (1995) Breeding success and territory features of Buzzards *Buteo buteo* in Snowdonia and adjacent uplands of North Wales. *Welsh Birds*, **1** (2): 69–78.

Dare, P.J. (1998) A Buzzard population on Dartmoor, 1955–1993. *Devon Birds*, **51**: 4–31.

Dare, P.J. (1999) Large movements and ground assemblies of Buzzards in Devon. *Devon Birds*, **52** (2): 3–9.

Dare, P.J. (2006) A Buzzard nest rescue. *Welsh Birds*, **4** (5): 454.

Dare, P.J. (2006) Spring movements of Common Buzzards along the Suffolk coast. *Suffolk Birds*, **56**: 27–38.

Dare, P.J. (2008) Common Buzzards breeding again in north-east Suffolk. *Suffolk Birds*, **58**: 34–35.

Dare, P.J. (2013a) Buzzards on Dartmoor at Postbridge 70 years ago. *Devon Birds*, **66**: 25–27.

Dare, P.J. (2013b) A recolonising Buzzard population in north-east Suffolk. *Suffolk Birds*, **63**: 15–19.

Dare, P.J. & Barry, J.T. (1990) Population size, density and regularity in nest spacing of Buzzards *Buteo buteo* in two upland regions of North Wales. *Bird Study*, **37**: 23–29.

Davis, P.W. & Davis, P.F. (1973) The ecology and conservation of the Red Kite in Wales. Part III. Feeding habits and food. *British Birds*, **66**: 241–270.

Davis, T.A.W. (1955) Buzzards following the plough. *British Birds*, **48**: 413.

Davis, T.A.W. & Saunders, D.R. (1965) Buzzards on Skomer Island 1954–1964. *Nature in Wales*, **9** (3): 116–124.

Davis, P.E. & Davis, J.E. (1992) Dispersal and age of first breeding of Buzzards in Central Wales. *British Birds*, **85**: 578–587.

Davis, P. & Davis, J. (2002) Bigamous Buzzards in Central Wales. *Welsh Birds*, **3** (3): 205.

Davis, P.R.K. & Seel, D.G. (1983) Cuckoo taken by Buzzard. *British Birds*, **76**: 314.

Del Hoyo, J., Elliott, A. & Sartagal, J. (1994) *Handbook of Birds of the World, Vol. 2: New World vultures to guineafowl.* Lynx Ediciones, Barcelona.

Devon Bird-Watching & Preservation Society, *Annual Reports, 1929–2009*. Exeter.

Dittrich, W. (1985) Gefeidervariationen beim Mäusebussard (*Buteo buteo*) in Nordbayern. *Journal für Ornithologie*, **126**: 93–97.

Dixon, N. (2013) Peregrine aggression towards Buzzards at St. Michael's Church, Exeter. *Devon Birds*, **66** (1): 30–31.

Driver, J. (2004) Exceptionally aggressive Buzzards in North Wales. *Welsh Birds*, **4** (1):60–64.

Driver, J. (2006) Raven *Corvus corax* population census of of north-west Wales, 1998–2005. *Welsh Birds*, **4** (5): 442–453.

Driver, J. & Dare, P. J. (2009) Population increase of Buzzards in Snowdonia, 1977–2007. *Welsh Birds*, **6** (1): 38–48.

Drost, R. & Schuz, E. (1940) Von den Folgen des harten Winters 1939–40 fűr die Vogelwelt. *Der Vogelzug*, **11**: 161–191.

D'Urban, W.S.M. & Mathew, M.A. (1892) *The Birds of Devon*. R.H. Porter, London.

Dykstra, C.R., Hays, J.L. & Simmon, M.M. (2009) Spatial and temporal variation in reproductive rates of the Red-shouldered Hawk in suburban and rural Ohio. *Condor*,**111** (1):177–182.

Elliott, G.D. & Avery, M.I. (1991) A review of reports of Buzzard persecution 1975–1989. *Bird Study*, **38**: 52–56.

Elton, C. (1942) *Voles, Mice and Lemming: Problems in Population Dynamics*. Oxford.

Erlinge, S., Göransson, G., Hansson, L., Högstedt, G., Liberg, O., Nilsson, I.N., Nilsson. T., von Schantz, T. & Sylvén, M. (1983) Predation as a regulating factor on small rodent populations in southern Sweden. *Oikos*, **40**: 36–52.

Evans, D.R. (1957) Buzzard nests with weasels and stoats. *Nature in Wales*, **3** (2): 444.

Eylert, J. (1986) Untersuchungen zur Nährungsbiologie des Mäusebussards. *Zeitschrift für Jagdwissenschaft*, **32** (1): 29–41.

Fenn, C. (1957) Buzzards in north Breconshire. *Nature in Wales*, 3 (3): 485–486.

Fitch, H.S., Swenson, F. & Tillotson, D.F. (1946) Behaviour and food habits of the Red-tailed Hawk. *Condor*, **48**: 205–237.

Forrest, H.E. (1907) *The Vertebrate Fauna of North Wales*. London.

Forsman, D. (1999) *The Raptors of Europe and the Middle East: A Handbook of Field Identification*. T.& A.D. Poyser, London.

Fox, R., Lehmkuhle, S.W. & Westendorf, D.H. (1976) Falcon visual acuity. *Science*, **192** (Issue 4236): 263–265.

Frank, F. (1957) The causality of microtine cycles in Germany. *Journal of Wildlife Management*, **21** (2): 113–121.

Fryer, G. (1986) Notes on the breeding biology of the Buzzard. *British Birds*,**79**: 18–28.

Fryer, G. (1986) Buzzard and crows at Magpie nest. *British Birds*, **70**: 40–41.

Fryer, G. (1974) Aggressive behaviour by Buzzards at nest. *British Birds*, **67**: 238–239.

Garcia-Rodriguez, T., Ferrer, M., Carrillo, J. & Castroviejo, J. (1987) Metabolic responses of *Buteo buteo* to long-term fasting and refeeding. *Comparative Biochemistry & Physiology*, **87**: 381–386.

Gibbons, D. W., Reid, I. B. & Chapman, R. A. (1993) *The New Atlas of Breeding Birds in Britain and Ireland: 1988–1991*. T. & A. D. Poyser, London.

Gilbert, H. A. (1951) Display of Common Buzzard. *British Birds*, **44**: 411.

Glading, B., Tillotson, D.F. & Selleck, D.M. (1943) Raptor pellets as indicators of food habits. *California Fish & Game*, **29**: 92–121.

Godfrey, G.K. (1955) A field study of the activity of the mole (*Talpa europea*). *Ecology*, **36**: 678–685.

Goszczyynski, J. (1997) Density and productivity of Common Buzzard *Buteo buteo* and Goshawk *Accipiter gentilis* populations in Rogów, Central Poland. *Acta Ornithologica*, **32**: 149–154.

Graham, I.M., Redpath, S.M. & Thirgood, S.J. (1995) The diet and breeding density of Common Buzzards *Buteo buteo* in relation to indices of prey abundance. *Bird Study*, **42**: 165–173.

Green, J. (2002) *Birds in Wales 1992–2000*. Welsh Ornithological Society.

Gregory, C. (2006) The return of the Buzzard to Suffolk. *Suffolk Birds*, **56**: 22–26.

Hagemeijer, W. J. M. & Blair, M. J. (eds.) (1997) The EBCC Atlas of European Breeding Birds: *Their Distribution and Abundance*. T. & A. D. Poyser, London.

Halley, D.J. (1993) Population changes and territorial distribution of Common Buzzards *Buteo buteo* in the Central Highlands, Scotland. *Bird Study*, **40**: 24–30.

Hanski, I., Hansson, L, & Henttonen, H. (1991) Specialist predators, generalist predators and the microtine rodent cycle. *J. Animal Ecology*, **60**: 353–367.

Hardey, J., Crick, H., Wernham, C., Riley, H., Etheridge, B. & Thompson, D. (2005) *Raptors: a field guide to survey and monitoring*. Scottish Natural Heritage, Edinburgh.

Harris, S., Morris, P., Wray, S. & Yalden, D.W. (1995) *A review of British mammals: population estimates and conservation status of British mammals other than cetaceans*. Joint Nature Conservation Committee, Peterborough, 183 pp.

Hayes, S.R. & Gessaman, J. A. (1980) The combined effects of air temperature, wind and radiation on the resting metabolism of avian raptors. *Journal of Thermal Biology*, **5** (2): 119–125.

Hayman, R.W. (1970) Persistent ground-feeding by Buzzards. *British Birds*, **63**: 133.

Hayworth, A.G. (1984). Buzzard stunned in flight. *British Birds*, **77**: 73.

Herberigs, H. (1953) Note sur la comportement de la Buse dans ses quartiers d'hiver. *Gerfaut*, **43**: 132–142.

Hewson, R. (1981) Scavenging of mammal carcasses by birds in West Scotland. Journal of Zoology, London, **194**: 525–537.

Heywood, A. (1986) Buzzards talon-grappling and falling to ground. *British Birds*, **79**: 429.

Hill, M.O., Evans, D.H. & Bell, S.A. (1992) Long-term effects of excluding sheep from hill pastures in North Wales. *J. Ecology*, **80**: 1–13.

Hills, P. (1956) Buzzard catching Lapwing in the air. *Nature in Wales*, **2** (1): 234.

Hodder, K.H., Kenward, R.E., Walls, S.S. & Clarke, R.T. (1998) Estimating core ranges: a comparison of techniques using the Common Buzzard (*Buteo buteo*). *Journal of Raptor Res*earch, **32** (2): 82–89.

Holstein, V. (1956) *Musvågen Buteo bute (L).* Copenhagen.

Holdsworth, M. (1971) Breeding biology of Buzzards at Sedbergh during 1937–67. *British Birds*, **64**: 412–420.

Holmes, J. (2012) A survey of Common Buzzards in ST66 south of Keynsham. *Bristol Ornithology*, **31**: 28–30.

Hubert, C. & Gallo, A. (1995) Modification of parental behaviour during the nesting period in the Common Buzzard (*Buteo buteo*). *J. Raptor Research*, **29** (2): 103–109.

Hurrell, H.G. (1929) Census of Buzzards. *Western Morning News*, 28 August 1929, p 6. Plymouth, Devon.

Hurrell, H.G. (1946) Devon Bird-Watching & Preservation Society, *Annual Report*, **19**: 30.

Hurrell, H.G. (1952) Census of Buzzards, 1929. *Devon Birds*, **5**: 34–37.

Hurrell, H.G. (1954a) Devon Bird-Watching & Preservation Society, *Annual Report*, **27**: 15.

Hurrell, H.G. (1954b) The Buzzard population in Devon and Cornwall. *Devon Birds*, **7**: 35–38.

Hurrell, H.G. (1974) The white Buzzard of Buckfastleigh. *Devon Birds*, **27** (1): 2–5.

Insley, H. & Dugan, D. (1973) Buzzard and Golden Eagle feeding on other avian predators. *British Birds*, **66**: 310.

James. D. (2000) Collective ground feeding of Welsh Buzzards. *Welsh Birds*, **2** (5): 292.

Jedrzejewski, W., Szymura,A. & Jedrzejewska, B. (1994). Reproduction and food of the buzzard *Buteo buteo* in relation to the abundance of rodents and birds in Bialowieza National Park, Poland. *Ethology, Ecology & Evolution*, **6** (2): 179–190.

Jones, C. G. (1985) Heavy hippoboscid infestation on Buzzards. *British Birds*, **78**: 185.

Jones, E.B.G. (1957) Buzzard taking Wood Pigeon in flight. *Nature in Wales*, **3** (2): 444.

Jones, P.H. & Whalley, P. (2004) *Birds of Anglesey*. Menter Môn, Llangefni, Wales.

Kenward, R.E. (2006) *The Goshawk*. T. & A.D. Poyser, London.

Kenward, R.E., Walls, S.S., Hodder, K.H., Pahkala, M., Freeman, N. & Simpson, V.R. (2000) The prevalence of non-breeders in raptor populations: evidence from rings, radio tags and transect surveys. *Oikos*, **91**: 271–279.

Kenward, R.E., Walls, S.S. & Hodder, K.H. (2001) Life path analysis: scaling indicates priming effects of social and habitat factors on dispersal distance. *Journal of Animal Ecology*, **70**: 1–13.

Kenward, R.E., Hall, D.G., Walls, S.S. & Hodder, K.H. (2001) Factors affecting predation by buzzards *Buteo buteo* on released pheasants *Phasianus colchicus*. *Journal of Applied Ecology*, **38**: 813–822.

King, B. (1986) Food-seeking Buzzard following combine-harvester. *British Birds*, **79**: 429.

Kinley, R. I. K. & Thexton, D.B. (1985). Opportunistic food acquisition by Buzzard while mobbed by Peregrines. *British Birds*, **78**:193.

Koch, G.J. (2006) Using a Doppler light detection and ranging (lidar) system to characterize an atmospheric thermal providing lift for soaring raptors. *Journal of Field Ornithology*, **77** (3): 316–318.

Kostrzewa, R. & Kostrzewa, A. (1991) Winter weather, spring and summer density, and subsequent breeding success of Eurasian Kestrels, Common Buzzards, and Northern Goshawks. *The Auk*, **108**: 342–347.

Kostrzewa, A. (1996) A comparative study of nest-site occupancy and breeding performance as indicators for nesting habitat quality in three European raptor species. *Ethology, Ecology & Evolution*, **8** (1): 1–18.

Kruckenhauser, L., Haring, E., Pinsker, W., Riesing, M.J., Winkler, H., Wink, M. & Gamauf, A. (2004) Genetic vs. morphological differentiation of Old World Buzzards (genus *Buteo*, Accipitridae). *Zool. Scr.*, **33**: 197–211.

Kruger, O. & Lindström, J. (2001) Lifetime reproductive success in common buzzard, *Buteo buteo*: from individual variation to population demography. *Oikos*, **93** (2): 260–273.

Kruger, O. (2004) The importance of competition, food, habitat, weather and phenotype for the reproduction of Buzzard *Buteo buteo*. *Bird Study*, 51: 125–132.

Lack, D. (1957) *The Natural Regulation of Animal Numbers.* Oxford.

Lambin, X., Petty, S. J. & Mackinnon, J. L. (2000) Cyclic dynamics in field vole populations and generalist predation. *Journal of Animal Ecology*, **69**: 106–119.

Lambin, X., Bretagnolle, V. & Yoccoz, N.G. (2006) Vole population cycles in northern and southern Europe: is there a need for different explanations for single pattern? *Journal of Animal Ecology*, **75** (2): 340–349.

Lees, A.C., Newton, I. & Balmford, A. (2013) Pheasants, buzzards and trophic cascades. *Conservation Letters*, **6**: 141–144.

Lewis, S. (1934) Brood of five in the Common Buzzard. *British Birds*, 28 (2).

Lockley, R.M. (1955). Buzzards following the plough. *British Birds*, **48**: 412–413.

Lockley, R.M. (1955) Mallard attacking Buzzard. *Nature in Wales*, **1** (3): 141.

Löhmus, A. (2003) Are certain habitats better every year? A review and case study on birds of prey. *Ecography*, **26** (5): 546–552.

Lovegrove, R., Williams, G. & Williams, I. (1994) *Birds in Wales.* T. & A.D. Poyser Ltd., London.

MacNally, L. (1964) Food at a Buzzard's nest. *Scottish Birds*, **3** (1): 26–27.

Madge, G. (1992) Buzzard with live common eel. *British Birds*, **85**: 187.

Mallord, J.W., Orsman, C.J., Cristinacce, A., Butcher, N., Stowe, T. & Charman, E. (2012) Mortality of Wood Warbler *Phylloscopus sibilatrix* in Welsh oakwoods: predation rates and the identification of nest predators using miniature nest cameras. *Bird Study*, **59** (3): 286–295.

Mayo, A.L.W. (1948) Nesting season and clutch-size of Common Buzzard. *British Birds*, **41**: 349.

Mebs, Th. (1964) Zur Biologie und Populationsdynamik der Mäusebussards (*Buteo buteo*). *Journal für Ornithologie*, **105** (3): 248–306.

Melde, M. (1956) *Der Mäusebussard.* Wittenberg-Lutherstadt.

Mikkola, H. (1976) Owls killing and killed by other owls and raptors in Europe. *British Birds*, **69**: 144–154.

Moore, N.W. (1957) The past and present status of the Buzzard in the British Isles. *British Birds*, **50**:1 73–197.

Musgrove, A., Aebischer, N., Eaton, M., Hearn, R., Newson, S., Noble, D., Parsons, M., Risely, K. & Stroud, D. (2013). Population estimates of birds in Great Britain and the United Kingdom. *British Birds*, **106**: 64–100.

Newton, I., Davis, P.E. & Davis, J.E. (1982) Ravens and Buzzards in relation to sheep-farming and forestry in Wales. *Journal of Animal Ecology*, **19**: 681–706.

Newton, I. (1979) *Population Ecology of Raptors.* T. & A. D. Poyser, Berkhamsted.

Newton, I. (1979) Distances between birthplace and breeding place in Sparrowhawks and other European raptors. *Journal of Raptor Research*, **13** (4): 97–101.

Newton, I. (1991). Habitat variation and population regulation in Sparrowhawks. *Ibis*, **133** (Suppl.1): 76–88.

Newton, I. (2013) Organochlorine pesticides and birds. *British Birds*, **106**: 189–205.

Niethammer, G. (1938). *Handbuch der deutschen Vogelkunde.* Leipzig.

Nore, T. (1999) Vingt ans de marquage des nichées de buses variables *Buteo buteo* dans le centre de la France. *Alauda*, **67** (4): 307–318.

North, F.J., Campbell, B. & Scott, R. (1949) *Snowdonia. The National Park of North Wales.* Collins, Lomdon.

Olendorff, R.R. (1974) Some quantitative aspects of growth in three species of Buteos. *Condor*, **76**: 466–468.

Olstad, O. (1934) Iakttagelsar over fjellvaken. *Norsk. Jaeg. -og Fiskforen. Tidsskr.*, 63: 567–579.

Olsson, V. (1958) Dispersal, migration, longevity and death causes of *Strix aluco, Buteo buteo, Ardea cinerea* and *Larus argentatus. Acta Vertebratica*, **1** (2): 87–189.

Owen, J. (1956) Buzzard killing Herring Gull. *Nature in Wales*, **2** (2): 280.

Panting, P.J. (1955) Buzzards following the plough. *British Birds*, **48**:412.

Park, K. J., Graham, K. E., Calladine, J. & Wernham, C. W. (2008) Impacts of birds of prey on gamebirds in the UK: a review. *Ibis*, **150**: 9–26.

Parslow, J.L.F. (1967) Changes in status among breeding birds in Britain and Ireland. *British Birds*, **60**: 1–47.

Petty, S.J., Lambin, X., Sherratt, N., Thomas, C. J., Mackinnon, J. L., Coles, C. F., Davison, M. & Little, B. (2000) Spatial synchrony in Field Vole *Microtus agrestis* abundance in a coniferous forest in northern England: the role of vole-eating raptors. *Journal of Applied. Ecology*, **37**, Supplement 1: 136–147.

Picozzi, N. & Weir, D. (1974) Breeding biology of the Buzzard in Speyside. *British Birds*, **67**: 199–210.

Picozzi, N. & Weir, D. (1976) Dispersal and causes of death of Buzzards. *British Birds*, **69**: 193–201.

Piechocki, R. (1953) Die Beeinflussung der Ernährung des Mäuse- und Rauhfussbussards durch den Tiefstand zyklischer Massenvermehrungen von Feldmäusern. *Wiss. Z. Univ. Halle, Math.-nat.*, **1**(3): 59–69.

Piechocki, R. (1970) Todesursache, Gewicht und Masse von *Buteo buteo buteo* (L.). Beitr. Vogelk, **16**: 313–327.

Piotrowski, S. (2003) *The Birds of Suffolk*. Helm, London.

Porter, R. & Abrams, C. (2013) Common Buzzard survey in north Norfolk 2012. *Norfolk Bird & Mammal Report*, **46**:43–45.

Potapov, E.R. (1997) What determines the population density and reproductive success of Rough-legged Buzzards, *Buteo lagopus*, in the Siberian tundra? *Oikos*, **78** (2): 362–376.

R.P.C.. (1957) Buzzard struck down crow in flight. *Nature in Wales*, **3** (2): 444.

Prestt, I. (1971) An ecological study of the viper *Vipera berus* in southern Britain. *Journal of Zoology, London*, **164**: 373–418.

Pring, C.J. (1947) Nesting season of Common Buzzard. *British Birds*, **40**: 182–183.

Prytherch, R.J. (2009) The social behaviour of the Common Buzzard. *British Birds*, **102**: 247–273.

Prytherch, R. J. (2013) The breeding biology of the Common Buzzard. *British Birds*, **106**: 264–279.

Ransom, P.L. (1956) Buzzard taking trout from Heron. *Nature in Wales*, **2** (1): 234.

Ratcliffe, D.A. (1965) Organochlorine residues in some raptor and corvid eggs from northern Britain. *British Birds*, **58**: 65–81.

Ratcliffe, D. A. (1980) *The Peregrine Falcon*. T. & A.D. Poyser, Calton.

Ratcliffe, D. A. (1997) *The Raven*. T. & A. D. Poyser, London.

Redpath, S. (1990) Hen Harrier facilitating predation of Red Grouse chicks by Buzzard. *British Birds*, **83**: 116.

Reif, V., Tornberg, R., Jungell, S. & Korpimäki, E. (2001) Diet variation of common buzzards in Finland supports the alternative prey hypothesis. *Ecography*, **24**: 267–274.

Reif, V., Jungell, S., Korpimäki, E., Tornberg, R. & Mykra, S. (2004) Numerical response of common buzzards and predation rate of main alternative prey under fluctuating food conditions. *Ann. Zool Fennici*, **41**: 599–607.

Reynolds, R.A.W. (1948) Nesting season and clutch-size of Common Buzzard. *British Birds*, **41**: 349–350.

Riddle, G. (2011) *Kestrels for Company*. Whittles Publishing, Dunbeath, Scotland.

Roberts, J.L. & Jones, M.S. (2009) Spacing and breeding production of Buzzards *Buteo buteo* in north-east Wales, 1978–2008. *Welsh Birds*, **6** (1): 9–24.

Robinson, J.S.C. (1951) Buzzard capturing prey in flight. *British Birds*, **44**: 412.

Robinson, W. (1945) Buzzards in the Postbridge area, Dartmoor, 1941–44. *MS unpublished*, Edward Grey Institute Library, University of Oxford.

Rochard, J.B.A. & Horton, N. (1977) *Birds killed by aircraft in the United Kingdom, in 1966–76*. Report to the 12th Meeting of the Bird Strike Committee, World Conference on Bird Hazards to Aircraft, Paris, October 1977.

Rockenbauch, D. (1975) Zwölfjährige Untersuchungen zur Ökologie des Mäusebussards (*Buteo buteo*) auf der Schwalbischen Alb. *Journal für Ornithologie*, **116**: 39–54.

Rooney, E. & Montgomery, W. I. (2013) Diet diversity of the Common Buzzard (*Buteo buteo*) in a vole-less environment. *Bird Study*, **60**: 147–155.

Ryves, B.H. (1948) Nesting season of Common Buzzard. *British Birds*, **41**: 53–54.

Ryves, B.H. (1948) *Bird Life in Cornwall*. Collins, London.

Saunders, D.R. (1960) Buzzard killing Little Owl on Skomer. *Nature in Wales*, **6** (4): 121.

Schifferli, A. (1951) Bericht der Schweis. Vogelwarte Sempach für die Jahre 1949 und 1950. *Orn. Beob.* **48** (6): 181–210.

Schmaus, A. (1938) Der Einfluss Mäusejahre auf das Bratgeschaft unserer Raubvögel und Eulen. *Beitr. FortPflBiol. Vogel*, **14**: 181–184.

Schuster, L. (1949) Beobachtungen über Aufsuchen und Verlassen des Schlafplatzes beim Mäusebussard (*B. buteo*) nebst einigen allgemeinen Bemerkungen über das Zurruhegehen der Vögel. *Festschrift von Erwin Stresemann, Heidelberg*. pp. 211–216.

Selås, V. (2001) Predation on reptiles and birds by the common buzzard, *Buteo buteo*, in relation to changes in its main prey, voles. *Canadian Journal of Zoology*, **79**: 2086–2093.

Selås, V., Tveiten, R. & Aanonsen, O. M. (2007) Diet of Common Buzzards (*Buteo buteo*) in southern Norway determined from prey remains and video recordings. *Ornis Fennica*, **84**: 97–104.

Sergio, A. & Newton, I. (2003) Occupancy as a measure of territory quality. *Journal of Animal Ecology*, **72**: 857–865.

Sharrock, J.T.R. (1976) *The Atlas of Breeding Birds in Britain and Ireland*. British Trust for Ornithology, Tring.

Shrubb, M. (1993) *The Kestrel*. Hamlyn, London.

Shrubb, M. (2000) An increase in the Buzzard *Buteo buteo* population in north Breconshire. *Welsh Birds*, **2** (5): 251–256.

Sim, I.M.W., Campbell, L., Pain, D.J. & Wilson, J.D. (2000) Correlates of the population increase of Common Buzzard *Buteo buteo* in the West Midlands between 1983 and 1996. *Bird Study*, **47**: 154–164.

Simmons, R. E., Avery, D. M., & Avery, G. (1991) Biases in diets determined from pellets and remains: correction factors for a mammal and bird-eating raptor. *J. Raptor Research*, **25** (3): 63–67.

Sitters, H.P. (ed.) (1988) *Tetrad Atlas of the Breeding Birds of Devon*. Devon Bird Watching and Preservation Society, Plymouth.

Smith, K. (1955) Buzzards following the plough. *British Birds*, **48**: 412.

Smith, M.H. (1986) Buzzards following and alighting on working plough. *British Birds*, **79**: 429.

Soltz, R.L. (1984) Time and energy budgets of the Red-tailed Hawk in southern California. *Southwestern Naturalist*, **29** (2): 148–156.

Southern, H.N. (1954) Tawny Owls and their prey. *Ibis*, **96**: 384–410.

Southern, H.N. (1959) Mortality and Population Control. *Ibis*, **101**: 429–436.

Southern, H.N. (ed.) (1964) *The Handbook of British Mammals*. Blackwell, Oxford.

Spaar, R. & Bruderer, B. (1996) Soaring migration of Steppe Eagles *Aquila nipalensis* in southern Israel: Flight behaviour and various wind and thermal conditions. *Journal of Avian Biology*, **27** (4): 289–301.

Spidsø, T.K. & Selas, V. (1988) Prey selection and breeding success in the Common Buzzard *Buteo buteo* in relation to small rodent cycles in southern Norway. *Fauna norv. Ser. C, Cinclus* **11**: 61–66.

Stewart, R.E. (1949) Ecology of a nesting Red-shouldered Hawk population. *Wilson Bulletin*, **61**: 26–35.

Stresemann, E. (1927–32) *Aves. Handbuch der Zoologie*, **7**, 2. Berlin.

Sumner, E.L. (1933) The growth of some young raptorial birds. *University of California Publications in Zoology*, **40**: 277–308.

Sumption, K.J. & Flowerdew, J.R. (1985) The ecological effects of the decline in Rabbits (*Oryctolagus cuniculus* L.) due to myxomatosis. *Mammal Review*, **15**: 151–186.

Suomus, H. (1952) Näringsundersökninger över ormvraken. *Papers on Game-Research, Helsingf*ors, **8**: 121–127 (English summary).

Suomus, H. (1953) Food of the Buzzard – in Finnish. *Suom. Riista*, **8**: 36–41.

Sutcliffe, S. J. (1998) A review of raptors and owls on Skomer Island from 1960 to 1995. *Welsh Birds*, **2** (1): 21–34.

Swann, R.L. & Etheridge, B. (1995) A comparison of breeding success and prey of the Common Buzzard *Buteo buteo* in two areas of northern Scotland. *Bird Study*, **42**: 37–43.

Sylvén, M. (1982) *Reproduction and survival in Common Buzzards (Buteo buteo) illustrated by the seasonal allocation of energy resources.* PhD dissertation, 102pp. University of Lund, Sweden.

Tattersall, F.H., Avundo, A.E., Manley, W.J., Hart, B.J. & Macdonald, D.W. (2000) Managing set-aside for field voles (*Microtus agrestis*). *Biological Conservation*, **96**:123–128.

Taylor, K., Hudson, R. & Horne, G. (1988) Buzzard breeding distribution and abundance in Britain and Northern Ireland in 1983. *Bird Study*, **35**: 109–118.

Taylor, M., Seago, M., Allard, P. & Darling, D. (1999) *The Birds of Norfolk*. Pica Press, Sussex.

Trout, R.C. & Tittensor, A.M. (1989) Can predators regulate wild Rabbit *Oryctolagus cuniculus* population density in England and Wales? *Mammal Review*, **19**: 153–173.

Tubbs, C.R. (1972) Analysis of nest record cards for the Buzzard. *Bird Study*, **19**: 96–104.

Tubbs, C. R. (1974) *The Buzzard*. David & Charles, Newton Abbot & London.

Tubbs, C.R. & Tubbs, J.M. (1985) Buzzards *Buteo buteo* and land use in the New Forest, Hampshire, England. *Biological Conservation*, **31**: 41–65.

Tucker, V.A. (2000) The deep fovea, sideways vision and spiral flight paths in raptors. *Journal of Experimental Biology*, **203** (24): 3745–3754.

Turner, C. V. (2007) The fate and management of Pheasants (*Phasianus colchicus*) in the U.K. Unpublished Ph.D thesis. Imperial College, University of London.

Tyack, A.J., Walls, S.S. & Kenward, R.E. (1998). Behaviour in the post-nestling independence period of radio-tagged Common Buzzards *Buteo buteo*. *Ibis*, **140**: 58–63.

Tyler, M. W. (2000) Common Buzzard feeding on apple. *British Birds*, **93**: 90.

Üttendorfer, O. (1939) *Die Ernährung der deutschen Raubvögel und Eulen und ihr Bedeutung in der Heimischen Natur*. Berlin.

Üttendorfer, O. (1952) *Neue Ergebnisse über die Ernährung der Greifvögel und Eulen*. Stuttgart.

Village, A. (1990) *The Kestrel*. T. & A D. Poyser, London

Walls, S.S. & Kenward, R.E. (1995) Movements of radio-tagged Common Buzzards *Buteo buteo* in their first year. *Ibis*, **137**: 177–182.

Walls, S.S. & Kenward, R.E. (1998) Movements of radio-tagged Buzzards *Buteo buteo* in early life. *Ibis*, **140**: 561–568.

Walls, S.S., Manosa, S., Fuller, R.M., Hodder, K.H. & Kenward, R.E. (1999) Is early dispersal enterprise or exile? Evidence from radio-tagged buzzards. *Journal of Avian Biology*, **30**: 407–415.

Walls, S.S. & Kenward, R.E. (2001) Consequences of relatedness and age in buzzards. *Animal Behaviour*, **61**: 1069–1078.

Walls, S., Kenward, R. & Holloway, G. (2004) How common is the common buzzard, *Buteo buteo*? *Biologist*, **51** (1): 23–26.

Watson, A. (1957a) The behaviour, breeding and food-ecology of the Snowy Owl *Nyctea scandiaca*. *Ibis*, **99**: 419–462.

Watson, A. (1957b) The breeding success of Golden Eagles in the North East Highlands. *Scottish Naturalist*, **69**: 153–169.

Warncke, K. & Wittenberg, J. (1959) Über Siedlungsdichte und Brutbiologie des Mäusebussards *Buteo buteo*. *Vogelwelt*, **80**: 101–108.

Weir, D. & Picozzi, N. (1975) Aspects of social behaviour in the Buzzard. *British Birds*, **68**: 125–141.

Weir, D. & Picozzi, N. (1983) Dispersion of Buzzards in Speyside. *British Birds*, **76**: 66–77.

Wendland, V. (1933) Vermehrung, allgemeine Brutbiologie und Ernährung des Mäusebussards (*Buteo b. buteo*). Beitr. *FortPflBiol. Vogel*, **9**: 157–167.

Wendland, V. (1952) Populationsstudien an Raubvögeln. *Journal fur Ornithologie, Leipzig*, **93**: 144–153.

Wernham, C., Toms, M., Marchant, J., Clark, J., Siriwardena, G & Baillie, S. (2002) *The Migration Atlas. The Movements of the Birds of Britain and Ireland.* T. & A. D. Poyser, London.

Wheeler, P. (2008) Effects of sheep grazing on abundance and predators of field voles (*Microtus agrestis*) in upland Britain. *Agriculture, Ecosystems & Environment*, **123**: 49–58.

Whittle, C. (2013) A review of British regional Buzzard research. *Cumbria Bird Club*, **24** (3): 62–77.

Williams, G. A. & Coan, D. (1973) Buzzard attacking observers at nest. *British Birds*, **66**: 31.

Wilson, G.R., Cooper, S.J. & Gessaman. (2004) The effects of temperature and artificial rain on the metabolism of American Kestrels (*Falco sparverius*). *Comparative Biochemistry & Physiology – Part A: Molecular & Integrative Physiology*, **139** (3): 389–394.

Witherby, H.F., Jourdain, F.C.R., Ticehurst, N.F. & Tucker, B.W. (1943) *The Handbook of British Birds*, vol. 3. Witherby, London.

Wooltorton, G.C. (1955) Buzzard killing Tawny Owl. *British Birds*, **49**: 149.

APPENDICES

APPENDIX 1

SCIENTIFIC NAMES OF SPECIES MENTIONED IN THE TEXT

BIRDS

American Kestrel *Falco sparverius*
Blackbird *Turdus merula*
Buzzard, Common *Buteo buteo*
Buzzard, Long-legged *Buteo longipes*
Buzzard, Rough-legged *Buteo lagopus*
Capercaillie *Tetrao urogallus*
Crow, Carrion/Hooded *Corvus corone*
Chaffinch *Fringilla coelebs*
Chough *Pyrrhocorax pyrrhocorax*
Common Sandpiper *Tringa hypoleucos*
Common Snipe *Gallinago gallinago*
Cormorant *Phalacrocorax carbo*
Crossbill *Loxia curvirostra*
Cuckoo *Cuculus canorus*
Curlew *Numenius arquata*
Dipper *Cinclus cinclus*
Domestic Fowl *Gallus gallus domesticus*
Dunlin *Calidris alpina*
Dunnock *Prunella modularis*
Feral Pigeon *Columba livia*
Gannet *Sula bassana*
Goldcrest *Regulus regulus*
Golden Eagle *Aquila chrysaetos*
Goldeneye *Bucephala clangula*
Golden Plover *Pluvialis apricaria*
Goldfinch *Carduelis carduelis*
Goshawk *Accipiter gentilis*
Grey Heron *Ardea cinerea*
Grouse, Black *Lyrurus tetrix*
Grouse, Hazel *Tetrastes bonasia*
Grouse, Red *Lagopus lagopus*
Guillemot *Uria aalge*
Gull, Great Black-backed *Larus marinus*
Gull, Herring *Larus argentatus*
Hen Harrier *Circus cyaneus*
Hawk, Red-shouldered *Buteo lineatus*
Hawk, Red-tailed *Buteo jamaicensis*
House Sparrow *Passer domesticus*
Jackdaw *Corvus monedula*
Jay *Garrulus glandarius*
Kestrel *Falco tinnunculus*
Kite, Black *Milvus migrans*
Kite, Red *Milvus milvus*
Lapwing *Vanellus vanellus*
Linnet *Acanthis cannabina*
Little Grebe *Tachybaptus ruficollis*
Magpie *Pica pica*
Mallard *Anas platyrhynchos*
Manx Shearwater *Puffinus puffinus*
Merlin *Falco columbarius*
Moorhen *Gallinula chloropus*
Mute Swan *Cygnus olor*
Osprey *Pandion haliaetus*
Owl, Barn *Tyto alba*
Owl, Eagle *Bubo bubo*
Owl, Little *Athene noctua*
Owl, Short-eared *Asio flammeus*
Owl, Snowy *Nyctea scandiaca*
Owl, Tawny *Strix aluco*
Oystercatcher *Haematopus ostralegus*
Peregrine Falcon *Falco peregrinus*
Pheasant *Phasianus colchicus*
Pied Flycatcher *Ficedula hypoleuca*
Pied Wagtail *Motacilla alba*
Pipit, Meadow *Anthus pratensis*
Pipit, Tree *Anthus trivialis*
Pomarine Skua *Stercorarius pomarinus*
Puffin *Fratercula arctica*
Raven *Corvus corax*
Red-legged Partridge *Alectoris rufa*
Redpoll *Acanthis flammea*
Redshank *Tringa totanus*
Redstart *Phoenicurus phoenicurus*
Reed Bunting *Emberiza schoeniclus*
Ring Ouzel *Turdus torquatus*
Robin *Erithacus rubecula*
Siskin *Carduelis spinus*
Skylark *Alauda arvensis*
Sparrowhawk *Accipiter nisus*
Starling *Sturnus vulgaris*
Stock Dove *Colunba oenas*

Stonechat *Saxicola torquata*
Teal *Anas crecca*
Thrush, Mistle *Turdus viscivorus*
Thrush, Song *Turdus philomelos*
Tit, Blue *Parus caeruleus*
Tit, Coal *Parus ater*
Tit, Great *Parus major*
Treecreeper *Certhia familiaris*
Tufted Duck *Aythya fuligula*
Warbler, Garden *Sylvia borin*
Warbler, Grasshopper *Locustella naevia*
Warbler, Willow *Phylloscopus trochilus*
Warbler, Wood *Phylloscopus sibilatrix*
Wheatear *Oenanthe oenanthe*
Whinchat *Saxicola rubetra*
Whitethroat *Sylvia communis*
Woodcock *Scolopax rusticola*
Woodpecker, Great Spotted *Dendrocopus major*
Woodpecker, Green *Picus viridis*
Wood Pigeon *Columba palumbus*
Wood Warbler *Phylloscopus sibilatrix*
Wren *Tyroglodytes troglodytes*
Yellowhammer *Emberiza citrinella*

MAMMALS

Badger *Meles meles*
Brown Hare *Lepus europaeus*
Brown Rat *Rattus norvegicus*
Deer, Roe *Capreolus capreolus*
Fox, Arctic *Alopex lagopus*
Fox, Red *Vulpes vulpes*
Goat, Feral *Capra hircus*
Hedgehog *Erinaceus europaeus*
Mole *Talpa europaea*
Mouse, House *Mus musculus*
Mouse, Wood *Apodemus sylvaticus*
Otter *Lutra lutra*
Rabbit *Oryctolagus cuniculus*
Sheep *Ovis aries*
Shrew, Common *Sorex araneus*
Shrew, Pygmy *Sorex minutus*
Shrew, Water *Neomys fodiens*
Stoat *Mustela erminea*
Squirrel, Grey *Sciurus carolinensis*
Squirrel, Red *Sciurus vulgaris*
Vole, Bank *Clethrionomys glareolus*
Vole, Common *Microtus arvalis*
Vole, Water *Arvicola amphibius*
Weasel *Mustela nivalis*

REPTILES

Adder *Vipera berus*
Common Lizard *Lacerta agilis*
Grass Snake *Natrix natrix*
Slow-worm *Anguis fragilis*

AMPHIBIANS

Common Frog *Rana temporaria*
Common Toad *Bufo bufo*

FISH

Eel *Anguilla anguis*
Salmon *Salmo salar*
Trout, Brown *Salmo trutta*
Trout, Rainbow *Onchorhynchus mykiss*

TREES

Alder *Alnus glutinosa*
Ash *Fraxinus excelsior*
Beech *Fagus sylvaticus*
Birch *Betula pubescens*
Crab Apple *Malus sylvestris*
Douglas Fir *Pseudotsuga menziesii*
Hawthorn *Crataegus monogyna*
Larch *Larix decidua*
Oak, English *Quercus robur*
Oak, Sessile *Quercus petraea*
Rowan *Sorbus aucuparia*
Sitka Spruce *Picea sitchensis*
Scots Pine *Pinus sylvestris*
Sycamore *Acer pseudo-platanus*
Willow *Salix caprea*

OTHER PLANTS

Bilberry *Vaccinium myrtillus*
Bracken *Pteridium aquilinum*
Cotton-grass *Eriophorum sp.*
Gorse *Ulex europaeus/gallii*
Heather *Erica spp.*
Ivy *Hedera helix*
Purple Moor-grass *Molinia caerulea*

APPENDIX 2a

BUZZARD STUDIES: AIMS AND METHODS

Outlined below is the range of investigations that were undertaken in my three study areas during various periods between 1956 and 1993. The notes may also provide a guide for enthusiasts contemplating studies of Buzzards in their own localities.

Dartmoor (Postbridge)

The main aims of the academic research from 1956 to 1958 were related to the advent of the 1953–54 myxomatosis Rabbit disease pandemic in the British countryside, and its initial impacts upon the diet, numbers and breeding success of Buzzards. In particular, the project set out to assess how Buzzards were adapting their food habits to cope with the myxomatosis era, and to measure any effects of the sudden and drastic reduction in Rabbit numbers upon Buzzard survival and breeding. It was necessary also to study their social behaviour and attempt to measure how much food individual birds needed to catch daily in order (a) to survive in good condition, and (b) for the adults to breed successfully. For such an ambitious programme, finding a study site with an adequate Buzzard population within a 'manageable' area free from persecution and excessive disturbance were major considerations. The Postbridge area on Dartmoor fulfilled all these criteria.

Information was collected every month by repeated observation of individual birds (recognised from plumage differences) so as to map their daily locations, movements and, ultimately, territories; to observe hunting methods, pair relationships and social interactions; and to record the dispersal of juveniles. Food habits were assessed by analyzing regurgitated pellets found beneath regularly-used perches, by prey capture observations, and from prey remains found on or seen being brought to nests. Details of each activity are given in relevant chapters. The seasonal pattern of the field work and the relative effort spent on each activity during a year is shown, very approximately, in the schematic chart.

The average daily food requirements were measured by captive feeding experiments with two full-grown juvenile Buzzards during their first autumn and winter. Also assessed were pellet production frequency and the different extents to which principal prey species were digested and subsequently identifiable in pellets. These last findings would provide a more realistic interpretation of prey remains in pellets of wild Buzzards. The breeding season required additional effort for locating and monitoring nests (clutch and brood sizes, fledging success). Tasks included measuring growth rates and survival within broods, recording preys brought to broods, and observing the roles of the sexes in hunting and caring for their offspring.

Such a full field schedule necessitated frequent visits to, or stays in the study site (using an old gypsy-style caravan located in a Buzzard territory) but especially during the 7–8 weeks when young were in nests. Near-daily inspections were made of two or three broods virtually throughout the nestling period in each of two seasons. During the most intensive phase, in June, older broods were examined four times daily for 2–3 week periods (details in Appendices 2a and 2b). This involved daily cycling 35–45 km along hilly lanes and tracks to make eight (sometimes more) unaided climbs to the tree nests. Over the full three seasons, a total of 426 brood inspections were made, equivalent to climbing almost 5,500 m (18,000 ft); to which could be added a further *c.*300 m (1,000 ft) when checking clutches.

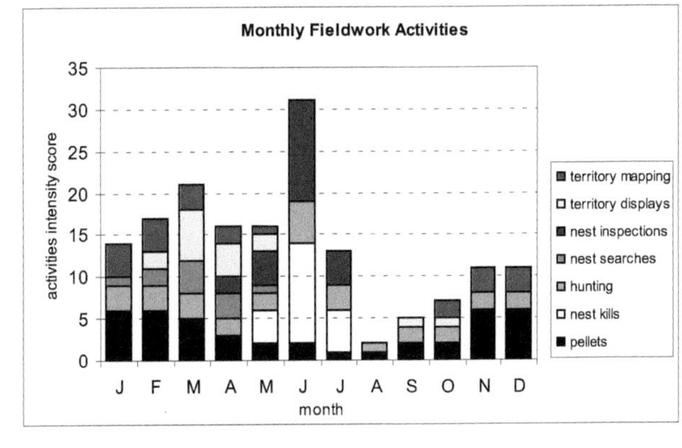

On monitoring visits in the 1960s and early 1990s (when I was living far from Devon) only the population size and final breeding performance were assessed. The aims then were restricted to counting the total production of young fledged each year in relation to the total number of pairs present and those which bred. This could be done mainly from the ground by flushing incubating birds off nests (to confirm breeding) followed later by observing either fully-feathered youngsters standing on nests or by finding newly-fledged juveniles nearby.

North Wales

Unlike my Dartmoor research, the Wales project of 1977–84 was entirely a leisure time enterprise. It concentrated on carrying out a census of the Buzzard populations in the Snowdonia mountains and around the adjoining Migneint-Hiraethog moors. This was undertaken in conjunction with a census of Raven populations. The main aims were, first, to map the numbers and distribution of territorial Buzzard pairs, and then to assess their breeding densities and performance in the widely different terrains and habitats. Information on territorial and hunting behaviour, nest sites and breeding behaviour, as well as opportunistic observations of preys brought to feed broods, also was collected. Three woodland nests containing young were observed from hides on several days.

Nest searches began in winter (January) when the many and extensive (leafless) deciduous woods in valleys were combed to locate old nests, including any under repair, and new nests being built. Most nests in trees, and some on small rock faces, were accessible either by climbing (unaided) or could be viewed from higher vantage points. Those with broods on high cliffs usually could be viewed only from 100 m or more away using a pocket telescope (x20 magnification). The breeding season field work ended in August, when it was judged that the last fledged broods and used nests had been located.

These two study areas encompassed 1,366 km^2 of rugged countryside sustaining a Buzzard population of some 150 pairs. Total coverage each year was impractical, especially given the challenging terrains and weather of Snowdonia. In the best year, 57 occupied nests were located. In general, however, different annual samples of 25–40 breeding pairs, widely scattered across the region, could be monitored adequately by repeat inspections in any one season. On average, each nest inspection took about 45 minutes, and often entailed rough hill scrambling, to and from the site; eight 'active' nests could be checked on a good day.

APPENDIX 2b

ROUTINE INSPECTION OF BUZZARD BROODS IN THE DARTMOOR STUDY

Brood age (days)	Inspection tasks
1–15	one visit a day, in the evening was sufficient to record food and the condition of the chicks.
15–23	2 visits daily were necessary, usually about noon and in late evening; prolonged hide observations at nests proved very informative.
23–47	4 visits daily, at around 0700, 1300, 1700 and 2100 BST; nest screen introduced at 24–26 days old, when young feathered on backs (App. 2c).
47–fledging	Necessary to remove nest screen about 6 days before expected fledging date, to allow young to exercise wings fully; as a result nest visits reduced to 1–2 a day.
Post-fledging	usually one daily visit for a few days, to check progress of the fledglings, and for casual recording of larger preys still being brought to the nest.

At each nest inspection the following checks were made:

(i) Preys – whole kills were weighed or, where impractical to do so, estimated.

(ii) Whole kills were 'marked' to prevent duplicate recording; especially important during early nestling stages when prey supplied may exceed brood demand, and some items stay uneaten for more than a day. Small mammals, birds and amphibians were tagged by clipping off a foot; Rabbits by clipping the tail (effective since rear parts usually were eaten last).

(iii) Discarded prey remains removed to avoid duplication; feathers, scales and other uncertain traces were collected for later identification.

(iv) Pellets were collected and date labelled for subsequent analysis.

(v) Parental behaviour noted, e.g. whether at or near nest, vocal reactions, threat display, etc.

(vi) Brood – weighed at the nest until too large to handle *in situ*; plumage and behavioural development recorded, including hunger state. Any visible food bulge in crop estimated by reference to vole size unit. [Where a nest screen was in use, young Rabbits and other large kills were carved up and fed to the large chicks in manageable portions for them to swallow or tear apart].

(vii) Miscellaneous observations – state of nest – hygiene; presence of fresh green foliage; weather conditions. Check ground below for prey remains and pellets.

Disturbance to parents and brood was kept to a minimum, particularly during bad weather and when chicks were small. Each inspection lasted about 10 minutes except when a nest screen was in use. Then, the evening visit could be prolonged by the need to feed the young should a fresh Rabbit kill have recently been brought to the nest.

APPENDIX 2c

NEST PREYS: QUANTITATIVE ASSESSMANT METHODS

A set routine of nest inspections was adopted for the detailed Dartmoor studies at carefully selected tree nests. The daily frequency of visits was raised to four as the brood grew, in order to keep pace with the increasing amounts of prey brought and with faster consumption of kills. When a brood was about 25 days old, well feathered dorsally, and capable of swallowing smaller preys, it became necessary to prevent the parents from passing kills to the young directly. The nest was therefore partitioned into two areas: the habitual landing area for the parents, and a living space for the single chicks. This enabled a near-complete record of daily diets to be obtained. Unlike the Polish box cage system (Czarnecki & Foksowicz 1954), a simple screen of 1.5 cm diameter mesh flexible wire netting was placed across the nest. Preys were dropped by parents in front of the screen, and then fed to the chicks by the observer at his next visit. Screen dimensions varied with brood size and nest area. Provision had to be made for parents to land and leave food at the front of the nest and for the young to move freely around at the back; sometimes the nest platform was extended manually. All broods fledged successfully.

At all screened nests, however, within 2–3 days the females began to pass food through the mesh to their young. This 'problem' was overcome by reducing the mesh openings by half. Even then, one female endeavoured to feed the young through the barrier. Such parental tenacity was reported also in the similar Polish study. At all nests where food was 'smuggled' to the young, the preys were usually larger mammals (Rabbits especially) or birds which left ample traces (fur or feathers) of their presence. Any small preys leaving no traces on nests often were detected later in the young's pellets; or by the visual state of the chicks' crops, and were logged as 'unidentified small vertebrate' species. Errors resulting from smuggling food to broods were considered to be comparatively small in the final assessments of brood diets.

This intensive programme would not have been possible without a base or field station in the study area – an old wooden caravan beside a stream on Cator Common. From here, nests were visited by bicycle in 1957 and by motor-cycle in 1958. On average, a 16-hour day (0600–2200 BST) was worked during the busiest month. The 1957 study nest entailed cycling almost 40 km a day; and some 850 km in total. In this intensive kind of study it is clear that nest distances limit the number of nests that can be monitored without motor transport. Nowadays, it could be feasible to keep several nests under continuous surveillance using webcams and video recording equipment.

APPENDIX 3

ENERGY CONTENT OF THE FLESH OF PREY SPECIES

	Energy content of the flesh of prey species (kcalories/g fresh weight)	
Small Mammals		
Microtus arvalis	1.46	ref.1
M. ochrogaster	1.42	ref.3
Clethrionomys gapperi	1.69	ref.2
Rabbit, wild spp.	1.44–1.53	culinary data
Squirrel sp.	1.49	culinary data
Wild Birds		
Pigeon	1.45	culinary data
Pheasant	1.4	culinary data
Sheep carrion		
Lamb	1.67	culinary data
Amphibians		
Frog, Rana sp. (legs)	0.75	culinary data
Invertebrates		
Earthworms (Lumbricidae)	0.81	ref. 4
caterpillars (Lepidoptera)	1.33	ref. 4
leatherjackets (Tipulidae)	0.98	ref. 4

1 Gorecki, A. (1965). Energy values of body in small mammals. Acta Theriologica 10: 333–352.

2 Bergeron, J.M. (1976). Caloric values of small mammals in south eastern Quebec. Acta Theriologica 21: 157–163.

3 Fleharty, E., Krause, M.E. & Stinnett, (1973). Body composition, energy content and cycles of four species of rodents. J. Mammalogy, 54: 426–438.

4 Westerterp, K., Gortmaker, W. & Wijngaarden, H. (1982). Energetic optimum in brood-raising in the Starling Sturnus vulgaris: an experimental study. Ardea, 70: 153–162.

APPENDIX 4

CHARACTERISTIC TYPES OF BUZZARD PELLETS

Four basic types were recognisable in the Dartmoor study area, based on texture and prey content, though marked variation in size and appearance was noted.

Fur

Commonest type: Medium-large and elongate pellets of compacted fur from one or more mammal species, and normally containing small amounts of bone and traces of other prey groups (both vertebrate and invertebrate). The largest pellets were all of this type: average size 45 x 21 x 16 mm (maximum 73 x 23 x 22 mm). The smallest - 12 mm diameter highly compressed balls of triturated hair – were secondary castings. These were produced by both wild and captive Buzzards.

Vegetable matter & Frog bones

Frequently found type in spring, and indicating heavy predation on Frogs. These were loosely constructed pellets comprising Frog bones bound together by varying amounts of grass, roots and moss. Most of the vegetable matter apparently was ingested purposely as 'roughage'. Reptile scales and invertebrate traces were sometimes associated with Frog remains.

Invertebrate

Composed entirely or largely of terrestrial insect larval and beetle remains (earthworm remains rare). Frequent in spring and early summer in some territories, and indicating targeted ground foraging, perhaps during warm dry weather. Some pellets were entirely of numerous skins of lepidopterous and tipulid larvae (noctuid moth caterpillars and crane-fly 'leatherjackets'). The largest pellet measured 55 x 18 x 15 mm.

Vegetable fibres

Medium size pellets (largest 55 x 18 x 16 mm) entirely of fibrous plant materials mixed with mineral grains; always associated with abundant earthworm setae, thus reflecting intensive ground foraging in pasture fields. Most frequently found in winter and wet weather. Vegetable matter, acting as 'roughage', was mainly grass, roots and mosses, but sometimes also dead leaves, conifer needles and twig fragments.

Additionally, occasional but distinctive pellets were composed mainly or entirely of sheep wool; occasionally small pellets contained numerous small feathers or reptile scales.

Dimensions of Buzzard pellets (from a small mammal diet)

Source	Number	Mean (mm)	Maximum	Minimum
Wild birds (Dartmoor)	100	45 x 21 x 18	73 x 23 x 22	21 x 17 x 13
			71 x 28 x 25	19 x 17 x 17
			70 x 28 x 22	17 x 15 x 15
Captive birds	34	46 x 20 x 18	68 x 23 x 20	29 x 16 x 15
			63 x 22 x 19	29 x 14 x 10
			48 x 21 x 18	15 x 15 x 9

APPENDIX 5

PREY SPECIES' BODY WEIGHTS

In a raptor study one needs to know the average body weight of each prey species so as to determine:

- their relative dietary importance in terms of biomass as well as by numbers.
- the weight of food brought to broods in a given time (it is rarely possible to weigh all kills)
- the daily food consumption, estimated from pellet material

On Dartmoor, weight data were collected from small mammals live-trapped, preys found on nests, and from the literature. Prey weight values used in this Buzzard study are tabulated below.

Mean Weights for vertebrate preys used in the food analyses

Prey Species	Mean Wt.(g)	Prey Species	Mean Wt.(g)
Mammals:		*Birds:*	
Rabbit, juvenile	250	Song Thrush	70
Brown Rat, immature	200	Mistle Thrush	100
Wood Mouse	20	Blackbird	90
Water Vole	100	Wheatear	25
Short-tailed Vole	20	Robin	15
Bank Vole	20	Grasshopper Warbler	13
Common Shrew	10	Whitethroat	15
Small mammal, unidentified	20	Dunnock	20
Mole	100	Meadow Pipit	18
Reptiles:		Starling	80
Adder	100	Magpie	225
Slow-worm	10	Carrion Crow, pullus	200
Common Lizard	5	Great Tit	15
Small reptile, unidentified	10	Wood Pigeon	475
Amphibians:		Feral Pigeon	400
Common Frog	25	Chaffinch	22
Common Toad	25	House Sparrow	25
		Small passerine sp.	25*

(* in adult Buzzard pellet; 20g used for nest prey items)

APPENDIX 6

BUZZARD CLUTCH SIZES IN DIFFERENT REGIONS OF BRITAIN

Area	Years	Main Prey	Clutches	Clutch Sizes (as % of samples)						Mean	SD	Source
				c/1	c/2	c/3	c/4	c/5	c/6			
Uplands												
Dartmoor	1956-69	SM	21	4.8	52.4	42.9				2.38		Dare (1999)
Snowdonia	1979-82	SM	46	19.6	52.2	28.3				2.09	0.69	Dare (1995)
Snowdonia	1977-2009		186	4.3	57.1	38.6				2.34		J. Driver (in litt.)
Migneint-Hiraethog	1979-82	SM	39	7.7	43.6	48.7				2.40	0.46	Dare (1995)
NE Wales	1980-2008	R, SM	229	6.6	41.5	50.2	1.6			2.47	0.7	Roberts & Jones (2009)
mid-Wales	1975-79	R, SM, LB	467							2.1		Newton *et al.* 1982
Lake District		SC ?	60	1.7	13.3	83.3	1.7			2.85		Coombs (1948)
NW Pennines	1937-67	R*, SM	56	1.8	17.8	61.0	17.8	1.8		3.03		Holdsworth (1971)
Speyside	1969-72	R	72		27.8	48.6	23.6			2.96	0.72	Picozzi & Weir (1974)
Glen Urquhart	1977-89	SM, SB	162	5.6	51.9	38.9				2.41		Swann & Etheridge (1995)
West Moray	1977-88	R, LB	64	4.7	17.2	57.8	20.3			2.94		Swann & Etheridge (1995)
mid-Argyll	1989-90	SM, LB	73	8.2	61.6	27.4	2.7			2.24		Austin et al. (1997)
Kintyre	1970s ?	?	89	6.7	32.6	56.2	4.5			2.58		Maguire (1979)
Lowlands												
W. Midlands	1994-95	R, LB	82	6.1	64.6	28.0	1.2			2.2	0.06	Sim *et al.* (2001)
New Forest	1961-71	B	70	18.6	67.1	14.3				1.86		Tubbs (1974)
Somerset/Devon*	1930s-40s	R*	58	1.7	29.3	58.6	5.2	3.4	1.7	2.84		Pring (1947)
	1930s-40s	R*	60	1.6	25.0	63.3	6.6	3.3		2.85		Mayo (1948)
Devon*	1940s*	R*	33	3.0	18.2	72.7	6.0			2.82		Reynolds (1948)
Coastal												
Skomer (island)	1954-64	R*	20	5	40.0	45.0	10.0			2.60		Davis & Saunders (1965)
Totals/averages =			**1887**	**6.4**	**42.0**	**45.6**	**5.6**	**0.3**	**<0.1**	**2.64**		

note - c/5 and c/6 might be product of 2 females with a bigamous male; ref. 2 laying 4 eggs in one nest in mid-Wales (Davis & Davis 2002). Cornwall - 1930s-40s: 'commonest' clutch was 3 eggs, 4-egg clutches were 'rare (Ryves 1948). Preys R - rabbit; R* - rabbit, pre-myxo; SM - small mammals; LB - large birds (corvid size); SB - smaller birds; SC - sheep carrion based mainly on remains at nests.

APPENDIX 7

BUZZARD EGG LAYING DATES IN DIFFERENT REGIONS OF BRITAIN

Region	Years	Clutches	Earliest	Median	Peak	Latest	Source
Dartmoor	1956-69	22	Apr-06 (Apr 1)*		Apr 16-25	May 15 *	Dare (1999)
Snowdonia & Migneint-Hiraethog	1977-83	40	Apr-01 (Mar 27)*	Apr 18*	Apr 15-20*	Apr-26 (May 8)*	Dare (1989)
Snowdonia	1977-2006	60	Apr-07 (Mar 26)*	Apr 17*	Apr 11-25*	May-01	J. Driver (in litt.)
NE Wales	1980-2009	202	Mar-01	Apr 14 *	Apr 10-19*	May-01	J.L. Roberts (in litt.)
Lake District		60	Apr-10		Apr 19-29		Coombs (1948), Brown (1948)
NW Pennines	1937-67	56	Apr-08	Apr-21			Holdsworth (1971)
mid-Argyll	1989-90	73	Apr-02	Apr-14			Austin et al. (1997)
Speyside	1969-72	72			Apr 10-20		Picozzi & Weir (1974)
Kintyre			Mar-27	Apr-20			Maguire (1979)
W. Midlands/ Welsh Border	1994-95	82	Apr-02	Apr-17	Apr 12-17	May-04	Sim et al. (2001)
Somerset/ Devon	1930s-40s	118	Apr-07		Apr 15-25		Pring (1948), Mayo (1948)
Devon	1930s-40s	33	Apr-04				Reynolds (1948)
Cornwall	1930s-40s		Apr-05		Apr 9-20		Ryves (1948)
New Forest	1961-71	70	Apr 6-8	Apr-18	Apr 10-26	May 4-6	Tubbs (1974)

note: ( ) * back calculated from fledging date, assuming mean periods of 46 days for fledging & 35 days incubation (Dare 1989)

NE Wales data include 2 years (2008-09) when nestling ages were estimated from wing length using method of Bijlsma (1999).

APPENDIX 8

ASPECTS OF BUZZARD PARENTAL CARE AND NESTLING BEHAVIOUR

TWO SAMPLE LOGS OF NEST OBSERVATIONS

These observations were made on Dartmoor, at the 1957 Bellever territory nest, from a hide situated on a slope overlooking the nest, and using a telescope of x20 magnification. The large nest was in a Scots pine at the bottom of a steep scrubby clearing in the spruce forest. Attention is directed to two behavioural and developmental features of particular interest:

(a) The progress of the brood towards independence, and the consequent emancipation of the female from many nest duties, thus enabling her to participate more in hunting.

(b) The dominating behaviour of one nestling following a presumed temporary deterioration in the food supply, and despite the very close similarity in their sizes and development.

(c) New prey items and sex of captor are highlighted.

DAY 1. 31 MAY (1300-2115 BST). BROOD AGE = 15 DAYS. WEATHER: CLOUDY BUT WARM.

13.02 Male brought an adult Short-tailed Vole and left it on the nest; female absent.

14.05 Pair soaring over the forested valley, male display-diving. Chicks active, sitting up alertly or shuffling about over their toilet.

16.47 Female flew into tall fir trees near nest and began preening.

16.58 Male in with a small kill, paused a few seconds on the nest, then flew into a nearby pine for a moment's rest before returning to its hunting grounds.

17.02 Female left her watch-point and flew into a pine close by, where she broke off a foot-long twig for the nest. Nestlings were then fed for 13 minutes with 50 and 67 morsels, in the rotation – chick I, I & II, II – after which they were brooded for 11 minutes. Female then returned to look-out station but soon returned to the nest area.

18.13 Female brought a small kill, paused a moment until chicks awoke and lined up to be fed; She then fed brood for 23 minutes, not on the fresh prey but from the remains of a Rabbit brought yesterday. Chicks received 89 and 87 morsels apiece, including some fur, in the rotation – chick I (24), II (89), I (63). Female also ate some meat, but mostly fur. After the meal, female dug vigorously into the nest bottom and swallowed several objects – presumably food scraps, pellet debris and possibly invertebrate nest fauna. Chicks were pushed aside during the clean-up, after which female brooded them for 48 minutes.

19.35 Female fed chicks again: 34 morsels in 7 minutes (a light meal). Chicks then slept with female standing silently beside them.

20.21 Male brought a Short-tailed Vole; no reaction whatsoever from female.

20.38 Female left nest after standing silently for 55 minutes – had been on nest for very nearly 2.5 hours; she departed the nest area.

20.55 Female returned and settled on top of a fir overlooking the nest.

21.04 Female glided onto nest and ate a Rabbit foot; gave some pieces of meat to brood, but chicks apparently not very hungry.

21.15 Observation period terminated.

21.16 **Total kills = 4 small preys in 8.25 hours; 3 of them caught by the male.**

DAY 2. 9.6.57 (11.35–19.30 BST). BROOD AGE = 24 DAYS. WEATHER: DULL AND COOL WITH PROLONGED HEAVY SHOWERS.

11.35 One chick is eating a recently brought Short-tailed Vole; no other prey on the nest today.

13.26 **Female** brought a fledgling **Chaffinch;** one chick seized the kill and swallowed it whole after plucking a few feathers (retrieved later for identification). Female remained only 20 seconds at nest before returning to hunting area. Chicks quiet and alert between visits, their dorsal feather covering affording effective protection against even heavy rain.

16.06 **Male** arrived with a large **Short-tailed Vole** which was seized by one chick - other chick apparently uninterested. Male resumed hunting after a 10 seconds pause on the nest. 17.15 **Male** returned with a **small mammal** which was swallowed immediately by same nestling that had eaten the last kill. Nest-mate now began squealing hunger calls.

17.30 Another small prey swallowed by dominant youngster after a brief dispute with its hungry companion.

18.02 The dominated chick now giving frequent hunger calls, having received no food for at least 4.5 hours. Occasional scuffling between the chicks, with pecking at bills and heads. 19.04 A large **Short-tailed Vole** was dropped onto nest in haste (parent not identified) and was pounced on by the hungry chick, which disposed of it voraciously. The dominant chick showed no interest in this kill, presumably being satiated!

19.30 Observations terminated.

Total kills = 5 small preys in ca. 8.25 hours.

(Footnote: Both youngsters fledged successfully).

APPENDIX 9

NESTLING DEVELOPMENT AND BEHAVIOUR OF BUZZARDS: POSTBRIDGE, DARTMOOR

Age (days)	Plumage	Behaviour
1–2	thin cover of silky whitish down or filoplumes	sight weak; very little strength; feeble cheeping sleep for long periods
3–5		can hold head up briefly to beg by day 3, when 'fighting' also begins. can hold head up briefly to beg by day 3, when 'fighting' also begins. sight better by day 4 when can follow movements of parents low over nest. By day 5 - pecks quite strongly at fingers or nest mates.
6–10	second coat of down appears around day 8.	respond to parental alarm calls by crouching quietly with 'glazed' look in eyes from day 8-9. feet grip nest lining firmly when body lifted. pecking order develops between siblings
11–15	down coarse and thicker, greyer. Primary quills on day 12 or 13, followed by secondaries.	sits up alertly by day 15, but still sleeps for long periods. pecking order now strongly established voice changes from cheeping to hunger whistles at 2 weeks.
16–20	primary quills open ca day 17; tails quill ca. day 18, followed by scapulars & mantle feathers.	rapid development of beak and feet incipient threat display towards intruders may begin
21–25	first flank feathers appear from day 21, ear coverts on day 25. By day 24 wings, scapulars & tail areas are well scattered with feathers. Head & breast still pure down.	increasing activity & curiosity; stand momentarily to shake plumage & stretch wings. by day 23. Can tear up small mammals; siblings may dispute kill by day 24. frequent toe flexing exercises when reclining on tarsi.
26–30	flank feathers appear ca. day 27; sometimes a week later; side of breast feathers show ca. day 28; crown feathers start by day 30.	can stand well for short periods & totter about nest by day 29; frequent preening; well developed threat display by day 26.
31–35	central breast & ear coverts show ca. day 31; cheek ca. day 35; breast, belly & flanks well covered by day 35, & all upperparts complete.	mantle over prey when very hungry, but unable to tear rabbit flesh until ca. day 34; stands for long periods at times; first fully immature hunger calls.
36–40	underparts almost fully feathered by day 40; head also well feathered down now only around bill & face,also under wings & over crop.	stand frequently; active about nest; wing exercises begin; still unable to pierce skin of moles.
41–45	almost full plumage by day 45; only a few traces of down adhering around base of bill & central breast.	becoming increasingly restless frequent vigorous wing exercises, stretching & preening

Appendix 9 table (*cont.*)

Age (days)	Plumage	Behaviour
46–50	Immaculate plumage by day 50.	frequent wing exercising; very active; now able to tear up most of a young rabbit very active; may 'jump' from nest if alarmed by human untrusion; now able to tear up most of a young rabbit without help from female.
50 – fledging		very restless, jumping out onto side branches; still squats on tarsi sometimes to rest; incipient adult calls developing.

Note: 1. development rate and fledging age are variable according to food availability and relative ranking in the brood.
2. maximum feather development/growth occurs during weeks 4 & 5.

APPENDIX 10

BUZZARDS AT POSTBRIDGE: PRODUCTIVITY RATINGS OF 13 TERRITORIES; FROM 17 YEARS OF FULL RECORDS (1959-69 AND 1990-93)

Territory	(size, ha)	Ocupancy by pairs	Breeding attempts	Breeding successful	No. young fledged	No. young median	No. young % of total	Annual Productivity per territory	Annual Productivity per breeding attempt	Annual Productivity per pair successful
Archerton	106	17	13	11	15 (21)	18	14.4	1.06	1.33	1.64
Blackaton	126	17	16	12	15 (20)	17.5	13.9	1.00	1.04	1.46
Soussons	188	17	16	10	16 (18)	17	13.5	1.00	1.06	1.25
Cator Court	73	16	12	12	14 (16)	15	12.0	0.88	1.25	1.25
Grendon	69	15	14	9	11 (16)	13.5	10.8	0.79	0.96	1.50
		max. 85 82 96.5%	**71 86.6%**	**54 76.1%**	**69 (91)**	**81**	**64.7**	**0.95**	**1.14**	**1.50**
Bellever	200	14	13	6	7 (10)	8.5	6.8	0.05	0.65	1.41
Runnage	171	16	9	5	7 (8)	7.5	6.0	0.44	0.84	1.50
Postbridge	159	12	9	6	7 (8)	7.5	6.0	0.44	0.84	1.25
Riddon	163	13	10	6	7	7	5.6	0.41	0.70	1.16
		max. = 68 55 80.9%	**41 60.30%**	**23 33.3%**	**28 (33)**	**30**	**24.4**	**0.44**	**0.68**	**1.50**
Webburn Wood	53	15	8	4	4 (6)	5	4.0	0.29	0.63	1.25
Powder Mills	237	15	7	2	4	4	3.2	0.24	0.57	2.00
Challacombe	216	15	5	3	4	4	3.2	0.24	0.80	1.33
Rowden	106	9	3	2	2	2	1.6	0.12	0.67	1.00
		max. = 68 54 79.4%	**23 33.3%**	**11 16.2%**	**14 (16)**	**15**	**12.0**	**0.22**	**0.65**	**1.36**
	All terrs.	**max. 221 191 86.4%**	**135 70.7% of pairs**	**88 65.2% of breeders**	**111 (140)**	**126**		**0.57**	**0.71**	**1.43**
								using median fledged values		

Summary: two thirds (65%) of young fledged were reared in just one third (35%) of the 13 territories.

APPENDIX 11

NATURE OF PREY REMAINS IN BUZZARD PELLETS

The characteristic remains of each prey species found in pellets of the captive Buzzards are described below and compared with those of wild birds on Dartmoor, at Postbridge. The effects of differential digestion, delayed pellet ejection ('holding over'), and of prey-handling behaviour before eating a kill are all important in determining pellet contents.

Brown Rat (6 eaten) Most bones were readily dissolved. Pellets were composed of much fur, once with vibrissae, but only one contained mandibles, though in a rather fragile state; this was the only set eaten. Otherwise, all pellets contained merely bone fragments, even when one bird devoured an entire rat (except the mandibles). Claws appeared in three pellets. These results agreed with the findings from the Postbridge pellet samples. There, rats were rare preys and thus could be assessed with little error.

Short-tailed Vole (312) The nature of vole remains in pellets of captive and wild Buzzards were almost identical. The only (partially) resistant parts were the mandibles, dentition and palate, but even the teeth were dissolved at times. Other bones were usually missing though occasionally broken skulls and limb bones were recovered. Two extreme examples of digestive power were recorded. Buzzard 'A' ate a total of 9 adult voles (mean weight 18.4 g) from which only three molar teeth were found. On another day, the same bird ate a further 9 voles (14.2 g mean weight). The pellet remains comprised 1 palate, 2 mandibles, 12 loose molars and sundry bone fragments. Vole remains in pellets thus represent only a small fraction of the numbers eaten. At Postbridge, where this vole is a common prey, its dietary importance may be under-estimated on the basis solely of pellet traces. The same problems would also apply to Bank Voles, if taken in any numbers by Buzzards.

Wood Mouse (24) Twelve were eaten by each captive Buzzard during meals of mixed small mammals; with not more than three eaten by either bird in a day. The pellets contained a total of 18 molars, 2 incisors and a dentary bone. Mouse fur and bones could not be distinguished from those of the other small mammals.

Common Shrew (53) Pellet remains were similar to those from voles. Limb bones, girdles and vertebrae were rarely found. Of head structures, the mandibles with teeth at times were well preserved, and formed the main basis for pellet analyses. Maxillary tooth rows appeared occasionally but in a very eroded condition.

Small Birds (19) Bones were rapidly digested and none survived. Ceratin protected mandibles (bill) and feet occasionally appeared entire in pellets, but more often were ground to small fragments. Most pellets contained few feathers, but several comprised a mass of feathers. Where the prey had been plucked thoroughly, no pellet appeared. Twice, even when feathers were swallowed in quantity (thrush and warbler), no pellet was cast, and no signs were found in pellets after the next meal. On four occasions when two or more birds were eaten in a day it was not always possible to identify species and number of items by feathers alone; colours were destroyed and structure fragmented by gastric trituration.

Bird remains in pellets thus were minimal, and therefore numbers eaten will be under-estimated should predation be heavier, as during the breeding season. On the other hand, when birds are caught infrequently the errors should be small.

Common Frog (33) Remains in pellets of captive and wild Buzzards were similar. Only small numbers of bones survived even when voles were added to provide some fur bulk and induce pellet formation. The total bone counts from 27 Frogs eaten were: 3 pelvic girdles, 6 radio-ulnae, 3 humeri, 3 coracoids, 12 vertebrae, and single scapula and pes, plus fragments. Skulls were never found. Counts of frogs eaten were based therefore on the numbers of pelvic girdles supplemented, when necessary, by fore-limb bones and occasionally others. Numbers of Frogs taken will be considerably under-estimated, especially in early spring when predation is visibly heaviest.

Reptiles (2) Only one Grass Snake and a Slow-worm were eaten by the captive Buzzards. No pellet was produced from the latter which was eaten without other preys. The snake, eaten with some other species, was represented by just a few scales. Digestive effects on the skeleton were similar to those for birds, but scales were more resistant than feathers. Study area pellets produced similar traces, and scale shape and pattern were used to identify reptile species. Estimation of the numbers of reptiles involved in pellets presented similar problems to those encountered when assessing bird remains.

APPENDIX 12a

DIFFERENTIAL DIGESTION AND RECOVERY CONVERSION FACTORS (RCF) OF COMMON PREYS: FROM FEEDING EXPERIMENTS WITH TWO CAPTIVE JUVENILE BUZZARDS.

Digestion of Common Frogs

	Bird 'A' No. of Frogs			Bird 'B' No. of Frogs		
Expt.	Eaten	In Pellets	%	Eaten	In Pellets	%
5	0	0	0	4	0	0
6	2	1	50.0	2	0	0
8	12	2	16.5	13	5	38.5
	14	3	21.4	19	5	26.3
'A' + 'B'	**33**	**8**	**24.2 = x 4 Recovery Conversion Factor**			

Digestion of Shrews (Sorex sp.)

	Bird 'A' No. of Shrews			Bird 'B' No. of Shrews		
Expt.	Eaten	In Pellets	%	Eaten	In Pellets	%
2	11	4	36.4	10	3	30.0
5	2	1	50.0	9	1	11.1
6	5	0	0	10	2	20.0
11	2	0	0	4	0	0
	20	5	25.0	33	6	18.2
'A' + 'B'	**53**	**11**	**20.8 % = x 5 Recovery Conversion Factor**			

Digestion of Short-tailed Voles

	Bird 'A' No. of Voles			Bird 'B' No. of Voles		
Expt.	Eaten	In Pellets	%	Eaten	In Pellets	%
1	30	14	46.7	20	5	25.0
2	16	6	37.5	14	4	28.6
3a	43	14	32.6	33	10	30.3
5	18	7	38.9	26	10	38.5
6	22	5	22.7	23	11	47.8
11	38	11	29.0	29	7	24.2
	167	57	34.1	145	47	32.4
'A' + 'B'	**312**	**104**	**33.3% = x 3 Recovery Conversion Factor**			

APPENDIX 12b

COMPARISON OF PELLET CONTENTS WITH KNOWN DIET OF CAPTIVE BUZZARDS: ESTIMATES USING RECOVERY CONVERSION FACTORS (RCF)

	Numbers			Weight %		
Preys	**Eaten**	**Ident.**	**RCF Est.**	**Diet**	**Pellets**	**RCF Est.**
Short-tailed Vole	157	52	156	62.3	62.0	68.1
Wood Mouse	27	6	24	10.8	7.0	10.6
Brown Rat	6	4	4	2.3	4.8	1.8
Rabbit (juvs.)	1	0	0	0.4	0	0
Shrews	32	5	25	12.7	6.0	11.0
Birds	19	15	15	7.4	17.9	6.6
Common Frog	8	1	4	3.1	1.2	1.8
Reptiles	2	1	1	0.8	1.2	0.4
	252	**84**	**229**			

APPENDIX 13

EXPERIMENT: RELATION BETWEEN DAILY CONSUMPTION & PELLET RECOVERY RATE OF SHORT-TAILED VOLES

voles/day eaten	frequency	total eaten	total recovered	proportion recovered
1	7	7	7	1.00
2	6	12	8	0.67
3	8	24	11	0.46
4	18	72	19	0.26
5	14	70	23	0.33
6	7	42	13	0.31
7	4	28	6	0.21
8	6	48	15	0.31
9	1	9	2	0.22
		312	**104**	**0.33**
				RCF = 3

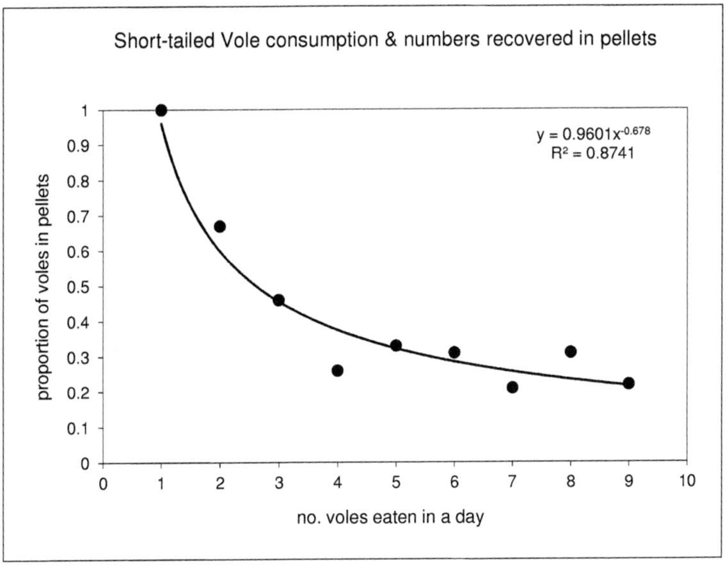

APPENDIX 14

THE DAILY FOOD CONSUMPTION OF TWO CAPTIVE BUZZARDS IN AUTUMN AND SPRING, AS MEASURED BY FEEDING EXPERIMENTS (DARE 1961).

Autumn (29 days)

	Hawk 'A'	Hawk 'B'
Mean body weight of hawk (g)	1,053	1,075
Mean daily weight of food eaten (g)	124 +/- 84	152 +/- 105
Mean daily consumption as % body weight	11.8	14.1
Maximum daily consumption (g)	267	340
Maximum daily consumption as % body weight	25.3	31.6
Days of complete fasting	2	4

[Ambient daily air temperatures: maxima 13–18°C, minima 3–8°C]

Spring (15 days)

	Hawk 'A'	Hawk 'B'
Mean daily weight of food eaten (g)	142 +/- 102	143 +/- 93
Mean daily consumption as % body weight	13.5	13.0
Maximum daily consumption (g)	340	378
Maximum daily consumption as % body weight	32.4	34.4
Days of complete fasting	2	2

[Ambient air temperatures: mild first week, wintry second week]

Summary

	Hawk 'A'				Hawk 'B'			
	Experiment			Mean	Experiment			Mean
	I	II	III	II&III	I	II	III	II&III
Mean daily weight eaten (g)	150	124	142	133	150	152	143	148
Mean weight as % body wt.	16.0	11.8	13.5	12.4	16.0	14.1	13.0	13.9
Maximum daily consumption (g)	265	267	340	303	265	340	378	359
Maximum as % body wt.	30.5	25.3	32.4	28.9	30.5	31.6	34.4	33.4

(Ages of birds: I = 5.5–8 weeks, fledging stage; II = 4–5 months; III = 9–10 months)

APPENDIX 15

IRREGULAR PELLET PRODUCTION

Two physiological anomalies can interrupt the regular production of pellets even when Buzzards are feeding amply every day. They need to be taken into consideration when attempting to estimate food intake rates.

Non-ejection or 'holding-over' of pellets

The term 'holding-over' denotes instances where ejection of the pellet for a particular meal (food-day) was either delayed beyond the normal 24 hours period, or failed to appear at all. In the latter case, any prey traces were probably mixed with those from the next food-day. The table shows the frequency of holding-over during the 8 experiments on differential digestion. Only occurrences where ample indigestible matter ('roughage') was taken to form a pellet are recorded. Similar behaviour in other captive Buteo hawks has been described in North America for both B. borealis (Glading et al. 1943) and B. jamaicensis (Fitch et al. 1946).

Here, holding-over occurred with 12% of food-days for Buzzard 'A' and 7.7% for 'B', but with a marked difference depending on whether the birds were fed a uniform diet of small preys or a mixed diet of large and small preys. No holding-over occurred at all with the small prey diet, but with a mixture of preys it was high – being 20.7% for 'A' and 13.3% for 'B'. Preys involved in 8 of the 10 cases were Brown Rats (3 times), juvenile Rabbit (1), medium-size birds (2) and voles (2). The remaining two cases involved amphibians mixed with other species.

Incidence of 'Holding-over' of pellets by two captive Buzzards

		No. Food-days		Holding-over		Preys Held-over	
Expt.	**Foods**	**'A'**	**'B'**	**'A'**	**'B'**	**'A'**	**'B'**
1	small preys	6	6	-	-		
2	(voles etc.)	4	4	-	-		
3	small preys	6	6	-	-		
5	small preys	6	6	-	-		
6	mixed preys	10	10	1	2	Brown Rat*	Brown Rat *, thrush sp.
7	mixed preys	5	5	2	1	Brown Rat, Wood mouse	Rabbit (juvenile), Turtle Dove
8	mixed preys	4	4	1	-	Frog (3), Toad	
9	mixed preys	10	11	2	1	Voles (6), Starling (2)	Voles (4)
		51	**52**	**6**	**4**		

Large preys and meals containing much fur or other indigestible material may need more time to digest. Holding-over also may be caused by lack of indigestible residues in preys with easily dissolved fragile bones (amphibians, reptiles) or small birds that have been thoroughly plucked. These results agree with those reported for B. borealis (Glading et al., 1943). The Red-tailed Hawk studied by Fitch et al. (1946) produced only 23 pellets in 61 days, but it was fed almost entirely on large preys.

Carry-over

Carry-over follows incomplete emptying of the stomach debris during pellet formation and ejection. The residues are then subjected to further gastric action and may continue to appear in pellets over successive days but in progressively greater states of dissolution. Extreme cases have been recorded, lasting more than

7 days with one captive Red-tailed Hawk (Fitch et al. 1946) and for at least 4 days with B. borealis Glading et al., 1943). Such processes could introduce errors of over-estimation when analysing pellets of wild Buzzards. Some experiments therefore were made with the captive Buzzards to determine its possible importance under natural conditions. Carry-over by one or other Buzzard occurred on 5 (7%) of 35 food-days, all being two-day carry-overs. Three involved Short-tailed Voles and two related to small birds (Blackbird and House Sparrow). With wild Buzzards, however, the Postbridge pellet data suggested that carry-over was more prevalent, particularly when feeding upon Rabbits, Moles, birds and Adders. With care, however, potential carry-over errors could be minimised by considering the temporal distribution pattern of each prey species in the pellet samples. For this population as a whole the errors were relatively minor compared to other sources of bias such as differential digestion.

APPENDIX 16

PELLET PRODUCTION RATES BY BUZZARDS: EXPERIMENTS WITH TWO CAPTIVE HAWKS

		Bird 'A'				Bird 'B'			
Expt.	**Diet**	**Mean wt/ day eaten (g)**	**Food-days**	**Pellets**	**Pellets per day**	**Mean wt/day eaten (g)**	**Food-days**	**Pellets**	**Pellets per day**
I	small prey (voles etc)	114	6	7	1.17	100	6	6	1.00
II		121	4	4	1.00	111	4	4	1.00
III		134	6	7	1.17	135	6	7	1.17
V		75	6	6	1.00	138	6	6	1.00
	totals/ means	**111**	**22**	**24**	**1.08 (A1)**	**121**	**22**	**23**	**1.04 (B1)**
VI	mixed preys	95	10	7	0.70	120	10	8	0.80
VII		130	5	3	0.60	100	5	3	0.60
VIII		100	4	3	0.75	105	4	4	1.00
XI		94	10	8	0.80	95	11	9	0.82
	totals/ means	**105**	**29**	**21**	**0.71 (A2)**	**105**	**30**	**24**	**0.80 (B2)**
	totals/ means	**108**	**51**	**45**	**0.90**	**113**	**52**	**47**	**0.92**

Notes: (a) overall mean pellet production for both birds = 0.91
(b) difference A1 : A2 = 0.37, is highly significant (t = 5.63; P <0.01)
(c) Difference B1 : B2 + 0.24, is highly significant (t = 2.65; P< 0.05)

APPENDIX 17

DAILY FOOD INTAKE (DFI) RATES OF WILD BUZZARDS ON DARTMOOR ESTIMATED FROM PELLETS (AFTER CORRECTING FOR DIFFERENTIAL DIGESTION)

Period	No. pellets (territories)	No. preys (corrected)	Wt. preys % (corrected)			DFI
			Rabbit	sm.mammals	others	prey (g)
Dec.-Feb.	90 (6)	338	6.0	79.8	14.2	97
Mar.-April	147 (9)	558	40.2	31.4	28.6	139
May-June	77 (8)	193	59.3	30.4	10.2	121
July-Aug.	27 (10)	106	43.8	47.0	9.4	148
Sep.-Nov.	37 (5)	131	25.4	59.2	15.2	106
	378	**1326**	**34.9**	**43.6**	**15.5**	**122**
Rabbit *						
Mar.-June	117 (6)	434	20.0	41.2	38.8	104
Nov.- Feb.	113 (5)	325	9.4	79.0	11.6	70
Rabbit ***						**87**
Mar.-June	107 (3)	213	74.2	21.8	3.9	135
Nov.-Feb.	22 (3)	55	41.0	50.8	8.2	83
						109
	349	**1027**	**36.1**	**48.2**	**15.6**	**98**

* in territories where Rabbits were scarce; *** Rabbits available

APPENDIX 18

AMOUNTS OF PREY BROUGHT TO TWO BUZZARD BROODS AT POSTBRIDGE, DARTMOOR

Brood age (days)	Cator 1958 b/3 - b/1 Prey wts. g/day *	Bellever 1957 b/2 Prey wts. g/day *	Brood age (days)	Cator 1958 b/3 - b/1 Prey wts. g/day *	Bellever 1957 b/2 Prey wts. g/day *
2	250	118	26	183	110
5	193	318	29	170	538
8	250 **	n.o.	32	295	252
11	167	n.o.	35	350	385
14	87 **	313	38	295	307
17	88	207	41	223	215
20	178	n.o.	44	403	302
23	340	110	47	193	320

*3-day means **one chick died during period n.o. = no observations

	Cator	Bellever
No. days	56	53
No. kills recorded	82	145
Est. total kills	99	197
Mean no/day	1.7	3.7
Wt of food recorded	11,000g	10,465g
Est. total weight *	12,967	14,257g
Mean wt/day	228	269

[* with interpolations when no observations possible]

APPENDIX 19

INITIAL WEIGHTS LOST BY TWO CAPTIVE BUZZARDS DURING A WINTER STARVATION PERIOD

		Buzzard 'A'			Buzzard 'B'		
Date	Day	Body Wt. (g)	Mean Loss/ day (g)	% Initial Wt.	Body Wt. (g)	Mean Loss/ day (g)	% Initial Wt.
16.1.58	0	1,016			1,132		
			28.5	2.8		31.0	2.7
18.1.58	2	959			1,070		
			21.5	2.1		24.5	2.2
20.1.58	4	916			1,021		
			11.0	1.1		12.5	1.1
22.1.58	6	894			996		
			14.0	1.4		14.0	1.2
23.1.58	7	880			982		

Total weight loss = 136g (13.4%) 150g (13.3%)
Mean daily loss = 19.4g (1.9%) 21.4g (1.9%)

Meteorological Data

	Air Temperatures in shade (°C)			Weather
	maximum	minimum	mean	
16.1.58	8.3	6.1	7.2	mild conditions
17.1.58	10.0	3.3	6.6	mild conditions
18.1.58	9.4	6.7	8.0	mild conditions
19.1.58	3.9	-1.7	1.1	light snow ahowers
20.1.58	5.0	-3.9	0.5	light snow showers
21.1.58	1.1	-3.6	-1.3	37mm snowfall
22.1.58	1.1	-5.6	-2.3	6mm snowfall
23.1.58	0.8	-7.2	-3.2	75mm snowfall
24.1.58	3.9	-8.3	-2.2	hard night frost

APPENDIX 20a

WEIGHTS OF HEALTHY AND STARVING WILD BUZZARDS IN GERMANY (PIECHOCKI 1953)

	Males			Females		
	No.	**Mean Wt. (g)**	**Range (g)**	**No.**	**Mean Wt. (g)**	**Range (g)**
Healthy birds	7	784	570–985*	10	1,083	929–1,206
Starved birds	7	523	430–610	6	612	535–712
Mean difference (g)		261			470	
Mean difference (%)		33.3			43.4	

* heaviest bird was 114 g above maximum recorded by other authorities)

APPENDIX 20b

WEIGHT OF VISCERAL FAT RESERVES IN 9 HEALTHY BUZZARDS IN GERMANY (PIECHOCKI 1953)

Sex	**Total Body Wt. (g)**	**Visceral Fat Wt. (g)**	**Fat as % Body Wt.**
Female	1,130	158	14.0
Male	900	105	11.7
Female	1,206	125	10.4
Male	985	79	8.0
Female	1,070	80	7.5
Female	1,028	60	5.8
Female	1,096	60	5.5
Female	929	45	4.8
Male	867	35	4.0

APPENDIX 21

SEASONAL PREDATION INDICES OF BUZZARDS AT POSTBRIDGE, DARTMOOR, 1956-58

Prey	J/F	M/A	M/J	J/A	S/O	N/D
Rabbit	0.03	0.23	0.29	0.26	0.13	0.13
Short-tailed Vole	2.07	1.23	0.81	2.34	3.21	2.13
Mole	0.09	0.03	0.05	0.19	0.13	0.13
Common Shrew	0.30	0.45	0.50	0.40	0.65	0.65
small mammals unid.	0.44	0.56	0.56	0.28	0.52	0.32
all small mammals	2.63	2.37	2.92	3.21	4.51	3.36
birds	0.02	0.07	0.10	0.11	0.07	0.04
Common Frog	0.32	1.16	0.16	0.44	0.13	0.12
reptiles	0.02	0.17	0.13	0	0	0

(index = estimated mean number of prey items per pellet after adjusting vole, shrew and Frog remains for differential digestion biases.

APPENDIX 22

SAMPLE LOG OF BUZZARD HUNTING ACTIVITY
SOUSSONS PAIR, POSTBRIDGE, DARTMOOR
20 June 1956

A 14.5-hour watch was carried out, from a Land Rover, between 04.00–18.30 BST while this pair was feeding a single chick, about 4 weeks old. The weather was clear and very cool at dawn with a light or moderate N-NW wind. The sun rose above the hills at 05.45 BST. The day was then sunny and warm with a fresh NW wind, but it became steadily duller in the afternoon with light mist and drizzle setting in by 16.00 hrs. The watch was curtailed by worsening conditions soon afterwards.

04.00 Observer in position at observation point (X) 75 m from the nest area located in a hillside copse.

05.12 First signs of activity: male emerged from near the nest tree and flew low to a perch on the edge of the nest copse to preen.

05.17 Female appeared from nest and perched on a tall look-out fir for 2 minutes and called, then flew down into the valley to pasture fields where she settled on top of a haystack.

05.29 Male rose and circled over the nest site, then flew down to its favourite valley bog hunting area by Grendon Bridge.

05.30 Female in area is hunting from fence posts and feeding on invertebrates in the pastures; up to 11 minutes spent at a perch, and 2 minutes on the ground.

06.14 Male brought a small vertebrate kill from the bog area to the nest, returning immediately to the same area. Female now on a hawthorn bush by the pastures.

06.29 Male brought a second small animal to nest from the bog in his talons with some grass; he stayed 15 seconds on nest, then flew off to Cator Brake to perch in the beech trees above the nestsite.

06.45 Observation point moved to position beside Soussons bog.

07.00 Female has shifted from pastures up the hill side to Cator Brake and now is near her mate.

07.25 Female flew down into nest site where she apparently stayed until nearly 10.00 hrs, presumably brooding and tending to the nestling.

08.10 After apparently resting for the last 1.5 hours, the male began to hover over the grassy hill slope between Cator Brake and the nest copse; he then crossed the valley to hover into a stiff wind above the NW slope of Blackaton Hill. Soon, he dropped into a ploughed field to 'grub' for invertebrates for a while before moving on to perches.

09.01 Male caught a small reptile (slow-worm?) by diving sideways off his perch into the hedge corner; prey taken in bill to nest, the hawk beating and gliding low over the valley across-wind. Male stayed 15 sec. on nest then began hovering nearby.

09.12 Male still hovering over hill slope below nest copse, then suddenly plunged into a pasture near the hedge; a small mammal was taken to a nearby post for a minute where part (head?) was eaten, apparently. Prey then taken up to the nest, the male staying a moment before returning to the same hunting area.

09.24 Male brought yet another catch from same area to the nest, his third in 23 minutes. He then crossed to the previous hill to hover and 'grub', as before, in the same ploughed field.

10.00 Female has left nest site after some 2.5 hours; now hovering over the common above nest wood.

10.17 Male returned briefly to nest area before dropping down to the boggy area beside the West Webburn river.

10.55 Female still in her same area but now perching in the Brake trees.

11.01 Female brought a small lizard-type reptile in her bill from the common to the nest; her first kill today.

11.02 Male caught a small vertebrate in the bog area; with the prey in his talons the hawk soared up into the wind to some 150 m, then descended 50 m in a wide loop before power-diving the last

25 m to the nest. In the final stoop, the wings were folded back and legs stretched downwards and forwards, the prey still grasped in the feet. The male, arriving at the nest so soon after his mate, departed almost immediately, whereas the female stayed 10 minutes. Male flew out over the valley floor and hovered above Soussons bog.

11.12 Female now hovering high (75 m) over the hill near the nest copse; then glided across the valley for more than 1 km to the west side of Challacombe Hill.

11.20 Male still hovering high above the expanse of bog and hill side.

11.30 **Male dived beside the road through area and rose with small prey** and grass in talons; he soared to gain height before gliding high across-wind to the nest. He returned to hang in the wind over exactly the same place, after being mobbed by a Lapwing en route.

11.40 **Male made yet another kill,** near the last spot, crossed to the nest in a leisurely manner, then went back to the same pitch.

12.00 The pair indulged in a short interlude of soaring together high above Blackaton Hill and the Soussons bog. Female then returned to her uneventful hunting, this time on the nest slope.

12.22 **Male plunged from 30 m with talons extended and caught a small mammal** near the site of his last two catches. Part of the prey was eaten on the ground, the rest being taken, very leisurely, in talons to the nest.

12.25 **Female returned to nest with her second small vertebrate kill** today, again from the common.

12.45 Male visited west side of Challacombe Hill for the first time today, and hovered over a favourite rough grassy slope.

12.54 **Male brought a small capture** to nest from his new station. Departing instantly from nest, he roamed about near the nest copse for a while before settling for a well-earned rest; the female is still with the chick.

13.30 Male active again – after hovering briefly near the nest area he flew across to Blackaton Hill.

13.55 **Male caught yet another kill** by the bog and, as he dropped on to the nest, the female joined him. Five minutes later the male was flying back to the hill via the Soussons bog.

14.10 While hovering about 30 m above the bog, the male plummeted to ground, but missed his intended victim this time.

14.29 Female left nest area and joined male in hovering over Blackaton Hill before proceeding on to Challacombe Hill where she was rejoined by her mate at 14.50 hrs; pair then began feeding on invertebrates by dropping from low hanging stations.

15.40 Male left female and returned to his ground on Blackaton Hill for a short time, then crossed to hover near the nest copse. A light misty drizzle is now setting in from the west.

16.07 Male returned yet again to Blackaton Hill.

16.50 Female left nest site and went up the hill side to the Cator Brake trees.

17.40 Male still hovering over Blackaton Hill but his efforts are now unrewarding; starts occasional 'grubbing' in the ploughed field used this morning.

18.20 Male hovering occasionally there but much time now spent on the ground as the weather deteriorates.

18.30 No prey has been brought to the nest in the last 4.5 hours, in contrast to frequent earlier successes. Pair is now becoming increasingly inactive as bad weather clamps down. Observations terminated in poor light with mist descending from the hill tops.

Summary of the day's events:
No. of small vertebrate kills brought to the brood in 14.5 hours = 13 (11 by the male, 2 by the female).

APPENDIX 23

FLEDGED BROOD SIZES OF BUZZARDS IN VARIOUS REGIONS OF THE BRITISH ISLES

Area	Years	Main Prey	Broods	f/1	f/2	f/3	f/4	Mean	SD	Source
Dartmoor	1956-93	SM	60	32	26	2		1.50		Dare (1998)
Snowdonia	1979-82	SM	95	63	27	5		1.39	0.59	Dare (1995)
Snowdonia	1977-2009	SM,SC	400	322	72	4		1.19		J. Driver (in litt.)
Migneint-Hiraethog	1979-82	SM	63	41	22			1.35	0.48	Dare (1995)
NE Wales	1980-2008	R, SM,B	197	83	76	36	2	1.78	0.8	Roberts & Jones (2009)
mid-Wales	1975-79	SM,LB,R	302					1.20		Newton et al. (1982)
Speyside	1969-72	R	63	5	24	23	11	2.64		Picozzi & Weir (1974)
Glen Urquhart	1977-89	SM, SB	174	97	71	6		1.48		Swann & Etheridge (1995)
West Moray	1977-88	R, LB	123	18	38	50	17	2.54		Swann & Etheridge (1995)
mid-Argyll	1989-90	SM, LB	66	17	34	14	1	1.98		Austin & Houston (1997)
S. England lowlands										
W. Midlands	1994-95	R, LB	64	25	32	6	1	1.74	0.08	Sim et al. (2001)
New Forest	1961-71	B	73	44	29			1.40		Tubbs (1974)
Offshore island										
Skomer	1954-64	R, P	18	6	9	3		1.83		Davis & Saunders (1965)
All Regions			**2000**	**753**	**460**	**149**	**32**	**1.69**		
			%	54	33	11	2			

R - rabbit; R* - rabbit, pre-myxo; SM - small mammals; LB - large birds (corvid size); SB - smaller birds; SC - sheep carrion, P - Puffins

APPENDIX 24

BUZZARD PRODUCTIVITY IN 10 STUDY AREAS IN BRITAIN

				Productivity (young fledged per pair)			
Area	**Period**	**No. Pairs (average)**	**% laying eggs**	**territorial**	**breeding**	**successful**	
Dartmoor	1956-58	12	76	0.5	0.7	1.3	Dare, 1998
	1961-69	8	72	0.8	1.0	1.4	Dare, 1998
	1990-93	16	68	0.9	1.4	1.6	Dare, 1998
Snowdonia							
all areas	1979-82	91	>64	0.6	1.0	1.4	Dare, 1995
Carneddau	1979-82	19	62	0.7	1.1	1.4	Dare, unpubl.
Carneddau	1998-2000	40	76	0.7	0.9	1.3	J. Driver, in litt.
Migneint-Hiraethog	1979-84	57	76	0.9	1.2	1.4	Dare, 1995
mid-Wales	1975-79	112	83	0.6	0.8	1.2	Newton *et al.*, 1982
NE Wales	1978-2008	63	86	1.3	1.5	1.8	Roberts & Jones, 2009
Speyside	1969-72	34		1.5		2.6	Picozzi & Weir, 1974
Moray, W	1977-89	14	72	1.6	2.2	2.5	Swann & Etheridge, 1995
Glen Urquhart	1977-89	16	80	0.9	1.1	1.5	Swann & Etheridge, 1995
mid-Argyll	1989-90					1.8	Austin & Houston, 1997
W. Midlands	1994-95	85	83	1.2	1.4	1.7	Sim *et al.*, 2001
NE Suffolk	2008-12	15	>76	0.8	1.1	1.2	Dare, 2013

APPENDIX 25

BUZZARD POPULATION ESTIMATES: NATIONAL AND LOCAL, 1929-2012

Survey			Total pairs min	max	Area (km^2) surveyed	Count unit	Sampling unit	Sponsor	Authors
National									
	1954	pre-myxo	8000	12000	14700	TP	variable	BTO/NC	Moore (1957)
	late 1950s	post-myxo	6000?	8000?					Dare (Chapter 15)
	1970		8000	10000		TP		NC	Tubbs (1974)
	1983		12000	17000	1166	SB	tetrad	BTO/NC	Taylor *et al.* (1988)
	2000		21000	44000		TP		BTO/NCC	www.bto.org
	2001		44000	61000		TP	habitats	0	Clements (2002)
	2009		57000	79000		P	transect	JNCC/BTO	Musgrove *et al.* (2013)
County									
Devon	**1929**		450	650	792	AF	variable	bird society	Hurrell (1952)
	1954		1700	3650	300	TP	variable	BTO/NC	Moore (1957) recalc. 2013
	1966		1850		486	AF	1 x 1 km square	0	Moysey (1966)
	1974		1380	1450	413	AF	tetrad	bird society	Dare, in Sitters (1988)
	1983		1530	1980	2620	SB	tetrad	BTO	Taylor *et al.* (1988)
Small Areas									
Dartmoor	**1955**		15		33	TP	SA	university	Dare (1998)
	1956-58		12		33	TP	SA	university	Dare (1998)
	1960-69		8		33	TP	SA	0	Dare (1998)
	1990-93		16		33	TP	SA	0	Dare (1998)
Somerset, N.	**1982**		13		75	TP	SA	0	Prytherch (2013)
	1991		26		75	TP	SA	0	Prytherch (2013)

	1996	56		75	TP	SA	0	Prytherch (2013)
	2001	83		75	TP	SA	0	Prytherch (2013)
	2006	90		75	TP	SA	0	Prytherch (2013)
	2012	103		75	TP	SA	0	Prytherch (2013)
Somerset, NE.	**1995**	32		60	TP	SA	0	Holmes (2012)
	1999	40		60	TP	SA	0	Holmes (2012)
	2004	56		60	TP	SA	0	Holmes (2012)
New Forest	**1962-71**	33		290	BP	SA	NC	Tubbs (1974)
	early 1990s	~18		290	BP	SA	0	Clements (2002)
Speyside	**1971**	14		94	TP	SA	ITE	Weir & Picozzi (1983)
	1988-89	21		94	TP	SA	university	Halley (1993)
Snowdonia	**1950s**	30	35	926	TP	SA	0	D. A Ratcliffe (in litt.)
	1977-84	96		926	TP	SA	0	Dare & Barry 1990
	1998-2007	244		926	TP	SA	0	Driver & Dare (2009)
Carneddau	**1950s**	5	10					
	1980	26		251	TP	SA	0	D. A. Ratcliffe (in litt.)
	1986	34		251	TP	SA	0	Driver & Dare (2009)
	1990	40		251	TP	SA	0	Driver & Dare (2009)
	1995	45		251	TP	SA	0	Driver & Dare (2009)
	2000	61		251	TP	SA	0	Driver & Dare (2009)
	2003	78		251	TP	SA	0	Driver & Dare (2009)
	2010	78		251	TP	SA	0	Driver & Dare (2009)

AF - adults flying; SB - soaring birds; BP - breeding pairs; TP - territorial pairs; P - pairs, SA - study area, Sponsors, 0 = author/s

APPENDIX 26a

BUZZARDS: POPULATION DENSITIES & OTHER STATISTICS IN DIFFERENT REGIONS OF BRITAIN

Region		Land Use/ Habitats (main)	Area (km²)	Territories or Pairs	Density (km²/pair)	Territory Occupancy	Breeding Pairs (as % occupancy)	NND (km)		Source
								mean	range/s.d.	
Dartmoor	1956-58	HF, GM, HM, CP	33	15	2.2	80-93	67-79	1.01	0.45-2.4	Dare (1961)
	1990-93	HF, GM, HM, CP	33	16-17	1.9-2.1	97	68-74	?	?	Dare (1998)
Migneint-Hiraethog	1979-82	HF, HM, GM, CP, DW	440	62	7.1	90-93	64-77	1.53	0.65-3.8	Dare (1995)
Snowdonia	1979-82	HF, GM, Mo, DW, CP	926	96	9.7	94-96	53-66	1.95	0.5-0.4	Dare (1995)
NE Wales	2000-08	HF, CL, DW, CP, HM	?	16-21	?	85-98	71-90	0.89	0.15-1.7	Roberts & Jones (2009)
mid-Wales (a)	1975-79	HF	135	58-62	3.4	85-90	68-89	0.87	0.03 sd	Newton *et al.* (1982)
mid-Wales (b)	1975-79	GM, CP	340	74-78	4.2	85-98	71-89	1.13	0.04 sd	Newton *et al.* (1982)
Welsh Border	1994-95	HF	100	81	1.2	95	80	0.83	0.27 sd	Sim *et al.* (2001)
W. Midlands	1994-95	CL, DW, CP, lowland	100	22	4.5	91	85	1.33	0.27 sd	Sim *et al.* (2001)
N. Somerset	1988-2007	CL, DW	75	19-92	3.9-0.8*	100	>99	0.97-0.6	0.12-2.86	Prytherch (2013)
NE Somerset	1995-2004	CL, DW	60	32-56	1.9-1.1*	100	?	?	?	Holmes (2012)

Speyside	1969-72	HF, CL, HM, DW, CP	173	31-38	4.6-5.6**	?	?	1.5	?	Picozzi & Weir (1974)
W. Moray	1977-88	CL, CP lowland	?	10 to 19	?	?	72	1.75	0.8-3.2	Swann & Etheridge (995)
Glen Urquhart	1977-89	HF, DW, CP	?	12 to 19	?	?	80	1.1	0.3-1.9	Swann & Etheridge (995)
New Forest	1962-66	DF, CL lowland	250	33-34	7.5	97	86	1.5	0.3-2.4	Tubbs (1974)

* Somerset populations increasing rapidly ** Speyside - 3.3 km^2/pair of the area actually occupied by Buzzard territories

Habitats Key : HF = hill farms (enclosed pastures); CL = cultivated land (usually lowland); GM & HM = grass & heather moorland (sheepwalk): Mo = steep montane grazing (high sheepwalk); DW = deciduous woods; DF = ancient deciduous forest; CF = natural coniferous forest: CP = conifer plantations.

APPENDIX 26b

SIZES (HA) OF BUZZARD TERRITORIES IN 6 UPLAND REGIONS OF BRITAIN

Region		Land use (main habitats)	Average size (ha)	Range	N
Dal moor, Postbridge		HF, M, CP	142	53 - 223	13
Migneint-Hiraethog		HF, M	220	60 - 340	17
Snowdonia: low	(a)	HF, DW, CP	260	150 - 390	17
	(b)		90	40 - 200	54
Snowdonia: high	(a)	HF, CP, MSW	440	260 - 630	8
	(b)		290	150 - 440	18
NE Wales		HF, DW, M	125	60 - 260	20
Welsh Border		HF, W	120	39 -221	81
Strathspey, Highlands		HF; DW; M, CP	175	75 - 350	38

HF - hill farm fields; M - moorland; MSW - mountain sheep walk; W - mixed woodland; DW - deciduous woodland; CP - conifer plantation Snowdonia (a) relates to 1977-84; (b) to 2003-04.

APPENDIX 27a

BUZZARD TERRITORIES, DARTMOOR: HABITAT COMPOSITIONS & BREEDING PERFORMANCE (1956-69 & 1990-93)

(13 original 'permanent' territories)

		Habitats (%)					Productivity			
Territory	**Area (ha)**	**fields**	**scrub**	**bog**	**woods**	**heath**	**pairs**	**bred**	**successful**	**fledglings**
5 best:										
Blackaton	126	40	1	7	1	52	17	16	12	15 (20)
Cator Court	73	83	0	3	8	5	16	12	12	14 (16)
Archerton	106	63	4	2	23**	8	17	13	11	13 (21)
Soussons	188	26	20*	15	1	40	17	16	10	16 (18)
Grendon	69	71	9	6	2	12	15	14	9	11 (16)
av. =		**57**	**7**	**7**	**7**	**23**	**16.5**	**14.2**	**10.8**	**13.8 (18.2)**
4 intermediates:										
Bellever	200	22	5	1	45**	27	14	13	6	7 (10)
Postbridge	159	82	0	8	1	9	12	9	6	7 (8)
Riddon	163	32	0	7	5	56	13	10	6	7
Runnage	171	39	18*	10	1	32	16	9	5	7 (8)
av. =		**44**	**6**	**6**	**13**	**31**	**13.7**	**10.3**	**5.8**	**7.0 (8.2)**
4 worst:										
Webburn Wood	53	62	8	19	2	8	15	8	4	4 (6)
Challacombe	216	16	1	3	0	80	15	5	3	4
Powder Mills	237	12	14*	7	0	67	15	7	2	4
Rowden	106	58	2	17	0	23	9	3	2	2
av. =		**37**	**6**	**12**	**<1**	**44**	**13.5**	**5.7**	**3.0**	**3.5 (4.0)**

* conifer plantation - open scrub stage in 1950s. ** conifer plantation - closed cover in 1950s

APPENDIX 27b

BUZZARD BREEDING PERFORMANCE IN 3 TERRITORY GROUPINGS OVER 17 YEARS

(1956-69 and 1990-93) at Postbridge, Dartmoor

Territory group	A	B	C	All
success	**most**	**medium**	**least**	
number	5	4	4	13
Occupancy by pairs	82	55	54	191
% years	96.5	80.9	79.4	86.4
Breeding attempts	71	41	23	135
% years	86.6	60.3	33.3	70.7
Attempts successful	54	23	11	88
% years	76.1	33.3	16.2	65.2
No. young fledged	81	30	15	126
% total	64.7	24.4	12.0	
Annual productivity per territory	0.95	0.44	0.22	0.57
breeding attempt	1.14	0.68	0.65	0.71
successful attempt	1.50	1.30	1.36	1.43

APPENDIX 28

EFFECTS OF MYXOMATOSIS ON THE BREEDING OF BUZZARDS IN DEVON: AVON VALLEY AND DARTMOOR, DURING 1954–58

	Avon Valley			Dartmoor			
	Pre-myxo	Post-myxo		Pre-myxo	Post-myxo		
Activity	**1954**	**1955**	**1956**	**1955**	**1956**	**1957**	**1958**
Pairs resident in April	21	14	12	c.16	12	14	14
Pairs preparing nests	19	13	9		10	12	12
Pairs breeding (eggs)	19	1	8	c.14	8	10	11
Pairs hatching eggs	17	0	5		7	7	7
Pairs fledging young	17	0	5	c.10	6	5	3
Feldglings reared	28(33)	0	7(10)	15	7	8	3
Fledglings per pair:							
Resident population	1.33 (1.67)	0	0.58 (0.83)	c.1.0	0.58	0.57	0.21
Breeding	1.47 (1.90)	0	0.88 (1.25)	c.1.1	0.88	0.80	0.27
Successful	1.65 (1.94)	0	1.40 (2.00)	c.1.5	1.17	1.60	1.00

notes: 1. myxomatosis reached Postbridge a year later than Avon Valley
2. 1955 Postbridge data from local farmer reports
3. Avon Valley values in parentheses are probable maxima

INDEX